AF654140

MARXIST ECONOMIC THEORY

MARXIST ECONOMIC THEORY

Volume I

Ernest Mandel

Translated by
Brian Pearce

AAKAR

MARXIST ECONOMIC THEORY (Vol. I)
Ernest Mandel

© The Merlin Press 1968
© Aakar Books for South Asia 2008

First Published in India 2008
Reprinted 2014
Reprinted 2024

ISBN 978-81-89833-46-6 (Set)
ISBN 978-81-89833-47-3 (Volume I)

Published in agreement with The Merlin Press Ltd., London for publication and sale only in the Indian Subcontinent (India, Pakistan, Bangladesh, Nepal, Maldives, Bhutan and Sri Lanka)

All rights reserved. No part of this book may be reproduced or transmitted, in any form or by any means, without prior permission of the publisher.

Published by
AAKAR BOOKS
28 E Pocket IV, Mayur Vihar Phase I, Delhi 110 091
Phone : 011 2279 5505 Telefax : 011 2279 5641
info@aakarbooks.com; www.aakarbooks.com

Printed in India at
D.K. Fine Art Press (P) Ltd.

Vol. I

CONTENTS

INTRODUCTION

Paradox of Marxism today 13
Responsibility of the Marxists 14
Economic theory and empirical facts 15
Economic theory and economic history 16
Method 17
The value and power of attraction of Marxism 19
Living Marxism: a promise 20

CHAPTER ONE

LABOUR, NECESSARY PRODUCT, SURPLUS PRODUCT

Labour, society, communication, language, consciousness, humanity 23
Necessary product 24
Beginning of the social division of labour 25
First appearance of a social surplus product 26
The neolithic revolution 28
Co-operative organisation of labour 30
Primitive occupation of the soil 33
The cultivation of irrigated land, cradle of civilisation 36
The metallurgical revolution 37
Production and accumulation 39
Is there an "economic surplus"? 42

CHAPTER TWO

EXCHANGE, COMMODITY, VALUE

Simple exchange 49
Silent barter and ceremonial gifts 50
Developed exchange 53
Trade 54
Production for use and production of commodities 57
Co-operatively organised society and society based on economy of labour-time 59
Exchange-value of commodities 63
Petty commodity production 65
Law of value in petty commodity production 67

CHAPTER THREE

MONEY, CAPITAL, SURPLUS-VALUE

Need for a universal equivalent 72
Evolution of the universal equivalent 74
Money 76
Evolution of social wealth and different functions of money 78
Circulation of commodities and circulation of money 79
Surplus-value emerging from the circulation of commodities 82
Surplus-value arising from commodity production 85
Capital, surplus-value and social surplus product 88
Law of uneven development 91

CHAPTER FOUR

THE DEVELOPMENT OF CAPITAL

Forms of agricultural surplus product 95
Accumulation of use-values and accumulation of surplus-value 98
Usurer's capital 100
Merchant capital 102
The commercial revolution 106
Domestic industry 110
Manufacturing capital 113
Creation of the modern proletariat 116
The Industrial Revolution 118
Special features of capitalist development in Western Europe 119
Capital and the capitalist mode of production 125

CHAPTER FIVE

THE CONTRADICTIONS OF CAPITALISM

Capital thirsting for surplus-value 132
The lengthening of the working day 135
Growth in the productivity and intensity of labour 136
Human labour-power and machine production 140
Forms and evolution of wages 143
Additional note on the theory of absolute impoverishment 150
Dual function of labour-power 154
Equalisation of the rate of profit in pre-capitalist society 156
Equalisation of the rate of profit in the capitalist mode of production 158
Price of production and value of commodities 160
Centralisation and concentration of capital 162
Tendency of the average rate of profit to fall 166
Supreme contradiction of the capitalist system 170
Free labour and alienated labour 172
Class struggle 174

CHAPTER SIX

TRADE

Trade, outcome of uneven economic development 182
Production and realisation of surplus-value 184
Annual amount of surplus-value and annual rate of profit 186
Commercial capital and commercial profit 189
Commercial capital and labour-power engaged in distribution 191
The concentration of commercial capital 192
Capital invested in transport 198
International trade 199
Costs of distribution 201
The Tertiary Sector 204

CHAPTER SEVEN

CREDIT

Mutual aid and credit 210
Origin of banking 211
Credit in pre-capitalist society 214
Supply and demand of money capital in the epoch of commercial capital 217
Supply and demand of money capital in the epoch of industrial capitalism 219
Interest and rate of interest 222
Circulation credit 226
Investment credit and the finance market 228
The Stock Exchange 230
Joint-stock companies and the evolution of capitalism 233
Consumer's credit 236
Credit and the contradictions of capitalism 237

CHAPTER EIGHT

MONEY

The two functions of money 242
Value of metallic money and price movements 243
Circulation of metallic money 244
Origins of private fiduciary currency 246
Origins of public fiduciary currency 248
Creation of public fiduciary currency: First source: discounting 250
Creation of public fiduciary currency: Second source: advances on current account (overdrafts) 251
Creation of public fiduciary currency: Third source: public expenditure 253

Socially-necessary stock of currency 254
Circulation of inconvertible paper money 255
Balance of payments 259
Central banks and bank credit 261
Currency manipulations 262
Three forms of inflation 264
Purchasing power, circulation currency and rate of interest 266

CHAPTER NINE

AGRICULTURE

Agriculture and commodity production 271
Pre-capitalist rent and capitalist ground-rent 272
Origins of capitalist ground-rent 273
Differential ground-rent 276
Absolute ground-rent 278
Ground-rent and the capitalist mode of production 280
Price of land and evolution of ground-rent 282
Landed property and the capitalist mode of production 286
Production-relations and property-relations in the countryside 288
Concentration and centralisation of capital in agriculture 290
The wretched lot of the agricultural worker 293
From the theories of Malthus to agricultural Malthusianism 294
Ground-rent and the marginal theory of value 298

CHAPTER TEN

REPRODUCTION AND GROWTH OF THE NATIONAL INCOME

New value, new income and transferred income 305
The State, surplus-value and social income 310
The sharing-out of surplus-value 312
Social product and social income 314
Distribution of incomes and realisation of commodities 317
Production and reproduction 320
Simple reproduction 322
Expanded reproduction 324
Expanded reproduction and the laws of development of capitalism 327
Expanded reproduction, economic growth and social accounting 329
Contracted reproduction 331
War economy 332
Redistribution of national income by the State 335

CHAPTER ELEVEN

PERIODICAL CRISES

Pre-capitalist and capitalist crises 342
General possibility of capitalist crisis 343
Law of markets 344
Cyclical progress of capitalist economy 345
Internal logic of the capitalist cycle 349
Extension of the basis of capitalist production 358
Under-consumption theories 361
Critique of "under-consumption" models 363
Theories of disproportionality 366
Outline of a synthesis 368
Conditions of capitalist expansion 371
No growth without fluctuations? 373

Vol. II

CHAPTER TWELVE

MONOPOLY CAPITALISM

The second industrial revolution 393
Industrial concentration accentuated 394
Monopoly agreements, groupings and combines 398
The forms of capitalist concentration 401
Bank concentration and finance capital 403
Monopolies 406
The empires of financial groups 411
Monopoly super-profits 419
Equalisation of the monopoly rate of profit 423
Origins of monopoly profit 426
Monopolies as fetters on economic progress 428
Monopolies and "oligopolies" 433
Monopoly capitalism and contradictions of capitalism 434

CHAPTER THIRTEEN

IMPERIALISM

Capitalism and inequality among nations 441
The world market and industrial capitalism 445
From export of goods to export of capital 448
Colonialism 450
Colonial super-profits 453
The world-wide division of labour 459
International trusts and cartels 465
Private trusts wield sovereign rights in under-developed countries 469
Economic structure of the under-developed countries 472
Imperialism as an obstacle to the industrialisation of under-developed countries 476
Neo-imperialism 480

CHAPTER FOURTEEN

THE EPOCH OF CAPITALIST DECLINE

Concentration and centralisation of capital on an international scale 485
Relative shrinkage and fragmentation of the world market 488
All-round cartellisation of industry 491
Forced cartellisation 496
The bourgeoisie and the state 498
The state as guarantor of monopoly profits 501
Increasing fusion between state and monopolies 507
Self-financing 511
Overcapitalisation 517
Growing importance of armaments and war economy 521
Permanent tendency to currency inflation 526
A crisis-free capitalism? 529
The laws of development of capitalism in its age of decline 534
Welfare State and Fascism 536
The age of the managers? 539
The bankruptcy of capitalism 541

CHAPTER FIFTEEN

THE SOVIET ECONOMY

Stages of the Soviet economy 548
What the Five-Year Plans achieved 557
The social character of the Soviet economy 560
The "economic categories" in the U.S.S.R. 565
The fundamental contradictions of Soviet economy 572
Disproportion between industry and agriculture 575
Planned economy and the material incentive of personal interest 584
The contradictions of bureaucratic management 589
Bureaucratic management and workers' conditions 593

CHAPTER SIXTEEN

THE ECONOMY OF THE TRANSITION PERIOD

The third industrial revolution 605
Need for a transition period 608
Sources of international socialist accumulation 612
Sources of socialist accumulation in industrialised countries 615
Sources of socialist accumulation in under-developed countries 618
Maximum and optimum rates of accumulation 621
Note on the "law of priority in the development of the capital goods sector" 627
Economic function of socialist democracy 631
Planned economy and market economy 632
Planning techniques 637
New production relations and socialised mode of production 643

Agriculture and distribution in the transition period 646
A mixed economy? 649

CHAPTER SEVENTEEN

SOCIALIST ECONOMY

Mode of production, mode of distribution, mode of life 654
Individual wages and social wages 656
Basic needs and secondary needs: freedom of consumption and rational consumption 660
Withering away of commodity production and money economy 664
Economic revolution and psychological revolution 668
Withering away of classes and the state 673
Economic growth not a permanent aim 677
Alienated labour and free labour 679
Man's limitations? 683

CHAPTER EIGHTEEN

ORIGIN, RISE AND WITHERING AWAY OF POLITICAL ECONOMY

Economic activity and ideology 690
The dawn of economic thought 692
Origins of the labour theory of value 693
Development of the labour theory of value 698
Climax and break-up of classical political economy 703
Marx's contribution 705
Attacks on the labour theory of value 707
The marginalist theory of value and neo-classical political economy 712
The "Keynesian revolution" 717
The econometrists 721
An apologetic variant of Marxism 722
New developments in economic thinking in the U.S.S.R. 726
The end of political economy 729

BIBLIOGRAPHY 735

INDEX 773

INTRODUCTION

THE attitude of the academic world towards Marxist economic theory is ruled by a strange paradox. Half a century ago, this theory was the subject of increasing theoretical interest and of fervent discussions in university circles, but it was said to lack all practical significance: a socialist economy "is impracticable", said the economists.[1] Today nobody denies that Marxist theory is capable of inspiring, and not unsuccessfully, the economic policy of states both large and small; but in academic circles it now meets only with indifference or contempt.* If it sometimes figures as the subject of more thorough studies, this happens not for its own sake but in so far as it is a sub-branch of the new "science" called "sovietology", or is included within a still stranger discipline, "marxology"...

Whoever regards as valid the Marxist method of investigation and the mass of results which it has produced—and the writer is unreservedly of that opinion—might obviously retort that there is nothing to be surprised at here. Is not academic science "in the service of the ruling class"? Is not the capitalist world "engaged in a fight to the death" with the "socialist camp"? Is not Marxist theory an essential weapon of this "camp"? Are not the servants of capitalism obliged to discredit systematically whatever is of service to their class foes? From this standpoint the discredit cast upon Marxism in the West is merely a manifestation of the class struggle itself, indirectly confirming the validity of the Marxist propositions. This method of reasoning runs the risk of producing the sort of dialogue between people who are impervious to each other's arguments which is what the exchange of "technical" invective between Marxist and psychoanalysts amounts to.

We shall not, of course, deny that there is a grain of truth in these allegations; but only a grain! If we consider objectively the entire realm in which ideas are shaped and defended, we shall not be able to deny that a fair number of cynics and careerists are to be met therein, people who sell their pens and their brains to the highest

* J. M. Keynes describes Marx's *Capital* as "an obsolete economic textbook ... not only scientifically erroneous but without interest or application for the modern world."[2] A. A. Berle, Jr., considers that Marx's political economy is outworn and refuted.[3] François Perroux declares that "none of the 'chronic tendencies' [of capitalism, revealed by Marx] is logically demonstrable or can be proved by resort to scientific observation."[4] Raymond Aron writes: "Marxism no longer holds any place in the culture of the West, even in France and Italy, where an important section of the intelligentsia openly supports Stalinism. It would be vain to seek an economist worthy of the name who could be described as a Marxist in the strict sense of the word."[5] And so on.

bidder, or who subtly modify the direction taken by their thought if it risks prejudicing their promotion. It must further be added that for some decades now the Soviet Union, in possession of increasing material power, itself also wields an influence of the same sort.

No Marxist worthy of the name, faithful to the great scientific tradition of Marx himself, would be capable, however, of reducing the problem of the evolution of ideas to mere matters of corruption, whether direct (working through personal interest) or indirect (working through the pressure of the surrounding milieu). Marx and Engels emphasised more than once that the history of ideas follows its own dialectic, that ideas evolve on the basis of data bequeathed by one generation to another, and by the clash of competing schools of thought (cf. Engels's letter to Franz Mehring, 14th July, 1893). The social determination of this process operates essentially on material provided in this manner, with its own contradictions and possibilities of "explosion" in different directions.

Commenting on Marx's *Theorien über den Mehrwert* [Theories of Surplus Value], which were to have constituted Volume IV of *Capital*, Rudolph Hilferding correctly stressed that what we have here is a study of the dialectical evolution of ideas in accordance with their own logic and their internal contradictions *(Selbstentwicklung der nationalökonomischen Wissenschaft)*. Marx did not bring in the social factor except as the explanation of this evolution in the last analysis, and not at all as its immediate explanation.[6]

Now, Marxist tradition sums up the evolution of bourgeois political economy, that is, of "official" or "academic" political economy, in three stages, each of which coincides with a stage in the evolution of capitalism. In the stage when the bourgeoisie is rising to the position of ruling class, political economy undertakes to master economic reality, and we have the working out of the theory of labour-value, from William Petty to Ricardo. Then comes the stage when the bourgeoisie is involved in an even more acute class struggle with the proletariat, without, however, having finally eliminated the former ruling classes: this is the period when the range of possibilities contained in the inherent contradictions of the bourgeois theory of labour-value is wide open, so that we have the birth of the Marxist school, on the one hand, and that of the various post-Ricardian schools of bourgeois economic thought, on the other. Lastly, in the third stage, the bourgeoisie, having finally consolidated its ruling position, has no other struggle to wage than a defensive one against the proletariat. This is the period of the decline of bourgeois political economy. It ceases to be scientific and becomes merely apologetic. The theory of labour-value is replaced, first by "vulgar (eclectic) economics", and then by the marginalist school or by mixed schools which synthesise eclecticism and marginalism.

When one analyses the evolution of official economic thought during the last thirty years, one perceives, however, that this schema is not complete. Since the great crisis of 1929–1933 a *fourth* stage in the evolution of bourgeois political economy can easily be discerned: the stage of *purely pragmatic theory*. Mere apologetics is an effective device only so long as the system is threatened in the theoretical sphere alone. It becomes absurdly inadequate as soon as the system is in danger of collapsing in practice.

From that moment on, political economy throws overboard most of its purely academic concerns, in order to become *a technique for the practical consolidation of capitalism*. This is in fact the function it has fulfilled since the "Keynesian revolution" and the working out of the various techniques of econometry.*

Here we touch upon one of the roots of the indifference shown nowadays by "official" economists towards Marxism. In their minds, Marxism appears as just one of the schools of "the old political economy" which were centred on problems of micro-economics and were content to "reason in the abstract", without offering any recipes for increasing the volume of employment or remedying a deficit in the balance of payments. More than that, the only contemporary economists who accord Marx an honourable place in the history of economic ideas are precisely those who see him as an ancestor of the macro-economic theories now fashionable.† Some Marxists too try to show that Marx's merit consists above all in his having "foreshadowed" Keynes, the theory of economic cycles and the calculation of the national income . . .

But though interest in "pure" economic problems detached from immediate practical concerns has undeniably diminished in our times, marked as they have been by tremendous social upheavals,[11] those who claim to be Marxists are themselves partly responsible for the decline in interest in Marxist economic theory. The fact is that, for nearly fifty years, they have been content to repeat Marx's teaching, in summaries of *Capital* which have increasingly lost contact with contemporary reality. Here we touch upon the second root of the paradox mentioned at the beginning: the inability of the Marxists to repeat in the second half of the twentieth century the work that Marx carried through in the nineteenth.

This inability is due above all to political causes. It results from the subordinate position in which theory was kept in the U.S.S.R. and in the Communist Parties during the Stalin era. Theory was then the handmaid of day-to-day politics, just as in the Middle Ages philosophy was the handmaid of theology. From this situation, theory suffered

* See Chapter 18, the paragraphs: "The Keynesian revolution" and "Econometry, or the Triumph of pragmatism."

† Notably, Schumpeter,[7] Henri Guitton,[8] Condliffe,[9] Alvin Hansen,[10] etc.

a distortion towards pragmatism and apologetics which especially showed itself in economic theory. As the Stalin era was also marked by a ban on independent theoretical research, a sterile dogmatism was laid down on top of this apologetical distortion, thus forming a structure which is repulsive to the young generations both in the East and in the West. Thinking which has been stopped and distorted for 25 years* does not get back into its stride otherwise than slowly, especially if the social conditions which, in the last analysis, have caused this stoppage have not been fundamentally abolished.

Moreover, there is a secondary reason for this cessation of development in Marxist economic thought, not only in the U.S.S.R. and in the parties connected with it but also in the West, in all the Marxist schools which have remained independent of the Soviet Union. This derives from a misunderstanding regarding the Marxist method itself.

In a famous passage in his introduction to the *Contribution To The Critique Of Political Economy*, Marx explains the method that a scientific exposition of political economy must follow—proceeding from the abstract so as to reconstitute the concrete.[13] Popularisers without number have been inspired by this passage, as also by the structure of the three volumes of *Capital*, to renew again and again, in abridged and often unsatisfactory form, the economic explanations which Marx elaborated last century.

Now, *one ought not to confuse method of presentation with origin of knowledge*. While Marx insists on the fact that the concrete cannot be understood without first being analysed into the abstract relationships which make it up, he equally stresses that these relationships themselves cannot be the outcome of a mere brilliant intuition or superior capacity for abstraction; they must emerge from the study of empirical data, the raw material of every science. To grasp what Marx's opinion really was, it is enough to put beside the passage on method in the introduction to the *Contribution To The Critique Of Political Economy* the following text from the second edition of *Capital*:

"Of course the method of presentation must differ in form from that of inquiry. *The latter has to appropriate the material in detail*, to analyse its different forms of development, to trace out their inner connexion. *Only after this work is done* can the actual movement be adequately described. If this is done successfully, if the life of the

* "In our country no fundamental creative work has been done in Marxism-Leninism. Most of our theoreticians busy themselves with turning over and over again old quotations, formulas and theses. What is a science without creative work? It is not so much science as scholasticism, a pupils' exercise, not a science; for science is above all creation, creation of something new and not repetition of what is old."[12]

subject-matter is ideally reflected as in a mirror, then it may appear as if we had before us a mere *a priori* construction." [Emphasis ours.][14]

It is thus apparent that a presentation which, in the middle of the twentieth century, restricts itself to summarising, more or less accurately, the chapters of *Capital*, written in the last century, is definitely insufficient, first and foremost from the standpoint of the Marxist method itself. Still less valid, of course, are the numerous peremptory declarations made by critics of Marxism, according to which the latter is out of date "because it relies on the data of the science of last century".

The scientifically correct position is obviously that which *endeavours to start from the empirical data of the science of today in order to examine whether or not the essence of Marx's economic propositions remains valid.** This is the method we have tried to follow in this book.

We must therefore issue a warning. The reader who expects to find numerous quotations from Marx and Engels or their chief disciples will close this book disappointed. Unlike all the writers of Marxist economic textbooks, we have *strictly abstained* (with very few exceptions) from quoting the sacred texts or interpreting these quotations. As against that, we quote abundantly from the chief economists, economic historians, ethnologists, anthropologists, sociologists and psychologists of our times, in so far as they express opinions on phenomena relating to the economic activity, past, present or future, of human societies. What we seek to show is that it is possible, on the basis of the scientific data of contemporary science, to reconstitute the whole economic system of Karl Marx. Furthermore, we seek to show that only Marx's economic teaching makes possible this synthesis of the totality of human knowledge, and above all a synthesis of economic history and economic theory, just as it alone makes possible a harmonious integration of micro-economic and macro-economic analysis.

The great superiority of the Marxist method compared with other schools of economic thought in fact consists of this dynamic synthesis

* Several writers, notably François Perroux, have frequently declared that the laws of capitalist development discovered by Marx have never been demonstrated by observation or by means of statistical data (see quotation *supra*). We try in this book to show that this is not so—making our point of departure, of course, Marx's own laws of development and not those which have been falsely attributed to him (such as that of "absolute impoverishment", of the permanent decline of real wages, or other such notions). We are curious to know whether the official economists will be able to refute the material we have brought together in this connexion, or if they will go on declaring dismissively that "Marx is out of date", thus revealing the same lack of scientific rigour as the pseudo-Marxists who confine themselves to repeating figures and examples from the last century.

of economic history and economic theory which it alone makes possible. Marxist economic theory ought not to be regarded as a completed outcome of past investigation but rather as the summation of a method, of the results obtained by using this method, and of results which are continually subject to re-examination. Such non-Marxist writers as Joseph Schumpeter and Joan Robinson have voiced their nostalgia for this synthesis.[15] Marxism alone has been able to achieve it. The Marxist method is morever inconceivable except as an *integration* of dialectical rationalism with empirical (and practical) grasping of the facts.*

The method must therefore be genetico-evolutionary, critical, materialistic and dialectical. *Genetico-evolutionary*, because the secret of no "category" can be discovered without study both of its origin and its evolution, which is nothing else but the development of its inner contradictions, that is to say, the revelation of its true nature.† *Critical*, because no "category" ought to be "taken for granted", neither the categories "society", "labour", and "necessary product" (subsistence) nor the categories "commodity", "exchange", "money" and "capital" whose secrets Marx himself revealed. In order to do this we have generally relied on the very profound though fragmentary remarks which are scattered through Marx's writings. Sometimes, however, we have had to proceed from scratch.

In any case, critical, genetico-evolutionary study of these "fundamental categories" has brought us face to face with anthropology, sociology and social psychology. So as not to put the reader off, and not to interrupt the logical course of the demonstration, we have put the bulk of this analysis in the penultimate chapter instead of the

* Cf. Marx in his letter to Engels dated 1st February, 1858. "He [Lassalle] will learn to his cost that to bring a science by criticism to the point where it can be dialectically presented is an altogether different thing from applying an abstract ready-made system of logic to mere inklings of such a system."[16]

† Cf. Hilferding: "What distinguishes Marx from all his predecessors is the social theory which underlies his system, the materialist conception of history. Not only because it implies understanding the fact that economic categories are equally historical categories; this understanding by itself is not yet the essential thing; but rather because it is only by revealing the law-governed nature of social life that one can reveal and show the mechanism of evolution, [that one can show] how economic categories are born, change and pass away, and how all that happens."[17] Here still, of course, there is conflict between the origin of knowledge and the method of its presentation. Before fully grasping the significance of a category in the phase in which it first appears one needs to have analysed it in its mature form. This is why Marx deliberately abandons the genetico-evolutionary method of presentation in the first chapters of *Capital*. Once, however, in possession of the key to the mystery, the contemporary researcher who wants to re-examine the validity of a category in the face of fresh empirical data has every reason to go over its evolution, starting from the beginning.

first.* An obvious dialectical temptation exists, moreover, to study the category of labour in the light of socialist society rather than in that of primitive society. Is it not in its negation, or rather in its surpassing, in the negation of its negation, that the nature of a phenomenon is seen in its full brilliance and richness?

Finally, the method is *materialistic* and *dialectical*, since the ultimate secret of any economic category is not to be found in men's heads; it is in every instance to be found in the social relations which men have been obliged to establish among themselves in the production of their material life. And this life, together with these relations, is examined both as an indissoluble entity and as a contradictory entity which evolves under the pressure of its own contradictions.

An objection will doubtless be urged against the method which the author has followed and the results to which it has led. It will be said that though he has certainly based himself on empirical data of contemporary science, he has done this selectively. He has chosen the data which fit into "his" preconceived system, and not *all* the data. He has interpreted *some* facts but not *the* facts.

This objection is valid only to the extent that the author has indeed tried to get away from the childish obsession for "writing history with *all* the details", that obsession which Anatole France ridicules so wittily in *Le Livre de mon Ami*. The task is not merely impossible in the material sense—several men's lives would be needed to read all the books and all the sources, in all the languages of the world, which relate to the economic activity of mankind—it is also quite pointless.

At the level of the various disciplines, valid syntheses have been worked out. The Marxist who wants to study the conclusions that are to be deduced from the primitive ways in which land was held in mediaeval France need not consult a lot of sources for this purpose; he can rely sufficiently on such works as Marc Bloch's *Les Caractères Originaux de l'Historie Rurale Française*.

It is moreover obvious that selecting one's facts is characteristic of every science, the natural sciences no less than the social sciences.†

* See Chapter 17, paragraphs: "Alienated labour, free labour, withering away of labour", "Social revolution, economic revolution and psychological revolution", and "Man's limitations?"

† "Science is not a set of facts but a way of giving order, and therefore giving unity and intelligibility to the facts of nature," declares Dr. Bronowski, chairman of the British Association.[18] "Unless I am seriously mistaken, the prevailing view among statisticians is that the theory to be tested determines the statistical procedure to be adopted . . . It is logically impossible, except by accident, to bring the testing of theories into the problem as one proceeds along the road, as a sort of by-product of a more general examination of facts," says the economist Metzler.[19] And the economists Edey and Peacock stress that "the facts with which we are concerned in most fields of knowledge are many in number and exhibit great complexity in their relationships one with

What is anti-scientific is not the unavoidable choice of "significant facts", it is the deliberate suppression (or falsification) of experiments and observations, so as to "deny" phenomena which do not fit into the schema. We have tried to avoid all subjectivism of that sort.

It remains true that the attempt we have made to "de-Westernise" the material, except that relating to nineteenth-century capitalism, *that is to say, to discover the common features of pre-capitalist economic categories in all the civilisations which have reached the stage of developed international trade*, may seem rash. We have neither the knowledge of languages nor the knowledge of history needed for success in undertaking such a task. Nevertheless, it is indispensable, both because the public to which Marxism appeals today is no longer essentially a Western public, and also because the popularisers of Marxism have brought a tremendous confusion into this sphere with their theory of the "successive stages" that society is supposed to have passed through, or must necessarily pass through, in all parts of the world, a theory which was explicitly repudiated by Marx himself (see especially his letters to the *Otechestvennie Zapiski*, November 1877, and to Vera Zasulich, 8th March, 1881.[21]*

This is therefore merely an attempt, at once a draft which calls for many corrections and an invitation to the younger generations of Marxists, in Tokyo and Lima, in London and Bombay, and (why not?) in Moscow, New York, Peking and Paris, to catch the ball in flight and carry to completion by team work what an individual's efforts can obviously no longer accomplish. If this work succeeds in causing such consequences, even if in the form of criticisms, the author will have fully achieved his aim, for he has not tried to reformulate or discover eternal truths, but only to show the amazing relevance of living Marxism. It is by collective synthesis of the empirical data of universal science that this aim will be attained, far more than by way of exegesis or apologetics.

ERNEST MANDEL

another. To know in detail all the facts relating to a particular study and to be able to trace their individual relationships would be normally impossible for any person, however industrious. It seems to be the natural reaction of the human mind in such circumstances to classify, with varying degrees of precision depending upon the man and the nature of the problem, the relevant facts and relationships into a sufficiently small number of categories for them to be comprehended and considered together, after which they can be used as a basis for judgments about the nature of the world and its inhabitants; and, perhaps, for purposes of prediction."[20]

* It must be noted, however, that, starting a few years ago, some historians in the Chinese People's Republic have seriously questioned this non-Marxist dogma of world-wide "successive stages", and, in particular, have returned to Marx's ideas regarding "Asiatic society".

REFERENCES

1. E. Lippincott, introduction to: Oskar Lange and Fred M. Taylor: *On the Economic Theory of Socialism*, p. 3.
2. J. M. Keynes, *Essays in Persuasion*, p. 300.
3. A. A. Berle, Jnr.: *The XXth Century Capitalist Revolution*, pp. 13-24.
4. Fr. Perroux: *Le Capitalisme*, p. 109.
5. Raymond Aron: *L'Opium des Intellectuels*, p. 115.
6. R. Hilferding: *Aus der Vorgeschichte der Marxschen Oekonomie*, in *Die Neue Zeit*, Vol. XXIX, pt. 2, p. 574.
7. J. Schumpeter: *History of Economic Analysis*, p. 391.
8. Henri Guitton: *Les Fluctuations économiques*, pp. 329-32.
9. J. B. Condliffe: *The Commerce of Nations*, p. 241.
10. Alvin Hansen: *Readings in Business Cycles and National Income Theories*, p. 129.
11. Paul M. Sweezy: *The Theory of Capitalist Development*, p. 209.
12. Mikoyan at the 20th Congress of the C.P.S.U. *Die Presse der Sowjet-Union*, 1956, Vol. XXIII, p. 559.
13. K. Marx: *Zur Kritik der politischen Oekonomie*, ed. Kautsky, p. xxxvi.
14. K. Marx: *Das Kapital*, Vol. I, p. xvii.
15. J. Schumpeter: op. cit., p. 4; Joan Robinson: *The Accumulation of Capital*, p. 56.
16. K. Marx-F. Engels: *Briefwechsel*, II, p. 243.
17. R. Hilferding: op. cit., p. 626.
18. *Manchester Guardian*, 8 September 1955.
19. *Social Research*, September 1947, p. 375.
20. H. C. Edey and A. T. Peacock: *National Income and Social Accounting*, p. 155.
21. K. Marx-F. Engels: *Selected Correspondence* (1953), pp. 379, 412.
22. See especially articles by Fan Wen-lan and Jiang Quan in *Neue Chinesische Geschichtswissenschaft—Zeitschift für Geschichtswissenschaft*, Sonderheft 7, Jahrgang, 1959.

CHAPTER ONE

LABOUR, NECESSARY PRODUCT, SURPLUS PRODUCT

Labour, society, communication, language, consciousness, humanity

MAN alone, of all species, is unable to survive by adapting himself to the natural environment, but has instead to try to bend this environment to his own needs.[1] Labour, an activity at once conscious and social, born of the possibility of communication and of spontaneous mutual aid between the members of this species, is the means whereby man acts upon his natural environment.

The other animal species adapt themselves to a particular environment through development of specialised organs. Man's specialised organs, a hand with an opposable thumb and a developed nervous system, do not give him the means of directly obtaining his food in a particular natural environment. But they enable him to use tools and, through the development of language, to construct a social organisation which ensures the survival of the human race in an indefinite number of different natural environments.* Labour, social organisation, language, consciousness, are thus the distinctive characteristics of man, inseparably linked each with the others and mutually determining one another.

The tools without which man cannot produce, that is, in the first place, obtain the food needed for the survival of the species, appear at first as artificial prolongations of his natural organs. "Man needs tools to make up for the inadequacy of his physiological equipment."[3] At the dawn of mankind, these tools were very crude: sticks, chipped stones, sharpened pieces of bone and horn. In fact, prehistory and ethnology classify the primitive peoples in accordance with the raw materials from which they make their chief tools. This classification usually begins with the epoch of chipped stone, though among the prehistoric inhabitants of North America an age of bone seems to have preceded the stone age properly so called.

* "A creature which has become perfectly adapted to its environment, an animal whose whole capacity and vital force is concentrated and expended in succeeding here and now, has nothing left over with which to respond to any radical change . . . It can therefore beat all competitors in the special field but equally on the other hand should that field change it must become extinct. It is this success of efficiency which seems to account for the extinction of an enormous number of species."[2]

Production techniques emerge progressively from the continual repetition of the same work-movements. The most important technical discovery in human prehistory was undoubtedly that of the production and maintenance of fire. Though there are no longer any primitive tribes which were ignorant of fire before their contact with external civilisation,* innumerable myths and legends testify to an age without fire, followed by a period in which man did not yet know how to keep it going.

Sir James Frazer brought together the myths about the origin of fire of nearly two hundred primitive peoples. All show the great importance at the dawn of mankind of the discovery of a technique for generating fire and conserving it.[5]

Necessary Product

It is by labour that men satisfy their basic needs. Food, drink, rest, protection against inclemencies and excesses of cold or heat, ensuring the survival of the species by procreation, exercise for the muscles—these are the most elementary needs, according to the ethnologist Malinowski. All these needs are satisfied *socially*, that is to say, not by a purely physiological activity, by single combat between the individual and the forces of nature, but by activity which results from mutual relations established between the members of a human group.[6]

The more primitive a people the bigger is the share of its labour, and indeed of its entire existence, absorbed by seeking and producing food.[7]

The most primitive methods of food production are the gathering of wild fruit, the catching of harmless little animals, and elementary forms of hunting and fishing. A people living at this primitive stage, such as the aborigines of Australia or, better, the primitive inhabitants of Tasmania, who completely disappeared three-quarters of a century ago, know neither permanent dwellings nor domestic animals (except sometimes the dog), neither weaving of clothes nor making of containers for food. They have to traverse a very extensive territory in order to gather together sufficient food. Only the old men who are physically incapable of constant movement may be to some extent released from direct gathering of food, so as to busy themselves with making tools. The majority of the most backward communities that still survive today, such as the inhabitants of the Andaman Islands in the Indian Ocean, the Fuegians and Botocudos of Latin America, the Pigmies in Central Africa and Indonesia, the Kubu savages in Malaya, lead lives similar to those of the Australian aborigines.[8]

* In the sixteenth century the explorer Magellan came upon communities in the Mariana Islands in the Pacific who did not know fire. In the eighteenth century, Steller and Krasheninnikov visited the Kamchadales, inhabiting the Kamchatka Peninsula, who also were ignorant of fire.[4]

If it be accepted that mankind has been in existence for a million years, at least 980,000 years of that period were spent in a state of extreme poverty. Famine was a permanent threat to the survival of the species. The average production of food was inadequate to meet the average need for consumption. The keeping of reserves of food was unknown. Infrequent periods of plenty and good luck led to substantial wasting of food.

"The Bushmen, Australians, Veddahs of Ceylon and Fuegians hardly ever hoard for the future. The Central Australians want all their food at once, so as to have a good gorge; then they are resigned to 'go one big fella hungry' . . . When they move they leave their stone utensils lying about. If they need more they make them . . . A single tool is enough, until it wears out, for a Papuan; he has no idea of providing a successor before-hand . . . Insecurity prevented hoarding all through the primitive time. Periods of repletion and of semi-starvation regularly succeeded one another."[9]

This "improvidence" is not due to intellectual shortcomings in primitive man. It is rather the result of thousands of years of insecurity and endemic famine, which urged him to gorge himself to the full whenever opportunity occurred, and which did not allow him to work out a technique for hoarding food. Production as a whole provides the *necessary product*, that is to say, food, clothing, the community's dwelling-place, and a more or less stable stock of tools serving to produce these good things. There is no permanent surplus.

Beginning of the social division of labour

So long as an adequate supply of food is not ensured, men cannot devote themselves consistently to any other economic activity than the production of food. One of the first explorers of Central America, Cabeza de Vaca, encountered Indian tribes who knew how to make straw rugs for their dwellings but never undertook this work.

"They wish to give their full time to getting food, since when otherwise occupied they are pinched with hunger."[10]

Since all the men devote themselves to producing food, no true social division of labour, no specialisation into different *crafts*, can occur. For certain peoples it is quite incomprehensible that everybody should not be able to make all the objects in current use. The Indians of Central Brazil were always asking the German explorer Karl von der Steiner whether he had made his trousers, his mosquito-net and many other things himself. They were very surprised when he told them that he had not.[11]

Even at this level of social evolution there are individuals gifted with a special aptitude for a particular kind of work. But the economic situation, that is to say, the lack of a permanent reserve of foodstuffs, does not yet permit them to exercise these special aptitudes exclusively.

Describing the activities of the islanders of Tikopia, in the Solomon archipelago in the Pacific, Raymond Firth writes:

"Every Tikopia man is an agriculturist and a fisherman, and to some extent a worker in wood; every woman weeds plantations, uses her scoop net on the reef, beats bark-cloth and plaits mats. Such specialisation as exists is the development of extra capacity in a craft and not the practice of the craft to the exclusion of others."[12]

What is true of comparatively advanced society, where agriculture is already known, is even truer of a still more primitive society.

But the social organisation described by Raymond Firth reveals at the same time the existence of a rudimentary division of labour that can be observed at all the stages of mankind's economic development: *the division of labour between the sexes*. Among the most primitive peoples, the men devote themselves to hunting, the women gather fruit and harmless little animals. Among communities which have developed a little, certain of the techniques acquired are employed exclusively either by the men or by the women. The women undertake those activities which can be carried on near the dwelling-place: maintaining the fire, spinning, weaving, pottery-making, etc. The men go further out, hunting larger game, and work up basic raw materials into tools, using wood, stone, ivory, horns and bones.

The absence of such a division of labour as would lead to the formation of specialised crafts prevents the working out of techniques requiring a long apprenticeship and special knowledge, though it makes possible a more harmonious development of the body and of human activity. Those peoples who do not know as yet the division of labour, but who have been able to overcome famine and the worst epidemics, thanks to favourable natural conditions (Polynesians, some North American Indians before the white conquest, etc.), have developed a human type admired by modern civilised man.

First appearance of a social surplus product

The slow accumulation of inventions, discoveries and knowledge makes it possible to increase the production of food while reducing the physical effort needed from the producers. This is the first sign of an *increase in productivity of labour*. The invention of the bow and arrow, along with that of the harpoon, makes it possible to improve the technique of hunting and fishing and thus to regularise mankind's supply of foodstuffs. Henceforth, these activities become more important than the gathering of wild fruit, which is now nothing more than a supplementary economic activity. The skins and hair of animals regularly caught, along with their horns, bones and tusks, become raw material which man possesses the leisure to work up. The discovery of particularly rich hunting-grounds or fishing-beaches makes possible transition from the nomadic state to that of hunters or fishermen who are semi-settled (with seasonal alternation of dwelling-place) or even completely settled. This is the position with communities such as the Minkopies (inhabiting the shores of the Andaman Islands), the Klamath (Indians of the Californian coast), some tribes in Malaya, etc.[13] The transition to a settled way of life, whether temporary or permanent, made possible by the development of the productivity of labour, in turn makes it possible to increase the latter. It now becomes feasible to accumulate tools over and above the limited amount that a migratory community could carry with it.

Thus there gradually appears, alongside the product necessary for the survival of the community, a first permanent surplus, a first form of *social surplus product*. Its essential function is to make possible the formation of food reserves, so as to prevent or at least to mitigate the periodical return of famine. Through thousands of years primitive peoples tried to solve the problem of storing food. Numerous tribes found the solution only through contact with higher civilisations. Thus, those communities which have remained nomadic hunters and who as a rule do not produce any regular surplus, are all ignorant of salt, the most effective material for keeping meat.[14]*

The second original function of the social surplus product is to enable a more advanced division of labour to take place. From the moment that the tribe has more or less permanent reserves of food at its disposition, some of its members can devote a more considerable part of their time to producing objects which are not for eating: tools, ornaments, containers for food. What was previously just a personal inclination or talent for a certain technique now becomes a specialisation, the embryo of a craft.

The third original function of the social surplus is to make possible a more rapid increase of population. Conditions of semi-famine practically limit the population of any tribe to able-bodied men and women. The tribe cannot keep alive more than a minimum of small children. Most primitive peoples know about and extensively apply artificial birth-control, which is absolutely indispensable because of the inadequate food supply.[15] Only a limited number of sick or disabled people can be looked after and kept alive. Infanticide is commonly practised. Prisoners of war are usually killed, if not eaten. All these efforts to restrict the growth of population do not show that primitive man is innately cruel, but testify rather to an effort to avoid a greater danger, the disappearance of the entire people for lack of food.

From the moment, however, when a more or less permanent food

* Before the discovery of the preservative functions of salt, a discovery which was decisive for the establishment of permanent reserves of protein, a wide variety of methods were used to preserve meat. It was dried, smoked, kept in bamboo vacuum containers, etc. All these methods have been found inadequate for long-term preservation.

reserve makes its appearance, a new equilibrium between the food available and the number of the population can be achieved. Births increase, and with them the number of children surviving infancy. Sick people and the aged can live longer, increasing the average age of the tribe. The density of the population on a given territory will increase with the productivity of labour, and this is an excellent index of economic and social progress.[16] With the growth of the population and the specialisation of its labour the productive forces at mankind's disposal are increased. The appearance of a social surplus is an essential condition for this increase.

The neolithic revolution

The formation of a permanent surplus of foodstuffs is the material basis for the carrying through of the most important economic revolution man has known since his appearance on earth: the beginning of agriculture and of the domestication and rearing of animals. In accordance with the period of prehistory during which this revolution occurred, the period of polished stone, or neolithic period, it is known as the neolithic revolution.

Agriculture and cattle-raising presuppose the existence of a certain surplus of food, and this for two reasons. First, because their technique demands the utilisation of seed and animals for purposes not directly concerned with food consumption, so as to produce more plants and more meat at a later stage. Peoples who have lived for thousands of years on the brink of famine do not easily agree to diverting towards a more distant goal whatever is immediately edible, unless they possess other stocks of food.*

Besides, neither agriculture nor cattle-raising immediately produce the food needed for the tribe's existence, and a food reserve is needed to cover the period between seed-time and harvest. For these reasons, neither primitive agriculture nor cattle-raising could be adopted straight away as the principal production system of a people. They make their appearance by stages, being at first regarded as activities secondary to hunting and the gathering of fruit, and they long continue to be supplemented by these activities, even when they have become the basis of the people's livelihood.

It is generally thought that the raising of domestic animals (beginning: *c.* 10,000 B.C.) came later than the first attempts at systematic agriculture (beginning: *c.* 15,000 B.C.), though the two activities may appear simultaneously or, with certain peoples, the order of appearance may even be reversed.[18] The most primitive form of agriculture,

* "Agriculture calls for . . . an ascetic self-discipline which does not follow automatically from a knowledge of tools," Gehlen points out. The author wonders whether, for this reason, the first crops were perhaps protected by being exclusively devoted to religious purposes.[17]

still practised today by a number of peoples of Africa and Oceania, consists of scratching the surface of the soil with a pointed stick, or digging it with a hoe. Since the soil is rapidly exhausted by such methods of cultivation, it is necessary to leave the land thus worked, after a few years, and occupy fresh land. Several peoples, for example, the mountain tribes of India, acquire this fresh land for cultivation by burning the jungle, the ashes forming a natural fertiliser.[19]

The neolithic revolution brings the production of means of subsistence, for the first time since the dawn of mankind, under man's direct control: this is its main importance. The gathering of fruit, hunting and fishing are *passive* methods of providing food. They reduce, or, at least, maintain at a given level, the quantity of resources that nature puts at the disposal of man on a given territory. Agriculture and cattle-raising, however, are *active* methods of providing food, since they increase the natural resources available to mankind, and create new ones. With the same expenditure of labour, the amount of food at man's disposal can be increased tenfold. These methods thus constitute a tremendous increase in the social productivity of human labour.

The neolithic revolution also gives a powerful stimulus to the development of tools. By creating a *permanent surplus* it creates the possibility of a professional body of craftsmen.

"The preliminary condition for the formation of craft (technical) abilities is a certain amount of leisure which can be taken from the time devoted to producing means of subsistence."[20]

The beginning of agriculture and the raising of domestic animals leads, moreover, to the first great social division of labour: pastoral peoples appear alongside agricultural peoples.

Undoubtedly, the decisive progress due to the practice of agriculture must be ascribed to women. The example of the peoples who still exist as primitive agriculturists, as well as numberless myths and legends,* confirm that women, who in primitive society devote themselves to gathering fruit, and usually remain close to the dwelling-place, were the first to sow the seeds of the fruit they had collected, so as to facilitate the provision of food for the tribe. The women of the Indian Winnebago tribe were, moreover, compelled to *hide* the rice and maize destined for sowing, as otherwise the men would have eaten them. In close connexion with the development of agriculture by the women there appear, among numerous primitive agricultural peoples, religions based on the worship of goddesses of fertility.† The

* "The appellation *pasigadong*—the means of getting *gadong*, or food—is jocosely applied by the Batak to his wife . . ."[21]

† Cf. the following observation by Robert Graves: "The whole of neolithic Europe, to judge from surviving artifacts and myths, had a remarkably homogeneous system of religious ideas, based on worship of the many-titled Mother-goddess, who was also known in Syria and Libya. Ancient Europe had no

institution of the matriarchate, the existence of which can be shown among a number of peoples at the same level of social development, is also connected with the part played by women in the creation of agriculture. Sumner and Keller and Kritz Heichelheim[24] list a large number of proved instances of matriarchate among primitive agricultural peoples.

Co-operative organisation of labour

Hobhouse, Wheeler and Ginsberg studied the mode of production of all the primitive peoples who were still surviving at the beginning of the twentieth century. They found that all the tribes who know only a rudimentary form of agriculture and cattle-raising—and, *a fortiori*, all those peoples who have remained at a lower stage of economic development—are ignorant of the use of metals and possess only a very crude technique of pottery-making and weaving.

Archaeological data confirm those of ethnography. In the neolithic epoch we find in Europe only the crudest forms of pottery. In India, in North China, and in North and West Africa, we find traces of similar societies between the sixth and fifth millennia B.C.[25] The non-existence of advanced pottery or weaving indicates the absence of a fully separate body of craftsmen. The surplus that agriculture and cattle raising supplies to society does not yet make it possible to free the craftsman completely from the task of producing his own food.

Thus, even today, in the Chinese village of Taitou:

"None of the artisans . . . makes his living entirely from his trade . . . All the masons, carpenters, weavers, workers in the small foundry, the village schoolteacher, the crop watcher, and the several village officers work on their land with their families during the sowing and harvesting seasons or whenever they happen not to be engaged in their professional work."[26]

Just as at more primitive stages of economic development, society remains based on the co-operative organisation of labour. The community needs the labour of every one of its members. It does not yet produce a surplus sufficiently large for this to become private property without jeopardising the survival of the whole community. The customs and code of honour of the tribe are opposed to any *individual* accumu-

gods. The Great Goddess was regarded as immortal, changeless, and omnipotent; and the concept of fatherhood had not been introduced into religious thought. She took lovers, but for pleasure, not to provide her children with a father. Men feared, adored, and obeyed the matriarch: the hearth which she tended in a cave or hut being their earliest social centre, and motherhood their prime mystery."[22] The Indian writer Debiprasad Chattopadhyaya has made an extensive analysis of the relationships between the part played by women as the first cultivators of the soil, the matriarchate, and the magico-religious cult of goddesses of fertility, on the basis of the history and literature of his country.[23]

lation in excess of the average. Differences in individual productive skill are not reflected in distribution. Skill as such does not confer a right to the product of individual work, and the same applies to more diligent work.[27]

"Maori distribution," writes Bernard Mishkin, "was fundamentally dominated by one aim: to meet the needs of the community. No one could starve so long as anything remained in the community storehouses."[28]

Special institutions were developed—for instance, the ceremonial exchange of gifts and the organisation of feasts after the harvest—to ensure an equitable sharing of foodstuffs and other necessary products among all the members of the community. Describing the feasts organised among the Papuan people of Arapesh, Margaret Mead considers that this institution "is actually an effective measure against any one man's accumulating wealth disproportionate to the wealth accumulated by others."[29]

Georges Balandier writes to the same effect regarding the Bakongo tribes in Equatorial Africa:

"An institution like the one called *malaki* throws light on this ambiguous situation. At the start, it was in the nature of an annual feast (in the dry season) which extolled the unity of the kindred by honouring ancestors, and made possible the reinforcement of alliances . . . On this occasion, a quantity of good things which had been accumulated during the year were consumed collectively in a true atmosphere of rejoicing and celebration. Thrift operated, upheld by the heads of the kindreds, in the form of *renewal of relationships of consanguinity and alliance*. The *malaki* functions, by its regular periodicity and the amount of wealth needed for it, as one of the driving forces and regulators of the Bakongo economy . . . It testifies to a moment (hard to date) in economic evolution when the surplus of products presented men with new problems: their products came between them and distorted the system of personal relations."[30]

James Swann, describing the customs of the Indians of Cape Flattery (Washington State, U.S.A.), says that whoever has produced a plentiful supply of food, in whatever form, customarily invites a series of neighbours or members of his family to come and consume it with him. If an Indian has gathered sufficient stocks of food, he has to give a feast, which goes on until this stock is exhausted.[31] A society of this kind puts the accent on the quality of *social solidarity* and regards as immoral an attitude of economic competition and ambition for individual enrichment.

Solomon Asch, who has studied on the spot the customs of the Hopi Indians, observes:

"All individuals must be treated alike; no one must be superior and no one must be inferior. The person who is praised or who praises himself is automatically subject to resentment and to criticism . . . Most Hopi men refuse to be foremen . . . The play behaviour of children is equally instructive in this respect. From the same source I learned that the children, young and old, are never interested in keeping score during a game. They will play basket-ball by the hour without knowing who is winning or losing. They continue simply because they delight in the game itself . . ."[32]

The co-operative organisation of labour implies, on the one hand, the carrying-out in common of certain economic activities—building huts, hunting the larger animals, making paths, felling trees, breaking up new land—and, on the other, mutual aid between different families in daily life. The American anthropologist John H. Province has described such a work-system in the Siang Dyak tribe, who live in Borneo. All members of the tribe, including the witch-doctor, work alternately on their own paddy field and on that of another family. They all go hunting and firewood-collecting and all carry out domestic tasks.[33]

Margaret Mead describes a similar system prevailing among the Arapesh, a mountain people of New Guinea.[34] The co-operative organisation of labour in its pure form means that no adult holds back from participating in labour. It thus implies the absence of a "ruling class". The work is planned by the community in accordance with custom and with ancient rites based on a deep knowledge of the natural environment (climate, composition of the soil, habits of game, etc.). The chief, if there is one, is merely the embodiment of these rites and customs, the correct fulfilment of which he ensures.

Labour co-operation continues, as a rule, throughout the slow process, prolonged through hundreds (if not thousands) of years, of disintegration of the village community.[35] It must be stressed that the custom of carrying out tasks in common which is found very late in class-divided societies is doubtless the origin of *corvée*, that is, of unpaid extra work which is carried out on behalf of the State, the Temple, or the Lord. In the case of China, the evolution from one to the other is perfectly clear.

Melville J. Herskovits[36] mentions a very interesting transitional case in Dahomey. *Dókpwê*, communal work, is usually carried out for the benefit of every native household. But, contrary to tradition, and to official statements, a request for help from a relatively prosperous household is answered before one from a poor household. Furthermore, the head of the *dókpwê* has become a member of the ruling class. The Dahomeyans are, moreover, aware of the evolution which his taken place, and themselves told Herskovits the following:

"The *dókpwê* is an ancient institution. It existed before there were kings. In the olden times there were no chiefs and the *dókpwêgâ* [directing the communal work] was in command of the village. The male members of the village formed the *dókpwê* as today, and the cultivation of the ground was done communally. Later, with the coming of chiefs and kings, disputes arose as to their respective authority . . ."[37]

According to Nadel, in the Nigerian kingdom of Nupe, communal work, called *egbe*, is carried out first (and above all!) on the lands of the chiefs; Joseph Bourrilly mentions a similar evolution of the *touiza*, as co-operative work is called among the Berbers.[38]

Primitive occupation of the soil

At the moment when tribes start to practise agriculture they are usually organised on the basis of kinship. The oldest form of social organisation seems to be that of the *horde*, such as still exists among the aborigines of Australia.

"[A horde] is a body of persons who jointly possess, occupy and exploit a certain defined area of country. The rights of the horde over its territory can be briefly indicated by saying that no person who is not a member of the horde has the right to any animal, vegetable or mineral product from the territory except by invitation or consent of members of the horde."[39]

Later, the large family, the clan, the tribe as a confederation of clans, the confederation of related tribes, are the normal forms of organisation of the primitive peoples, at the moment when they begin to apply themselves to agriculture. It is therefore not surprising that the primitive occupation of the soil, and the establishment of one or other form of authority (ownership) over the latter, are first and foremost influenced by this predominant form of social organisation.

So long as the people concerned have not yet reached the stage of intensive agriculture, with manuring and irrigation, the occupation of the soil usually takes the form of occupation of a village by a large family, a group of men and women united by kinship. In Northern Rhodesia, Audrey I. Richards notes that the Bemba people "live in small communities, the average village consisting of 30 to 50 huts . . . Each village is a kinship unit under the rule of a headman . . ."[40]

Among the settled Berbers of Morocco, "the typical state is not the tribe but what we call, inaccurately enough, the fraction of a tribe [the large family] . . . All the members of the fraction say they are descended from the same ancestor, whose name they bear."[41] In the Slavonic countries of the sixth to ninth centuries the tribes "lived each with its own clans and on its own lands, each clan being its own master."[42]

Describing country life in mediaeval France, Marc Bloch concluded: "To sum up, the village and its fields are the work of a very large group, perhaps . . . of a tribe or a clan; the *manses* (English *hides*, German *Hufe*) are the shares allotted to smaller sub-groups. What was this secondary collectivity, of which the *manse* formed the shell? Very probably, it was the family, as distinct from the clan . . . , a family still patriarchal in type, large enough to embrace several collateral couples. In England the word *hide* has as its Latin synonym *terra unius familiae* [the land of one family]."[43]

Speaking of agricultural life in Lorraine, Ch. Edmond Perrin confirms "that the *manse* was, in the beginning, the share of land cultivated by a single family, is proved sufficiently by the practices of the Merovingian period; in the seventh century, indeed . . . it was by head of family and not by *manse* that the obligations of tenants were calculated on the lands of the Church and of the Crown."[44]

It is thus the large family, the clan, that occupies the village, and the family strictly so called that builds the farm. Now, primitive agriculture was confronted above all by the problem of periodical clearing of new land, a task carried out in common by the entire village, as is testified by the example of those peoples who have remained to this day at the given stage of development, and as is celebrated in old Chinese songs. It is logical, within the framework of a co-operative organisation of labour, that the cultivable land, cleared communally, should remain common property and be redistributed periodically. Only the garden around the dwelling, cleared by the family alone, or the fruit tree they have planted, evolves towards the stage of private property.[45] *Garden* means, moreover, "enclosed place", that is, "field closed to others", in contrast to the fields which are common property and are not divided up by fences.*

The allotment and periodical redistribution of the cultivable land by drawing lots are confirmed by numerous pieces of historical and linguistic evidence. The cultivable lands in Lorraine were first called *sors* (lots); the lands distributed by lot in Old Testament Palestine were called *nahala* (lots), a word which later came to mean property, etc. The same is true of ancient Greece.[47]

When, with the development of more advanced agricultural methods, the cultivated area at last became stabilised and the collective clearing of new land ceased to play an important part in the life of the village, private property in land began to appear. Even then, however, so long as the village community had not been dissolved, the ancient communal ownership survived in various forms. A third of the village—over and above the houses and gardens, on the one hand, and the cultivable fields, on the other—made up essentially of pastures and woods, remained common property. The right to graze, that is, the

* When the T'ang dynasty came to power in China (A.D. 618), thanks to a peasants' revolt, it re-established the system of periodical redistribution of the cultivable land, but left the gardens (about one-fifth of all the land of each farm) as hereditary property of the peasant families.[46]

use of all the fields, before sowing began, by the cattle of all the members of the community; the right to glean after the harvest; the right to build and use mills or wells in common; the constitution of the village as a unit collectively responsible for the payment of taxes; the keeping up of customs of mutual aid; the right to set up new farms on cleared portions of woodland; all these phenomena show that for centuries a strong collective solidarity continues in village life, a solidarity the roots of which lie deep in the communal ownership of olden times.

It is not possible to list all the sources that confirm the existence of this common ownership of the land among all civilised peoples, at a certain phase of their agricultural evolution; we will briefly mention some of the chief sources. The Japanese village community called the *mura* is described by Yoshitomi. Yosoburo Takekoshi, in his monumental work *Economic Aspects of the History of Civilisation in Japan* describes the common ownership of the land in ancient times, with division of the soil by lot. In Indonesia "the village community represents the original community", writes Dr. J. H. Boeke. Wittfogel has analysed the *tsing-tien* system of dividing the fields of the Chinese villages into nine squares, and discovered there the village community which has descended from the collective appropriation of the soil.[48] The work of Professor Dyckmans on the ancient empire of the Egyptian Pharaohs states explicitly that there the land was originally clan property with periodical redistribution of the holdings. Professor Jacques Pirenne says the same thing in his *History of Institutions and Private Law in Ancient Egypt*.[49] M. Jacques Weulersse, describing the agricultural system of the Arab people called the Alaouites, has found among them even today traces of collective ownership, which was formerly predominant throughout the Islamic world:

"Those villages are called *mouchaa* villages in which the whole of the land belongs collectively to the whole village community. No member of the latter possesses any land as his own, but only a right in the entire territory. This right guarantees him a definite share of the soil when the periodical redistribution of land takes place . . . usually every three years."[50]

In respect of all Central and East Africa the semi-official *African Survey* states that:

"It is true to say that throughout that part of Africa with which we are concerned, there is a prevailing conception of the land as the collective possession of the tribe or group."[51]

Speaking of the Polynesian economy of Tikopia, Raymond Firth notes "the traditional ownership of orchards and garden plots by kinship groups."[52]

Historical research confirms the existence of collective ownership of the land in Homeric Greece, in the Germanic *Mark*, in the ancient

Aztec village, in the ancient Indian village of the time of the Buddhist writings; in the Inca village where the ploughed fields are called *Sapslpacha*, that is, "the land (*pacha*) which belongs to everyone"; in the villages of the Byzantine Empire, notably in Egypt, Syria, Thrace, Asia Minor and the Balkans, before the Slav colonisation; in ancient Russia, with its village community the *obshchina*; among the South Slavs, the Poles, the Hungarians, etc. In a study undertaken for the F.A.O., Sir Gerald Clausen confirms, furthermore, that everywhere, in the beginning, agriculture was carried on within the framework of an agrarian system based on communal ownership, with periodical redistribution of land.[53]

The cultivation of irrigated land, cradle of civilisation

Agriculture was initially clumsy and irregular; man did not know how to preserve the soil's fertility. The discovery of irrigation and of the effect of letting land lie fallow completely revolutionised agricultural technique.

The consequences of this revolution in agriculture were incalculable. The breeding of domestic animals and the first beginnings of agriculture had enabled men to take control of the means of subsistence. The systematic application of the practice of letting land lie fallow, and above all, of irrigation, linked with the use of draft animals, enabled mankind to guarantee itself permanently a substantial surplus of foodstuffs, dependent only on man's own work. Each seed sown in Mesopotamia was repaid a hundredfold at harvest-time.[54]

The existence of this permanent surplus of foodstuffs made it possible for craft techniques to become independent, specialised and perfected. Society was able to support thousands of men who no longer participated directly in the production of foodstuffs. The town could separate itself from the country. Civilisation was born.

Already the ancient Greeks of Homer's time regarded civilisation as the product of agriculture.[55] The Chinese of the classical epoch attributed the "invention" of agriculture, of trade and of civilisation, all to the mythical emperor Chen-Nung.[56] It is interesting to note that in Aztec tradition the origin of the people's prosperity is to be found in a communication received by the high priest in a dream, a communication "which ordered the Mexicans to dam a great river which flowed round the foot of the hill, so that the water spread over the plain."[57] Over and above these limited examples, the historian Heichelheim does not shrink from stating, with justification, that *agriculture has been the foundation of all civilisations down to modern capitalism.*[58] And the American Encyclopaedia of the Social Sciences says:

"History and archaeology have so far brought to light no great civilisation not largely dependent upon one of these three grains [wheat, maize and rice]."[59]

The transition to cultivation of the land by irrigation, and the appearance of town life, which resulted from it, occurred in several parts of the world where natural conditions made it possible. It is still difficult to determine to what extent this evolution took place among different peoples independently of each other; but this independence seems established as regards some of them. We find the development of agriculture by irrigation of the land, of a large permanent surplus of foodstuffs, of specialisation of crafts and of the rise of towns, successively in the valley of the Nile and in the valley of the Euphrates and Tigris in the fifth millennium B.C.; in the valley of the Hwang-ho in China, in Iran and on the island of Cyprus in the fourth millennium; in the valley of the Indus, in Central Asia and on the island of Crete in the third millennium; in mainland Greece, in Anatolia, in the Danube valley and in Sicily in the second millennium; in Italy and in Southern Arabia (the kingdom of Minea* and the Sabaean civilisation) in the first millennium B.C.; and in West Africa (civilisations of Ghana, Mali and Songhai in the valleys of the Niger and the Senegal) and also in America (in Mexico, Guatemala and Peru) in the first millennium A.D.

The metallurgical revolution

The agricultural revolution coincided broadly with the end of the age of polished stone. Men, released from the degrading servitude of hunger, were able to develop their innate qualities of curiosity and technical experimentation. They had long since learnt that it was possible to cook certain kinds of clay in the fire to make pots. By subjecting different kinds of stone to the fire they discovered metals, and then their wonderful capacity for being made into tools. The successive discovery of copper (sixth millennium B.C., in the valley of the Euphrates and Tigris and also in that of the Nile), of tin, then of the appropriate mixture of copper and tin called bronze (third millennium B.C., in Egypt, Mesopotamia, Iran and India), and at last of iron (*c.* 1300 B.C., among the Hittites, after a sporadic use of it among the coastal peoples of the Black Sea) constitute the most important stages in this technical revolution.

The effects of the metallurgical revolution were important first of all in the field of agriculture itself, which continued to be the basic economic activity of society. With the introduction of metal implements in agriculture, especially the plough with a metal share, the

* Etymologically, Minea means "spring water".[60] In the same period, Germany and Gaul were opened to civilisation thanks to the use of the fallow system.

employment of animal power for draft purposes became necessary, and the productivity of agricultural labour made a fresh leap forward. The use of the iron plough made possible extensive agriculture and the appearance of towns on the heavy soils of Europe in the eighth to seventh centuries B.C.[61] The introduction of metal tools in Japan in the eighth century A.D. made possible a considerable extension of the cultivated area and consequently a notable increase in the population.[62]

Thus was created the material condition for the rise of craft techniques and for the separation of town and country. The growth of population, made possible by the general increase in well-being,* provided the labour force. The increase in the surplus of foodstuffs supplied the means of subsistence for this urban labour-force. The metals themselves constituted the main raw material for the work of these craftsmen. At first essentially a technique of luxury and ornamentation, the metal-working craft later became specialised in the

* As for every species of life, this increase of the population is indeed the most objective index of progress. The geographer Ratzel[63] gives the following table of the density of population corresponding to the different ways of life at the beginning of this century. We have slightly simplified it:

	Inhabitants per square mile
Tribes of hunters, and of fishermen in the peripheral parts of the inhabited world (Eskimos)	·1–·3
Tribes of fishermen and hunters inhabiting steppe-land (Bushmen, Australian aborigines, Patagonians)	·1–1·5
Tribes of hunters with rudimentary agriculture (Dyaks, Papuans, Indian hill tribes, the poorest Negro tribes)	1–20
Tribes of fishermen settled on the coasts or river-banks (North-West American Indians, peoples of small Polynesian islands, etc.)	Up to 100
Nomadic shepherds	40–100
Agriculturists with beginnings of crafts and trade (Central Africa, Malay Archipelago)	100–300
Nomads with agriculture (Kordofan, Persia, Sennaar)	200–300
Peoples carrying on extensive agriculture (Moslem countries of Western Asia and the Sudan, Eastern European countries)	200–500
Tribes of fishermen carrying on agriculture (Pacific islands)	Up to 500
Regions carrying on intensive agriculture (peoples of Central Europe)	2,000
Regions of Southern Europe where intensive agriculture is carried on	4,000
Regions of India where irrigation agriculture is carried on	Over 10,000
Regions of Western Europe where large scale industry is carried on	Over 15,000

making of tools and weapons of all kinds. The crafts won final independence with the labour of the smith.*

Production and accumulation

Agriculture which can preserve and increase the fertility of the soil creates a permanent surplus of foodstuffs, a substantial *social surplus*. This surplus is not only the basis for the social division of labour, for the separation of the crafts from agriculture, of town from country. It is also the basis of the division of society into classes.

So long as society is too poor to be able to accumulate a permanent surplus, social inequality cannot develop on any great scale. To this day, in the countries of the Levant, whereas on the fertile land the property-right of lords has been established, taking from the peasant half and even more of his crop, on the mountain land "the crops are so poor that the land would not be able to bear the double burden of a share-cropper and a landlord."[65]

"Under primitive conditions it [slavery] does not exist. It has no economic basis at a time when a pair of hands can produce only as much and no more than one mouth consumes. It comes into being when the cumulative results of labour can be stored, or integrated into large works of construction."[66]

After examining the social institutions of 425 primitive tribes, Hobhouse, Wheeler and Ginsberg found that slavery was completely absent among peoples ignorant of agriculture and cattle-raising. They found the beginnings of slavery among one-third of the peoples who had reached the pastoral stage or the initial stage of agriculture, and a generalisation of slavery at the stage of fully developed agriculture. Thirty years later, C. Darryl Forde arrived at the same conclusions.[67]

As soon as a considerable surplus has been formed, the possibility appears for a part of society to give up productive labour, obtaining leisure at the expense of the remainder of society.† The use of

* In mediaeval Europe the smith appears as the first craftsman who works professionally for the market. The Latin word *faber* = "smith", and the German word *Schmied* = "smith" meant originally just "craftsman".[64] In Western and Central Europe, however, the Bronze Age did not see the appearance of an urban civilisation; only the iron plough created a plentiful surplus there. In Central America, on the other hand, the climatic conditions and the low density of population made possible a rise of civilisation already before metal tools came into use. These exceptions show, however, that the production and concentration of a large social surplus constitute indeed the condition for the appearance of civilisation. The differentiation of the natural environment inevitably entails differences in the methods of producing this surplus and differences as to the epoch in which different peoples attain to this.

† This is obviously only a *possibility*; it is equally possible that the leisure thus won may reduce the working time of all of the producers and be put to use for extra-economic activities by everyone. This seems to have been the

prisoners of war or captives of any kind as slaves (in Polynesia, slave means *Tangata-Taua* = "man obtained by war"[69]) constitutes one of the two most common forms in which society is first divided into classes. The other form of this same primitive division is the payment of an imposed tribute to part of society.

When advanced agriculture is carried on in a large number of small villages, each of them produces a surplus which, taken separately, is quite insufficient for the formation of a body of professional craftsmen, and still less sufficient for the foundation of towns.* The concentration of this surplus becomes the preliminary condition for its effective utilisation:

"The surplus produced by an individual family above the requirements of domestic consumption is liable to have been exceedingly small under a rural economy so backward that a large proportion of each season's calves had simply to be eaten. For a community to acquire any substantial quantity of foreign material a concentration of the surplus would be requisite. Historical testimony from the Bronze Age civilisations of the Ancient East and ethnographic evidence from Polynesia and North America show that one way of effecting this concentration is the institution of chieftainship, another the cult of a deity. Offerings made by each family of followers or votaries from its tiny surplus, the real chief or the representative of the imaginary god can accumulate quite a substantial surplus."[71]

Something which is at first voluntary and intermittent later becomes obligatory and regular. By the application of force, that is to say, by the organisation of the state, a social order is established which is founded on the surrender by the peasants of their surplus of foodstuffs to the new masters.†

Speaking of the most primitive peoples, Malinowski explains:

"These people have no centralised authority nor any tribal policies. Consequently they have no military force, no militia, no police; and they do not fight as between one tribe and another. Personal injuries are avenged by stealthy attacks on individuals, or by hand to hand

case among the Siane of New Guinea, among whom the replacement of their old stone axes by steel ones cut down the share of their working time devoted to the production of means of subsistence from 80 per cent to 50 per cent, according to Salisbury.[68]

* According to the American Assyriologist A. L. Oppenheim, the first Mesopotamian towns were only big villages, and retained a structure exactly the same as that of the village community.[70]

† In the Nigerian kingdom of Nupe, the rent paid to the chiefs is still called a gift, *kynta*, in the villages, whereas it is already called a tithe, *dzanka*, in the environs of the capital, Bida.[72] It is significant that the Arabic word *makhzen*, which means "government", comes from the verb *khazana*, "to accumulate", "to store", and that it has given us the French and Spanish words *magasin* and *almacén*!

fighting . . . War does not exist among them." C. Darryl Forde describes similarly the primitive clan communism, without hereditary chiefs, among the Tungus in North-East Siberia.[73]* Heichelheim notes, in contrast, the appearance of a state organisation in the first towns:

"The majority of the town population . . . lived from rents and tributes [that is, by appropriating the surplus product of agricultural labour]. Some belonged to the ruling class, princes, priests and nobles. The upper class had in its employ a large range of officials, agents, servants, tradesmen . . ."[75]

Beyond concentrating and accumulating the social surplus, these new possessing classes fulfilled other socially-necessary and progressive functions. They made possible the development of art, a product of the luxury crafts working for the new lords. They made possible the differentiation of the surplus product as a result of its accumulation, and the differentiation of the surplus product meant also the differentiation of production itself. They made possible, and to some extent themselves ensured in person, thanks to their leisure, the accumulation of techniques, knowledge and rules which guaranteed the maintenance and development of the productive forces of agriculture: astronomical and meteorological knowledge regulating the control of the waters, the approximate most favourable moment for starting the harvest, and in certain circumstances the forbidding of it: geometrical knowledge making possible the division of the fields; carrying out of works of initial cultivation made necessary by the growth of population, on a scale exceeding that of the power of a village or a group of villages; construction of canals, dykes and other hydrographical works essential for irrigation, etc.†

The technique of accumulation has been used to justify the appropriation of extensive material privileges. Even if it be historically indispensable, there is no reason to believe that it could not have been applied eventually by the collectivity itself. As for the privileges, they were in any case felt as exactions by the people who were the victims of them, and they inspired protests such as those of the peasant of the ancient Egyptian empire who speaks in the *Satire of the Crafts*.[77]

* Among the Nambikwara Indians the chief (*nilikande*: he who unites) enjoys an authority based on consent, and possesses no power of coercion. When Lévi-Strauss asked an Indian what were the privileges of the chief he received the same answer ("He's the first man to march off to war") as Montaigne had received in 1560—four centuries earlier!—to a similar question which he put to an American Indian.[74]

† 2,400 years ago, Kautilya, prime minister to the Indian King Maurya Chandragupta, explained in his work *Arthashastra* the origin of all civilisation as springing from the work of the peasantry: "For the fact that the villages supply their own needs and that men find their only pleasure [!] in the fields makes it possible to increase the King's treasury, merchandise [trade!], corn and moveable property."[76]

The Marxist category of "historical necessity" is moreover much more complex than popularisers commonly suppose. It includes, dialectically, both the accumulation of the social surplus which was carried out by the ancient ruling classes, and also the struggle of the peasants and slaves against these classes, a struggle without which the fight for emancipation waged by the modern proletariat would have been infinitely more difficult.

Is there an "economic surplus"?

The idea of a social surplus product, which is rooted in that of a permanent surplus of means of subsistence, is essential for Marxist economic analysis. Now, this idea has until recently been accepted not only by the majority of economists but, what is more significant, by all anthropologists, archaeologists, ethnologists and specialists in primitive economy. The numerous references to the work of these specialists which are scattered through the first chapters of this work testify that the empirical data of contemporary science confirm the validity of the basic hypotheses of Marxist economic analysis.

The only serious scientific attack directed against the ideas of economic surplus and social surplus product in pre-capitalist economy has been launched by Professor Harry W. Pearson, in a chapter of the collective work published under the editorship of Karl Polanyi, Conrad M. Arensberg and Pearson himself: *Trade and Market in the Early Empires*. It deserves refutation in detail.

Professor Pearson's criticisms can be summarised in five points:

1. The idea of "economic surplus" is a muddled one, since it in fact covers two different entities: the absolute surplus, in the physiological sense of the word, without which society cannot exist, and the relative surplus, which society has decided to form.

2. Now, an "economic surplus" in the absolute, biological, sense of the expression, does not exist. It is impossible to determine the minimum level of subsistence below which an individual would perish; it is impossible to determine this for society as a whole.[78] In any case, this level is so low that there is no proof that any human society has ever lived as a whole at this level.

3. As for the relative surplus, this is not the result of an economic evolution, in particular of the increase in the average productivity of labour. There are always and everywhere potential surpluses. The decisions to create or increase resources not assigned for consumption by the producers are social decisions which may be taken for quite non-economic reasons (religious, political, prestige).

4. There is "not a shred of evidence" to show that the appearance of "private property, barter, trade, division of labour, markets, money, commercial classes and exploitation" is due to the appearance of an economic surplus at crucial moments in the development of human

society. Such statements can be justified only by the assumption that "the logical course of economic development . . . is toward the market system of nineteenth-century western Europe."[79]

5. Furthermore, this whole conception is founded on the crudest materialism, which "bases social and economic development upon 'the narrow capacity of the human stomach'."[80] At every level of material existence, economic resources have been employed for non-economic ends.

Professor Pearson's argument proceeds from the distinction between "absolute surplus" and "relative surplus", a distinction which he has himself, of course, introduced into the discussion. To our knowledge, neither the physiocrats nor the British classical economists, nor, above all, Marx and Engels, ever regarded the "subsistence level" as an absolute biological notion. But one cannot thereby conclude that this idea has no definite historical significance in each specific instance, that one may arbitrarily reduce the level regarded as the minimum by a particular people at a particular time. For this reason it is wrong to state that every society possesses a potential source of surplus, regardless of an increase in the average productivity of labour.

True, no society can continue to exist if, after providing the most modest of livelihoods to its members, its production is inadequate to maintain the supply of tools. In this "absolute" sense of the word, no society reduced to the mere "biological" level of subsistence could survive. But so long as man *is not in control of* his means of subsistence—or in other words, so long as we are dealing with hordes, or primitive tribes who live by gathering fruit, hunting and fishing—this "surplus" is both precarious and extremely limited. The reason for this is quite simple: any exceptional increase in current production would not produce a "permanent surplus" but, on the contrary, a famine, upsetting the ecological balance of the inhabited area.

When Professor Pearson writes that no human society has ever lived at such a level of poverty he commits in reality a mistake similar to that for which he rightly blames the neo-classical economists. Just as the latter conceive all economic activity as a function of a market economy, Professor Pearson sees the entire economic past of humanity in the light of the economy of primitive peoples on the threshold of civilisation or already civilised, that is, of peoples who have already accomplished their "neolithic revolution" and are carrying on agriculture and cattle-raising. But when one considers that the period since that revolution occupies only a small fraction of the time that man has existed on the earth, when one recalls that hundreds, if not thousands, of primitive tribes have disappeared before reaching the stage of the neolithic revolution, in particular because they have not been able to solve the problem of subsistence in a modified natural environment, one realises how untenable this statement is.

Proof, both logical and empirical, shows the contrary, that the majority of human societies previous to the neolithic revolution* had to carry on a permanent struggle for subsistence; that they were obsessed by this struggle, which seemed never to reach a victorious conclusion, and that all the social institutions quoted by Professor Pearson in support of the opposite view (especially the important place held by magic and religion in these societies) had definitely economic *functions*, that is, were supposed to contribute precisely to the solution of the agonising problem of subsistence. "The universal occurrence of magical and religious practices in association with productive processes reveals . . . that anxiety with respect to food supply is universal."[81]

That is where the key importance of the neolithic revolution lies. For the first time in human prehistory, control over mankind's means of subsistence passes from nature to man. For the first time, henceforth, these means can be multiplied, if not without limit, then at least in a proportion quite unknown before. For this reason, an important fraction of society can be released from the need to contribute directly to the production of food. There are no archaeological or anthropological data to bring into question today this obvious proof of the connexion between the appearance of a *permanent and substantial surplus of food*, on the one hand, and, on the other, the separation of the crafts from agriculture and of town from country, and the division of society into classes.

True, the growth in the average productivity of labour creates only the *necessary material conditions* for social evolution and transformation. There is no economic automatism, independent of social forces.† Men make their own history; an existing society defends itself against forces of transformation. Primitive society defends its egalitarian structure. There must then be a social revolution to break up egalitarian primitive society and give birth to a society divided into classes. But this social revolution is not *possible* unless a level of productivity has been reached which enables part of society to release itself from material work. So long as this material condition, this potential surplus, does not exist, the social revolution in question is impossible.

Professor Pearson will retort that, after all, the decisive driving force has been social, the replacement of one "model" of social organ-

* Except tribes living in an exceptionally favourable natural environment, usually described as "developed hunters".

† See Chapter 2, paragraph: "Co-operatively organised society and society based on economy of labour-time."

isation by another.* We readily agree to this primacy of the social. But would a confederation of tribes of primitive hunters have been able to build the Roman Empire, or even the Babylon of Hammurabi? Would the Mesopotamian peasants have been able to create modern industry? To answer these questions is to appreciate the strategic role of the increase in the economic surplus and the social surplus product in human history, through the growth in the productivity of labour.

* George Dalton[82] has endeavoured to enlarge upon the ideas of Professor Pearson in this connection. He is obviously right in opposing the anachronistic use, in relation to a primitive society, of motives like the *unlimited* search for material means. He is also right in opposing the use, in this different social setting, of categories derived from a commodity or money economy. But he is wrong when he concludes that the shortage of material goods is a purely "ideological" notion, or that there is no rational economic explanation of the socio-economic conduct of primitive peoples. To allege that "transactions of material goods in primitive society are expressions of social obligations which have neither mechanisms nor meaning [!] of their own apart from the social ties and social situations they express"[83] is to forget that primitive people are obliged, after all, to keep themselves alive, no less than modern ones; that their survival demands a certain amount of production of material goods; that social organisation is not independent of the need to produce these material goods; that the economic motive, that is, the striving to ensure that a certain *limited* amount of production takes place is thus definitely present in this primitive society; and that if it is often difficult to analyse this socio-economic structure, nobody ought to declare it an impossible task from the outset, because this would make impossible the scientific study of the evolution of societies in general.

REFERENCES

1. J. Grahame Clark: *From Savagery to Civilisation*, p. 26; A. Gehlen: *Der Mensch*, p. 24.
2. G. Heard: *The Source of Civilisation*, pp. 66-67. See also Gehlen, op. cit., pp. 35, 91, etc.
3. Gordon Childe: *Man Makes Himself*, p. 49. Cf. also Prof. Oakley in *An Appraisal of Anthropology Today*, p. 235.
4. G. Renard: *Le Travail dans la Préhistoire*, p. 67: R. Furon, *Manuel de Préhistoire générale*, p. 174.
5. Sir James Frazer: *Myths of the Origin of Fire*.
6. B. Malinowski: *A Scientific Theory of Culture*, p. 95.
7. Raymond Firth: *Primitive Polynesian Economy*, pp. 37-38.
8. L. T. Hobhouse, G. C. Wheeler and M. Ginsberg: *Material Culture of the Simpler Peoples*, pp. 16-18.
9. W. G. Sumner and A. G. Keller: *The Science of Society*, Vol. I, pp. 163-4.
10. M. J. Herskovits: *The Economic Life of Primitive Peoples*, p. 48.
11. Kaj Birket-Smith: *Geschichte der Kultur*, pp. 143-4.
12. Raymond Firth: op. cit., pp. 112-13.

13. Heinrich Cunow: *Allgemeine Wirtschaftsgeschichte*, Vol. I, pp. 103-23; C. Darryl Forde: *Habitat, Economy and Society*, p. 374.
14. H. Cunow: op. cit., Vol. I, p. 95.
15. Raymond Firth: op. cit.; Cl. Lévi-Strauss: *Tristes Tropiques*, pp. 297-8.
16. Gordon Childe: op. cit., pp. 15-19.
17. A. Gehlen: op. cit., pp. 433-4.
18. Fritz Heichelheim: *Wirtschaftsgeschichte des Altertums*, p. 36; C. Darryl Forde: op. cit., p. 397. See in *Historia Mundi*, Vol II, pp. 66-80, the discussion of the present state of this question by Karl J. Narr.
19. L. T. Hobhouse: et al., op. cit., p. 22.
20. R. Thurwald: article *"Handwerk"* in *Reallexicon der Vorgeschichte*, Vol. V, pp. 98. These ideas are nowadays generally accepted by the specialists: see *An Appraisal of Anthropology Today*, pp. 40-41.
21. W. G. Sumner: et. al., op. cit., Vol. I, p. 134.
22. Robert Graves: *The Greek Myths*, p. 13, Vol. I, Penguin Books, revised edition 1960.
23. Debiprasad Chattopadhyaya: "Lokayata", People's Publishing House, 1959, pp. 251-65 and 273-92.
24. W. G. Sumner: et al., op. cit., Vol. III, pp. 1954 sqq.; F. Heichelheim; *Antike Wirtschaftsgeschichte*, Vol. II, p. 898. See also F. Kern: *Mutterrecht einst und jetzt*, in *Theologische Zeitschrift*, Basel, 6, 1950, and *Historia Mundi*, Vol. I, p. 389, and Vol. II, pp. 91-92, 94.
25. R. Furon: op. cit., passim.
26. Martin C. Yang: *A Chinese Village*, p. 27.
27. R. Firth: op. cit., p. 63.
28. Margaret Mead: *Co-operation and Competition among Primitive People*, p. 445.
29. Ibid., p. 29.
30. Georges Balandier: *"Structures sociales traditionnelles et changements economiques"*, in *Revue de l'Institut de Sociologie Solway, U.L.B.*, No. 1, 1959, pp. 38-39.
31. *Smithsonian Contributions to Knowledge*, Vol. XVI.
32. Laura Thompson: *A Culture in Crisis*, pp. 94-95.
33. M. J. Herskovits: op. cit., pp. 72-77.
34. Margaret Mead: *Sex and Temperament*, pp. 26-27. See also the description by Jomo Kenyatta of communal work among the Kikuyu: *Facing Mount Kenya*.
35. *Les Populations aborigènes*, published by the International Labour Office, p. 225.
36. M. J. Herskovits: *Dahomey, An Ancient West African Kingdom*, Vol. I, p. 64.
37. Ibid., Vol. I, p. 65.
38. S. F. Nadel: *A Black Byzantium, The Kingdom of Nupe in Nigeria*, p. 49; Joseph Bourrilly: *Eléments d'ethnographie marocaine*, p. 139.
39. A. R. Radcliffe-Brown: *Structures and Functions in Primitive Society*, p. 33.
40. Audrey I. Richards: *Land, Labour and Diet in Northern Rhodesia*, p. 18.
41. Henri Terrasse: *Histoire du Maroc*, p. 28.
42. *The Russian Primary Chronicle*, trans. S. H. Cross (1930), p. 8.

43. Marc Bloch: *Les caractères originaux de l'histoire rurale française*, p. 163.
44. Ch. E. Perrin: *Recherches sur la seigneurie rurale en Lorraine*, p. 639.
45. C. Darryl Forde: op. cit., p. 375; René Grousset: *Histoire de la Chine*, p. 9.
46. Stefan Balazs: *Beiträge zur Wirtschaftsgeschichte der T'ang-Zeit*, in *Mitteilungen des Seminars für Orientalische Sprachen*, 1931–32.
47. See in particular J. Caesar: *De Bello Gallico*, Vol. IV, 21, 23; Perrin: op. cit., p. 629: *Old Testament*, Numbers 26, verses 55, 56, Joshua 18, verse 6, Micah 2, verse 5, etc.
48. M. Yoshitomi: *Etude sur l'histoire économique de l'ancien Japon*, p. 67; Yosoburo Takekoshi: *Economic Aspects of the History of the Civilisation of Japan*, pp. 26-27; J. H. Boeke: *Theorie der Indische Economie*, p. 30; K. A. Wittfogel: *Probleme chinesischer Wirtschaftsgeschichte*, p. 304. See also a recent Chinese publication, *An Outline History of China*, p. 19.
49. G. Dijckmans: *Histoire économique et sociale de l'Ancienne Egypte*, Vol. I, p. 128; Jacques Pirenne: *Histoire des Institutions et du Droit Privé de l'Ancienne Egypte*, Vol. I, p. 29.
50. Jacques Weulersse: *Le Pays des Alaouites*, p. 357.
51. *African Survey*, pp. 833-4 (1st and 2nd editions only).
52. R. Firth: op. cit., pp. 57-58.
53. G. Glotz: *Le Travail dans la Grèce antique*, pp. 14-15; J. Kulischer: *Wirtschaftsgeschichte des Mittelalters*, Vol. I, pp. 12-32; G. C. Vaillant: *The Aztecs of Mexico*, p. 113; *Cambridge History of India*, Vol. I, p. 200; H. Cunow: *Geschichte und Kultur des Inka-Reiches*, p. 138; M. V. Levtchenko: *Byzance*, p. 48; P. I. Lyastchenko: *History of the National Economy of Russia*, p. 70; Sir Gerald Clausen: *La Tenure Communautaire*, passim, pp. 23-25.
54. Gordon Childe: *What Happened in History*, p. 90.
55. G. Glotz: op. cit., p. 48.
56. Chen Huan-Chang: *The Economic Principles of Confucius*, p. 122.
57. Ramirez Ms.: *Histoire de l'Origine des Indiens*, p. 13.
58. F. Heichelheim: *Vormittelalterliche Geschichtsepochen*, pp. 163-4.
59. *Encylopaedia of Social Sciences*, Vol. I, article "Agriculture", p. 572.
60. P. K. Hitti: *History of the Arabs*, pp. 49-58.
61. F. Heichelheim: *Wirtschaftsgeschichte des Altertums*, Vol. I, p. 205.
62. M. Yoshitomi: op. cit., p. 208; Sir George Sansom: *A History of Japan to 1334*, p. 14.
63. Ratzel, *Anthropogeography*, Vol. II, pp. 264-5. (1st German edition, 1891).
64. J. Kulischer: op. cit., Vol. I, p. 71.
65. J. Weulersse: op. cit., p. 357.
66. B. Malinowski: *Freedom and Civilisation*, p. 301.
67. L. T. Hobhouse: et. al., op. cit., pp. 235-6; C. Darryl Forde: op. cit., p. 391.
68. Salisbury: *From Stone to Steel*, passim. Melbourne University Press, 1962.
69. H. Cunow, *Allgemeine Wirtschaftsgeschichte*, Vol. I, p. 411.
70. In Karl Polanyi et al., *Trade and Market in the Early Empires*, pp. 30-31.

71. Gordon Childe: *Scotland before the Scots*, p. 48.
72. S. F. Nadel: op. cit., p. 190.
73. B. Malinowski: *Freedom and Civilisation*, p. 278; C. Darryl Forde: op. cit., p. 359.
74. Cl. Lévi-Strauss: op. cit., p. 330.
75. F. Heichelheim: *Wirtschaftsgeschichte des Altertums*, Vol. I, p. 171.
76. *Kautilya's Arthashastra*, German trans. by J. J. Mayer, pp. 61-62.
77. G. Maspéro: *Histoire ancienne des peuples de l'Orient classique*, Vol. I, p. 331.
78. K. Polanyi: et al., op. cit., p. 324.
79. Ibid., p. 327.
80. Ibid., p. 325.
81. Marvin Harris: "The Economy has no surplus?", in: *American Anthropologist*, Vol. LXI, nr. 2, April 1959, p. 194.
82. George Dalton: "Economic Theory and Primitive Society", in: *American Anthropologist*, Vol. LXIII, nr. 1, February 1961, pp. 1-25.
83. Ibid., p. 21.

CHAPTER TWO

EXCHANGE, COMMODITY, VALUE

Simple exchange

THE conditions for occasional exchange were created by encounters between hordes gathering different fruits or hunting different animals. "Barter and trade develop in areas of contrasted produce, where bush and sea-coast, forest and plain, mountain and lowland, offer each other novelties and encourage the exchange of goods."[1]

Speaking of the Bemba people of Rhodesia, who trade very little, Audrey I. Richards notes that "the environmental conditions of the Bemba account to some extent for their poor development of trade, since conditions are, generally speaking, so uniform in this area that there is little reason for one district to exchange goods with another".[2]

The origin of exchange is thus to be found *outside* the primitive social unit, whether this be horde, clan or tribe. Within it there prevail originally mutual aid and labour co-operation, which exclude exchange. The service each person owes to the community is laid down by custom or religious rite; it varies with age and sex and with the system of consanguinity. But it does not depend on any expectation of a precise reciprocal payment, whereas *a measured reciprocal payment is what constitutes the essential characteristic of exchange.*

The measurement involved here is not necessarily an *exact* one. Indeed, it cannot be exact at the stage of simple exchange, which is casual and occasional. Hordes and tribes who know little about the nature, origins, conditions of production, or precise use of a product which they receive "in exchange" for another, inevitably let themselves be ruled by arbitrariness, caprice or mere chance in determining the conditions of such exchange. Exchange, the most precisely "measured" operation in modern economic life, was born in material conditions that excluded any possibility of precise measurement.

Simple exchange is casual and occasional exchange; it cannot form part of the normal mechanism of primitive life. It may result either from the chance appearance of surplus or from a sudden crisis in the primitive economy (famine).*

In either case, a primitive group which knows other groups are liv-

* Speaking of the Bachiga tribe in East Africa, May Mandelbaum Edel notes that "as a rule trade occurs only when it is necessary, as the result of a lean harvest, to eke out the food supply."[3]

ing nearby will try to establish exchange-relations, either by violent methods or by peaceful ones. This encounter between two occasional surpluses, varying in natural qualities, utility and *use-value*, creates the most usual conditions for a simple exchange transaction.

Silent barter and ceremonial gifts

When a primitive group regularly has a surplus of certain products, after meeting its own consumer needs, simple exchange can become developed exchange. This is no longer a casual exchange operation happening at exceptional moments, but a more or less regularised series of exchange operations.

The establishment of strict rules of exchange is only the culmination of a long transition which starts from a situation in which sporadic exchange takes place without any precise measurement. To the two ways of acquiring foreign products—simple exchange and war for plunder—there correspond two transitional forms of exchange among primitive groups: ceremonial gifts and silent barter.

Contacts between primitive groups not related by blood are hardly ever contacts between groups of equal strength. They imply relations near the brink of hostility, and this brink is quickly crossed.

Experience teaches the weaker groups that it is wisest to flee before the approach of formidable strangers. To the latter it teaches that if they decimate weaker groups whose products they want, this entails the risk of losing all chance of obtaining these products.* Thus conventionally regulated exchange-relations, known as silent barter, are established at the borderline of open hostility. The weaker group leaves its products for exchange in an uninhabited spot and goes away until the partner has left its own products in the same place.

Economic history is full of examples of this silent barter. The case of the relations between Moors and Negroes to the west of Gibraltar, mentioned by Herodotus, and that of the relations between Persian, Tartar and Greek merchants in South Russia with the inhabitants of the frozen steppes of North Russia, mentioned by the traveller Ibn Batuta, figure in the classical literature on the subject. Today, silent barter is to be found in several parts of the world: among the Chukchi tribes of Siberia, in their relations with the inhabitants of Alaska; among the *negritos* who live in the valleys in the north of the island of Luzon, in the Philippines, in their relations with the Christian inhabitants of the same area; among the Awatwa tribe, in Northern

* "The Mundugumor [headhunters of New Guinea] wander far afield not only in search of enemies to ambush, but in search of trade-acquaintances . . . From the emaciated, half-starved, rickety peoples who inhabit the eastern swamps, they buy cooking-pots, carrying baskets, mosquito-bags . . . They said they were careful not to kill all of them, for then there would be no makers of pots left alive."[4]

Rhodesia, in the relations between the inhabitants of the interior and those of the marshlands; in New Guinea, in the New Hebrides, in India, in Indonesia, etc.[5]

Silent barter, and still more the exchange operations which are derived from relations of open hostility, originate in contact between different primitive groups unconnected by ties of blood. Within the group, as we have seen, exchange relations are absent, in primitive conditions. Food and other primary necessities are not exchanged but shared.[6] What exists is a mere giving of gifts, presents (precious objects, talismans, ornaments) which are conventionally returned, just as today within a modern family, without any exact calculation of equivalent values.

However, when groups with a common ancestry grow large and spread themselves over a territory which is too extensive to be administered by a single leadership, they split into fragments. The exchange of presents, consisting of different products specially found in the respective territories on which these sub-groups live, is institutionalised, repeated periodically in a solemn manner, and becomes regular. The ceremony expresses the relations of real material interdependence which exist between these sub-groups, one being unable to live without the help of another, or else merely the existence of ties of blood.[7]

This institution of ceremonial exchange of gifts survives among primitive groups which have already reached the stage of individual agriculture but remain settled together in village communities. The difference between individual harvests within one and the same community, or between the harvests of a number of villages related by ties of blood, will be offset from time to time by exchange of gifts; numerous relations involving solemn exchange of gifts, the economic function of which appears today vague or even invisible, had a functional origin like this.

In his *Structures élementaires de la parenté*, Claude Lévi-Strauss has convincingly shown how these exchanges of presents, like exchanges of women, are integrated in economic life at this stage of social evolution, and how these two parallel circuits—which the primitive people regard as the same, the women being themselves considered as presents—are indispensable for *maintaining the social cohesion of the group*. The division of labour being still essentially the division of labour between the sexes, any disorganised choice of wives would lead to the weakening of certain groups, and even to their disappearance.

This is why the rules of reciprocity imply that a man "may not receive a wife from any other group than that from which he has the right to obtain one, because in the previous generation a sister or a daughter was lost; while a brother owes the outside world a sister (or a father owes a daughter), because in the previous generation a wife was acquired".[8]

"Exogamy," concludes Lévi-Strauss, "provides the only means of maintaining the group as a group, avoiding the endless break-up and separation that consanguine marriages would mean".[9]*

Among the Ozuitem Ibo of Southern Nigeria, the exchange of presents of food is explained by members of the tribe themselves as follows:

"The people of Ozuitem claim that in the past, before cassava was first introduced at the beginning of this century, there was often a severe food shortage in the three months (June-August) before the annual yam harvest. A long-established system of food transfers during this period is still practised whereby food gifts are made by those having available supplies on the understanding that money gifts will be made in return. Men are also under obligation to make food gifts to their wives and female kinsfolk which ultimately benefit the households of these women."[11]

The practice of ceremonial exchange may proceed beyond the limits of a single tribe and extend to several tribes or peoples inhabiting a particular region. Just as ceremonial exchange within a narrow group merely gives expression to the close bonds of solidarity and co-operation in labour, its extension to several tribes and peoples expresses an effort to stabilise peaceful relations of co-operation among them.[12]

"The tribute-missions began as the gestures of the princes of the countries of the Nanyang [south-east Asia] sending envoys to the Chinese capital with gratulatory or ceremonial messages to the Chinese court. They were always received as humble emissaries conveying the submission of their masters to the Sun of Heaven. They brought presents, of course, usually of native produce, and the emperor, out of the benevolence of his heart, bestowed presents upon them in return. It happened that these return presents were often more valuable than those brought from Java, Borneo or Malacca, as the case might be; but even if they were only of equal value it was clear that here ready established was an embryonic foreign trade."[13]

When individual economic activity—above all, agriculture—comes

* Lévi-Strauss argues against Frazer, who explains the exchange of women by the fact that primitive people were unable to pay any other "price" [*sic*] for them. He is right in blaming Frazer for supposing the existence in the past of "calculations" which are found only in much more "advanced" societies. But he is wrong when he concludes: "In exchange of women there is nothing like a reasoned solution to an economic problem . . . It is an act of primitive and indivisible consciousness . . ." Actually, Lévi-Strauss himself has shown what a vital economic role was played by women in primitive economy. The desire to regulate the "circulation of women" so as to ensure the maximum equality of opportunity to marry for all the able-bodied men thus fully corresponds to an *economic* need for social equilibrium.[10]

to take a more and more important place in the life of the village community, when relations of ceremonial exchange of presents and of silent barter become frequent and are regularised, increasingly numerous elements of *measurement*, of *calculation* of the presents exchanged are introduced into the community, so as to maintain its economic equilibrium. In the *desa*, the Indonesian village community, two forms of economic activity thus coexist: the *samba sinambat*, unpaid activity directed towards the satisfaction of vital needs, and the *toeloeng menseloeng*, activity directed towards the realisation of individual needs for which one has the right to expect a more or less equivalent counter-payment.[14] Schechter,[15] having examined most of the examples of ceremonial exchanging of presents, found that in the majority of cases the principle of equivalence, and so of precise measurement of the counter-payment, already plays a preponderant part. True, this is still a long way from a market economy, based on commodity production, but equivalence is generally accepted and even institutionalised, as appears in Hammurabi's code.[16]

Developed exchange

Silent barter and ceremonial gifts are transitional forms between simple exchange and generalised exchange, which can be included under the common heading of *developed exchange*.

Developed exchange results from an encounter between surpluses of different products which are no longer casual but habitual. Both silent barter and ceremonial gifts can take the form of developed exchange, and can also outgrow this form and appear as part of generalised exchange properly so called.

In primitive society in which the crafts have not yet won their independence, a *regional specialisation*, a regional division of labour, can appear in consequence of specific peculiarities of a given territory. The tribe occupying this territory may devote itself to a large extent to producing this speciality, and appear in the eyes of neighbouring tribes as a collective specialist. It will produce a considerable surplus of the goods in question, and exchange it against the special products of other tribes. Prehistory and ethnography show that *tools* and *ornaments* are the first products likely to spread in substantial quantity from a given centre of production, through operations of developed exchange.

Thus, before the colonial conquest of their country, the Gouro tribe of the Ivory Coast used to exchange with the people of the savannah mainly cola nuts, which they produced, for iron rods, called *sompe*, which they used both as raw material for making agricultural tools and weapons and as media of exchange. Cola and *sompe* were elements in a trade between the South and the North which was genuinely complementary, between two different geographical zones.[17] It should further be noted that, at the same time as they carried on this genuine trade, the Gouro kept up relations of ceremonial exchange of gifts with tribes, such as the Baoulé, whom they regarded as their kindred.[18]

Already in the old stone age, real workshops for the production of stone implements were organised, notably at Saint-Acheul and on the island of Bömlo, in South-West Norway. In the new stone age, real flint quarries existed in Egypt, Sicily, Portugal, France (Grand Pressigny), at Grime's Grave and Cissbury in England, at Obourg and Spienne in Belgium, in Sweden and in Poland (Eastern Galicia and Kielce district). On the island of Marua remains have been found of workshops producing stone implements which supplied the needs of a large part of New Guinea.[19] Heichelheim mentions a number of sources which seem to confirm the circulation of ornamental objects within a very wide radius, from the earliest times.[20]

With the progress of the productivity of labour and the formation of small regular surpluses among many neighbouring tribes and communities, this system of regional specialisation can expand into a regular network of exchange and lead to a true regional division of labour. In the Amazon basin, for instance, various tribes each have their own specialities: the Menimels are particularly well-known for their pottery, the Karahone produce especially virulent poisons, the Boro specialise in the making of rugs, ropes and pipes; the Nitoto excel in the making of hammocks.[21] Exchange becomes more and more regularised between these tribes, on the basis of these specialities.

For each of the tribes concerned, however, the making of special products constitutes only a supplementary and secondary activity in their economic life. The latter remains based essentially on fruit-gathering, hunting and fishing (with sometimes the beginning of some agriculture), that is, on looking for food. No craft specialisation yet exists within the tribe, where developed exchange is completely absent, except perhaps in the form of ceremonial gifts. Those who today are making pots must tomorrow go hunting or cultivate the land, if the tribe is to escape falling victim to famine.

Trade

With the neolithic revolution, the development of agriculture and the formation of permanent surpluses create the possibility of permanent exchange with peoples who have not yet acquired such surpluses, and exchange enters a new phase. Exchanges are no longer restricted to a few rare products which are the specialities of certain regions. They henceforth embrace all the products of a whole region; *local markets* make their appearance. Each tribe or each village continues to provide for its own needs to a large extent, but none is any longer entirely independent of a supply of foreign products.

"Many communities (in Southern Nigeria) dispose of a surplus of foodstuffs and other goods in daily use, such as pottery, matting and wooden utensils, which find their way through the multitude of local market places to purchasers in other communities . . . Thus, the Agoi forest villages on the slopes of the Oban hills . . . trade smoked bush meat to the markets of the villages close to the Cross river in which they purchase yams, some of which may have been grown not by the people of these villages but by the Ibo living several miles on the far side of the river. Similarly, pot-making villages, which are relatively few and far between, are nearly all surplus producers, their wares being distributed over areas of a hundred square miles or more. Thus, though in general, the household, and still more the village community as a whole, is largely self-sufficient in food supplies and most other household needs, few, if any, are completely so."[22]

The system of *generalised exchange* coincides with the beginnings of professional crafts within the village or tribe. But this specialisation is a specialisation within a *village community*. The craftsmen who increasingly give up agricultural work receive their food in reward for their services. Exchange within the village or the tribe thus remains *rudimentary*. This is the situation, for example, among the inhabitants of the Marquesa Islands in the Pacific, or among the Kafflitcho and Gougo tribes in East Africa. Some craftsmen have already become fully independent, others not yet. The craftsmen in the first category receive a certain quantity of food, clothing and ornaments every year from the village community, in reward for all their work. The craftsmen in the second category are helped by other members of the tribe in the work they have to do on the land which is to supply them with means of existence.[23] In neither case have we here exchange in the strict sense.

Generalised exchange between different villages, tribes and communities is carried on in a more or less collective way, by the producers themselves, by a section of the community (for example, the women*), or by representatives of the community. It is not yet in itself a specialised economic activity.

"In mediaeval Europe, as in agricultural areas of our own day, the average producer was able to dispose of the petty surpluses of his household (eggs, cheese, hens, vegetables, milk, cattle, and even grain) without the assistance of a professional trader. Similarly, wherever an industry happened to be organised in small handicraft units and goods

* In so far as it was women who first undertook the cultivation of the soil, it is understandable that they should have been the first to undertake the exchange of food surpluses in a regular way. According to Chinese tradition, women were the first to engage in trade. Quite recently, all trade was in the hands of the women among the following peoples: the Togo, Somali, Galla and Masai in Africa, the Tatars and Tibetans in Asia.[24] Forde, Scott and Nadel note the same phenomenon in Nigeria. In pre-Columbian Nicaragua, only the women were allowed to appear in the market-place.[25] Similarly, only women sold in the local market in the kingdom of Dahomey.

were made in small quantities, or to order, producers and consumers could deal with each other without the intervention of a trader. Not only the village smith and potter, but the urban butcher, baker and candlestick-maker themselves disposed of their produce."[26]

This situation changes with the metallurgical revolution. The first metals that man found how to use, copper and tin, are not found in all countries, nor, in particular, in those which, thanks to irrigation agriculture, saw the first rise of civilisation. The mines are located in certain well defined areas, especially in mountainous parts, where the metals in question may well have been used over a long period for purposes of decoration, without giving rise to a metallurgical revolution in the economic sense of the word.

In order to acquire these minerals, the agricultural peoples who possessed adequate food surpluses, techniques and leisure had to go and seek them where they were to be found, first, no doubt, by way of plunder, then later through normalised exchange.[27] Exchange over long distances, international exchange between regions separated by hundreds of miles, could no longer be a supplementary activity, alongside the work of the crafts and agriculture. A new division of labour took place, the carrying-out of exchange was separated from other economic activities: trade was born.

Among the primitive peoples, the metallurgical revolution caused the appearance of professional crafts to coincide with the generalisation of exchange. The first craftsmen wholly detached from agricultural work are *itinerant smiths* (they are still found among the Bantu of equatorial Africa and the Peuls in West Africa). Among these peoples, the metallurgical revolution, by making trade independent, separates it completely from the crafts, just as it separates the latter from agriculture.

It is interesting to observe that the two forms of exchange, generalised exchange which has not yet become a specialised activity, and specialised trade properly so called, are usually found together in agricultural regions. Thus, among the Indians of the Chorti tribe, in Guatemala, the peasants and craftsmen themselves go to the local market once a week, and to the cantonal market once a month, or once every two months, to sell their small surpluses. But the trader who imports products from outside the region itself is a professional trader. The same distinction is observed among the Nupe, in Nigeria.[28]

From the age of copper onward, trade developed, notably in the first pre-dynastic civilisation in Egypt; in the first, "pre-diluvian" civilisation in Mesopotamia; in the most ancient of the civilisations discovered on the site of Troy, in Asia Minor; in the Creto-Mycenaean civilisation in Greece; in the civilisation of the Aztecs in Mexico, before the Spanish conquest; in the ancient Chinese, Indian and Japanese civilisations, etc.

In a work of Chinese classical literature, the *Appendix to Confucius's Book of Changes*, it is reported that markets (that is, trade) were invented in the same period as the plough, i.e. at the same time as the important changes in agriculture which result from the metallurgical revolution.[29]

With the bronze age, the development of trade relations becomes the preliminary condition for the productive use of technical knowledge. By a careful study of the deposits of copper and tin available in that period, Gordon Childe showed that in proportion as the Mediterranean peoples went over to the making of bronze objects they necessarily had to enter into international trade relations with a number of countries. From India to Scandinavia there are in fact only four regions where these two metals can be found together, namely, in the Caucasus, in Bohemia, in Spain, and in Cornwall.[30] However, the bronze age did not begin in any of these four regions.

The peoples who presided over the rise of the bronze age were obliged, in order to obtain these precious metals, to organise tremendous trading expeditions—in so far as they were not periodical raids, such as those which subjected the mines of the Sinai peninsula to Egypt from the time of the second dynasty.[31]* The wheeled chariot and the sailing ship were invented in the bronze age, and accompanied the progress of civilisation throughout the ancient world. Regular caravans linked Egypt with Mesopotamia across the Sinai peninsula, Palestine and Syria, and linked Mesopotamia with India across Iran, the north of Afghanistan and the Indus valley. From the bronze age onward, in a Europe which was still barbarous, extensive trade relations were formed between the Baltic and the Mediterranean, the Danube valley, the Pannonian Plain and the British Isles.

When this international trade became stabilised and peaceful, it continued none the less to be a State matter, and was carried on at first through merchants who were State servants. A neutral entrepôt provided the meeting-place for the two nations.[32]

Production for use and production of commodities

Production in primitive societies is essentially production to meet needs. The producers work in order to satisfy the needs of their community, whether this be large (tribe or clan) or small (family). This is true of the peoples who are still at the stage of gathering their food and also of those who are already producing it in the strict sense

* China, where copper and tin are plentiful, was able to enter the bronze age very soon. Internal trade therefore developed *earlier and further* than external trade. The decisive role of the metallurgical revolution in the development of trade is thus confirmed by this exception, too. In America copper and tin are found on the high plateaux of Peru and were basic to the Inca civilisation.

of the word. The first empires built up on the basis of irrigation agriculture do not show any economic features fundamentally different from the latter. The kings or priests who centralise the surpluses use them to satisfy their own needs or those of the community as a whole. It is significant that the King of Babylon was called, in official inscriptions: "Peasant of Babylon", "Shepherd of Men", "Irrigator of the Fields". In Egypt, the Pharaoh and the governmental administration were called *Pr'o*, meaning the big household. In China, one of the legendary emperors who were supposed to have founded the nation was called Héou-tsi, millet-prince.[33] The whole of the economy appeared indeed like a great estate producing *use-values* to satisfy its needs.[34]

With the independent crafts a new kind of production appeared. Producers who were peasant-craftsmen living in a village community, brought to the market only the *surplus* of their production, that is, what was left over after the needs of their families and their community had been met. The specialist craftsmen detached from a community, the itinerant smith or potter, no longer produces use-values to meet his own needs. *The whole of his production is intended for exchange*. It is in exchange for the products of his labour that he will acquire the means of subsistence, clothing, etc., to meet the needs of his family and himself. The independent craftsman detached from the village community no longer produces anything but *exchange-values, commodities* destined for the market.

Someone who essentially produces use-values, intended to satisfy his own needs or those of his community, lives by the products of his own labour. Production and products, labour and products of labour, are identical for him, in practice as in his mind. In commodity production this unity is broken.

The producer of commodities no longer lives directly on the products of his own labour: on the contrary, he can live only if he *gets rid* of these products. *He lives*, as Glotz says of the Greek craftsmen of the Homeric age, *exclusively by his labour*. This is all the truer in that these first craftsmen went to the homes of their clients and received from them the raw material for their production.[35] It was the same in most societies when the first development of commodity production took place: notably in Egypt, in China, in Japan, in India and at the beginning of the European Middle Ages.[36]

Commodity production does not appear all at once or over the whole of society. After the crafts have become professional and some craftsmen have become commodity producers detached from the village community, the peasants and the remainder of the craftsmen may for centuries go on living as producers of use values. They will exchange only small surpluses of their products in order to acquire the few commodities which they need. These commodities consist essentially of *salt* and *iron* (or other metals). It was so in China, in mediaeval Europe, in mediaeval Russia,* in mediaeval Japan, in the Indian village community, in Africa, in pre-Columbian America, etc.[37]

Generalised and specialised exchange, trade, is at first restricted to the metals and ornaments (luxury products) more or less reserved for the State (king, prince, temple). But commodity production attains a higher level from the moment that it supplies both craft and agricultural products to trade. The invention of the wheel, for chariots, makes it possible to use the principle of rotation in pottery-making technique. The potter's wheel is the first tool that makes possible "mass production" of commodities exclusively intended for trade.

Ethnography shows in most cases that, while women are the first to make pottery so long as this is merely a domestic or village technique, men are the first to use the potter's wheel and become specialists working for the market.[38] As regards agricultural products transformed into commodities, these first appear when human communities are formed that are completely separated from production of means of subsistence, communities of craftsmen, merchants and administrators, that is, *urban communities*. According to Polanyi, it was probably in Lydia, and then later at Athens, that the first local markets for foodstuffs were established. We have the impression, however, that in China such markets were also in existence in the fifth century B.C., if not earlier.[39]

Co-operatively organised society and society based on economy of labour-time

In primitive society producing little or no surplus, the co-operative organisation of labour is based on custom and religious rites which serve to regulate the essential economic activities. In poorly-favoured regions, where food supplies are hard to come by, labour co-operation may mean incessant economic activity, carried to the limits of human strength. In regions better favoured by nature, such as the Pacific islands, production of the necessary product may take up relatively little of the time available, the rest being devoted to leisure pursuits.

As a rule, no community will voluntarily give up a substantial part of its leisure to work and produce more if it is not forced to by economic and social necessity.† Economic necessity means the need to obtain a bigger surplus of products so as to acquire, through ex-

* The old Russian word for a merchant engaged in internal trade, *prasol*, indicates trade in salt, though later on the name came to be the general word for any retail trader.

† "Despite the frequency of famines no Mkamba (a Negro tribe) thinks of ever sowing more than is necessary to carry him on to the next rains."[40]

change, goods needed for the well-being of society and which the community itself does not produce (certain kinds of food, salt, raw materials for making tools, ornaments for ritual use, etc.). Social necessity means that which compels the community regularly to give up a surplus to a centralising authority, either in the interests of the community (to carry out irrigation works, etc.) or as the result of a conquest which has forcibly imposed such a tribute.

These two necessities may be combined. Speaking of the Mojo and Baure tribes, which live in eastern Bolivia, Alfred Métraux writes: "So great was the desire for metal, which eased the daily struggle for life, that the Indians, lacking other commodities acceptable to the whites, soon turned into slavers . . ."[41]

In other words: the growth of the surplus product beyond narrow limits (food reserves) is not the result of an independent development of the economy. It results from the intervention of *outside pressures,* either economic (exchange) or social (appropriation of the surplus by a central power or a ruling class).*

So long as primitive society, co-operatively organised, does not know any division of labour other than that between the sexes, the rhythm of labour is fixed by custom and religious rites. When a more consistent division of labour has been established, the contribution to the community made by each producer has to be measurable by a common yardstick. Otherwise, labour co-operation would tend to break up through the emergence of privileged and unprivileged groups. This common measure of organisation cannot be other than *economy of labour-time.*

The village can be regarded as a big family. Its total annual production has to correspond more or less to its needs in means of subsistence, clothing, housing and tools. To avoid any imbalance between these different forms of production, to ensure that the peasants do not devote an excessive share of their time to producing pots or leather articles, while leaving part of their land uncultivated, it is necessary that the community compile a record of the amount of labour-time available and allot this labour-time first and foremost among the essential sectors of production, indispensable for the well-being of the community, while leaving everyone free to employ the rest of his time as he pleases.

Ethnography and economic history show that the village community which has experienced the beginning of a division of labour

* This does not contradict the proposition we were defending earlier, according to which the development of a ruling class presupposes the existence of a social surplus. Though a primary development of the surplus does precede any formation of a ruling class, the latter thereafter in turn brings about a major expansion of this surplus, and a fresh development of the productive forces.

does indeed organise its social life on the basis of an economy of labour-time. Primitive peoples consider that only labour is something "scarce", says Ruth Bunzel.[42] According to Boeke, the economy of the Indonesian *desa* (vilage community) is based on calculation of hours of labour expended.[43]

In the economy of the Japanese village, "the principle of exchange is people and days. Thus, if household A has two people at work on household B's field for two days, household B is expected to provide its equivalent on A's fields—this may be three people one day and one person another day or any other combination to equal two people working two days . . . When four or five families work together in one *kattari* group [team for transplanting rice], the figuring is on the same basis. This requires a book to check days and workers."[44]

Among the Negro tribe called Heh, peasants who order a spear from the smith (who is himself a peasant as well as a smith), work on the smith's land while he is making the spear.[45] In ancient India, in the Maurya epoch, labour and products of labour governed the rules of organisation of economic life.[46]

When the first forms of social subordination were established, with appropriation of the surplus by a privileged section of society, the reckoning of exploitation was also based on an economy of labour-time. Among the Incas, "tribute was to consist solely of labour, time and skill as a workman, artisan or soldier. All men were equal in this respect, he being held to be rich who had children to aid him in making up his appointed tribute, and he who had none being considered to be poor. Every craftsman who laboured in the service of the Inca, or of his *curaca* (superior), must be provided with all the raw materials, and his employment in this way must not exceed two or three months in the year."[47]

It was the same in Europe in the early Middle Ages, when a large section of the peasantry lived under serfdom. The villagers were governed by a strict economy of labour-time: three days a week, on the average, being spent in work in the lord's land, and three days on the serf's own land.*

Similarly, the serfs' wives had to work a fixed number of days in the workshops of the manor, spinning, weaving, sewing, etc. Each craftsman had his own field, in exchange for which he had to render specific services to the manor and to the other tenants.

The social organisation based on the economy of labour-time has left numerous traces, even in the language. In central Europe in the Middle Ages the most common unit of area is the *Tagewerk*, the area

* We read, for example, in the old laws of Bavaria, that the "serfs of the Church" have to spend three days a week in work on the demesne (of their lord) and that "they do three days' work for themselves." *Opera vero 3 dies in ebdomada in dominico operet, 3 vero sibi faciat.*[48]

that a man can plough in one day. In mediaeval English the word "acre" had the same meaning. In the Kabyle mountains, holdings are evaluated in terms of *zouija*, days of ploughing carried out with a plough drawn by two oxen. In France, the "carrucata" signified the amount of land a man can normally plough in a single day. The "pose", the Swiss unit of area, is similar in meaning.[49]

The extent to which the economy of labour-time regulated the whole of economic life emerges clearly from the description given by Dollinger of the disappearance of the serf day-workers.

"These exemptions from service [as day-worker] did not, of course, leave the serf idle: they implied that he received from his lord a holding which he cultivated for himself on his free days . . . Undoubtely, this holding was as a rule proportionate to the time at his disposal. The serf who had only one free day a week probably obtained a very small piece of land, whereas the one who had two or three days free might perhaps receive an entire *manse*."[50]

Analysing the mediaeval peasants' obligations as a whole, Marc Bloch came to the same conclusion:

"The peasants, or at least some of them, had to render to the lord every year a fixed number of manufactured products: wooden articles; fabrics; clothing; in the case of certain *manses* where, from generation to generation, the income from a skilled trade was accumulated, even metal tools. Sometimes the supply of raw material was, like the labour, at the expense of the tenant: this was probably usual in the case of wooden articles. But where fabrics were concerned, the materials were often provided by the lord: the peasant or his wife *gave only their time* [my emphasis, E.M.], their efforts and their skill."[51]

In many instances, the description of the peasants' dues takes forms which are interchangeable, in labour-time or in quantity of products. Thus, the dues owed to the lordship of St. Gall by the serf women are sometimes—as in the ancient *Lex Alemannorum*—indicated by the number of days of labour to be performed, and sometimes by the number of products to be produced during these days.[52] The Aztecs imposed on the other peoples of Mexico a tribute calculated in working days, in amount of craft products, or in area of land to be cultivated.[53] In Japan there were in the eighth century A.D. two kinds of non-agricultural obligatory labour, called *cho* and *yo*. The statute of Taiho fixed the amount of these two obligations both in length of labour-time (ten days), in quantity of cloth (26 *shaku*, i.e. approximately 10 yards) and in quantity of corn (1 *To*, i.e. approximately two bushels).[54] Thus, among the producers in a society of this kind, the length of time needed to produce a given commodity was quite clear. Similarly in Western Europe, when from the twelfth century onward direct cultivation of the manor was more and more replaced, on the

Continent, by leasehold farming, it was *half the crop* that had to be given to the lord in place of the classic three days of work each week. In China the chronicles of the Tang dynasty calculate exactly how much work has to be devoted to growing millet (283 days a year) and wheat (177 days), the land tax being payable in kind.[55] In the mediaeval commune, notes Espinas, there is a strict equivalence between the working day and the (quantitative) amount of the work to be done.[56]

We find this same economic accounting based on the duration of labour in Spanish America, at the time when the forced labour of the Indians was transformed into rent in kind, in the system of *repartimiento-encomienda*,[57] and also in Indonesia at the time of the introduction of the *cultuurstelsel*. The population had no longer to pay "land rent" but to plant one-fifth of its land with products to be sold to the Government: indigo, sugar, coffee, tobacco, etc. "If one had no land, one had to work 66 days a year on the Government's plantations."[58] In Vietnam, during the dead season of the year, loans are made which are repayable in working days: 1·5 piastres, to be repaid by ten days' work at the time when there is much to be done, etc.

Exchange-value of commodities

Now, generalised exchange, trade, appears only at a stage of social development marked by this economy of labour-time. Those peoples who have escaped the need to observe this economy are satisfied with a small surplus product and exchange which is merely rudimentary or ritual.* It follows that this exchange is guided by the same objective standard which underlies all social organisation, namely, *that the exchange-value of commodities is measured by the labour time needed to produce them.*

We observe the transition from a social organisation *consciously governed* by the economy of labour time to one with exchanges regulated half-consciously, half-objectively, by the same principle, in the case of the trading relations established in the Nilgiri Hills, in the South-West of the Indian peninsula, between four tribes: the Toda, Karumba, Badaga and Kota.

* This is why numerous primitive peoples whose development has been stopped before the appearance of petty commodity production do not exchange their products in accordance with objective standards or on the basis of an economy of labour-time. This fact has led many ethnologists to false conclusions as regards economic analysis. Margaret Mead records, however, that the inhabitants of Manua (Samoa), who practise ceremonial exchange of finely woven mats, had originally fixed an exchange value for these mats which corresponded to the labour-time spent on producing them. Later, this value was greatly increased. This Samoan people, like the inhabitants of many other Pacific islands, consists of emigrants who have come from inhospitable countries to countries of plenty, where exchange no longer plays an economically important role.[59]

The Toda are shepherds; the Karumba still live in the jungle; the Badaga are agriculturists; and the Kota are primarily craftsmen who are already acquainted with metal-working and make knives. They supply these knives to the three other tribes, together with pots and musical instruments needed for religious ceremonies. In exchange they receive from the Toda buffaloes and other cattle; from the Karumba, honey, wild fruits, and (magical) protection; and from the Badaga, wheat. But the Kota are not mere craftsmen; they themselves possess land which they cultivate. Religious rites determine the traditional quantity of wheat—the outcome of long experience—which must be exchanged for the metal utensils provided by the Kota smiths. "Should a Badaga wish more of these utensils, he would have to work in the field of the Kota iron-worker of whom he requested them, while they were being forged."[60]

In the same way, among the people of Dahomey, "the practice among the iron-workers, for example, is for one smith to buy a quantity of scrap iron and keep it until such time as it is his turn to benefit from the labour of his fellows, for whom he has been working in the meantime. When this time arrives, all the members of the craft of forgers convert the iron he has acquired into hoes, axes, bush-knives, and other saleable goods. The owner of the iron then is free to sell these implements, and to keep the proceeds gained from selling them. This money he will use for living expenses and the purchase of scrap iron, meanwhile working for his associates, until it is once more his turn to have the use of the combined labour-power of his craft of forgers."[61]

Exchange which is simple, occasional, ritual and without economic importance may well disregard strict equivalence. It is not the same with generalised exchange. Lack of an objective criterion of equivalence would prevent any regulation of exchange-relations. It would lead to disorganisation and the dissolution of any society which included a substantial number of commodity producers. The producers would give up the kinds of work in which they received less for their products than in other kinds of work. Strict relations of equivalence between the products and commodities being exchanged are therefore indispensable.

But a relation of equivalence between two products, two commodities, demands a common gauge, a common commensurable quality. The *use-value* of a commodity depends on the totality of its physical qualities, which determine its utility. The existence of this use-value is an indispensable condition for the appearance of an exchange-value; nobody will accept in exchange for his own product a commodity which has no utility, no use-value, for anyone. But the use-value of two commodities, expressed in their physical qualities, is incommensurable; one cannot measure with a common gauge the *weight* of corn, the *length* of cloth, the *volume* of pots, the *colour* of flowers. For reciprocal exchange between these products to be possible, a quality must be found which they all possess, which can be measured and expressed quantitatively, and which must be a *social quality*, acceptable to all members of society.

Now, the totality of the physical qualities of commodities which give them their use-value, is determined by the *specific labour* which has produced them; the labour of a weaver determines the dimensions, fineness and weight of the cloth; the labour of a potter determines the durability, shape and colour of the pot. But if these commodities are each the products of a specific kind of labour, they are also the products of *social human labour*, that is, of a part of the total labour time available to a particular society, and on the economy of which society is based, as we have just shown. This is the fact that makes commodities commensurable; it is this general human labour —called abstract labour because abstraction is made from its specific nature, just as when one adds together three apples, four pears and five bananas one has to abstract from their specific qualities so as to be left with merely twelve *fruits*—that is the basis of exchange value.* It is the measurement of this work—the duration of the labour-time needed to produce the commodity—that provides the measurement of exchange-value.

Petty commodity production

So long as independent craft work, trade, and division of society into classes have developed only slightly, commodity production occupies a relatively limited place in society. It is only when trade and town life have reached a certain stage of development, when they have created a *sufficiently extensive market*, that commodity production develops and becomes general in its turn, in the towns.[63] We then enter a period of history marked by the fact that commodity production has become general in the towns while production for use is slowly breaking up in the country. This commodity production carried on by

* Since the dawn of petty commodity production, about 3,000 B.C., all labour has been considered equivalent, regardless of its special character. On the tablets, inscribed in a Semitic language, found at Susa, the wages in the household of a prince are fixed uniformly at 60 *qua* of barley for the cook, the barber, the engraver of stones, the carpenter, the smith, the cobbler, the tailor, the cultivator, the shepherd and the donkey man.[62] At this early phase of the production of exchange-values, however, men were not able to arrive at the notion of "abstract labour"; the equivalence of different skilled trades was conceived as such. The idea of "abstract labour" could not arise until the appearance of the *mobility of labour-power* in the capitalist era. This implies not merely that one hour of the labour of a textile worker produces as much as one hour of the labour of a brickmaker, but also that these jobs have been *interchangeable* in large-scale industry. See also Chapter 5, section: "Human labour-power and machine production".

craftsmen who own their own means of production (tools) is called simple or petty commodity production. It became preponderant in periods of urban civilisation, notably in Antiquity, from the sixth century B.C., in Greece; about the eighth century A.D. in the Islamic world; and from the eleventh century A.D. in Western Europe, where it reached its most characteristic development in the Southern Netherlands and in Italy in the thirteenth to fifteenth centuries.

In petty commodity production, labour no longer results directly in satisfying the producer's needs; labour and product of labour are no longer identical for him. But the producer remains owner of the product of his labour; he gives it up only in order to acquire for himself the goods which will ensure his existence. The division of labour has already separated the producer from his product, but it does not yet oppress the former by means of the latter. Commodity production develops slowly within society, while production of use-values pure and simple is slowly shrinking.

The more production of commodities extends, the more necessary becomes exact reckoning in hours of labour. In primitive society where only a rudimentary division of labour exists, accounting is of vital importance for the community survival only as regards the essential kinds of work. Apart from them, as we have seen, it matters relatively little whether two hours or three are spent on producing a particular object. This is what explains the quite extensive freedom enjoyed by members of such societies, within the framework of strict rules which govern the activities that produce food. Herskovits has given a striking picture of this mixture of strict accounting and wide freedom in the cycle of production and consumption among the Talensi, a people living by fruit-gathering and agriculture in Ghana.[64]

Once, however, commodity production has become widespread within a primitive community, the reckoning of labour-time takes place more strictly. On the market where the products of the labour of different villages, even different regions, meet, exchange-values establish themselves henceforth in accordance with *social averages*. It is not the number of hours actually spent on making an object that determine its value, but the number of hours of labour necessary to make it in the average conditions of productivity of this society in this period. Commodities would indeed become incommensurable if their value were determined by the *actual* time spent, by chance, by each individual producer on producing them. "He [the mediaeval artisan] has to produce, in accordance with fixed conditions, cloth which is 'not personal but official, municipal'; his labour, one might say, is expressly objective not subjective."[65]

Since the value of commodities is established by the amount of labour *socially necessary* to produce them—that is, since this average becomes fixed by the experience of repeated acts of exchange, by the simultaneous appearance of products from several different producers competing with each other—producers who are clumsy, slow, or who employ out-of-date methods, are penalised. They receive in exchange for the labour-time they have individually given to society only an equivalent produced in a shorter length of time. Greater discipline and stricter labour accounting thus accompany the development of commodity production.*

With the development of petty commodity production, human labour begins to be differentiated according to quality. *Composite, skilled* labour separates off from simple labour. As the crafts, becoming more and more specialised, necessitate a more or less lengthy period of apprenticeship, the cost of which can on longer be borne, as in primitive societies, by the whole community, but has to be met by the apprentice's family or by himself personally, no one would devote himself to the prolonged apprenticeship to a craft if, in exchange for an hour of skilled labour, he were to receive the same equivalent as for an hour of unskilled labour. Skilled labour is regarded as composite labour, into which there enters not only the labour expended by the craftsman at the moment when he is producing something as a qualified man, but also part of his expenditure of unpaid labour in the days when he was an apprentice (social depreciation of the overhead costs of apprenticeship).

Law of value in petty commodity production

The *law of value* which regulates the exchange of commodities in accordance with the amount of abstract, simple, socially-necessary human labour they contain, at last begins to fulfil a supplementary function. Primitive society and the village community, with their rudimentary division of labour, were organised on the basis of *conscious* labour co-operation, in which custom, religious rites, the counsels of elders or elected administrators, determined the rhythm of production; on these being grafted in due course the unpaid labour or tribute to be surrendered to the possessing classes.

But when petty commodity production has developed, we have

* This is clearly seen in the petty commodity production of the Guatemala Indians of Panajachel, as described by Professor Sol Tax. Men, women and even small children are continually on the alert to make a few pence by trade. It is not surprising that exchanges and equivalences are strictly calculated in this society where, Professor Tax tells us, a woman who could not read or write was able to state almost to within a penny the exact cost of production of a carpet on which she had worked the whole of one day. Under conditions like this, if land is sometimes rented in exchange for unpaid labour, sometimes in exchange for a part of the harvest, and sometimes for a money rent, one must suppose that in each case strict equivalences have been worked out, which could only be based on labour-value.[66]

before us producers who are free from any subordination to a collective social organisation. Each producer, within the limits of his physical strength and his capacity to produce (tools, etc.), can produce as much as he likes. These producers are no longer producing use-values for the consumption of a closed community; they are now producing commodities for a market which is more or less extensive, more or less impersonal. The law of value, which co-ordinates exchanges on an objective basis and ensures only equivalents for each commodity exchanged thus *reorganises*, through successful exchanges and unsuccessful ones, the distribution among the different branches of production of the totality of hours of labour at society's disposal. Human labour in primitive societies was *directly social* labour. In petty commodity society, individual labour acquires its quality as social labour only *indirectly*, through the mechanism of exchange, by the operation of the law of value.*

If a craftsman produces more cloth than the market of his society can absorb, part of his production will remain unsold, not exchanged, which will show him that he spent too great a share of the labour-time at society's disposal on producing this cloth, or, in other words, that he wasted social labour time. This waste, in a consciously co-ordinated society, would have been realised in advance, by custom or the observations of other members of the community. On the market, the law of value reveals it only after the event, to the disadvantage of the producer, who does not receive an equivalent for part of his exertion and its products.

These rules nevertheless remain quite obvious at the beginning of the period of commodity production. The proof is to be seen in the fact that in the corporations of Antiquity and in those of China, of Byzantium, of the European and Arab Middle Ages, etc., fixed rules, known to all, laid down alike the labour-time to be devoted to the making of each object, the length of apprenticeship, its cost, and the equivalent normally to be asked for each commodity.[67]†

This obviousness merely gives expression to the fact that with petty commodity production we have reached only a transitional stage between a society consciously governed by labour co-operation, and a society in which the complete dissolution of community ties leaves no room for anything but "objective" laws, that is, laws which are blind, "natural", independent of men's will, as the regulators of economic activity.

* See, in Chapter 18, refutation of current criticisms of the labour theory of value.

† Nadel mentions that in the Kingdom of Nupe the value of commodities is broadly proportional to the labour time spent on producing them.[68]

REFERENCES

1. Hingston Quiggin: *A Survey of Primitive Money*, pp. 21-22.
2. Audrey I. Richards: *Land, Labour and Diet in Northern Rhodesia*, p. 222.
3. Margaret Mead: *Competition and Co-operation among Primitive People*, p. 134.
4. Margaret Mead: *Sex and Temperament*, pp. 170-1.
5. Thurwald: *L'économie primitive*, p. 201; article *"Handel"* in *Reallexicon der Vorgeschichte*, Vol. V, p. 74; Herskovits: *The Economic Life of Primitive People*, p. 160; Quiggin: op. cit., p. 11.
6. M. Mauss: *"Essai sur le don"* in *Sociologie et Anthropologie*, p. 214.
7. Polanyi: et al., op. cit., p. 88.
8. Cl. Lévi-Strauss: *Les Structures élémentaires de la parenté*, p. 168.
9. Ibid., p. 593.
10. Ibid. , pp. 178-180, 48-49.
11. C. Darryl Forde and R. Scott: *The Native Economics of Nigeria*, p. 68.
12. M. Mauss: op. cit., pp. 277-8.
13. Victor Purcell: *The Chinese in Southern Asia*, p. xxvii.
14. J. H. Boeke: *De Theorie der Indische Economie*, p. 39.
15. Schechter: The Law and Morals of Primitive Trade, in Herskovits: *Economic Life of Primitive People.*
16. Polanyi: et. al., op. cit., pp. 20, 269.
17. Claude Meillassoux: *Anthropologie économique des Gouro de Côte d'Ivoire*, pp. 267-9.
18. Ibid., pp. 266-7.
19. Heichelheim: *Wirtschaftsgeschichte des Altertums*, p. 21; Gordon Childe: *What Happened in History*, p. 61, and *Cambridge Economic History of Europe*, Vol. I, p. 4; J. Graham Clark: *L'Europe préhistorique*, pp. 363, 371; J. C. Van Eerde, *Inleiding tot de Volkenkunde van Ned. Indië*, p. 57.
20. Heichelheim: *Wirtschaftsgeschichte des Altertums*, Vol. I, pp. 26-27.
21. Herskovits: *The Economic Life of Primitive People*, p. 129.
22. Forde and Scott: op. cit., p. 43.
23. Herskovits: *The Economic Life of Primitive People*, p. 125; Thurwald: article *"Lohn"* in *Reallexicon der Vorgeschichte*, Vol. VII, pp. 308-9.
24. W. G. Sumner and A. G. Keller: *Science of Society*, Vol. IV, p. 46.
25. Forde and Scott: op. cit., p. 79; S. F. Nadel: *A Black Byzantium*, p. 254; *Histoire du Commerce*, Vol. IV, p. 148; Polanyi: et al., op. cit., pp. 178-83.
26. M. M. Postan: "Trade of Mediaeval Europe: the North", in *Cambridge Economic History of Europe*, Vol. II, pp. 168-9.
27. Gordon Childe: *Man Makes Himself*, pp. 120-2; *What Happened in History*, pp. 96-97.
28. Charles Wisdom: *The Chorti Indians of Guatemala*, pp. 24-25, 199; S. F. Nadel: op. cit., p. 321.
29. Chen Huan-Chang: *The Economic Principles of Confucius*, p. 122.
30. Gordon Childe: *The Bronze Age*, p. 8.

31. G. Dijckmans: *Histoire économique et sociale de l'ancienne Egypte*, Vol. II, p. 226; Polanyi: et. al., op. cit., pp. 41 et. al.
32. Polanyi: et al., op. cit., pp. 51-55. D. D. Kosambi, *An Introduction to the Study of Indian History*, p. 151, *et al.*
33. Heichelheim: op. cit., Vol. I, p. 179; René Grousset: *Histoire de la Chine*, p. 9.
34. Boeke: op. cit., p. 44.
35. G. Glotz: *Le Travail dans la Grèce antique*, p. 53.
36. Dijckmans: op. cit., Vol. II, p. 236; K. A. Wittfogel: *Wirtschaft und Gesellschaft Chinas*, p. 514; Yoshitomi: *Etude sur l'histoire économique de l'ancien Japon*, p. 203; G. B. Jathar and S. G. Beri: *Indian Economics*, p. 104; Josef Kulischer: *Allgemeine Wirtschaftsgeschichte des Mittelalters*, Vol. I., p. 75.
37. Wittfogel: op. cit., p. 497; P. I. Lyashchenko: *History of the National Economy of Russia*, p. 162; M. Takizawa: *The Penetration of Money Economy in Japan*, p. 24; Jathar and Beri: op. cit., p. 103; Herskovits: op. cit., p. 187; Audrey I. Richards: op. cit., p. 22; Paul S. Martin: George L. Quimby and Donald Collier: *Indians Before Columbus*, p. 67.
38. Gordon Childe: *What Happened in History*, p. 85.
39. Polanyi: et al., op. cit., pp. 84-85; *An Outline History of China*, p. 28.
40. Sumner and Keller: op. cit., Vol. IV, p. 53.
41. Alfred Métraux, in: *Handbook of South American Indians*, Vol. III, p. 418.
42. Ruth Bunzel: in Franz Boas, ed., *General Anthopology*, p. 346.
43. Boeke: op. cit., p. 64.
44. John Embree: *Mura, A Japanese Village*, pp. 100-1.
45. Ralph Piddington: *An Introduction to Social Anthropology*, p. 275.
46. Kautilya's *Arthashastra*: German trans. by J. J. Mayer, p. 147.
47. John Collier: *The Indians of the Americas*, pp. 61-62.
48. See other articles in the Polyptique of Saint Germain-des-Prés and the *descriptio villarum* of the Abbey of Lobbes.
49. Joseph Bourrilly: *Eléments d'ethnographie marocaine*, pp. 137-8; Roger Grand and Raymond Delatouche: *L'Agriculture au moyen âge*, p. 79.
50. P. Dollinger: *L'évolution des classes rurales en Bavière*, p. 270.
51. Marc Bloch: *Caractères originaux de l'histoire rurale française*, p. 77.
52. Herman Bikel: *Die Wirtschaftsverhältnisse des Klosters St. Gallen*, pp. 133-239.
53. H. Cunow: *Wirtschaftsgeschichte*, Vol. I, pp. 270-1.
54. Y. Takekoshi: *Economic Aspects of the History of the Civilisation of Japan*, Vol. I, p. 117.
55. L. Génicot: *L'Economie rurale namuroise au bas moyen âge*, pp. 236-85; Grand and Delatouche: op. cit., pp. 105-35; Jacques Gernet: *Les aspects économiques du bouddhisme dans la société chinoise du Ve au Xe siecle*, p. 98.
56. Georges Espinas: *Les Origines du capitalisme*, Vol. I, p. 140.
57. Robert S. Chamberlain: "Castilian Backgrounds of the Repartimiento Encomienda", in *Contributions to American Anthropology*, Vol. V, pp. 25-26.

58. H. J. De Graaf: *Geschiedenis van Indonesië*, p. 406.
59. Margaret Mead: *Social Organization of Manua*, pp. 73-75, p. 65.
60. David Mandelbaum: "Notes on Fieldwork in India", in Herskovits: *Economic Life of Primitive Peoples*, pp. 136-7.
61. M. J. Herskovits: *Dahomey, an ancient West African Kingdom*, Vol. I, pp. 75-76.
62. Clement Huart and Louis Delaporte: *L'Iran antique*, p. 83.
63. Gordon Childe: *What Happened in History*, p. 156.
64. Herskovits: *Economic Life of Primitive Peoples*, pp. 248-51.
65. Espinas: op. cit., Vol. I, p. 142.
66. Sol Tax: *Penny Capitalism*, pp. 18, 15, 80.
67. Espinas: op. cit., Vol. I, pp. 118, 140-2.
68. Nadel: op. cit., p. 318.

CHAPTER THREE

MONEY, CAPITAL, SURPLUS-VALUE

Need for a universal equivalent

SIMPLE or developed exchange is carried out in the form of barter, that is, direct encounter between the products being exchanged. For primitive peoples, accustomed to exchanging the same products in accordance with procedures that were traditional and even ritual, barter created no economic "problem".[1]

It is different with generalised exchange and commerce. No longer is a single product, the tribe's surplus, exchanged for other products; a great number of a great variety of products are now exchanged for many other products. The relations of equivalence concern no longer just two products, or two categories of product, but an infinite variety of different goods. It is no longer the labour-time of the potter that is compared with that of the agriculturist; ten, twenty, thirty different crafts have to compare their respective productive efforts from time to time. In order that these exchanges may go on without interruption, the owners of the commodities must be able to get rid of their goods before they have had the luck to encounter purchasers who possess the products they themselves want to obtain in exchange for these goods. For exchanges to be carried out on the basis of equivalence, a commodity is needed in which all the others can express their respective exchange values. This function is fulfilled by the *universal equivalent* commodity.

The appearance of a universal equivalent, of money in all its forms, accompanies the generalisation of exchange and the beginnings of trade. The need for such an equivalent is obvious. Sir Samuel Baker tells of hearing country people shouting in the market-place of Unyoro, in Uganda:

"Milk to sell, for beads or salt! Salt to exchange for lance-heads! Coffee, coffee, going cheap, for red beads!"[2]

If the owners of salt do not want milk but red beads; if the owners of red beads do not want either salt or coffee but milk, none of these exchanges can take place, because there are no owners of commodities in proximity to one another here who are ready to exchange their goods reciprocally. What is characteristic of the universal equivalent is that it is a commodity for which *any other* commodity can be obtained. Suppose that salt became the universal equivalent. At once, the three operations could be carried through without difficulty. The trader will readily exchange his red pearls for salt, not because he wants to realise the use value of salt but because in exchange for salt, the universal equivalent, he can get the milk he wants.

The universal equivalent is thus itself a commodity; its own exchange-value is determined, like that of any other commodity, by the amount of labour socially necessary to produce it. It is in relation to this real exchange-value that all other commodities will henceforth express their own exchange-value. As a commodity, the universal equivalent also retains a use value which is determined by its natural qualities: when it has finished circulating, the salt ends up by being used for the salting of meat. But alongside its own natural, physical value, the universal equivalent commodity acquires a supplementary use value—that of facilitating the mutual exchange of other commodities, of being a means of circulation and a measure of value.

Thus, in Egypt in the days of the Ramassides, cattle served as universal equivalent, and

1 mat 5 measures of honey and 11 measures of oil	were equal in value to a bull.[3]

At the beginning of the second millennium B.C., in the reign of King Bilalama, silver had become the universal equivalent at Eshuna, in Mesopotamia. On the tax tablets discovered in 1947 at Tell Harmal, we find inscribed the following equivalences (converted into those of the metric system):

12 litres of sesame oil 300 litres of wheat 600 litres of salt 5 kilogrammes of wool 1 kilogramme of copper	were equal in value to one shekel (about 8 grammes) of silver.

In the Hittite code, 500 years earlier than that of King Bilalama, we find a long list of equivalences, from which we extract the following examples.

1 sheep 1 "zimittani" of butter 1 hide of a large ox 4 minas of copper 20 lambskins 2 "pa" of wine ½ "zimittani" of good oil	were equal in value to one shekel of silver.

3 goats were worth 2 shekels of silver.
1 divided robe was worth 3 shekels of silver.
1 large piece of cloth was worth 3 shekels of silver.
1 cart horse was worth 20 shekels of silver.[5]

What we have here is a real *price list*. The price is nothing but the exchange value of a commodity expressed in a definite quantity of the equivalent commodity. The universal equivalent has become money; price is the expression of exchange-value in money terms.

Evolution of the universal equivalent

Often, the commodities which were most commonly exchanged in a given region became, at the dawn of petty commodity production, the first universal equivalents. These commodities fall into two categories: the products which are of maximum importance for the people concerned (foodstuffs, tools, salt), and ornaments, which are among the first objects involved in any human exchange.

Those peoples who are engaged in both agriculture and cattle-raising usually choose as their universal equivalent either cattle, wheat or rice. Thus, Greeks and Romans adopted the ox as first universal equivalent down to the sixth and fifth centuries B.C. The Indians' word for their national currency, *rupee*, is derived from *rupa*, meaning a herd. The Iranians of the *Avesta* and the Germans of the *Lex Saxonum* also chose the ox as universal equivalent, which indicates the predominance of cattle-raising in the epoch when this happened. In North, East and South Africa, cattle, in the shape of camels, sheep, goats or cows, likewise constituted the universal equivalent among people who were essentially cattle-breeders. The horse played the same part among the Kirghiz, the buffalo in Annam and the sheep in Tibet.

In those cases where cultivation of the land was more important than cattle-raising at the time when the universal equivalent appeared, various products of the soil fulfilled this function. In ancient Japan, rice was for centuries the only universal equivalent. In China it was at first wheat and millet, later rice as well. In Mesopotamia it was wheat. In Egypt, wheat prepared as food, that is, loaves baked in a certain form, soon ousted the ox.

In India too, wheat took the place of the ox as universal equivalent from the fifth century B.C., and in the countryside it retained this function until the nineteenth century. In the Sudan, dates were for a long time used as universal equivalent. In Central America it was maize. In Newfoundland and in Iceland down to the fifteenth century, it was dried fish; in the Nicobar Islands, coconuts; among the primitive tribes of the Philippines, rice; and on the Hawaiian Islands, before Western penetration, salt fish.

The principal tools have also been used as universal equivalents: bronze or copper axes and bronze tripods in Crete; bronze vases in Laos; iron shovels and hoes in Central and East Africa; fish-hooks in the Solomon and Marshall Islands of the Pacific, etc. In China, the names of two of the oldest coins, "pu" and "tsian", meant originally "farming tool", and come from the names of bronze tools.[6] In Japan, in the seventh and eighth centuries A.D., iron shovels or hoes were the essential forms of movable wealth.[7]

The raw materials from which these tools were made could often in their turn, play the part of universal equivalent. Stone was the universal equivalent on the island of Yap, in the Pacific. In Homeric Greece, when bronze vases were beginning to be used as universal equivalent among the Achaeans of the mainland, the inhabitants of the island of Lemnos already regarded bronze, the metal, as itself the universal equivalent. Ingots and small sticks of iron have played the same role among the more advanced communities in Africa.

With the development of exchange, products of primary necessity, such as the chief foodstuffs or most important tools, may be replaced as universal equivalent by the local *commodity*, that is, the product chiefly bought or sold in relations with foreign traders. Thus we find as universal equivalents packets of compressed tea among the Tatars and Mongols of the nineteenth century; cocoa beans in Mexico in the time of the Aztecs; salt in Abyssinia, in West, Equatorial and East Africa, in Burma, in mediaeval Tibet and among some Indian tribes of North America; pelts in Canada down to the eighteenth century; white squirrel skins in Russia; hempen fabrics in mediaeval Japan; measures of cloth in certain communities of Western Europe in the Middle Ages, and so on. In China, a foot of cloth (*tch'e*) was worth a bushel (*che*) of grain and was used as universal equivalent, alongside wheat, millet and copper money, under the T'ang emperors.[8]

Ornaments, the first use of which may well have been magical,* were often used as universal equivalent in the early days of petty commodity production. Alongside utilitarian objects of bronze, small tripods of bronze thus made their appearance in the Creto-Mycenaean civilisation as universal equivalents. Bronze rings similarly come on the scene in Egypt. Jade fulfilled a similar function among the pre-Columbian Indians of Central America, and turquoises among the Pueblo Indians. Glass or enamel pearls were used for the same purpose in Egypt, and spread from there to Mediterranean Europe. They spread through Africa as a real currency.

The ornament which enjoyed the widest circulation as universal equivalent was the *cowrie* shell. From China and India these shells spread over the Pacific Islands, into Africa and Europe and even into the New World.

"Cowries surpass all other shell currencies in solidity and uniformity.

* The exchange of ornaments or other objects of value in a primitive society, as a magical phenomenon, also has an economic origin. In his *Essai sur le don*, Marcel Mauss explains that these objects "are regarded as replicas of inexhaustible instruments, creators of food, which the spirits have given to one's ancestors."[9]

They are fairly constant both in size and weight, and equal in these respects to foodstuffs such as kidney beans, broad beans, rice, wheat or barleycorns which provided the earliest units of weighing gold and silver."[10]

The precious metals as universal equivalent thus represent a coincidence of the object of primary necessity as universal equivalent and the ornament as universal equivalent. Copper, bronze, silver, gold have always served first of all as raw materials for the making of ornaments. Only with the progress of metal-working are these metals also used to make objects of primary necessity. As soon as this stage was reached, these metals played a vital part in the economy. At the same time they retained a religious, ritual, even magical significance, inherited from the era when they were used only to make ornaments. These factors facilitated the adoption of the precious metals as universal equivalent of all commodities.

Money

The development of international trade usually coincides with the metallurgical revolution. Metals are the chief objects of this trade. The need for a universal equivalent is felt more strongly now. It is not surprising that it should be precisely metals that are most often chosen to fulfil this function. At the start it is still objects made of metal that are used as universal equivalent, but if exchanges become frequent this means complications and extra costs.

In East Africa, iron hoes serve as universal equivalent. The tribes which live in areas rich in iron ore make these hoes, and exchange them for the products of other areas, and in the latter the local smiths often reforge them into weapons or ornaments.[11] In this way, they come to take as their universal equivalent *pure unwrought metal*, measured by weight. Hence the role of weighers of gold, who are synonymous with money-changers, bankers and usurers at the start of every money economy.

But it is tedious to weigh metal, whether or not in the form of ingots, whenever one makes an exchange. After a certain level of commercial development has been reached the State adopts the practice of stamping ingots of precious metal with a mark indicating their weight. Such officially weighed ingots appear from the third millennium B.C. in Mesopotamia and Egypt, and from the second millennium in Europe, in Crete and the Peloponnese, in the centres of the Creto-Mycenaean civilisation. Much later, about 700 B.C., the idea appears of adapting the form of the ingot to the needs of transport over long distances. The King of Lydia, who wanted to attract the trade of the Greek cities to the great entrepôts of his capital, Sardis, undertook the minting of small gold coins, each weighing only a few grammes. One of these coins, henceforth, could be used for the exchange against money of commodities of comparatively high value. The spread of trade was thus encouraged; peasants and small craftsmen could from now on sell their surpluses for money instead of having to barter.[12] This system of minting coins spread to the Persian Empire, to the Greek cities, and through these civilisations made its way throughout the world affected by their trade. In India and China it seems to have developed independently of Asia Minor. In China, metal coins were in circulation about 1,000 B.C. and were given official weights from 65 B.C. onward.[13]

If the precious metals established themselves everywhere as universal equivalents, this was because they possess a series of intrinsic qualities which merchants and administrators discovered empirically and which make them especially suitable for this purpose.

1. They are easily *transportable*: their high specific weight enables them to concentrate in a modest volume a quantity of metal representing a fairly large exchange-value. This value remains stable: comparatively few technical changes have occurred in the way they are produced, over several millennia.

2. They are *durable*, owing to their resistance to wear and tear, rust, etc.

3. They are easily *divisible*; and the fragments can be easily melted down into larger units.

4. They are easily *recognisable*, owing to specific physical qualities, and any counterfeiting can be detected fairly easily (by changes in weight).

However, while these intrinsic qualities of the precious metals predestine them, in a sense, for the role of universal equivalent as soon as trade has grown to a certain extent, their effective use as such remains dependent on their being produced in adequate quantity in a definite territory. As a rule, gold is produced before silver, and, at the start, even at lower cost. It was so in Egypt of the Pharaohs, in ancient India, in pre-Columbian America, etc.[14]

When the precious metals are hard to come by, other metals are normally employed as universal equivalent. In ancient Greece, before the gold mines of Laurium and Strymon were discovered, which brought riches first to Athens and then to the Kings of Macedonia, gold coins were very rare; silver, copper and sometimes even iron, were the most usual materials for coins. In Laconia, rich in iron, iron money predominated until the third century B.C. In China, where silver and gold are very rare, copper remained until the fifteenth century A.D. the metal base of the currency, and was sometimes replaced by iron. The same scarcity of gold and silver in Japan determined the use there of copper as the general measure of value, from the seventh to the seventeenth century A.D. Then the discovery of big deposits of gold and silver made it possible to mint plenty of coins from precious metals.[15] It is interesting to observe that even countries which possess great resources in precious metals do not usually start exploiting them until the development of trade really calls for a plentiful supply of currency made of these metals. This is easily explained by the fact that it is only at that stage that people apply themselves actively to looking for these deposits.*

So long as the universal equivalent consists of commodities which possess their own use-value—objects of primary necessity, ornaments, metallic raw materials—their new use-value, which is that of providing a universal equivalent for all other commodities, is only a subsidiary one, which may disappear when the purchaser of this special commodity wants to realise its natural use-value. It is otherwise with precious metals in the form of ingots bearing an official stamp, and later metal coins struck by a public authority. As soon as they appear, the use-value which is common and exclusive to this new commodity consists in its function as universal equivalent of the other commodities. For stamped ingots or minted coins to serve afresh as raw materials for the making of jewellery, they must first be melted down again, ceasing to exist as ingots or coins. We have thus arrived, at the end of the evolution of the universal equivalent, at a commodity which has no other use-value than that of serving as universal equivalent. This commodity is called *currency* or *money*.

Evolution of social wealth and different functions of money

A society which essentially produces use values has as its index of social wealth the accumulation of these same use-values. Among primitive peoples or in a primitive village community, the accumulation of foodstuffs is the best understood expression of wealth and the criterion of social prestige. Among pastoral peoples, social wealth is reckoned in cattle or horses; among agricultural peoples, in amount of wheat, rice, maize, etc. At the beginning of the seventeenth century in Japan, the wealth of the whole country and of each lord was still calculated in weight of rice (*koku* of rice). The accumulation of use values makes possible a concentration of wealth which should not be underestimated. A single family, that of the Tokugawa shoguns, possessed in those days 8 million *koku* of rice, out of 28 million *koku* which was the annual production of all Japan, i.e. a big proportion of the entire national income.[16]

With the spread of trade, the generalisation of exchange, the more and more current use of money, the latter becomes increasingly the main or even the only index of the wealth of individuals, families and nations. Its function is no longer merely to serve as universal equivalent in exchange transactions. Money fulfils at the same all the following functions:

* See on this subject, Chapter 4, as regards Western Europe.

1. It is the *universal equivalent*, i.e. it makes it possible to acquire all the commodities available on the market;

2. It is the *means of exchange*, i.e. it makes possible the circulation of commodities even between owners of commodities who do not want to realise the use-values of their respective commodities;

3. It is the *measure of value* and *gauge of prices*. The value of each commodity is expressed in a quantity, a particular weight of the precious metal, i.e. expressed in money. The price is nothing but this monetary expression of value. As such, *ideal money* can express the price of any commodity at all. To do this one need not *possess* a sum of money, it is enough to *name* it.

4. It is the universal *means of payment*: debts and fines owed to the State, the clergy or individuals, the counter-value of all commodities, services or payments, can be rendered by means of money, in contrast to primitive society in which there are special products for carrying out these different functions.*

Here, "ideal" money is of no use; coins that ring and weigh as they should are needed.

5. It is the *means of accumulating values* and the *means of forming hoards*. Every society needs to possess reserves to meet its requirements in case of natural disasters, such as epidemics, floods, harvest failures, earthquakes, fires, etc., or social disasters, such as wars, civil strife, etc. The original function of the social surplus is to constitute this reserve fund. In a society producing essentially use-values, these reserves consist of stored-up products.

In a society which is beginning to produce commodities on a large scale, it is precious metals, or metal coins, that are accumulated as hoards. In case of need, this hoard, a store of values and counter-values, makes it possible to obtain all the goods that are lacking, even if distant countries have to be applied to. The precious metals are indeed universally recognised as universal equivalents. Experience teaches the peoples that a metal reserve is much more reliable and less perishable than a reserve of wheat or of cattle.[18]

Circulation of commodities and circulation of money

In a society producing simple commodities, money serves as universal equivalent only in a fairly limited number of commercial transactions. Its function is above all to serve as a hoard. It is jealously kept by those who possess it and who utilise it, at most, for increasing or improving their personal consumption. "Down to the end of

* At the beginning of the era of petty commodity production, these different functions of money can be fulfilled by *different* products. Thus, in Babylon in Hammurabi's time, barley was the universal means of payment, silver the measure of value, gauge of prices and doubtless also means of accumulation, while as universal equivalent they used barley, wool, oil, silver, wheat, etc.[17]

the wars with Persia," says Glotz, "Greek society remained in the hoarding stage. Money was accumulated and not set to work."[19] It was the same in Western Europe in the early Middle Ages.[20] In fact, in a mode of production which is essentially based on co-operative organisation of labour within a patriarchal family and a village community, and on the individual work of the town craftsman, money, even when it circulates, is employed only for acquiring use-values. It remains a subordinate element, an *instrument of commodity circulation.* The latter takes place according to this diagram:

$$\begin{array}{ccccc} C^1 & — & M & — & C^2 \\ \text{Commodity} & & \text{Money} & & \text{Commodity} \end{array}$$

In the municipal market of the Chorti Indians, in Guatemala, a cabinet-maker appears, the possessor of some wooden chairs. He does not want to (or he cannot) realise the use-value of his commodity; on the contrary, he wants to get rid of it, that is, to realise its exchange-value. In order that this operation may take place, he must meet the possessor of a sum of money, M, who will be willing to realise the exchange value of the chairs. It is further necessary that this possessor of money be ready to get rid of his money because he wants to realise the use-value of the wooden chairs. Thus the sale of the chairs, $C^1 — M$, takes place to the satisfaction of both partners.

But the possessor of the wooden chairs wanted to sell his commodity so as to acquire another one, for example, some woven mats from Amatilla district which he needs for his home. Taking the money he has obtained by selling his chairs, he goes in search of a producer-possessor of woven mats, in order to buy them from him. If such a producer-possessor turns up in the municipal market, the purchasing transaction $M — C^2$ can as a rule take place. At the end of these two successive operations of sale and purchase, the cabinet-maker has, instead of a commodity which he did not want to realise the use-value of, a new commodity which is of use to him. Two commodities, the wooden chairs and the woven mats, have disappeared from the market because their use-value has been successively realised by two purchasers. On the other hand, the sum of money, M, has passed through the hands of three persons: from the purchaser of the chairs to the cabinet-maker, and from the cabinet-maker to the maker of woven mats. At the start of the era of petty commodity production, the last owner of this sum of money, the maker of woven mats, will in his turn be able to use this money for two purposes only: either to put it by as a reserve, a hoard, savings, against a rainy day; or to use it to buy some other commodity.

But when a society at the stage of petty commodity production makes contact with a more advanced trading civilisation, owners of money who want to make this possession of theirs "circulate", "work", "pay", appear alongside owners of commodities who merely want to get rid of these commodities in order to meet some needs. Thus, the professional traders among the Chorti visit a certain number of districts, often three or four between them, with a sum of money sufficient to buy all the surplus of the craftsmen they meet. This surplus they transport to the markets of the provincial capitals. They do not buy commodities in order to realise their use-values, like the small producers of chairs and woven mats. On the contrary, they buy commodities in order to *sell them again at a profit* to the inhabitants of the towns whose markets they visit.

The circulation of commodities, that is, the operations carried out successively by the owners of commodities in a society based on petty commodity production, consists in *selling in order to buy*, selling one's own products in order to buy products whose use-value one realises.

The circulation of money, that is, the operations carried out successively by the owners of *money capital* in a society in which professional trade already exists alongside petty commodity production, consists, on the contrary, in *buying in order to sell*, buying another's products so as to sell them again at a profit, that is, to increase by a *surplus-value* the money capital one possesses. *Capital is, by definition, any value that is increased by surplus-value.*

If we ask again the question we asked regarding the maker of woven mats—what will he do with the money he has just received from the cabinet-maker?—there are no longer two but three replies we can give, when it is a matter of the money increased by surplus-value which the Chorti professional trader has obtained at the conclusion of his activities and travels. He can, as before, use it simply to obtain what he needs to feed, clothe and house himself and his family, or to form a hoard. If he does either of these we have not left the limits of petty commodity production.

But he can also act in a different manner: he can use his money, increased by surplus-value, either wholly or in part, to go to other districts, buy other craft products, sell them again, dearer, in other markets, and find himself at the end of his transactions in possession of more money than he started with. In this case we have left the limits of petty commodity production strictly so called and entered the stage of the circulation of money, the *accumulation of money capital*, which takes place according to the formula:

$$\underset{\text{Money}}{M} \quad - \quad \underset{\text{Commodity}}{C} \quad - \quad \underset{\text{Money + surplus value}}{M^1}$$

The difference between the circulation of commodities, $C^1 — M — C^2$, and the circulation of money, $M — C — M^1$, consists then in this; in the circulation of commodities, the *equivalence* of the commodities C^1 and C^2 which are found at the extreme ends of the circulation process is the necessary condition for the two operations to be carried through. No simple producer of commodities can acquire commodities of a value higher than that of the commodities he has himself produced and sold. In the circulation of money, on the contrary, the appearance of a surplus-value ($M^1 - M$) is the necessary condition for circulation to take place: no owner of money-capital is going to "circulate" his money only to see come back to his pocket exactly the same amount which left it!

Surplus-value emerging from the circulation of commodities

Surplus-value has just appeared, then, in the course of the circulation of money. It seems, indeed, to be the essential aim of this circulation. But where has it come from?

In a society based on petty commodity production, the surplus-value obtained by owners of money comes either from *trade* or from usury. It is only when trade and usury have developed extensively that the possessing classes becomes conscious of the need to "make their money pay". The fifth century B.C. saw the rise of petty commodity production not only in ancient Greece but also in China. During this century, Chi-Jan, teacher of the great merchant, Fan-lin, instructed him in "the laws of accumulating capital" and explained to him that, above all, "one must not allow money to be idle".[21] Eighteen hundred years later, when petty commodity production had attained an unprecedented development in the empire of Islam, the historian Ibn Khaldun judiciously noted that "trade, regarded as a way of earning one's livelihood .... consists in artful tricks performed in order to establish between the buying price and the selling price a difference from which one can make a profit".[22]

It was no different in Ancient Greece, in China in the classical epoch, or in mediaeval Europe. The Odyssey speaks of the Phoenicians, the typical trading people of antiquity, as "clever navigators, deceitful traders". The biographer of St. Godric of Finchale, who engaged in trade at the end of the eleventh century, explains that "he bought in various countries goods which he knew were scarce and therefore dearer elsewhere, and carried them into other regions where they were almost unknown to the inhabitants and therefore seemed to them more desirable than gold".[23]

In fact, large scale trade consisted in going to buy goods at low prices from peoples at a lower stage of economic development, or perhaps not even arrived yet at the stage of general exchange, and who for this reason sold their products very cheap. Then one went to sell these same goods at a much higher price wherever they were very scarce and in demand, where their real value (the labour-time needed to produce them) was unknown, where fashion made certain goods especially attractive, or, better still, where as a result of disasters, famines, etc., a particularly marked shortage of these goods prevailed.

The surplus-value of the traders in an epoch like this comes from their buying goods below their real value and selling them above this real value. There is nothing surprising in the fact that in these conditions Mercury, lord of trade, is also regarded as the king of thieves. It is not surprising that among the African people called the Hereros, "who have no words for 'buy' and 'sell' but merely for 'barter', a merchant in the European sense 'is always a deceiver' because he seeks to win something by exchange."[24] It is not surprising that the Navajo Indians always have the impression that an unusually rich man has obtained his wealth by dishonest means.[25] All folk wisdom repeats the same thing, in all the languages of the earth. As getting something cheap is the basis of this trader's profit, pure plundering and piracy are to be found at the cradle of surplus value.

"More typical still of repeated enrichment at the expense of others which is, so to speak, admitted, is the frankness with which Ulysses relates that he conducted nine piratical expeditions before the Trojan war, or the way he questions the shade of Agamemnon, asking him whether he fell in battle for his city or while he was 'stealing the oxen or the sheep of the State', as though there were little difference between these two activities."[26]

From the earliest times, "piracy is the first phase of trade. This is so true that from the end of the ninth century, when they stopped their plundering, they [the Norsemen] transformed themselves into traders."[27] We know that Aristotle still regarded piracy and highway robbery as legitimate ways of earning one's livelihood. Solon gave the law's protection to associations of pirates, just as the British and French monarchies did 2,000 years later in relation to privateers.[28] The Aztec merchants, combining the function of traders with that of conquerors, imposed tributes to be paid wherever they could, and provide a typical example of the inextricable ties linking the origins of trade with brigandage. Here are clearly revealed the origins of commercial surplus-value![29]

The trade-brigands called Varangians (the word *varyag* means in Slavonic "cattle-merchant"), men of Scandinavian origin who ravaged Russia from the eighth to the eleventh century of our era, are another typical example of the same phenomenon: "The trading and plundering parties of Norsemen-Swedes penetrated into Slavic territory. As merchants of the eighth and tenth centuries, they went there in quest both of trade and plunder. Robbery and conquest were alike a source of trade, with trade supplementing robbery."[30]

Trade and plundering are inextricably connected in the Sahara:

"The hostile tribes organised against their foes, and those protected by the latter, plundering operations planned as real trading expeditions, which is why they have a place in this treatise. They were governed by customary law, which laid down in detail the role of the capitalists who financed the expedition, that of those who carried it into effect, and the profits of each, in proportion to his participation. It was a typical contract of a very ancient kind which was still in use, with the same features, thirty years ago, in Upper Mauretania as well as in the Sahara."[31]

This system makes possible an extremely rapid enrichment of a few merchants, or of the merchant class of a people. The profits are very high, often exceeding 1,000 per cent on a single transaction. In the fourteenth century merchants bought Tatar horses in the Crimea for one dinar and sold them in India for 25 or even sometimes 50 dinars, we are told by the great Arab traveller Ibn Batuta.[32] The Dutch East India Company bought spices in the seventeenth century for 7·5 cents a pound, in the Moluccas, and sold them in Holland for 300 cents.[33] Such differences between prices are possible only if the backward condition of a people implies that it is unaware of the exchange value of a commodity on the world market. The Phoenicians knew what they were doing when they regularly preferred to do business with barbarian peoples whom they could oppress politically.[34]

Under the Sung dynasty "the peoples of the North [of China] whose usual food was meat, cheese and milk, liked tea to drink. To get it they used to come and sell their horses on the 1st and 2nd of February and March. At the start, when exchanges of tea against horses began, they would offer a good horse for a dozen pounds of ordinary tea. The Chinese tea monopoly drew substantial profits from these transactions. Soon smuggling began, and the foreigners, informed as to prices, demanded ten times as much for their horses."[35]

However, a circulation of money which results in surplus-value that originated in this way is *sterile* from a global point of view; it does not increase the total wealth of human society.* It consists in fact of a *transfer* of wealth, pure and simple; what one gains the other loses, in absolute value. Social wealth remains unchanged.

Let us represent by C the value of a quantity of amber produced by the inhabitants of the Baltic coast; by M the price paid by the Phoenician merchants to the producers of amber; and by M' the

* At least from the static standpoint. From the historical point of view, the concentration of surplus-value obtained by plundering, direct or indirect, made possible a development of merchant capital and world trade which undoubtedly favoured the spread of culture and the growth of productive forces. It must also be stressed that the surplus-value of merchant and usurers' capital represents to some extent the appropriation by these new possessing classes of part of the agricultural surplus-product which was the income of the old possessing classes (of the Egyptian lord in the example which follows).

selling price obtained by these same Phoenicians in Egypt. Before these exchanges took place, the three partners possessed altogether the values $C + M + M^1$: C belonged to the Danes, M to the Phoenician merchants and M^1 to some rich Egyptian lord. When the exchanges have been completed, the Danes have M, the Egyptian lord has C, and the Phoenician merchants have M^1. The total of these three values is still $C + M + M^1$. Society has been neither enriched nor impoverished. A transfer of value has taken place, that is all.

The Danes have been impoverished by the difference in value between C and M and the Egyptian lord by the difference between M^1 and C, whereas the Phoenician merchants have enriched themselves by the difference in value between M^1 and M, which represents exactly their surplus-value (or the sum of the losses of value suffered by their two trading partners). It is always the same when surplus-value is acquired through the circulation of money: it is created at the expense of a partner, and does not lead to the enrichment of society as a whole.

It may be objected that the Danes have suffered no real impoverishment unless they are already living in a trading economy, and the very barbarism that causes them to accept this unequal exchange implies that they are unaware of this "loss of value". Moreover, this whole argument supposes a unified system of values, whereas in reality what we have before us are different civilisations, with different systems of production and different values, which touch only at their peripheries.

This objection is not valid if one regards exchange value as something *objective* and not subjective. It is precisely trade that unifies values by establishing international markets, in which nations at different levels of development may well participate. It is, furthermore, enough to study the history of certain peoples in certain periods to realise that the idea of impoverishment by *transfer of value* is an obvious reality (cf. West Africa from the sixteenth to the nineteenth century, etc.).

Surplus-value arising from commodity production

When petty commodity production is at its beginning, social wealth remains almost stationary, and the surplus grabbed by the owners of money may simply arise from an absolute impoverishment of the successive buyers and sellers. The history of Antiquity is to a large degree the history of the successive conquest of the hoards of various kingdoms and then their concentration, also by way of conquest, by the Kings of Persia and by Alexander the Great. "The new wealth with which imperialism enriched Babylonia and Egypt was really just loot, and represented no addition to the total supply of real wealth available to humanity . . ."[36] The increase of real social wealth in that period is chiefly a function of the increase in the productivity of agricultural labour and the spreading knowledge of craft techniques, both connected with the growth of population. As the agricultural and craft techniques concerned are fairly simple and do not require costly equipment, the expansion of trade in ancient times towards the barbarian parts of the world ended by introducing there the same conditions of production as at the centre, and so itself put an end to the inequality in levels of economic development which had made this trade profitable. One of the chief reasons for the blind alley which ancient merchant capital got into, and for the decline of the Roman empire, is to be found in this simple fact. In the same way, *usury*, while it is a frequent source of individual enrichment, does not in the least signify an enrichment of society as a whole, since it represents, even more clearly than pre-capitalist trade, a simple *transfer of values* from one person to another.

Now, when we examine the evolution of certain societies based on petty commodity production, such as Greece from the sixth to the third century B.C., China from the eight to the third century B.C., the Islamic world from the eighth to the twelfth century A.D., or Western Europe from the eleventh to the fifteenth century, we observe that enrichment of the entire society did in fact occur. This enrichment exceeded by far the increase in agricultural and craft production; nor was it the mere result of looting economically backward countries, since it involved the totality of the countries linked by trade relations. It could, then, have resulted only from a mass of *new values* making their appearance in money economy. How could the creation of new values occur during the circulation of money M — C — M[1]?

We know already that value is only crystallised human labour. Money cannot, it would seem, create fresh values. But instead of buying commodities which he will sell for more than their value, the merchant can use his money to buy *a commodity which has, as its use-value, the quality of producing new values*: human labour-power.*

In the fifth and fourth centuries B.C. the purchase price of an adult male slave varied in Athens between 180 and 200 drachmas. Suppose a merchant buys such a slave. The average net daily income, after deduction of maintenance costs, obtainable from a slave amounts, according to Xenophon and Demosthenes, to an obolus a day, or allowing for holidays, 300 oboli or 50 drachmas a year.[37] After ten years' work this slave will thus have earned his master 500 drachmas,

* On this matter Aristotle and also the authorities of the Catholic Church, from the Council of Nicœa to St. Thomas Aquinas, had quite correct ideas, not as advocates of the labour theory of value but as representatives of an essentially natural economy which was defending itself against the dissolving invasion of money and usury.

or 300 drachmas of surplus value.* Buying a slave thus constitutes a source of surplus value of a special kind. This surplus value is not the result of a mere appropriation of existing values, a mere transfer of values from one pocket to another. It results from *the production of new values*, the appropriation and sale of which are the source of surplus value.

In fact, the biggest fortunes in Athens came from the employment or hiring-out of slaves for work in the mines. Possessing or hiring-out as many as 1,000 slaves, Kallias the Athenian was able to accumulate 200 talents, Nikias 100 talents.[40] At one obolus a day of net income produced by a slave, 100 talents (36,000 oboli) represents the income from 36,000 days worked by these slaves, without taking into account the recovery of the purchase price. The orator Demosthenes makes exactly the same calculation when he records the income received by his father, who owned two manufactories, one making furniture, with 20 slaves who each brought him, net, one obolus a day, and the other making swords and knives, with 30 slaves who each brought him, on the average, 1·5 oboli a day.[41]

The surplus value produced by a slave, leaving out of account the recovery of his purchase price, represents the difference between the value of the commodities he produces (and which his master appropriates) and the cost of production of these commodities (cost of raw material, overheads, including depreciation of tools, and maintenance costs of the slave himself). The figures quoted above show that this difference can be considerable. Otherwise, there would not have been the thousands of entrepreneurs and landowners that there were in the ancient world, ready to buy slaves in order to set them producing a large quantity of craft and agricultural products, the sale of which brought in a substantial surplus value to these slave-owners.

Two thousand years later there are no more slaves in Western Europe. Herr Fugger—like Messrs. Nikias and Kallias, a concession-holder and later owner of mines—does not buy slaves any more. He does not have to invest a small capital, outright, recoverable only over

* We do not know what the daily maintenance costs of a Greek slave amounted to. But De Castro records that in the British West Indies in the eighteenth century the food for a black slave for whom £50 had been paid cost only 25s. a *year*.[38] And Juan Leon Africano tells how, two centuries earlier, the Portuguese planters reduced to zero the maintenance costs of the slaves on Sao Thomé: "The slaves were compelled to work the whole week long for their masters, except Sunday: that day they worked for themselves, sowing millet, yams or sweet potatoes, and lots of vegetables, such as lettuces, cabbages, leeks and parsley. They kneaded cakes of millet flour; their drink was water or palm wine, and sometimes goats' milk; their only clothing was a cotton loin-cloth which they wove themselves. Thus, the masters had to pay nothing for the livelihood of their servants."[39]

a dozen years, in order to acquire a potential labour force.* He recruits *wage* workers in the villages of Bohemia and the Tyrol. He pays them by the week or by the day. This wage, while a little more than the value of the food given to the slaves of Messrs. Nikias and Kallias, is no more than the minimum necessary for the subsistence of the worker and his family.

The new value created by the workers whose labour power Herr Fugger buys by the day or by the week, must of course exceed the value their employer spends on their wages, or else he would not be interested in employing them. It must even be confessed that this difference was considerable, for, just like Messrs. Nikias and Kallias, Herr Fugger became the richest man of his age, to whom barons, dukes, princesses, kings, even the Emperor in person, owed real fortunes.

The individual enrichment of merchants and manufacturers by the exploitation of labour-power, whether it be servile, half-free or free, is achieved by transferring to the pockets of these entrepreneurs the *new values* created by this labour-power. It is an enrichment which is accompanied by an overall increase in social wealth.

The surplus value which makes its appearance in the circulation of money is thus not created in this circulation. It is the result either of the appropriation through trade or usury of a value belonging to others, or of the appropriation of new values created by the labour power which has been bought. In the latter case, the surplus value is nothing but *the difference between the value created by the worker and the cost of maintaining him.* The totality of the capital existing in the world is only the accumulated result of this dual appropriation, as was soon appreciated by sharp observers. Fifteen hundred years before Proudhon borrowed from the Chartist leader O'Brien his famous sally: "What is property? Theft!" the golden-mouthed bishop John Chrysostom told the rich merchants of Antioch: "You possess the results of theft, even if you are not yourselves the thieves."

Capital, surplus-value and social surplus product

Primitive man learns by long and painful experience how to avoid famines and guarantee himself regular nourishment which will enable him to increase the productivity of his labour and bring the production of the means of life under his own control. For this reason he produces a surplus in excess of his necessary product. "On the whole it may be said that capital in Tikopia is accumulated by surplus production over immediate requirements rather than by abstinence *per se*," states the anthropologist Raymond Firth.[43]

* A slave-owner, indeed, runs a risk. He buys only a *potential* labour force; slave labour has always involved an enormous wasting of human labour. The Roman writer Varro estimated that in his day 13 out of 45 of a slave's working days were a dead loss.

We do not intend to discuss at this point whether the word "capital" is correctly used here. But the historical survey we have carried out has made it possible for us to affirm that nowhere in the world have social enrichment, the generalisation of trade, primitive accumulation of money and the production of a growing mass of surplus value been the result of voluntary abstinence on the part of producers who thus make savings and become rich. Everywhere the generalisation of commodity production, the primitive accumulation of money capital and its circulation at a more rapid rate so as to obtain surplus value, have been the outcome of an appropriation, a *grabbing by one part of human society of the social surplus product which has been produced by the rest of this same society.* This appropriation may, indeed, be the result of an "abstinence", namely, that of the producers, reduced to subsistence level by the grabbers of the surplus product. Unfortunately, it has been the grabbers and not the unwilling heroes of this abstinence who have emerged enriched from the ordeal.

The growth of the productivity of labour is an indispensable condition for the appearance of capital and surplus value. Surplus value which has emerged from the process of production, as we have seen, represents only the difference between the product of labour and the cost of maintaining labour. So long as the product of labour is more or less equal to the cost of maintaining labour (that is, to the means of subsistence of the producer and his family), there is no objective basis for the lasting and organised exploitation of labour power. It is only when growth in the productivity of labour has made it possible to recognise such a difference, such a surplus product, that the struggle to appropriate it can break out.

While, however, capital is the historical result—not an automatic result, but arising in particular conditions that can be specifically defined—of growth in the productivity of human labour, it is not synonymous with the *means* that ensure such growth. This confusion is still made even by specialists who are well informed regarding the historical facts. Thus, for the historian Fritz Heichelheim the neolithic revolution, the transition to agriculture and cattle-raising, means the appearance of "capital, . . . that is, the creation of the first reliable way of transferring human work into something which gave rent for a longer time and even for the duration of generations".[44]

A peasant who had sown 1,000 seeds of wheat on the banks of the Euphrates harvested 100,000. But this 'rent' no more made a capitalist of him than striking a banana tree with a stick to make the fruit fall sooner makes an industrialist of a chimpanzee.

Each important technical invention represents an important saving of human labour for society, and each tool that makes it possible to produce at less cost can be regarded as a "store of accumulated labour" which brings in a more or less permanent "rent" in saving of labour. All this, however, relates only to the progress of the productivity of labour in *the production of use-values.**

Capital and surplus value do not appear until *exchange* and *money* have developed, and until an increased average productivity of labour is used no longer so as to enable *the whole of society* to achieve a saving in labour-time but so as to ensure for *one part of society* the products of this increased productivity, by subjecting the rest of society to a heavier burden of work. Capital is the culmination of the history of the appropriation of the social surplus product by one part of society at the expense of another, and not the culmination of the history of the saving of human labour accomplished for the benefit of human society as a whole.

Appropriation of the surplus value produced during the process of production assumes the existence of a market economy and the sale of commodities produced by producers who do not own the products of their labour. Surplus value, in this sense, is the *monetary form of the social surplus product*. In a society producing use values, the social surplus product which a possessing class appropriates is appropriated directly, either in the form of labour (*corvée*) or of products (land rent, tribute). In a society producing commodities, the social surplus product appropriated by the possessing class is indirectly appropriated, in the form of money, by the sale of commodities, from the results of which sale the costs of maintaining labour and the other costs of production have been deducted.

Like petty commodity production, capital developed originally within the pores of a society which was first and foremost engaged in producing use values. Surplus value appeared and developed in a society in which the social surplus product essentially retained the form of use-values. The entire history of capital, from its origins to its apotheosis in the capitalist mode of production, is the history of the slow disintegràtion of this fundamentally non-market economy, through the effect of trade, of usury, of money, of capital and of surplus value. Capital is embodied, in a non-trading society and in contrast to the old-established possessing classes, in a new class, the bourgeoisie. Capital is only a new social relation between producers and owners of capital, a relation which replaces the old social relations between small commodity producers, on the one hand, and

* It could be objected that this is merely a matter of definition. If so, it would be necessary to find *another expression* to indicate capital and surplus value which arise from commodity production and the circulation of money. The confusion consists in the simultaneous use of the same term, capital, for every technique of growth in the productivity of labour, on the one hand, and for specific social relations, based on exploitation, on the other. Etymology meets economics here, moreover, since H. Sée says that the word "capital" means originally only *a sum of money which is to be invested so as to earn interest.*[45]

between peasant producers and those who take the surplus product of agriculture, on the other.

The law of uneven development

The study of the origin and development of economic categories is necessarily a study of economic history, and an analysis of the economy of those peoples of our own day which have remained at stages of historical evolution long since left behind in the capitalist world. It actually isolates "pure" forms which in real life are combined, or have more or less degenerated. To reduce economic history to a series of "stages" or to the successive appearance of "categories" is to make it excessively mechanical, to the point of rendering it unrecognizable. But to eliminate from historical study any allusion to successive stages of economic organisation and any reference to the progressive appearance of these "categories" is to make it merely incomprehensible.

Marxism has often been compared to Darwinism, and the evolution of societies to that of species. Like any other comparison, this one includes points of resemblance and of difference. In biology, too, however, a *dialectical* conception of evolution is gradually taking the place of the mechanical, unilateral and linear conception.* The Marxist conception of economic and social change has no place for any fatalism or automatism. No phase of social organisation "must" necessarily succeed another.

Alongside linear progress there is progress by leaps. Economic evolution can lead to blind alleys or age-long stagnations, especially through excessive adaptation to a specific environment; that seems to have happened with the agricultural peoples of South-East Asia.[47] Moreover, Marxism would not be dialectical if it did not recognise, alongside societies which are progressing (from the standpoint of the average productivity of labour), societies in marked regression.[48]

The law of uneven development, which some have wished to restrict in application to the history of capitalism alone, or even merely to the imperialist phase of capitalism, is thus a universal law of human history. Nowhere in the world has there been a straight-line progressive evolution, starting from the first stages of fruit-gathering and ending with the most advanced capitalist (or socialist) industry. The peoples which reached the highest level of development of productive forces at the stage of food-gathering, hunting and fishing—the

* The idea of a straight-line progress from the anthropoid apes up to the emergence of man has now been dropped. Today it is supposed either that the anthropoid apes and man have simian-like ancestors in common, or that man is descended from an anthropoid ape less specialised than any of those that exist today. Thus, there has been progress combined with stagnation, retardation or proterogenesis.[49]

Eskimos, and, above all, the Indians of the North-West coast of America—did not invent agriculture. This first appeared in the well-watered valleys of Abyssinia, Anatolia, Afghanistan, Transcaucasia, and North-Western India.[49] But it was not there, either, that agriculture gave birth to civilisation, which is the child of irrigation.*

Agricultural civilisation reaches its most advanced phase in Egypt, Mesopotamia, India and China. It was not however, in these countries, but rather in Greece, at Rome, at Byzantium, and in mediaeval Europe (Italy and Flanders) that the progress of the productivity of labour culminated in the most advanced forms of crafts and trade within the framework of petty commodity production. And for petty commodity production to produce the industrial revolution and the capitalist mode of production, we have to move still further north, to England, a country which had long remained backward as regards crafts and trade, and which in the seventeenth century was still far from being the richest in the world or in Europe. Nor was it in Great Britain or in any other advanced capitalist country that capitalism was first overthrown, but in Russia, a typical backward country at the beginning of the twentieth century. May we venture a prophecy and say that it will not be in Russia, either, though this was the first country to introduce a planned economy based on socialisation of the chief means of production, that we shall first see the emergence of a completed socialist society, with the withering away of classes, commodities, money and the state?

* Gordon Childe, too, insists on the absence of any identical succession of stages passed through by the peoples in the neolithic epoch. "Evolution and differentiation go hand in hand," he concludes; but he also mentions a number of instances of convergence.[50] Is not evolution as a *combination of differentiation and convergence* an eminently *dialectical idea*?

REFERENCES

1. Hingston Quiggin: *A Survey of Primitive Money*, p. 5.
2. Sir Samuel Baker: *The Albert Nyanza* (1866), Vol. II, p. 182.
3. A. De Foville: *La Monnaie*, p. 9.
4. Jacques Lacour-Gayet: *"Le roi Bilalama et le juste prix"*; in *Revue des Deux Mondes*, 15th November, 1949.
5. Frédéric Hrozny: *Code Hittite*, p. 137.
6. Wang Yü-Chüan: *Early Chinese Coinage*, in *The American Numismatic Society*, p. 259.
7. Sir George Sansom: *A History of Japan to 1334*, p. 88.
8. Jacques Gernet: *Les Aspects économiques du bouddhisme dans la société chinoise du Ve au Xe siecle*, pp. 88-89.
9. M. Mauss: *"Essai sur le don"*, p. 221.
10. Hingston Quiggin: *A Survey of Primitive Money*, p. 26.
11. Ibid., p. 92.

12. Gordon Childe: *What Happened in History*, pp. 192-3.
13. Nancy Lee Swann: *Food and Money in China*, pp. 217-22.
14. Herman Kees: *Kulturgeschichte des Alten Orients*, Vol. I, *Aegypten*, pp. 103-29; Louis Renon and Jean Filliozat: *L'Inde classique*, p. 378; *Histoire du commerce*, Vol. III, p. 142.
15. Gustave Glotz: *Le Travail dans la Grèce antique*, pp. 278-84; K. A. Wittfogel: *Wirtschaft und Gesellschaft Chinas*, pp. 96-104; M. Takizawa: *The Penetration of Money Economy in Japan*, pp. 30-33.
16. Takizawa, p. 20.
17. K. Polanyi: et. al., *Trade and Market in the Early Empires*, p. 266.
18. Gordon Childe: op. cit., p. 155.
19. Glotz: op. cit., p. 20.
20. P. Boissonnade: *Le Travail dans l'Europe chrétienne du Moyen Age*, p. 196.
21. Chen Huan-Chang: *The Economic Principles of Confucius*, p. 457.
22. Ibn Khaldoun: *Prolégomènes*, Vol. II, p. 325.
23. J. Kulischer: *Allgemeine Wirtschaftsgeschichte*, Vol. I, p. 89.
24. W. G. Sumner and A. G. Keller: *Science of Society*, Vol. I, p. 155.
25. A. H. and D. C. Leighton: *The Navaho Door*, p. 18.
26. A. Andréadès: *Geschichte der Griechischen Staatswirtschaft*, Vol. I, p. 27.
27. H. Pirenne: *Le mouvement économique et social du moyen âge*, p. 24.
28. F. Heichelheim: *Wirtschaftsgeschichte des Altertums*, Vol. I, p. 262.
29. V. W. von Hagen: *The Aztec and Maya Papermakers*, p. 12; W. H. Prescott: *History of the Conquest of Mexico*, p. 85.
30. P. I. Lyashchenko: *History of the National Economy of Russia*, p. 77.
31. H. Labouret: in *Histoire du Commerce*, Vol. III, p. 76.
32. Ibn Batuta: *Voyages*, Vol. I—, pp. 324-7.
33. S. I. Rutgers: *Indonesië*, p. 57.
34. Heichelheim: op. cit., Vol. I, p. 230.
35. J. Bonmarchand: in *Histoire du Commerce*, Vol. III, p. 312.
36. Gordon Childe: op. cit., p. 159.
37. Pauly-Wissowa: *Handwörterbuch der Altertumswissenschaften*, Supplementband VI, pp. 916-17.
38. J. de Castro: *Géopolitique de la Faim*, p. 139.
39. R. P. Rinchon: *La Traite et l'esclavage des Congolais par les Européens*, p. 50.
40. Heichelheim: op. cit., Vol. I, p. 392.
41. Ibid., p. 381.
42. R. H. Barrow: *Slavery in the Roman Empire*, p. 78.
43. Raymond Firth: *Primitive Polynesian Economy*, p. 274.
44. Heichelheim: op. cit., Vol. I, pp. 35-36.
45. H. Sée: *Les Origines du Capitalisme*, p. 7.
46. A. Gehlen: *Der Mensch*, pp. 133-6.
47. *An Appraisal of Anthropology Today*, pp. 42-143 passim.

48. A typical instance is quoted by Cl. Lévi-Strauss, in *Anthropologie structurale*, p. 126.
49. *An Appraisal of Anthropology Today*, pp. 70-72; Ralph Linton: *The Tree of Culture*, pp. 53-57.
50. Gordon Childe: *Social Evolution*, pp. 166-8.

CHAPTER FOUR

THE DEVELOPMENT OF CAPITAL

Forms of agricultural surplus product

AGRICULTURAL surplus product is the basis of all surplus product and thereby of all civilisation. If society had to devote all its working time to producing the means of subsistence, no other specialised activity, whether craft, industrial, scientific or artistic, would be possible.

Agricultural surplus product can appear in society in three different forms. In the fourth century B.C. the Chinese philosopher Mencius already distinguished between these three essential forms of agricultural surplus product: surplus product in the form of work (labour services), in the form of products (use values), or in the form of money.[1] *

Agricultural surplus product supplied in the form of unpaid work or labour services makes its appearance at the dawn of every class society. At the beginning of the Middle Ages in Western Europe, the land of the village was divided into three shares: the lands which the peasants cultivated for their own needs; the lands which the lord exploited directly by means of the unpaid work of peasants who were obliged to render labour services; the common lands, woods, meadows, wastes, etc., which remained more or less freely at the disposal of the peasants and of the lord.[2] The peasant had to divide his working week between work on his own fields and work on the lord's land. The former, *necessary labour* from the social point of view, provided the product needed for the subsistence of the producers. The latter, *surplus labour* from the social point of view, provided the surplus product needed for the subsistence of the possessing classes not participating in production.

A system similar to this has operated in innumerable countries at different epochs of history. Under the feudal system which existed in the Hawaiian Islands before the coming of the whites, the peasant had to work one day in five on the lands exploited by the landowner.[3] In Mexico, before the agrarian reform, there existed "the custom of paying rents for small subsistence holdings by two or three days per week of unpaid labour on the estates".[4]

* It is interesting to note that this same Mencius regards labour services as the most advantageous form of surplus product from the standpoint of a state which seeks to protect the peasantry from the exactions of the landowners, because it gives the peasants the maximum guarantees of stability.

Alongside surplus product supplied as unpaid work there may appear surplus product paid in kind. The serfs of the Middle Ages in Western Europe had to provide the lords not only with labour services but also with rent in kind (in agricultural or craft products). Similarly, in the Hawaiian Islands, rent in kind had to be supplied, over and above labour services.[5]

In Japan rent in kind (*so*) existed alongside labour services (*etachi*).[6] In China rent in kind appeared alongside labour services and gradually took their place, except as regards large-scale works of public utility. In fact, payment of rent in kind, that is, of agricultural surplus product in the form of use values (wheat, rice, wine, cloth woven in the peasant's household, etc.) fairly soon in history became the predominant form of surplus product, and remained in being for thousands of years, with little modification. In the history of Egypt, agricultural surplus product retained this form of provision of goods in kind from the time of the Pharaohs down to the empire of Rome and Byzantium. Each year for seven centuries, as payment of rent, 20 million *modii* of wheat were sent to Italy, then 24 million *modii* to Byzantium, or about 12·5 per cent of the total production of Egypt.[7]

So long as agricultural surplus product retains this form of rent in kind, trade, money, capital exist only *in the pores of a natural economy*. The bulk of the producers, the peasants, hardly ever appear on the market, consuming as they do only what they themselves produce, after deducting the surplus product.

The progressive increase in agricultural production is taken by the lords, who sell it on the market. But, for the same reason, the bulk of the population is unable to buy the products of craftsmen working in the towns. These products thus remain chiefly luxury goods. The narrowness of the market severely limits the development of craft production.

This was how ancient Greece, the Roman empire, the empires of Byzantium and of Islam, with India, China and Japan down to recent centuries, actually lived. The often remarkable splendour that petty commodity production and international trade were capable of attaining within these societies should not conceal from us their basically agricultural character.[8] So long as agricultural surplus product retains the form of goods in kind, trade, money and capital could develop only superficially within such a society.

The transformation of agricultural surplus product from rent in kind to money rent turns the social situation thoroughly upside down. In order to pay his rent, the peasant is henceforth obliged to sell his products himself on the market. He leaves the condition of a natural and closed economy and enters an essentially money economy. Money, which renders possible the acquisition of an infinite variety of goods, allows an infinite range of needs to develop.[9] Economic life quits its centuries-long torpor and relative equilibrium and becomes dynamic, unbalanced, spasmodic. Production and consumption develop along with the unprecedented expansion of trade. Money penetrates everywhere, dissolves all traditional bonds, transforms all established relationships. Everything is given a price. A man's worth is no longer estimated otherwise than according to his income. Universal venality accompanies the triumph of money economy, as Saint Thomas Aquinas observed early on.[10] At the same time, money begins to conceal the real economic relationship, formerly transparent, between serfs and lords, between necessary and surplus labour. Landowners and tenants, employers and wage-earners, meet on the market as free owners of commodities, and the fiction of this "free exchange" hides the continuation of the old relationship of exploitation under its new money forms.*

The transformation of agricultural surplus product from rent in kind into money rent is not the inevitable result of the expansion of trade and money economy; it results from *the existing relation of forces between the classes.*

"The rise of money economy has not always been the great emancipating force which nineteenth-century historians believed it to have been. In the absence of a large reservoir of free landless labour and without the legal and political safeguards of the liberal state, the expansion of markets and the growth of production is as likely to lead to the increase of labour services as to their decline."[11]

"The development of exchange in the peasant economy, whether it served the local market directly, or more distant markets through merchant middlemen, led to the development of money rent. The development of exchange in the lord's economy, on the other hand, led to the growth of labour services . . ."[12]

The typical example in this connection is the evolution of village economy in eastern Europe, including eastern Germany, from the fifteenth and sixteenth centuries onward; there, labour services, with the attachment of the serf-peasants to the land, continually increased,† following the development of production of agricultural commodities for the international market, on the lord's estates.

For money rent to take the place of rent in kind, the extension of money economy must be accompanied by economic, social and political conditions (the role played by the central authority, leaning for

* If the serf was attached to the land, the land was also attached to the serf. "The land holds him and he holds the land," said Fustel de Coulanges. In "freeing" the serf, the market economy also enables the landowner to separate him from his means of subsistence. This dialectical aspect of economic freedom is usually overlooked by liberal critics of the mediaeval economy.

† Duke Ferdinand I of Silesia proclaimed in 1528: "No peasants or gardeners, nor the sons or daughters thereof, may leave their hereditary lord without his consent."[13]

support on the urban bourgeoisie) such that the landowners find themselves obliged to leave in the peasants' possession a substantial part of their increasing production.

Accumulation of use-values and accumulation of surplus-value

So long as the agricultural surplus product retains the form of rent in kind, the accumulation of wealth by the possessing classes takes place essentially in the form of accumulation of use values. Agriculture supplies as use values only foodstuffs, clothing, wood and stone for building houses. Thus, the possessing classes have no interest in developing agricultural production to an unlimited extent. Their own *consumption capacity* constitutes the ceiling of the development of the productive forces:

"Having no means, for lack of outlets, to produce for sale, he [the large-scale mediaeval landowner] has thus no need to worry about obtaining from his men and his land a surplus which would only be an encumbrance to him. Compelled to consume his reserves, in person, he restricts himself to keeping them within his needs."[14]

In the Hawaiian Islands, where the surplus product takes the form, almost exclusively, of foodstuffs, the "demands (of the landowners) were further restricted by the perishableness of much of the produce (fish, bananas, sweet potatoes, *poi*); and in the circumstance that there was no reason for the chiefs to take more than they could themselves use . . . And although the *alü* (feudal lords) prided themselves justly upon their fatness and stature—the women especially were proud of their bulk—there was a limit to their power of consumption."[15]

When exchange and trade begin to develop, the possessing classes have a new interest in increasing production. In exchange for the part of the agricultural surplus product which they do not manage to consume themselves, they can acquire luxury products, jewels, domestic utensils of great value and beauty which they hoard in order to obtain both social prestige and security in the event of disasters. The Odyssey lists such treasures accumulated in the hero's storehouse, the *thalamos*: jars of old wine and vases of scented oil, heaps of gold, bronze and iron, rare weapons, rich fabrics, delicately carved cups, etc.[16]

With the generalisation of exchange and trade, the possessing classes receive a fresh stimulus to develop production. In exchange for that part of the agricultural surplus product which they do not themselves consume, they can now acquire rare consumer goods from distant countries. Their needs multiply, their tastes become more refined. Hoards of incalculable value are accumulated.

No longer are wheat, wine, oil or precious metals in the raw state subject to hoarding. Precious stones and works of art from the hands of the most famous craftsmen (or artists) are alone worthy to enter the palaces of the great. Hitti thus describes the wealth accumulated by the Egyptian caliph Al-Mustansir (1035–1094): "Precious stones, crystal vases, inlaid gold plates, ivory and ebony inkstands, amber cups, phials of musk, steel mirrors, parasols with gold and silver sticks, chess-boards with gold and silver pawns, jewelled daggers and swords and embroidered fabrics manufactured at Dabiq and Damascus."[17]

More impressive still are these treasures of the Byzantine court of the ninth century:

"He [the Emperor Theophilus, who reigned from 829 to 842] loved pomp and magnificence: to enhance the splendour of his palace receptions, he ordered from his craftsmen marvels of goldsmiths' work and mechanical ingenuity: the Pentapyrgian, a famous golden cupboard where the crown jewels were displayed; the golden organs that played on the days when the Emperor held solemn audience; the golden plane-tree that rose beside the imperial throne and on which mechanical birds fluttered and sang; the golden lions lying at the prince's feet, which at certain moments got up, waved their tails and roared; and the golden griffins of mysterious aspect which seemed, as in the palaces of Asian kings, to watch over the Emperor's serenity."[18]

The Empire of China and that of the Moguls in India knew luxurious displays of the same order. One has only to think of the walls of the Taj Mahal, covered with precious stones.

After all, though, all these treasures constitute hoarded use values, unconsumable and unused for the development of the productive forces. The concentration of a considerable share of social wealth for the mere purpose of luxury and waste is thus an important cause of the stagnation and decadence of societies of this sort.

The transformation of agricultural surplus product from rent in kind into money rent does not necessarily change this situation. It gives the ruling classes easier access to the market and possession of wealth even more excessive than before. But the money they receive continues to be wasted on *unproductive consumption*. Under these conditions, the development of money economy, and the powerful stimulus which this gives to the needs of the ruling classes, may become the cause of exactions which prove unbearable to the working classes, a factor of impoverishment and ruin for large sections of society. This was the case in Japan, after the development of money economy in the eighteenth century.[19]

But the money that the original possessing classes thus waste in extravagant luxury ends by leaving their pockets and becoming concentrated in those of usurers, traders and manufacturers. It is this concentration of wealth, in the form of money, in the hands of a new bourgeois possessing class that completely changes social evolution. In the hands of the original possessing classes, all accumulated wealth, including money, was merely wealth in use values, or means of acquiring use values. The object of accumulation was consumption (and hoarding with a view to future consumption). In the hands of the bourgeois classes, *accumulated money becomes capital.*

Money is accumulated in order to bring in surplus value. The surplus value thus accumulated, after deduction of the minimum necessary for subsistence at a level "in accordance with rank", is in its turn capitalised, transformed into capital, in order to bring in further surplus value. Such an accumulation of values which bring in new values is, in the long run, impossible to achieve by mere periodical transfers of wealth from one country to another or from one class to another. Either the accumulation of capital kept within the limits of such a transfer ends by ceasing, because its sources inevitably must dry up, or else it finds a new way forward thanks to the *introduction of capital into production itself,* the ultimate culmination of money economy. This penetration of capital into the sphere of production creates the conditions for an unlimited advance of the productive forces. No longer do the limited consumer needs of the possessing class restrict the productive forces—the need to increase the value which accretes to capital, a need without any limits by its very nature, makes possible on the contrary the abolition of every restriction on their development.

Usurer's capital

The first form in which capital makes its appearance in an economy which is still basically natural, agricultural, producing use-values, is that of usurer's capital. Usurer's capital, the hoard accumulated by an institution or an individual, makes up for the inadequacy of social reserves. Hesiod tells how the peasants of ancient Greece, when in need, borrowed wheat from their better-off neighbours, paying it back later with something more added.[20] Usurer's capital appearing in this way in the form of use values was common, all through the centuries, in essentially agricultural civilisations (Babylon, Egypt, China, India, Japan). In Sumerian the term *mas* (interest) means literally "young animal" (*Tierjunges*) and clearly testifies to the origin of usurer's capital in loans in kind.

What usurer's capital in the form of loans in kind is in relation to the peasants, usurer's capital in the form of advances of money is in relation to the lords and the kings.* During the period of transition from natural to money economy, the essential function of the usurers in France was to advance money to the kings on the security of taxes which were still essentially paid in kind.[22] Wars, famine, other natural

* Cf. the development of usury in China by the Buddhist temples from the fifth century onward: usury in kind at the expense of the peasants, usury in money at the expense of the lords and rich officials.[21]

and social catastrophes, necessitate exceptionally large concentrations of money. The transformation of hoards of objects made of precious metal into usurer's capital, or the use of the merchant's capital of foreign merchants as usurer's capital, provide the chief sources of these concentrations.

When exchange has started to become general and has already created a big money sector in the economy, but when at the same time the bulk of the producers and of the possessing classes still receive their incomes in the form of use values, usurer's capital has its golden age. Lending money at usurious rates becomes the chief source of profit. The ancient Hindu epic the *Mahabharata* mentions usury first among the sources of wealth:

"By usury, agriculture, trade and cattle-breeding may you acquire the power of wealth, O King of Kings."[23]

All the religious and political vetos are powerless to prevent usurer's capital from undermining the social relationships of such an epoch. The indebtedness of the great, the ruin of the small, the expropriation of peasants fallen into debt, or their sale as slaves, the concentration of landed property—these are the traditional calamities that usurer's capital provokes in this phase of social development. Most social disturbances are in this phase revolts against these disintegrating consequences of usurer's capital. In Greece in the fifth and fourth centuries B.C., the slogan generally accepted by the people was: "Redistribution of land and cancellation of debts."[24] Rome in the days of the Republic, Chinese society in the period of decline of each dynasty, Byzantium and India at several epochs of their history present a spectacle in no way different.

In vain did the legislation of Solon in Athens, that of the *decemviri* in Rome or of the Chinese minister Wang An-shi under the Sung dynasty, in vain did the Agrarian Law in Byzantium endeavour to check this encroachment by usurer's capital. They succeeded only in delaying the outcome, without being able to change the general direction of development. Caesar undertook his war of plunder against Gaul in order to rid himself of a burden of debt. The Roman citizens had to pillage the whole Mediterranean world and accumulate enormous wealth before they could free themselves to some extent from the pressure of usurer's capital during the first centuries of the Empire. When this Empire broke up, usurer's capital lasted a long time after the disappearance of large-scale trade[25] and the complaints of writers about usurious rates of interest follow one another monotonously from century to century.*

* One of the reasons why serfdom and feudal economy spread was that the free peasants were unable to pay taxes and fines fixed in money terms, when money had become very rare and extremely dear in relation to agricultural products. In the sixth century an ox was worth 1 to 3 *solidi*, but a *wergeld*

During the Middle Ages, the need to protect a basically natural economy from the disintegrating effects of money economy and usurer's capital led the Catholic Church in Western Europe to condemn vigorously the lending of money at interest. Usurer's capital then appeared in a special form, in order to get round this prohibition: *the purchase of land rent*. In exchange for a lump sum of money, a landowner surrendered to the lender the annual income from his land until he had repaid the capital advanced. The land became in fact the lender's property, recoverable by the owner when he had discharged his debt.[28]*

This was only a special form of the loan upon security which remained, in mediaeval Europe as in India, China and Japan, the most favoured operation of usurer's capital in a natural economy which was slowly breaking up. The purchase of land rent which played an important part in mediaeval European economy shows clearly what is the source of the surplus value obtained by usurer's capital: *the transfer of the incomes of the lords (or of the peasants) to the usurers.* The accumulation of usurer's capital at the expense of the landowners is essentially a transfer of agricultural surplus product into the hands of the usurers.

When money economy becomes widespread, usurer's capital in the strict sense loses its preponderant position and retreats to the dark corners of society, where it survives for centuries at the expense of the small man. It is not that the big man has less need of money—on the contrary, he needs more than ever. But in the meantime trade has become the essential field of action and source of profit for capital. Credit and trade are combined; it is the epoch of the great Italian, Flemish and German merchant financiers which opens with the thirteenth and fourteenth centuries in Western Europe.

Merchant capital

The appearance of a native merchant class in the midst of a basically natural economy presumes a primitive accumulation of money capital. This comes from two main sources: piracy and brigandage, on the one hand; on the other, the appropriation of part of the agricultural surplus product or even of the peasant's necessary product.

It was by raids into foreign territory, operations of brigandage and piracy, that the first merchant navigators assembled their little starting

might amount to as much as 800.[26] The same factor played an important role in the development of feudalism in the Islamic world, in Japan and in Byzantium.[27] Cf. what has been said above about the possibilities of extension of a money economy.

* The same form of usury is to be found among the Ifugao people in the Philippines. Its origins go back to the *antichresis* practised in ancient Greece. It is also found in China in the epoch of the rise of the Buddhist monasteries.[29]

capital. From the earliest times, the origins of maritime trade have been mixed-up with piracy.[30]* Professor Takehoshi observes that the first accumulation of money-capital in Japan (in the fourteenth and fifteenth centuries) was obtained by pirates operating on the coasts of China and Korea:

"While the government of Japan strove to get money by foreign trade, the Japanese pirates employed the more direct method of pillage, and as their booty consisted of gold and silver, copper coins and other treasure, it is impossible to estimate the value of the wealth they brought to Kyushu, Shikoku and the maritime regions of the islands in the central provinces of Japan. Subsequently these plundered treasures injected new life into the whole country."[31]

The accumulation of money capital by the Italian merchants who dominated European economic life from the eleventh to the fifteenth centuries originated directly from the Crusades,[32] an enormous plundering enterprise if ever there was one.

"We know for instance, that in 1101 the Genoese helped the Crusaders to capture and sack Caesarea, a Palestinian seaport. They reserved rich prizes for their officers and remunerated the shipowners with 15 per cent of the loot. They distributed the remainder among 8,000 sailors and soldiers, each receiving 48 *solidi* and two pounds of pepper. Thus each of them was transformed into a petty capitalist."[33]

The mediaeval chronicler Geoffroi de Villehardouin reports the reply given by the Doge of Venice to the Western nobles' request for help in the Fourth Crusade (1202):

"We will supply *vuissiers* (transports for horses) to carry 4,500 horses and 9,000 squires, and ships for 4,500 knights and 20,000 sergeants of foot. And we will agree also to purvey food for these horses and men during nine months. This is what we undertake to do at the least, on condition that you pay us for each horse four marks and for each man two marks . . . The sum total of your payment will thus be 85,000 marks. And we will do more. We will add to the fleet 50 galleys for the love of God [!], if it be agreed that, so long as this contract continues, we shall have the half (and you the other half) of all the conquests that we make by land or sea."

Later, in the fifteenth and sixteenth centuries, the primitive accumulation of money capital by the Portuguese, Spanish, Dutch and English merchants was to have exactly the same source.

In an economy essentially based on petty commodity production,

* N. S. B. Gras, professor of economic history at the Business Administration school attached to Harvard University, feels obliged to refute vigorously[34] this universally recognised truth, which seems to him incompatible with the dignity of capital. Equally unfounded is Schumpeter's assertion[35] that Marx and the Marxists are unable to solve the problem of the primitive accumulation of capital because they have a theory of interest based on exploitation. See also our quotations in the preceding chapter.

retail trade and even wholesale trade in articles of prime necessity is at first strictly limited and regulated.[36] Hardly separated from the crafts, it cannot give rise to a substantial accumulation of merchant capital.[37] Only foreign trade, international trade, allows of such an accumulation. This trade essentially involves *luxury products* intended for the possessing classes. It is through this trade that the merchants appropriate part of the agricultural surplus product on which the landowning classes live. The rise of trade in the Middle Ages in Western Europe, trade in spices and Eastern products, as also trade in Flemish and Italian cloth, is the rise of a typical luxury trade.[38]

The same is true of every society in which merchant capital develops. The customs inspector of the Chinese province of Fukien, Chan Ju-kua, left a picture of China's trade in the twelfth and thirteenth centuries A.D. He lists forty-three articles imported—camphor, incense, myrrh, amber, tortoise-shell, bee's wax, even parrots, all articles of luxury, or spices.[39] Trade in the earliest period of Japanese history was exclusively luxury trade, observes Georges Bonmarchand.[40] Andreades notes that Byzantine exports were almost exclusively luxury products.[41] The trade of the Islamic empire at the height of its greatness was in the same way largely confined to luxury products. Lopez lists as follows the commodities entering into this trade:

" 'Egyptian' emeralds, turquoises from Nishapur, rubies from Yemen, pearls from the Persian Gulf, coral from North-West Africa and Sicily, and marble from Syria and Azerbaijan . . . great quantities of linen from Egypt, Yemen and South-western Persia, of cotton from Merv, Eastern Persia and Spain, of silk from Turkestan and the South Caspian area, of carpets from various regions of Persia, of leather work from Andalusia, of pottery from Khurasan and other provinces, of glass ware from the Syrian coast, and of iron ware from Farghana . . . the scent of Iraqian violet water, of Persian rose water, of Arabian incense and ambergris . . . Maghrebine and Spanish figs, Iraqian and African dates, Turkestanian melons, Tunisian olive oil, Persian, Yemenite and Palestinian sugar, saffron from North-western Persia, sturgeon from the lake of Van, 'edible earth' from Kuhistan, and . . . excellent wine from Iraq and Spain."[42]

Before the coming of the Dutch to Indonesia, the Chinese merchants brought to the great trading centre at Bantam porcelain, silk, damask, velvet, silk thread, gold thread, cloth of gold, spectacles, costly fans, drugs, mercury, etc., and bought spices, musk, ivory, shells and indigo —both sides of this trade consisting of luxury goods.[43]*

* Pre-Columbian America had reached the threshold of the appearance of merchant capital at the moment of the Spanish invasion. The embryonic international trade which had been established between the Incas and the Aztecs concerned metals and luxury articles: "The Incas sell the Aztecs metals and alloys, bronze, *tumbaga* (an alloy of copper and zinc) and especially com-

In order effectively to realise surplus-value at the expense of the noble purchasers, the traders in luxury goods had to ensure for themselves real monopolies at both the buying and the selling end. "Seeking no territorial hegemony, they [the Phoenicians and the Carthaginians] did not wish to penetrate into the interior [of Africa], since they had ensured by long experience that they dominated the peoples of the interior through cleverly arranged trading monopolies."[45] All mediaeval trade in luxuries was a monopoly trade. The prosperity of Byzantium was based for six centuries on its role as exclusive entrepôt for the silks and spices of the East. The loss of this monopoly to Venice sounded the knell of Byzantine power.

When the Italian cities dominated Mediterranean trade, they had in their turn obtained monopolies of trade with Egypt, the new entrepôt for Eastern spices, and with the peoples of the Black Sea coast. The trade in herrings, wheat and timber in the Baltic and the Black Sea was transformed in the same period into trade in which large amounts of capital were employed, thanks to the *de facto* monopolies established by the German merchants in Scandinavia and in the regions recently colonised in the East. But these monopolies were broken owing to the fierce competition between the merchant bourgeoisies of different cities, and also, especially, by Dutch competition. This competition enabled the sellers to raise their prices, and at the same time compelled the merchants to lower their selling prices, thus sharply reducing their profit margin.[46]

The capital accumulated by the big merchants who operate in a society based on petty commodity production thus cannot be continually reinvested in international trade itself. When merchant capital has spread itself sufficiently, it has to endeavour to restrict all farther expansion, on pain of itself destroying the monopolistic roots of its own profits. The merchants of a period like this end by investing a considerable part of their profits in other spheres: landed property, usury, large-scale international credit. Cicero[47] advises the wholesale merchant to invest his profits in landed property. The Talmud—the Jewish commentary on the Old Testament—gives the advice, in the third century A.D., that one-third of one's fortune should be invested in land, and one-third in trade and craft production, with the remaining third kept available as ready money.[48]

Matters were no different in ancient India, in China, in Japan and in Byzantium. In the eleventh and twelfth centuries the Jewish merchants possessed nearly one-third of the land in the County of Barcelona.[49] Gras records that the Norwegian prose treatise *The King's Looking-*

pounds of silver, gold and copper. The Aztecs give the Incas in exchange precious stones such as amethysts, emeralds and obsidians, and to an even greater extent the highly specialised work of their most famous corporations: weapons, dyes, cloth made of embroidered cotton, jewellery . . ."[44]

Glass, compiled about 1260, advises itinerant merchants to invest two-thirds of their high profits in land.[50] In the city of Genoa in the thirteenth century "even the greatest of the merchants . . . backed their commercial investments with very considerable investments in real estate . . . behind the group interested in commerce was another, far larger and infected only slightly or not at all with the adventurous spirit of the capitalist, which based its financial system directly upon the land."[51]

As for the great Italian and German merchants of the thirteenth, fourteenth, fifteenth and sixteenth centuries, the Bonsignori, Scotti, Peruzzi, Bardi, Medici, Fugger, Welser and Hochstätter, the capital they acquired through trade was used for large-scale credit operations, and a substantial part of the profit realised was employed in the purchase of landed property.

The commercial revolution

The expansion of trade from the eleventh century onward had speeded up the development of a money economy in Western Europe. But coins remained very scarce. After the end of the economic decline which accompanied the Hundred Years War, the shortage of coins became oppressive. Everywhere, old mines that had been abandoned since Roman times were reopened, or new mines were sought for.[52] The advance of the Turks and the convulsions which were occurring along the old trade routes in Central Asia stimulated efforts to break the Venetian monopoly of the spice trade. At last an unexpected success was obtained. The discovery of America, the plundering of Mexico and Peru, the circumnavigation of Africa, the establishment of a sea link with India, Indonesia, China and Japan, completely transformed economic life in Western Europe. This was the commercial revolution, the creation of a world commodity market, the most important change in the history of mankind since the metallurgical revolution.

The precious metals, whose cost of production had been stable for a thousand years, were suddenly shrunk in value by important technical revolutions (separation of silver from copper by means of lead; use of draining machinery; digging of improved shafts; use of the stamping-mill, etc.).[53] There ensued an important price revolution, the same quantity of silver being now the equivalent only of a smaller quantity of goods. From the countries where these methods of exploitation were first applied[54]—Bohemia, Saxony and Tyrol in the fifteenth century—this price revolution spread rapidly into Spain in the sixteenth century. The plundering of the treasures of Cuzco and the opening of the silver mines of Potosi reduced still further the cost of production of the precious metals, by the use of slave labour. Subsequently, the increase in prices spread all across Europe, where the new mass of precious metals found its way.

The ruination of the nobility and of the wage-earning classes was thus hastened. For the first time in human history, landed property lost the economic predominance it had possessed from the dawn of civilisation. The fall in real wages—particularly marked by the substitution of cheap potatoes for bread as the basic food of the people—became one of the main sources of the primitive accumulation of industrial capital between the sixteenth and eighteenth centuries.

"In England and France the vast discrepancy between prices and wages, born of the price revolution, deprived labourers of a large part of the incomes they had hitherto enjoyed, and diverted this wealth to the recipients of other distributive shares. As has been shown, rents, as well as wages, lagged behind prices; so landlords gained nothing from labour's loss." Labour's loss thus benefited the capitalist entrepreneurs only. Between 1500 and 1602 in England, the index of wages rose from 95 to 124 whereas the index of prices rose from 95 to 243![55]

As a result of Spain's adverse balance of trade, and of the stagnation and decline of its crafts, the bulk of these treasures of gold and silver which had been plundered or acquired by the enslavement of Indians and Negroes, ended up in the hands of the bourgeoisie of Western Europe, of Germany, France, the Netherlands and Great Britain. The supply of materials of war for the numerous dynastic conflicts which tore Europe apart during these three centuries was another important lever for the accumulation of commercial capital. The brothers Pâris, the biggest French capitalists of the eighteenth century, owed their wealth to war contracts. The appearance of the public debt,* of loans in the form of state bonds negotiable on the stock exchanges—first, those of Lyons and Antwerp, then that of Amsterdam, which remained predominant over a long period—constituted another lever of this primitive accumulation of capital, provided by the pillage of America and India.†

Like the primitive accumulation of merchant capital, the primitive accumulation of commercial capital took place first and foremost by way of brigandage and piracy. Scott[57] notes that about 1550 there was

* The British national debt rose from £16 million in 1701 to £146 million in 1760 and £580 million in 1801. The public debt of the Netherlands increased from 153 million florins in 1650 to 1,272 million in 1810.

† "The fairs which played so big a part when large-scale trade was still merely periodic in character, gradually lose their old importance, in proportion as static, urban trade develops. From the sixteenth century onward we see the establishment of the world stock exchanges . . . which will more and more completely replace them. In the fairs, financial transactions occurred only on the occasion and as a result of commercial transactions. On the stock exchanges commodities are no longer dealt with in kind, business being carried on only in the values which represent them."[56]

a marked shortage of capital in England. Within a few years, the pirate expeditions against the Spanish fleet, all of which were organised in the form of joint stock companies, changed the situation. Drake's first pirate undertaking, in the years 1577–1580, was launched with a capital of £5,000, to which Queen Elizabeth contributed. It brought in about £600,000 profit, half of which went to the Queen. Beard estimates that the pirates introduced some £12 million into England during the reign of Elizabeth. The frightful barbarism of the Spanish *conquistadores* in the Americas is notorious. In a period of fifty years they exterminated 15 million Indians, if we are to believe Bartholomé de las Casas, or 12 million according to more "conservative" critics. Densely populated regions like Haiti, Cuba, Nicaragua, the coast of Venezuela, were completely depopulated.[58] The primitive accumulation of Portuguese commercial capital in India was marked by "civilising" activities of the same sort:

"Vasco da Gama's second voyage (1502–1503), at the head of a veritable war fleet of 21 vessels, resulted in the replacement of the Egyptian-Venetian monopoly (of the spice trade) by a new monopoly. This was not established without bloody incidents. It was a kind of crusade [!] by merchants of pepper, cloves and cinnamon. It was punctuated by horrible atrocities; everything seemed permissible against the hated Moslems whom the Portuguese was surprised to meet again at the other end of the world, after having driven them out of the Algarve and fought them in Barbary. Arson and massacre, destruction of rich cities, ships burnt with their crews in them, prisoners slaughtered and their hands, noses and ears sent in mockery to the 'barbarian' kings, these were the exploits of the Knight of Christ; he left alive, after mutilating him in this way, only one Brahmin, who was given the task of conveying these horrid trophies to the local rulers."[59]

Hauser mentions in this passage that the new commercial expansion remained based on monopoly. It is therefore not to be wondered at that the Dutch merchants, whose profits depended on their monopoly of spices obtained through conquests in the Indonesian archipelago, went over to mass destruction of cinnamon trees in the small Islands of the Moluccas as soon as prices began to fall in Europe. The "Hongi voyages" to destroy these trees and massacre the population which for centuries had drawn their livelihood from growing them, set a sinister mark on the history of Dutch colonisation, which had, indeed, began in the same style, Admiral J. P. Coen not shrinking from the extermination of all the male inhabitants of the Banda Islands.[60]

The source of the surplus value obtained by pre-capitalist commercial capital is thus identical with the source of surplus value accumulated by usurer's capital and merchant capital. A remarkable illustration of this is to be found in the following table of the purchase prices and selling prices of the French East India Company in 1691:

	Purchase price £	*Selling price* £
White cotton cloth and muslin	327,000	1,267,000
Silks	32,000	97,000
Pepper (100,000 lb.)	27,000	101,000
Raw silk	58,000	111,000
Saltpetre	3,000	45,000
Cotton thread	9,000	28,000
Total, including some smaller items	487,000	1,700,000

Or a rate of profit of nearly 250 per cent, and this in "ordinary" trade! [61]

One of the pioneers of Dutch large-scale trade, Willem Wisselinx, wrote plainly enough in a pamphlet published at the beginning of the seventeenth century:

"The trade on the Guinea coast was, indeed, profitable to the country in two ways: first, commodities of great value were obtained there from people who as yet were ignorant of their true value [!]; secondly, these commodities were obtained in exchange for European goods of much smaller value."[62]

While the commercial revolution brought about a general increase in the price of goods, it nevertheless also caused a relative reduction in the prices of the luxury products of the East. Alongside a larger supply, an extension of the market and of needs thus occurred. What had originally been the privilege of a few noble families now entered into the ordinary consumption of all the possessing classes (sugar, tea, spices, tobacco, etc.). Trade in colonial products increased substantially and was soon monopolised by a few joint-stock companies: the *Oost-Indische Companie* in the Netherlands, the *East India Company* and the *Hudson Bay Company* in Great Britain, the *Compagnie des Indes Orientales* in France.

As in the dark centuries of the Middle Ages and at the dawn of trade in Antiquity, these companies combined the spice trade with the slave trade. Enormous profits were realised in this way. Between 1636 and 1645 the Dutch West India Company sold 23,000 Negroes for 6·7 million florins in all, or about 300 florins a head, whereas the goods given in exchange for each slave were worth no more than 50 florins. Between 1728 and 1760 ships sailing from Le Havre transported to the Antilles 203,000 slaves bought in Senegal, on the Gold Coast, at Loango, etc. The sale of these slaves brought in 203 million *livres*.[63] From 1783 to 1793 the slavers of Liverpool sold 300,000 slaves for

£15 million, a substantial slice of which went into the foundation of industrial enterprises.[64]

All the well-to-do classes of the population sought to share in the rain of gold from the plundering of the colonies. Kings, dukes, princes, judges and notaries tried to invest their money with the big traders so as to get regular interest, or bought shares or holdings in the colonial companies. Hochstätter, the Nuremburg banker, Fugger's great rival, must have received such investments to the value of more than £100 millon in the sixteenth century.[65] The New Royal African Company, which was engaged down to 1698 in the slave traffic, had partners so distinguished as the Duke of York and the Earl of Shaftesbury, as well as the latter's illustrious friend, the philosopher John Locke.[66]

The rise in prices impoverished those people who were living on fixed incomes. The public debt,* speculation and wholesale trade concentrated capital in the hands of the bourgeoisie. Basically, international trade remained luxury trade.[68] However, government orders and the growing needs of the well-to-do classes stimulated the production of non-agricultural commodities. Alongside trade in colonial products and precious metals, trade in craft and manufactured products became more extensive than in the Middle Ages. The English clothing industry, the Lyons silk industry, the metallurgical industry of Solingen, the textile industries of Leyden, Brittany and Westphalia, were already working for international markets, including those of the overseas colonies, and going beyond the stage of luxury manufacture. This extension of the market hastened the accumulation of capital by big merchants and created one of the conditions for the flowering of capitalist industry.

Domestic industry

In spite of the extension of large-scale international trade from the eleventh century onwards in Western Europe, the mode of production in the towns remained basically petty commodity production. Master craftsmen, working with a few journeymen, produced a quantity of certain products in a certain labour-time, and sold them directly to the public at prices fixed in advance. The census of a district of the city of Ypres, in Flanders, in 1431, revealed 704 people working at 161 different trades. In the enterprises of 155 different occupations there were only 17 hired journeymen. Altogether, more than half

* "We see appearing in France from the seventeenth century onward the tax-farmers who, in exchange for advances to the royal treasury, are given the right to collect a given tax . . . The profits they realise at the expense of the treasury are enormous . . . If Boulainvilliers is to be believed, between 1689 and 1708, out of an amount collected of one milliard *livres*, 266 millions remained in their hands."[67]

of the persons covered by the census were independent entrepreneurs.[69] The differences of social condition between master craftsmen and journeyman were limited; every journeyman, at the termination of his apprenticeship, had the chance to rise to the dignity of master.

This mode of production encountered, however, a number of contradictions. In the first place, contradictions inherent in the system itself; the progressive increase in the town population and in the number of craftsmen was not balanced by an extension of the market. It led to increasing competition between one town and another, to an accentuation of the protectionist tendencies of each town and to the development of protectionist tendencies in the craft corporations themselves, which endeavoured to close their doors against new master-craftsmen. Apprentices had harder and harder conditions imposed on them as they strove to rise to the status of master. In fact, this rise soon became impossible. According to Hauser, this was the situation in France from 1580 onward.[70] Kulischer quotes numerous openly monopolistic declarations by craft corporations, from the fourteenth and fifteenth centuries.[71]

On the other hand, the craftsmen of Flanders and Italy who had begun by the twelfth century to work for markets wider than the mere urban market, ended by losing control of the products of their labour.[72] In order to carry his own products to a distant fair, a weaver or a brazier had to stop producing and could not start again until he returned. Inevitably, some of them, notably the richer ones who could provide themselves with a substitute at home, soon specialised in trade. At first they conveyed to the market their neighbours' products along with their own, simply as a favour. They ended by buying up directly the products of a large number of master craftsmen and undertaking the whole charge of selling them in distant parts. This system does not necessarily imply subordination of the craftsman to the merchant. But it promotes it, especially in the textile branch, in which numerous craft-guilds carry out one after the other a series of jobs on the same product, and thus find themselves at the end confronted by a single purchaser.[73] It was the same with the making of leather saddles in London, where the "saddlers" subordinated the secondary trades from the fourteenth and fifteenth centuries.[74]

This subordination was achieved by the thirteenth century in the Flemish clothing industry and in the Italian woollen and silk industries. The cloth merchant was still dealing with master-craftsmen, owners of their means of production. Wage-earners, in the strict sense, were an exception, elsewhere than in the Florentine woollen industry, where there were 20,000 day-workers by the middle of the fourteenth century.[75] But the master craftsmen had to buy their raw material from the cloth merchant, and were likewise obliged to sell him their finished products. "Having been able to sell at the highest prices, (the clothier) will insist on buying at the lowest prices."[76]* In his study of a great clothier of Douai at the end of the thirteenth century, Sire Jehan Boinebroke, Espinas notes that the clothiers were already tending to make the craftsmen lodge in houses belonging to themselves, and even beginning to buy means of production. The inevitable indebtedness of the craftsmen to the merchants provided a natural path to this subordination.†

The craftsmen did not accept without resistance a subordination like this, whether partial or complete. In the thirteenth and fourteenth centuries the Flemish and Italian communes were torn by violent class struggles which often ended with the victory of the craftsmen. But this could only intensify the decadence of urban petty commodity production, which had come to a blind alley. It often hastened this decline by protectionist measures. In order to escape from the strict regulations of the town guilds and the high wages of the craftsmen, the merchants began to put work out to craftsmen working at home in the country, who received raw material and means of production from the merchant entrepreneurs, and worked, no longer only *de facto* but also *de jure*, for a mere wage.

From the fifteenth century onward, this domestic industry spread to the countryside in Belgium, in Italy, in France and in Great Britain. The big merchants of Antwerp financed the "new draperies" of French Flanders and the carpet-making of Oudenarde and Brussels.[79] But progress remained slow. In the sixteenth century every English clothier still had to undergo a seven years' apprenticeship.[80] In the seventeenth century, in the Lyons silk industry, the merchant masters had no trades of their own, though they possessed the capital, supplied silk and patterns to the master-workers, and collected the finished product from them.[81]

In the mining industry, however, where large-scale costs of installation were inescapable, the commercial bourgeoisie succeeded more quickly in taking possession of the means of production.[82] At Liège, the chief coal-producing centre of the Continent, the independent associations of miners had almost completely disappeared by 1520, and been replaced by small capitalist enterprise, mostly belonging to merchants of the town. Most of the mining enterprises were transformed into joint-stock companies, the shares in which were bought by members of the well-to-do classes. The most important were taken over as

* The law, wherever it favoured the merchants, expressly granted them a selling monopoly. It was exceptional that in Venice a law of 1442 authorised weavers who had no apprentices or journeymen—and only these—to sell their products on the market.[77]

† It was inevitable only in so far as these clothiers, splendid embodiments of the capitalist spirit of money-making, squeezed and robbed the wretched producers in every imaginable way. Espinas paints a striking picture of this behaviour on the part of Jehan Boinebroke.[78]

concessions by rich commercial or banking families like the Fuggers.

The *Saigerhütten*, works where silver was separated from copper, in Saxony, Thuringia, Tyrol and Carinthia, were, through the cost of the installations and the concentration of wage-earning labour, the most important industrial enterprises of the sixteenth century. With them we have already passed from the realm of domestic industry to that of modern manufacture.[83] In the following century the richest Dutch merchants acquired immense fortunes by securing the monopoly of exploitation of the Emperor's mercury mines (the Deutz family) and the iron and copper mines in Sweden, combined with the manufacture of arms and munitions (the De Geer and Tripp families).[84]

It is interesting to note that this separation of the producers from their means of production by the merchant middlemen took place in a very similar way in other societies besides those of Western Europe. Bruno Lasker, basing himself on original fieldwork by Pieter H. W. Sitsen, describes the system operating in the countryside of Java: "In the Central lands of East Java, the quasi-independent home workers always had credit accounts in the finishing business and could draw against it in an emergency . . . The *Bakul*, or middleman . . . was the real financier and manager of the cottage industry . . . Through their debts to him, which he encourages in every possible way . . . he keeps the nominally independent producers so dependent on him that he can take the better part of their earnings. For example, in the furniture industry of the region, more than half of the gross return went to the *bakuls* when Dr. Sitsen made his study in 1936."[85]

Raymond Firth discovered an identical system in Malaya, where "in Trengganu the system of borrowing cash or equipment has often crystallised into a financial relationship between fishermen and fish-buyers, especially those who cure for export."[86]

S. F. Nadel found a similar system in the domestic industry making glass beads at Bida, in Nigeria. In India the *mahajans* advance the raw material and the other products needed for domestic industry. The textile industry of Soochow, in China, seems to have been organised in the same way in the sixteenth and seventeenth centuries, according to the chronicles of the Ming dynasty.[87]

Domestic industry is the logical culmination of the subordination of petty commodity production to money capital, in a money economy in which production for distant markets has destroyed all possibility of giving a stable foundation to the existence of the small producer.

Manufacturing capital

Domestic industry separates the small commodity producer first from control of his product and then from his means of production. But production increases only slowly, parallel to the slow extension of the market. The commercial bourgeoisie, like the merchant bourgeoisie before it, invests only a part of its capital and profits in domestic industry. The greater part is devoted to trade itself, to speculation, to the acquisition of landed property. The Fuggers, who began as mere weavers in Augsburg, made their fortune in the international trade in spices and fabrics, in which they continued after they had acquired the concessions for Central Europe's silver mines and had built the most important manufactories of their day. They ended by dedicating themselves essentially to credit operations for the house of Habsburg, which brought them to bankruptcy.

By the amount of labour it employed, domestic industry remained the chief form of non-agricultural production between the sixteenth and eighteenth centuries in Western Europe. Alongside it developed another system of production which constituted a sort of bridge to the modern big factory: the system of *manufacture.*

Manufacture means the assembling under one roof of workers who work with means of production which are provided for them and with raw material which is advanced to them. But instead of their being paid for the total value of the finished product, after deduction of the value of the raw material advanced and the cost of hiring the tools of labour, as with domestic industry, the fiction of the selling of the finished product to the entrepreneur is given up. The worker receives no more than what he was already earning *de facto* under the system of domestic industry: a mere wage.

This evolution can be followed step by step in the history of the cloth industry of Leyden, which has been analysed in masterly fashion by Posthumus. This industry was first organised on a craft basis. From the end of the sixteenth century it spread to the countryside and the merchants got the upper hand of the clothiers. The latter began to lose ownership, first of the raw material and the finished product, then of the means of production. Towards 1640 a fresh set of middlemen, the *reeders*, inserted themselves between the merchants and the clothiers. The stage of manufacture was reached, and around 1652 there is even talk of "manufacturers"! [88]

The new system presented two advantages for the suppliers of capital. On the one hand, they could do away with the overhead charges arising from the need to maintain a large number of middlemen to collect the finished products, distribute the raw material, etc. On the other, they could put a stop to the considerable embezzlement of raw material which inevitably occurred in domestic industry, as a means whereby the workers made up for inadequate wages. In manufactories the concentration of labour-power and its subjection to direct and continuous supervision by capital has already reached an advanced stage.

Manufacture also constitutes a considerable advance from the standpoint of the productivity of labour. In petty commodity production there is only a *social* division of labour between different crafts; *within* each craft, that is, during the process of production, division of labour hardly exists. Even when each craft is not completing a finished product, intended for direct consumption, as in the clothing or woollen industries, each craft does carry out one complete process of production: weaving, fulling, dyeing, etc.

Thanks to manufacture it becomes possible to *subdivide* each craft and each production process into an infinite number of labour operations, mechanised and simplified to the uttermost. This makes it possible at one and the same time to increase output, to increase the number of finished products completed in the same period of time, and to reduce the cost of production by substituting an unskilled labour-force of women, children, sick or old persons and even lunatics. This is the fact which appears as an entirely new social phenomenon, especially as regards the manufacture of textiles: the labour-force is largely composed of these wretched people. It is above all the low cost of such labour-power that makes it profitable to concentrate wage-earners in such numbers under one roof. One can compare the situation to some extent to the mines and large-scale state manufacturers in the ancient world, in China, India and elsewhere, in which slave or semi-slave labour predominates.

The utmost brutality, together with an amazing hypocrisy, were normally employed to compel these unfortunates to furnish a cheap supply of labour to young manufacturing capital.* In 1721 it was decided to set up a cloth manufactory in Graz "because hundreds of people are suffering from hunger and are idle". In order to provide the necessary labour-force, a suitable number of persons had to be "caught and locked up", from among the beggars who crowded the streets of the town. In Amsterdam, in 1695, on the proposal of the sheriffs, the municipal council considered "whether it was appropriate to seek a site for (the establishment) of a spinning mill where young girls could be employed so as to support themselves, along with other persons who were leading lives of idleness and beggary." As some merchants who wanted to set up woollen mills were offering favourable terms and as these worthy councillors considered that what was involved was a "very good and Christian work" [!], they authorised the Mayor to see to the putting of the scheme into effect.[90] Sombart[91] quotes numerous examples of the State's *compelling* the population to carry out veritable forced labour in manufactories,

* Already in the *arte di lana*, the Florentine woollen industry of the fourteenth century, where the wage-earner was tied to his employer by *debts*, a whole set of laws was introduced in order to compel him to do overtime. He was in particular forbidden by a law of 1371 to repay his debt in *money*; he had to do this in the form of *work*.[89]

notably in Spain, France, Holland, Germany, Switzerland, Austria, and, of course, England. In the countries where serfdom still existed, serfs were compelled to work in the manufactories, notably in Russia, in the copper manufactory in Tula.

The development of manufacture did not yet do away with manual labour as the preponderant means of production in industry: the greater part of the expenditure of manufacturing capital still went on wages. Nevertheless, manufacture developed most rapidly in the sectors in which costly apparatus had to be installed to an increasing extent. In the eighteenth century, in Rheims and Louviers, thousands of workers were already massed together in manufactories which had cost hundreds of thousands of *livres* to build.[92]

Leyden, which was the leading textile centre of Europe in the middle of the seventeenth century, saw its manufactories develop owing to the large-scale use of fulling-mills. The use of these mills was profitable, however, only on the basis of the employment of children or women as workers. For this reason, the entrepreneurs organised expeditions to places as far away as the Liège region to recruit labour.[93]

Creation of the modern proletariat

Alongside this broadening of the field of action of capital, which was steadily entering the sphere of production, from the sixteenth century onward a new social class came into existence, which had been present in the Middle Ages only in the form of a few uprooted "hirelings" who wandered from town to town. This class originated from the cutting down of the retinues of the feudal lords, itself a result of the impoverishment of the latter by the price revolution. It originated also from the decay of the urban crafts since the merchant entrepreneurs had started to put out their orders to men working in the countryside. Its development was speeded up by deep-seated changes in the field where the great majority of the producers were still concentrated: in agriculture.

In the mediaeval village the peasants' land was broken up into numerous plots. In order to work on these plots, the peasants had to have free access to the land separating them. This free access was linked with the right to gleaning and gathering straw, to free common pasture, the reservation of land for the benefit of new households, and compulsory rotation of crops, all of which were essential to the stability of a village economy based on the three-field system and marked with the imprint of the primitive village community.[94] At the same time, the common lands offered free amenities for pasturing cattle and collecting wood, both for fires and for building, etc.

From the fifteenth century onward, despite numerous governmental decrees and laws directed against this development, the landlords in England began to divide up the common lands and to rearrange the farmers' plots of land, so as to constitute farms for a single tenant. This movement was particularly encouraged by the rapid rise in the price of wool from the middle of the fifteenth century, which made sheep raising more profitable to the lords than cultivation of the soil.[95] But the practice of enclosure, of putting fences around fields, remained very sporadic until the eighteenth century.

It was then precipitated by a revolution in the agricultural mode of production itself: the abolition of fallow, transition from the three-field system to periodical cultivation of lucerne, turnips and fodder plants which restore the soil's productivity. This was a system of scientific agriculture, orginating in Flanders and Lombardy, which after several tentative attempts, now began to become general in England.[96] The agricultural surplus product increased markedly. The landlords, anxious to take this surplus for themselves, changed the system of tenancy, going over from long leases, which ensured a peasant family's tenancy for a century, to tenancies at will, or short leases, which implied a change of tenancy every nine years at most.[97]

From this resulted a large increase in ground rent, which hastened the expropriation of poor peasants and accompanied the enclosure movement, which was favoured also by the fact that with the ending of the three-field system the scattering of plots became burdensome to the cultivators. By about 1780 this movement had culminated in England in the quasi-liquidation of the class of independent peasants, who were replaced by big capitalist farmers working with wage labour. In France a similar movement for the break-up of the common lands occurred in the seventeenth and eighteenth centuries, but to a smaller extent,[98] until the French Revolution gave it a great impetus. Development followed similar lines to the French in Western Germany and Belgium.

The economic changes which, between the sixteenth and eighteenth centuries, created a mass of producers separated from their means of production in the towns, were thus accompanied by changes which in practice deprived part of the peasantry of land as a means of producing their means of life. In this way the *modern proletariat* appeared. This class was thus described, from the sixteenth century onward, by the entrepreneurs of Leyden:

"Poor and needy persons, many of whom have the charge and burden of wives and many children to support, and who have nothing but what they can get by the work of their hands."[99]

The ancestors of this proletariat were described already in 1247 as "those who earned money by the strength of their arms."[100] And in our own day, when the process of formation of the proletariat is being repeated among the backward peoples, they say in Malaya of a fisherman who has no net of his own (no means of production): "he has not a single thing; he only helps other people."[101] In other words, the separation of the producers from their means of production creates a class of proletarians who cannot live otherwise than by hiring out their strength, that is, by selling their labour-power, to the owners of capital, which enables the latter to secure for themselves the surplus-value produced by these producers.*

The Industrial Revolution

For capital to be able to penetrate into the sphere of industrial production, industry must be suddenly confronted with a market which is no longer stable but has expanded to the point where it seems ready to absorb a continuously increasing volume of products. The introduction of machinery into industry and transport, and the lowering of the cost of the products of large-scale factories resulting from this, have created such a market and signalised the definitive victory of the *capitalist mode of production.*

For thousands of years, the only two sources of power available for work were human power and the power of domestic animals. The ancient world was able to build the first machine which utilised another source of power: the water-mill. In the Roman mines, Archimedes' screw and Ctesibius's water-pump were used for draining purposes.[103] They were not widely employed, however, in agriculture. The Middle Ages inherited these machines, put them into general use from the tenth century onward, which resulted in a significant increase in the productivity of labour, and then received the windmill from the East.†

From the fifteenth century onward, a long series of small inventions and technical improvements increasingly transformed these machines, while still using water as the main source of power. Mills were built to make paper, to operate forge-hammers, to make silk, to pump out mines, to full cloth, to saw wood, etc.[104] Sombart lists about twenty different kinds of mills dating from that period.[105]

However, these technical improvements were only applied sporadically so long as economic and social conditions did not favour a large-scale flow of capital into industrial production. As mentioned above, it was above all in mining and metallurgy that progress was substantial, at the dawn of modern times. It was in the mines that the first kinds of railway were developed, to facilitate the carriage of coal.[106] The fifteenth century saw the building of the first blast furnace.[107] But the

* "The current analysis of the situation of the wage-earner points to its essential feature as being that labour is separated from and deprived of ownership of the means of production, and bases on this feature the difference between the wage-earner's situation and that of others."[102]

† In China, windmills were in use on a large scale in agriculture from the sixth century. As in Western Europe, they were the monopoly of rich landowners and of temples, and thus reinforced the exploitation of the peasants. In Europe windmills were the basis of the *banalités*, the additional burdens placed on the peasants which we also find in China.

development of these blast furnaces was hindered so long as the fuel they used was wood. In 1777 the use of the steam engine in the coal industry transformed the production process. It made possible a rapid increase in coal production and a reduction in prices which opened the way to the use of coke as fuel in blast furnaces. A few years later, about 1785, the making of iron by the puddling process again transformed the production process. The production of iron in England increased from 12,000 to 17,000 tons a year about 1750 to 68,000 in 1788, 244,000 tons in 1806 and 455,000 tons in 1823.[108]

The use of water power in the fulling mill and other mills, but still more and especially the invention of the mechanical loom, transformed the textile industry. At the same time, the expansion of Liverpool's maritime trade opened up to Lancashire overseas markets which seemed limitless. With the aid of new machines, the textile manufacturers produced their cottons at prices much lower than those of the craftsman and the domestic worker, and set out to conquer this immense market. Capital broke down first of all the internal customs barriers inherited from the feudal past: in 1776 by the formation of the United States, in 1795 in France, in 1800 in the United Kingdom, in 1816 in Prussia, in 1824 in Sweden and Norway, in 1834 by the creation of the Zollverein in Germany, in 1835 in Switzerland, in the 1850s in Russia and Austria-Hungary. Next, the world market was attacked. British exports of cotton grew from £5,915 in 1679 and £45,000 in 1751, to £200,354 in 1764, £19 million in 1830, £30 million in 1850, and £73 million in 1871.[109]

The iron and coal industries found enormous new outlets in the making and fuelling of steam engines. From 1825 onward, the building of railways made general this triumphal march of machine production and of the capitalist mode of production. By closely linking town and country they facilitated the penetration of commodities produced at low prices by big factories into the remotest corners of all countries. At the same time the building of railway lines constituted, for over half a century, the chief market for the products of heavy industry (coal, steel, metal products, etc.), first in Great Britain, then on the Continent, later in America and throughout the world.

Special features of capitalist development in Western Europe

Under petty commodity production the producer, master of his means of production and his products, can live only by selling these products in order to acquire the means of life. Under capitalist production, the producer separated from his means of production is no longer master of the products of his labour and can live only by selling, that is, by making a commodity of, his own labour-power, in exchange for a wage which enables him to acquire these means of life. The transition from petty commodity production to capitalist production properly so called is thus marked by two parallel phenomena: on the one hand, the *transformation of labour-power into a commodity*, and on the other, the *transformation of the means of production into capital*.* These two concomitant phenomena had never occurred on a large scale before they appeared, from the sixteenth century onward, and above all from the eighteenth century onward, in Western Europe, mainly in Great Britain.

Capital itself, in its primitive forms of usurer's capital and merchant capital, was, however, not at all a special feature of Western civilisation. Many civilisations which saw an advanced stage of petty commodity production saw with it a substantial flowering of capital: the ancient world, Byzantine society, the Mogul empire in India, the Islamic empire, China and Japan, to mention only the most important. The quantitative expansion of capital in these societies was in no way inferior to what occurred in mediaeval Europe.

In the middle of the fourteenth century King Edward III of England received 1,365,000 florins from the Florentine companies of the Bardi and the Peruzzi.[111] These were the richest bourgeois families of the West before the Fuggers. About the same period, a group of Karimi (Yemenite) merchants, who monopolised the spice trade with India in the Egypt of the Mamelukes, advanced 700,000 silver *dirhems* to some notables of Damascus, and then 400,000 gold *dinars* to the King of Yemen (coins which contained more pure metal than the European coins of the time).[112] In the ninth and tenth centuries, at the zenith of the Islamic empire, we find a number of merchants of Basra who have an *annual income* of over a million *dirhems*. A Baghdad jeweller, Ibn-al-Jassas, was still a rich man after 16,000 gold *dinars* of his had been confiscated.[113] In 144 B.C. the imperial prince Hsio, of Liang, died in China leaving 400,000 *catties* of gold (one *cattie* is about 600 grammes).[114] Why did this accumulation of usurer's and merchant capital not give birth to industrial capital in these various civilisations?

It was not that the forms of organisation lying between crafts in the strict sense and large-scale factories—the *Verlagssystem* of merchants putting out work to craftsmen, domestic industry, and manufacture—were unknown to these pre-capitalist civilisations. In Byzantium, real textile manufactories appeared, from the time of the Emperor Justinian, based, to be sure, on crafts and with a labour-force which, though concentrated in large establishments, remained in possession of its means of production.[115] But, already about the tenth century,

* This does not seem to be understood by Professor Sol Tax, who calls his work on the Guatemalan community of Panajachel *Penny Capitalism*. He examines the reasons for this definition, and discovers them above all in the "mental habit" of the natives of Panajachel to seek "maximum returns". In reality we have here a typical society where petty commodity production prevails, where neither the land nor labour-power have in practice become commodities.[110]

"the merchants of raw silk and the clothiers had a strong predominance over the other guilds, and some members of these two guilds were trying to rise above their colleagues and to become capitalist entrepreneurs. The guild of the dealers in raw silk . . . had brought under their control not only the impoverished silk spinners (*Katartarioi*) . . . but the whole guild of the *katartarioi*. As a matter of fact, a silk spinner could not sell the processed silk directly to the clothiers; he had to hand it over to a dealer in raw silk. Nor could he buy raw silk from the importers without the permission of the dealers . . . [and] he could buy only the quantity he could process in his own workshop . . . It is true that theoretically the dealers were forbidden to take over directly the spinning, or to do anything but buying and selling the raw material. But this prohibition . . . was practically nullified by the fact that a merchant of raw silk could hire workers, paying them in advance. It is hardly believable that these workers were employed just to assist him in buying and selling!"[116]

A no less impressive development of domestic industry and manufacture occurred in the Islamic empire. Over 1,000 workers are said to have been concentrated in the mercury mines of Moslem Spain. In Tinnis, the famous cloth-weaving town, domestic industry was in full operation from A.D. 815. The cloth merchants gave work to men and women for wages of half a dirhem a day.[117] China similarly had great mining and metal-working manufactories which employed slave labour, several centuries before our era. Rich entrepreneurs arose, especially in iron and copper working and in the exploitation of mercury and cinnabar.[118] Later, manufactories of porcelain and domestic textile work saw a great expansion, especially from the time of the Ming dynasty onward.[119] It was the same in India for a thousand years. Yet, nevertheless, the coexistence of these types of modern enterprise with a big accumulation of money capital did not result in the development of industrial capitalism.

Petty commodity production is already the production of commodities. But it is usually a production of commodities in the midst of production of use values. So long as the overwhelming majority of the population participates little or not at all in this commodity production, the latter inevitably remains restricted. Large-scale trade basically remains luxury trade. Faced with the narrow limits of this market, capital finds outlets more profitable than investment in production. This is what explains the fact that the manufactories and domestic industries of Byzantium, the Islamic world, China and India embraced almost exclusively luxury branches, unless they worked for State orders.

It was the penetration of money economy into the peasant economy, as a result of the changing of the agricultural surplus product from rent in kind, or labour services, to money rent that made possible a considerable expansion of commodity production in Western Europe, and so created the conditions for the flowering of industrial capitalism. Nowhere outside Western Europe did the agricultural surplus assume lastingly the form of money rent. Taxation in kind predominated in the Roman Empire and in Byzantium.[120] In the Islamic empire the land tax was paid partly in kind and partly in money, under the Abbasids, but soon afterwards rent in kind became preponderant again, and remained so in the Turkish period.[121] In India, land rent was generally paid in kind, except during a brief period of prosperity under the Moguls in the seventeenth century. In China, rent-tax in money, briefly general under the Mings towards the end of the fifteenth century, resumed the form of rent-tax in kind after the fall of this dynasty, to reappear definitely as tax-rent in money only in the seventeenth and eighteenth centuries in South China.[122]

Machine production, which alone enables the big factory to overcome the competition of domestic industry and the crafts, is the product of the application of natural science to production that, in turn, demands a ceaseless striving to economise human labour. The predominance of slave labour and the presence of an enormous mass of unproductive poor in the Roman Empire prevented any endeavour in this direction.* The significant comment of the Emperor Vespasian will be remembered, when he refused to allow the use of a mechanical crane: "I must feed my poor."[123]

As for the Islamic world, India, China and Japan, these were essentially agricultural civilisations, in which irrigation made possible the development of an extremely intensive agriculture which in turn led to a considerable growth of population. The competition of very cheap labour was to prevent for thousands of years any attempt to introduce machinery into the crafts. At the same time, the productive use of hydraulic power for non-agricultural purposes, the basis of the slow advance of machine production in Europe from the thirteenth to the eighteenth centuries, was much restricted in these agricultural civilisations because it came into conflict with the requirements of irrigation of the soil.†

* To this must be added the widespread contempt for manual labour, engendered by slavery and formulated in striking fashion by Xenophon in his *Economics*: "The arts which men call vulgar are generally held in low esteem and disdained by the state, and this for good reason. They utterly spoil the bodies both of the workers and their supervisors . . . And when men's bodies are exhausted, their souls become sick. *Further, these arts imply a total lack of leisure, and prevent men from leading a social and civic life*."

This last observation is most pertinent.

† These installations (water mills and automatic milling), which were a source of very big incomes for great lay families and for important monasteries, became numerous in the T'ang epoch [*i.e. four or five centuries sooner than in Europe!*], at the time when large landed property was also developing. The imperial administration had to fight against this new abuse, because the

The accumulation of money capital, usurer's capital, merchant capital and commercial capital took place in Western Europe between the tenth and eighteenth centuries, in the hands of a bourgeois class which progressively freed itself from the control of the feudal classes and the state, and ended by subjecting the state to itself and using it to accelerate the accumulation of capital for its own advantage. The formation of the bourgeoisie as a class, with a clear consciousness of its interests, took place in the free communes of the Middle Ages, where the bourgeoisie underwent its apprenticeship to political struggle. The establishment of centralised modern states from the fifteenth century onward did not result from a crushing of the urban bourgeoisie but from a new ascent of this class, which broke through the narrow confines of commune politics to confront, as the Third Estate, the old ruling classes on the national level (Russia, Spain, and to some extent the Austria of the Habsburgs, were in this respect interesting exceptions, something that had significant consequences for the later history of capitalism in these countries).

In the other pre-capitalist civilisations, however, capital remained unchangingly under the arbitrary power of the despotic and all-powerful state. In Rome it was the landed nobility that, thanks to the booty obtained in its plundering wars, ended by entirely subjecting the free capital of the ancient world.[125] In ancient India, the state monopolies made the king himself the chief banker, manufacturer and wholesale trader. Rostovtsev notes that the imperial treasury was the chief usurer in Rome.[126] The predominance of state manufactories in Byzantium, where the imperial treasure concentrated in its coffers the greater part of the available capital, is as well known as the pitiless taxation that crushed craft and industrial production in the Islamic world.[127] In China, under each successive dynasty, the state strove to monopolise whole sectors of industry.[128]

The nascent bourgeoisie underwent a strange life-cycle in all these societies. Each new fabulous accumulation of profits was followed by brutal confiscations and persecutions. Bernard Lewis notes that even the Islamic cities of the Middle Ages knew only an ephemeral existence, with a prosperity which lasted no more than a century and was followed by a long and pitiless decay.[129] The fear of confiscation of their capital haunts the owners of movable property in all these societies. It causes the bourgeois to conceal their profits, to invest them in ten small enterprises rather than one big one, to prefer the hoarding of gold and precious stones to public enterprises, and the purchase

paddle-wheels obstructed the flow of the rivers and caused some of the irrigation water to be lost. Moreover, they caused the depositing of mud in the canals. Accordingly, special laws restricted the use of mills to certain seasons of the year." The author quotes decrees and texts from the eighth century relating to the restriction and destruction of mills.[124]

of landed property to the accumulation of capital. Instead of concentrating, a bourgeoisie like this disperses itself as it disperses its capital. Instead of advancing towards autonomy and independence, it crouches in fear and servility.[130] "Never," says Istvan Balazs, "did the Chinese merchant class attain autonomy . . . the privileges of the big traders were never won in struggle, but were stingily granted by the state. The way of expressing their demands continues, for the merchant and the rest of the *misera plebs*, to be the petition, the timid request humbly submitted to the authorities."[131]*

Only in Japan, whose pirate merchants infested the China Sea and the Philippines from the fourteenth century on, and accumulated substantial capital while the state's authority was breaking down, did the supremacy of the commercial and banking bourgeosie over the nobility, and then the development of manufacturing capital, make it possible to repeat, starting in the eighteenth century, two centuries late, the evolution of capitalism in Western Europe, independently of the latter.†

The predominance of the absolute state in the non-European precapitalist civilisations was itself no result of chance. It followed from the conditions of irrigation agriculture, which necessitated a strict administration and centralisation of the social surplus. Paradoxically, it was the superior fertility of their soil and the greater growth of their population that doomed these civilisations to stop midway in their development. The much more primitive agriculture of mediaeval Europe could not carry the weight of a density of population comparable to that of China or the Nile valley in prosperous periods. But just for this reason it largely escaped the control of a centralising state.‡

In the mediaeval towns the bourgeoisie was favoured by a weakened

* The idea that in China, as against mediaeval Europe, the towns were subjected to the close supervision of the mandarins, whereas the villages enjoyed extensive administrative autonomy, was, says Balazs "brilliantly anticipated" by Max Weber. The author seems unaware that Marx expressed the same view three quarters of a century earlier, and that he also clearly defined the difference between Western and Oriental towns.[132]

† Even in Japan, however, the merchant Yodoya Tatsugoro, who had made an immense fortune during the Kwambuu era (1661–1672), had all his property confiscated "because he led too ostentatious a life."[133]

‡ It is interesting to note that in Black Africa the comparative abundance of land, which made possible an infinite spread of primitive agriculture, proved to be a barrier to the flowering of a black civilisation, except in the valleys of the Senegal, Niger and Zambesi.[134] It would seem that the relationship between land, water and population made possible the optimum combination *for agriculture* in the ancient Asian civilisations, and the optimum *economic* combination in Western Europe, starting in the sixteenth century. In this field too there is a striking parallel between the particular conditions in which agriculture developed in Japan (in contrast to the continent of Asia) and in Western Europe.[135]

central power which had to lean upon its support in order to recover the prerogatives it had lost at the dawn of feudalism. At first, the advance of this bourgeoisie was slow and interrupted. Many a Western financier ended up like his Islamic, Chinese or Indian colleague, by having his fortune confiscated by the kings he helped. But from the fifteenth century this interruption became the exception instead of the rule. The superiority of movable wealth over landed property was finally established, and with it the subjection of the state to the golden chains of the public debt. The road was clear for an accumulation of capital without political obstacles. Modern capitalism could be born.

These special features of the economic development of Western Europe (and to a certain extent of Japan) do not mean that the flowering of the industrial revolution was not *possible* in other regions: they merely explain why the capitalist mode of production appeared *first* in Europe. Thereafter it was the violent intervention of Europe in the economies of other parts of the world that smashed the elements that would have made possible more rapid economic progress there, so preventing or holding back their advance. The contrast between Japan on the one hand and India and China on the other shows the decisive role played in the nineteenth century by the maintenance or loss of real political independence, for the acceleration or retardation of the industrial revolution.*

Capital and the capitalist mode of production

Capital can appear as soon as there is a minimum of commodity circulation and of money circulation. It is born and develops within the framework of a pre-capitalist mode of production (village community, petty commodity production). Whatever dissolving effects it has on such a society, these are limited by the fact that it does not change the basic mode of production, especially in the countryside. Loaded with debts, harried by his creditors or by tax-collectors, the pre-capitalist peasant always finds in the solidarity of other villagers a support which guarantees him at least a meagre pittance:

"The Ifugaos [natives of the Philippines] are partial capitalists. Their wealth is rice land. It is prepared with a enormous labour, limited in quantity, and belongs to a class of rich men . . . Through a system of usury, the rich become richer and the poor poorer. Still, the poor are not entirely destitute. Yam gardens are by definition not 'wealth', and cannot be permanently owned. Anyone may plant as much as he wishes, and manage to live after a fashion . . ."[136]

The development of the capitalist mode of production implies the generalisation of commodity production for the first time in mankind's history. This production no longer embraces merely luxury

* See Chapter 13 for numerous examples of economic regression caused by imperialism.

products, the surplus of foodstuffs or other goods of current consumption, metals, salt and other products indispensable for maintaining and extending the social surplus product. Everything that is the object of economic life, everything that is produced is henceforth a commodity: all foodstuffs, all consumer goods, all raw materials, all means of production, including labour-power itself. Every outlet being closed, the mass of dispossessed people who no longer have their own tools are compelled to sell their labour-power in order to acquire the means of life. The entire organisation of society is fashioned so as to ensure to the owners of capital a regular and constant supply of wage labour, so as to facilitate the uninterrupted productive use of their capital.

During the process of its formation, industrial capital obtained, by the methods described above, the parallel formation of the modern proletariat. But when the capitalist mode of production had spread throughout the world, it experienced a need for wage labour before the primitive societies which it encountered were sufficiently disintegrated for this proletariat to be formed in the normal way. The intervention of state, law, religion and morality—if not of force pure and simple—made it possible to recruit the unhappy slaves of the new Moloch. The colonisers of Black Africa and Oceania repeated at the end of the nineteenth century the procedures whereby their slave-trading ancestors had assembled a mass of slave labour. This time, however, it was no longer a matter of sending this labour over the ocean to the plantations of the New World. It was on the spot, in capitalist agricultural, mining or industrial enterprises that this labour was employed to produce the surplus value indispensable to the life of Capital.*

The disintegrating action of money economy on primitive communities has in all civilisations favoured the primitive accumulation of usurer's capital and merchant capital. But it does not ensure by itself the development of the capitalist mode of production, of industrial capital.

However, the disintegrating action of money economy on primitive communities already confronted with the capitalist mode of production becomes the chief force for the recruitment of a native proletariat in the colonies. The introduction of an individual poll tax in money in primitive areas which are still living in conditions of natural economy has uprooted, in Africa and elsewhere, millions of natives from their customary centres and has forced them to sell their labour-power, their only resource, to get money. Where people do not find it necessary to sell their labour-power in order to obtain the means of life, the capitalist state has resorted to this modern form of compulsion in order to

* See Chapter 9, section: "Landed property and the capitalist mode of production."

supply proletarians to the bourgeoisies who are coming into existence in the colonies. For capitalism and the bourgeoisie are inconceivable without a proletariat. According to Alexander Hamilton, freedom is freedom to acquire wealth.[137] *But this freedom cannot be affirmed for one small part of society unless it be denied for the rest, even though this be the majority.*

REFERENCES

1. *Mong Dsi* (Mong Ko translated by Richard Wilhelm), pp. 51-52.
2. Boissonnade: *Le Travail dans l'Europe chrétienne du moyen âge*, pp. 99-107.
3. Theodore Morgan: *Hawaii, A Century of Economic Change*, p. 25.
4. International Labour Office: *Les Populations aborigènes*, p. 368.
5. Morgan: op. cit., p. 25.
6. Yoshitomi: *Etude sur l'histoire économique de l'ancien Japon*, pp. 139-40.
7. G. I. Bratianu: *Etudes byzantines d'histoire économique et sociale*, p. 133; A. Segré: *Essays in Byzantine Economic History*, p. 402.
8. F. Heichelheim: *Vormittelalterliche Geschichtsepochen*, pp. 163-4; J. C. Van Leur: *Eenige beschouwingen betreffende den Ouden Aziatischen Handel*, passim.
9. Gordon Childe: *What Happened in History*, p. 193.
10. E. Schreiber: *Die Volkswirtschaftlichen Anschauungen der Scholastik seit Thomas v. Aquino*, p. 23.
11. M. M. Postan: "Chronology of Labour Services", in *Transactions of the Royal Historical Society*, 4th Series, Vol. XX, 1937, pp. 192-3.
12. E. A. Kosminsky: "Services and Money Rents in the 13th Century", *Economic History Review*, Vol. V, 1934–5, No. 2, p. 43.
13. Günther Dessmann: *Geschichte der Schlesischen Agrarverfassung*, p. 58.
14. H. Pirenne: *Le mouvement économique et social au moyen âge*, p. 60.
15. Morgan: op. cit., p. 26.
16. Glotz: *Le Travail dans la Grèce antique*, p. 16.
17. P. K. Hitti: *History of the Arabs*, p. 626.
18. Ch. Diehl: *Les Figures byzantines*, Vol. I, pp. 147-8.
19. Takizawa: *The Penetration of Money Economy in Japan*, pp. 71-79; Hugh Barton: *Peasant Uprisings in Japan of the Tokugawa Period*, pp. 8-26.
20. *Handwörterbuch der Staatswissenschaften*, article by von Below on "Geschichte des Zinsfuss", Vol. VIII, p. 1017.
21. Jacques Gernet: *Les Aspects économiques du bouddhisme dans la société chinoise du Vᵉ au Xᵉ siecle*, p. 171.
22. H. Hauser: *Les Débuts du capitalisme*, p. 19.
23. *Mahabarata*, Vol. XII, pp. 62-69.
24. M. Rostovtzeff: *Social and Economic History of the Roman Empire*, p. 2.
25. R. S. Lopez: in *Cambridge Economic History of Europe*, Vol. II, p. 266.
26. J. Kulischer: *Allgemeine Wirtschaftsgeschichte*, Vol. I, p. 41.

27. F. Løkkegaard: *Islamic Taxation in the Classic Period*, pp. 66-68; Yoshitomi: op. cit., pp. 74-82, 131-5.
28. *Handwörterbuch der Staatswissenschaften*, art. cit.; Kulischer: op. cit., Vol. I, p. 336.
29. Paul Radin: *Social Anthropology*, p. 115; Gernet: op. cit., p. 131.
30. W. Sombart: *Der moderne Kapitalismus*, Vol. I, p. 116; Glotz: op. cit., pp. 63-67; A. Sapori: *Mercatores*, pp. 20-21; *Histoire du Commerce*, Vol. I, pp. 140-1 (Lacour-Gayet), etc.
31. Y. Takekoshi: *Economic Aspects of the History of the Civilisation of Japan*, Vol. I, p. 346.
32. Kulischer: op. cit., Vol. I, p. 275.
33. R. S. Lopez: op. cit., p. 306.
34. N. S. B. Gras: *Business and Capitalism*, p. 60.
35. J. Schumpeter: *Business Cycles*, Vol. I, p. 22.
36. K. Polanyi: et al., *Trade and Market in the Early Empires*, pp. 258-9, 269.
37. G. von Below: *Probleme der Wirtschaftsgeschichte*, pp. 307–8.
38. H. Pirenne: op. cit., p. 38.
39. Chan Ju-kua: *His Work on the Chinese and Arab Trade in the 12th and 13th Centuries*, pp. 191-239.
40. *Histoire du Commerce*: Vol. III, p. 397 (G. Boumarchand).
41. A. Andréadès: "The Economic Life of the Byzantine Empire", in *Byzantium*, p. 61.
42. R. S. Lopez: op. cit., p. 281.
43. S. I. Rutgers: *Indonesië*, p. 46.
44. *Histoire du Commerce:* Vol. IV, pp. 143, 149: cf. Polanyi: et al., op. cit., p. 115.
45. *Histoire du Commerce:* Vol. III, p. 34.
46. R. S. Lopez: op. cit., p. 46.
47. Cicero: *De Officiis*, Vol. I, pp. 150-1.
48. F. Heichelheim: *Wirtschaftsgeschichte des Altertums*, p. 709.
49. Abram Neumann: *Jews in Spain*, Vol. I, p. 164.
50. N. S. B. Gras: op. cit., pp. 38-39.
51. Margaret H. Cole: "The Investment of Wealth in 13th Century Genoa", in *Economic History Review*, Vol. VIII, 2nd May, 1938, p. 187.
52. H. Hauser and A. Renaudet: *Les Débuts de l'age moderne (Peuples et Civilisations*, Vol. VIII), pp. 52-53.
53. Robert C. West: *The Mining Community in Northern New Spain*, pp. 26 sqq.
54. K. Kautsky: *Die Vorläufer des neueren Sozialismus*, p. 201.
55. Earl J. Hamilton: "American Treasure and the Rise of Capitalism", *Economica*, November 1929, pp. 352, 355.
56. H. Sée: *Origines du capitalisme*, pp. 36-37.
57. W. R. Scott: *The Constitution and Finance of English, Scottish and Irish Joint Stock Companies, to 1720*, Vol. I, p. 17.
58. Barthélémi de las Casas: *Oeuvres*, Vol. I, pp. 9-10, 34-35, 75-76, etc.
59. H. Hauser and A. Renaudet: op. cit., p. 645.

60. H. T. Colenbrander: *Koloniale Geschiedenis*, Vol. II, pp. 117-229.
61. P. Kaeppelin: *La Compagnie des Indes Orientales*, p. 224.
62. Quoted in W. van Ravesteyn, Jnr.: *Onderzoekingen over de economische sociale ontwikkeling van Amsterdam gedurende de 16e eeuw*, p. 218.
63. Kulischer: op. cit., p. 265.
64. G. Lefebvre: et al., *La Révolution française* (*Peuples et Civilisations*, Vol. XIII), p. 349.
65. Hauser and Renaudet: op. cit., p. 349.
66. Kulischer: op. cit., Vol. II, p. 266.
67. Sée: op. cit., p. 92.
68. B. Nogaro and W. Oualid: *L'Evolution du commerce, du crédit et du transport depuis 150 ans*, p. 35.
69. H. Pirenne: *Histoire économique de l'Occident médiéval*, pp. 479-83.
70. Hauser: op. cit., pp. 34-36.
71. Kulischer: op. cit., Vol. I, p. 205; F. Vercauteren: *Luttes sociales à Liège*, pp. 102-3.
72. Sée: op. cit., pp. 15-17.
73. G. Espinas: *Les Origines du capitalisme*, Vol. I, p. 157.
74. Gras: op. cit., pp. 68-69.
75. Kulischer: op. cit., Vol. I, p. 218; A. Doren: *Italienische Wirtschaftsgeschichte*, Vol. I, p. 502.
76. Espinas: op. cit., Vol. I, p. 153.
77. Doren: op. cit., Vol. I, p. 497.
78. Espinas: op. cit., Vol. I, pp. 175-6.
79. Pirenne: *Histoire économique de l'Occident médiéval*, pp. 637, 646-7.
80. Kulischer: op. cit., Vol. II, p. 116.
81. J. Dénian: *Histoire de Lyon et du Lyonnais*, p. 87.
82. Kulischer: op. cit., Vol. II, p. 135.
83. J. U. Nef: "Mining and metallurgy in mediaeval civilisation", in *Cambridge Economic History of Europe*, Vol. II, pp. 475-80.
84. Violet Barbour: *Capitalism in Amsterdam in the 17th Century*, pp. 35-39, 41, 109.
85. Bruno Lasker: *Human Bondage in Southeast Asia*, pp. 127-8.
86. Raymond Firth: *Malay Fishermen*, p. 60.
87. S. F. Nadel: *A Black Byzantium*, p. 283; Cl. Lévi-Strauss: *Tristes Tropiques*, p. 148; Fan Wen-Lan: "*Einige Probleme der chinesischen Geschichte*", in *Neue chinesische Geschichtswissenschaft*, pp. 7-71.
88. N. W. Posthumus: *Bronnen tot de Geschiedenis van de Leidsche Lakennijverheid*.
89. Kulischer: op. cit.
90. F. Mayer: *Anfänge des Handels und der Industrie in Oesterreich*, p. 64; Wagenaar: *Amsterdam in zijn Opkomst*.
91. Sombart: op. cit., Vol. I, pp. 814-17.
92. Sée: op. cit., pp. 139-40.
93. Posthumus: op. cit.
94. Marc Bloch: *Les Caractères originaux de l'histoire rurale française*, pp. 37-48.

95. N. S. B. Gras: *A History of Agriculture*, p. 161.
96. Ibid., pp. 170, 183.
97. P. Sagnac: *La Fin de l'ancien régime et la révolution américaine* (*Peuples et Civilisations*, Vol. XII), p. 57.
98. H. Sée, *Histoire économique de la France*, Vol. I, pp. 189-200.
99. Posthumus: op. cit., Vol. V, document 201.
100. *Acte* of 2nd February, 1247, Tailliar: *Recueil d'Actes*, quoted in G. Espinas: op. cit., Vol. I, p. 37, note I.
101. R. Firth: op. cit., p. 136.
102. Simiand: *Le Salaire*, Vol. I, p. 148.
103. Vitruvius: *De architecture*, Vol. X, pp. 6, 7.
104. Hauser: op. cit., pp. 8, 9, 11, 15; Pirenne: *Histoire de Belgique*, Vol. IV, p. 421.
105. Sombart: op. cit., 1, 2, pp. 485-7.
106. J. H. Clapham: *An Economic History of Modern Britain*, Vol. I, pp. 86-99.
107. J. U. Nef: "Mining and metallurgy in mediaeval civilisation", in *Cambridge Economic History of Europe*, Vol. II, pp. 464-6.
108. Kulischer: op. cit., Vol. II, p. 452.
109. Clapham: op. cit., pp. 249-50; A. P. Usher: *An Introduction to the Industrial History of England*, p. 305.
110. Sol Tax: *Penny Capitalism*, pp. 13, 14, 16.
111. Sapori: op. cit., pp. 50 sqq.
112. Fischel: *Studia arabica*, Vol. I, p. 77.
113. Hitti: op. cit., p. 344.
114. Lien Sheng-yang: *Money and Credit in China*, p. 4.
115. C. M. Macri: *L'organisation de l'économie urbaine dans Byzance sous la dynastie de Macédoine*, pp. 18-19.
116. R. S. Lopez: "Silk Industries in the Byzantine Empire", in *Speculum*, Vol. XX, No. 1, pp. 18-19.
117. A. Metz: *Die Renaissance des Islams*, pp. 417, 442-3.
118. Nancy Lee Swann: *Food and Money in China*, pp. 265, 405, et seq.
119. *An Outline History of China*, pp. 175-7; Helmut Wilhelm: *Gesellschaft und Staat in China*, p. 73; Du Shen: *"Die Diskussion über das Problem der Keime des Kapitalismus in China"*, in *Neue Chinesische Geschichtswissenschaft*, pp. 130-7.
120. Rostovtzeff: op. cit., p. 95; Bratianu: op. cit., p. 139.
121. A. von Kremer: *Kulturgeschichtliche Streifzüge auf dem Gebiete des Islams*, p. 77 (Eng. trans. by S. Khuda Bukhsh, in "Contributions to the History of Islamic Civilisation", edited by the same author, second edition, 1929, University of Calcutta.)
122. Chen Huan-Chang: *The Economic Principles of Confucius*, p. 656; Lien Sheng-yang: op. cit., p. 3.
123. Suetonius: *Lives of the Twelve Caesars*, Book 8, 18.
124. Gernet: op. cit., p. 141.
125. Heichelheim: *Wirtschaftsgeschichte des Altertums*, pp. 507-8, 565.
126. J. J. Mayer: introduction to translation of Kautilya's *Arthashastra*, pp. 77-78; Rostovtzeff: op. cit., p. 172.

127: A. Mazahéri: *La Vie quotidienne des Musulmans au moyen âge*, p. 117.

128. Wilhelm: op. cit., pp. 40-41, 73.

129. Bernard Lewis: "The Islamic Guilds", in *Economic History Review*, Vol. VIII, No. 1, November 1937, p. 20.

130. Fischel: *Jews in the Economic and Political Life of Mediaeval Islam*, pp. 13-14 et seq.; A. Bonné: *State and Economics in the Middle East*, p. 48.

131. E. Balazs: *Les Villes chinoises*, in *La Ville, Recueils de la Société Jean Bodin*, pp. 237-8.

132. See especially his letter to Engels, 14th June, 1853 (p. 420 of Vol. I of the "Correspondence" published by Bebel and Bernstein), the first article on the Spanish revolution, a number of passages in *Capital*, etc.

133. *Histoire du Commerce*, Vol. II, 486.

134. Basil Davidson: *The African Awakening*, pp. 40-41.

135. Cf. Sir George Sansom: *A History of Japan to 1334*, pp. 4, 235, etc.

136. R. F. Barton: *Ifugao Economics*, summarized by Ruth Bunzel: "The Economic Organization of Primitive Peoples", p. 336.

137. For Alexander Hamilton's opinion, see: *Propositions for a Constitution of Government and Speeches in the Federal Convention*. (*The Works of Alexander Hamilton*, Vol. I, pp. 347-428).

CHAPTER FIVE

THE CONTRADICTIONS OF CAPITALISM

Capital thirsting for surplus-value

THE owner of slaves distributed food among them and in return took the entire product of their labour. The feudal lord took the products of the unpaid work which his serfs were obliged to render him in the form of labour services. The capitalist buys the worker's labour-power for a wage which is less than the new value produced by this worker. In each of these varying forms the possessing classes take for themselves the social surplus product, the product of the surplus labour of the producers.

The contract made at Liège in 1634 between Antoine de Jelly, master-weaver, and Nicolas Cornélis, states bluntly that the latter will be paid "half of what he makes, the other half being the master's profit."*

The wage-worker creates new value while he expends his labour-power to produce commodities in his employer's factory. At a certain moment he will have produced new value exactly equivalent to what he receives as his wages. If he were to stop working at that moment he would not have produced any surplus value. But the employer does not mean that to happen. He does not want to do a favour, he wants to do business. He does not buy labour-power in order to keep it alive, he buys it as he buys any other commodity, in order to realise its use-value.[2] And the use-value of labour-power, from the capitalist's standpoint, is precisely its capacity to create surplus-value, to provide surplus labour over and above the labour needed to produce the equivalent of the wage paid for it. In order to be hired by an employer, a worker must work longer than is needed to produce this equivalent. In doing this he will create new value for which he will be paid nothing. He is creating surplus value, which is the difference between the value created by labour-power and the value of labour-power itself.

* Apologists for slavery did not fail to stress the analogy between this daily, weekly or monthly alienation of a man's labour-power and the alienation for life that is slavery: "It is not essentially repugnant to justice and reason that a man should surrender to another, even for his whole lifetime, the labour that every day a workman pledges to his employer, his master, provided that the inalienable [!] rights of man are safeguarded," wrote in 1742 the Dutch captain Elias Joannes.[1]

The capitalist's aim is to accumulate capital, to capitalise surplus value. The very nature of the circulation of money implies this aim. Industrial capital pursues this aim of accumulation even more, much more insatiably than usurer's capital or merchant capital. It produces for a free and anonymous market, *dominated by the laws of competition.* A capitalist is not alone in offering his products on this market to possible customers. Under the rule of competition, each industrialist tries to grab as large a share of the market as possible. To succeed, however, he must reduce his prices. There is only one way to reduce selling prices without threatening profit: to reduce the cost of production, the value of commodities, to curtail the labour-time socially necessary for producing them, to produce more commodities in the same length of time.

"Last year already the expansion of the enterprise, which took only a few months, enabled us to maintain the profit on our cement business at the expected level, despite the fact that competition considerably cut down the price of cement. This experience has confirmed us in our decision to make up for the increasing decline in prices which we foresee by an increase in the amount we produce," was proudly proclaimed by the annual report of a German cement-works in the nineteenth century.

In order to bring about such an increase in production, equipment must be improved, the process of production rationalised, the division of labour within the enterprise carried to a higher level. All of which demands an increase in capital. But the increase in capital can come, in the last analysis, only from an increase in the surplus-value capitalised. Under the lash of competition, the capitalist mode of production thus becomes the first mode of production in the history of mankind the essential aim of which appears to be *unlimited increase in production,* constant accumulation of capital by the capitalisation of the surplus value produced in the course of production itself.

The capitalist's thirst for surplus value is not the thirst for use-values and luxuries of the old possessing classes; only a limited part of surplus value is consumed unproductively in order to keep the capitalist alive. It is a thirst for surplus-value to capitalise, a thirst to accumulate capital: ". . . that whole system of appetities and values, with its deification of the life of snatching to hoard, and hoarding to snatch . . ."[8]

There is nothing irrational or mystical in this thirst. The old possessing classes, who took the social surplus product essentially in the form of use-values, were assured of being able to go on doing this so long as the social edifice remained standing which had this particular form of exploitation as its foundation. They could be affected only by natural disasters, wars or social revolutions, disasters against which they tried to provide by constituting big reserves. The predominant form in which capital first appears in history—usurer's and merchant capital—is characteristic of the same striving for *stability and security*. It is significant that the investments made by the bourgeois in the Middle Ages were calculated so as to guarantee stable incomes, regardless of fluctuations in money or prices.[4] The classical type of bourgeois in the historical epoch of the primitive accumulation of money capital, the miser, is haunted by this same thirst for security. It is not the *return* on his capital that he is worried about but its *existence*.

It is otherwise with the capitalist properly so called, the capitalist entrepreneur. Carrying on business for a market which is anonymous, unknown, undefined, his enterprises are dominated by risk and uncertainty. Today a deal has been successful, tomorrow another may fail to come off. It is not only the fact of competition, but the very fact of production which is *free from any overall social regulation** that gives capitalist enterprise this aspect of uncertainty and that compels the capitalist to try and make the maximum profit on each separate deal, in face of the permanent danger that hangs over his business as a whole.

The landowner, the small commodity producer, the purchaser of ground-rents, all find in the certainty of their incomes an adequate reason for keeping their activities within given *limits*. The uncertainty of capitalist profit implies, on the contrary, the need for a continuous *expansion* of business, an expansion which in turn depends on maximum accumulation of capital, maximum realisation of profits. Thus there emerges the image of the capitalist, of whose mediaeval ancestor Georges Espinas has drawn this masterly portrait:

"To achieve the biggest possible gain while paying out the least possible amount in wages; to make the producers supply as much as possible while paying them as little as he can get away with, or even robbing them within the same limits; to draw to himself, to breathe in, to suck up, as it were, all he can take of the money which ought to go to the small employers (the producers) for the work which he alone can obtain for them and which they carry out for him alone—this is obviously the constant aim of the efforts of the 'capitalist' entrepreneur to secure the biggest profit he can, even at the expense of the utmost harm to the people in his employment. He is like a spider, in the centre of his web. To apply this 'sweating' system all means are good in his eyes, and every circumstance is favourable; he

* Such regulation existed for all the pre-capitalist crafts and even for the beginnings of the *Verlagssystem* (putting-out system) in several countries. In Carinthia and Styria in the middle of the fifteenth century "Duke Frederick III regulated afresh the way to be followed for iron, he fixed prices and taxes, restricted the number of forges and the amount of iron that each merchant could have, and laid down the terms of contracts (*Verläge*)."[5]

knows how to take advantage of everything; he cheats on materials, he violates agreements and steals from wages; business means other people's money."[6]

The lengthening of the working day

Thirst for surplus-value is thirst for surplus labour, for unpaid labour over and above the labour that produces the equivalent value of the worker's means of life. In order to get more surplus labour the capitalists can, in the first place, lengthen the working day to the utmost without increasing the daily wage. If we suppose that a worker produces the equivalent of his wages in 5 hours, then lengthening his working day from 10 to 12 hours without any increase in wages will increase the surplus labour from 5 to 7 hours a day, or by 40 per cent. This way of increasing surplus-value is called *increasing absolute surplus value*.

In every society where the obtaining of use values remains the basic aim of production, for both the producers and the exploiters, a constant lengthening of the working day must appear absurd. The limitation of needs and of markets imposes a limit no less narrow upon production. So long as the slavery of ancient times remained patriarchal, on estates which were self-sufficient, the lot of the slaves was quite tolerable, and was really little different from that of the poor relations of the estate-owning family. It was only when the slavery of ancient times became the basis of production for the market that barbarous treatment of slaves became general.[7]

In the Middle Ages, the communal laws placed strict limits on the working time of the craftsmen. In such laws we find, as a rule, besides prohibition of night work, also the stoppage of work on numerous religious holidays (saints' days) and at certain periods of the year. On the basis of a study of the by-laws of the small town of Guines, in Artois, Georges Espinas has estimated the number of actual working days in the mediaeval year at 240.[8] In the Bavarian mines there were in the sixteenth century between 99 and 190 holidays every year.[9] Hue concludes that, taking into account the numerous holidays, the average working week in the mines of the fifteenth century was 36 hours.[10]

As soon, however, as capitalist enterprise appears, a constant striving to lengthen the working day is to be observed. From the fourteenth century onward laws were passed in Great Britain to forbid too short a working day. English writing of the seventeenth and eighteenth centuries is full of complaints regarding the "idleness" of the workers, who, "if they earn in four days enough to provide food for a whole week, do not go to work for the three following days." All the leading bourgeois thinkers take part in this campaign: the Dutchman Jan De Witt, Spinoza's friend; William Petty, the father of

English classical political economy; Colbert, who speaks of the "idle people", etc. Sombart fills seven pages with quotations like this from the period under consideration.[11]

When the capitalist mode of production crosses the oceans and penetrates fresh continents, it finds itself up against the same natural resistance by the workers to the lengthening of their working day. In the seventeenth and eighteenth centuries the press of the virtuous Puritan colonists in North America resounded with complaints about the high cost of labour, "contrary to reason and equity". "'Tis the poor that make the rich," artlessly declared the *New York Weekly Journal*. In 1769 the *Maryland Gazette* complained that "the wages they receive for the labour of one day will support them (the workers) in intemperance for three days."[12] "The denunciations of the 'luxury, pride and sloth' of the English wage-earners of the seventeenth and eighteenth centuries are, indeed, almost exactly identical with those directed against African natives today."[13]

Alfred Bonné notes the amazement shown by Western observers when they behold poor Arabs who prefer to earn £1 a year as shepherds rather than £6 a month as factory hands.[14] Audrey I. Richards reports the same repugnance among the Negroes of Rhodesia: "Men who worked an intermittent three or four hours a day in their tribal reserves are now asked to do a regular eight to ten hours under white supervision on the big plantations or in industrial concerns."[15]

It was sufficient, however, to take advantage of the enormous mass of labour-power uprooted and unemployed as a result of the social and economic upheavals of the period between the fifteenth and eighteenth centuries to bring a pressure to bear on wages which brought them below subsistence level. In this way the bourgeoisie was able to advance from victory to victory in this "struggle against the idleness of the people".

From the eighteenth century onward we find that the normal working day in England is 13 or 14 hours.[16] In the English cotton mills the working week is between 75 and 80 hours in 1747; 72 hours in 1797; between 74 and 80 hours in 1804.[17] And since wages had fallen so low that every day without work was a day without food, Napoleon cuts a more generous figure than his minister Portalis when he rejects the latter's proposal to prohibit Sunday work: "Since the people eat every day they should be allowed [!] to work every day."[18]

The growth in the productivity and intensity of labour

However, absolute surplus-value cannot be increased without limit. Its natural limit is, first of all, the physical capacity of the workers. Capital is interested in exploiting but not in destroying the labour-power which constitutes its constant source of potential surplus labour.

Beyond a definite physical limit, the worker's capacity to produce declines rapidly towards zero.

Furthermore, the organisation of workers' resistance by the trade unions brought about from the middle of the nineteenth century the first regulation of the working day in the direction of laying down a maximum length. The legal limit of the working day was fixed first at 12, then at 10, and in the twentieth century at 8 hours, so as to give in some countries a 40-hour week; not without howls about economic ruin from the bourgeoisie at each reduction.*

Capital now falls back more and more upon a second way of increasing surplus-value. Instead of lengthening the working day, it tries to cut down the labour-time necessary to produce the equivalent of the worker's wages. Let us assume that with a working day of 10 hours, 4 hours are needed to create the amount of necessary value represented by the worker's wages. If this necessary labour can be cut from 4 to 2 hours, then surplus labour is increased from 6 to 8 hours, and exactly the same result is achieved as if the working day had been lengthened from 10 to 12 hours. This is what is called *increasing relative surplus value.*

The increase of relative surplus-value results essentially from *growth in the productivity of labour* thanks to the employment of new machinery, more rational methods of work, a more advanced division of labour, a better way of organising labour, etc.† Industrial capitalism has transformed economic life more than all the earlier modes of production put together. The fall in prices of articles of current consumption is clearly expressed in these figures:

In 1779 a certain quantity of No. 40 cotton thread cost 16s.

In 1784 it cost only 10s. 11d.

In 1799 it cost only 7s. 6d.

In 1812 it cost only 2s. 6d.

In 1830 it cost only 1s. 2·5d.[19]

No less eloquent is the following table, which relates to a slightly later period in the United States, where the triumphs of machine production occurred somewhat later than in Great Britain.

* These howls are to be compared to the well-known exclamation by the economist Senior: "Abolishing the last hour of work means abolishing profit."

† Surplus value is the difference between what is produced by labour-power and the cost of upkeep of this same labour-power. By gathering the workers together in factories and by introducing among them a more and more far-reaching division and co-operation of labour, capital increased their productivity (their production) even without changing the instruments of labour, and took the increased product for itself.

Labour-time necessary for making various articles (in thousands of minutes):

	Manual work		*Machine work*	
100 pairs men's shoes	1859	86·2	1895	9·2
100 pairs ladies' shoes	1859	61·5	1895	4·8
100 dozen collars	1855	81·0	1895	11·5
12 dozen shirts	1853	86·3	1894	11·3
100 dozen corn boxes	1865	6·5	1894	2·7
25,000 lb. soap	1839	25·9	1897	1·3
12 tables	1860	33·8	1894	5·0
50 doors	1857	83·1	1895	30·6
100,000 envelopes	1855	26·1	1896	1·9
Transporting 100 tons of coal	1859	7·2	1896	0·6[20]

By substantially reducing the value of all articles of primary necessity capital reduces the part of the worker's working day during which he is producing the equivalent of his wages. Also to be taken into account is the substitution of cheap articles for dear ones as consumer goods for the working classes—especially the substitution of potatoes for bread—together with a general deterioration in workers' food, housing and clothes, which facilitates the growth in relative surplus value.

Growth in absolute surplus value results, however, from *intensification of labour*, which is basically the same thing as lengthening the working day. The worker is obliged to expend in 10 hours of work the same productive effort as previously he expended in 13 or 14 hours. Such intensification can be brought about by various methods: speeding up the pace of work; speeding up the machinery; increasing the number of machines to be watched (e.g. of looms to be overlooked in textile mills), etc.

Particularly in the most recent phase of capitalist development, characterised by "scientific organisation of labour" (Taylor and Bedaux systems; piece-work; time and motion study, etc.), has the intensification of labour immensely increased the absolute surplus value obtained by capital. Georges Friedmann presents a striking picture of two methods used for this purpose by two great French motor-car firms, Berliet in Lyons and Citroën in Paris:

"Why has the Berliet works the reputation, in spite of the spacious beauty of its halls, of being a gaol? Because here they apply a simplified version of the Taylor method of rationalising labour, in which the time taken by a demonstrator, an 'ace' worker, serves as the criterion imposed on the mass of workers. He it is who fixes, watch in hand, the 'normal' production expected from a worker. He seems, when he is with each worker, to be adding up in an honest way the time needed for the processing of each item. In fact, if the worker's movements seem to him to be not quick or precise enough, he gives a practical demonstration, and his performance determines the norm expected in return for the basic wage . . . Add to this supervision in the technical sphere the disciplinary supervision of uniformed warders who patrol the factory all the time and go so far as to push open the doors of the toilets to check that the men squatting there are not smoking, even in workshops where the risk of fire is non-existent.

"At Citroën's the methods used are more subtle. The working teams are in rivalry one with another, the lads quarrel over travelling cranes, drills, pneumatic grinders, small tools. But the supervisors in white coats, whose task is to keep up the pace, are insistent, pressing, hearty. You would think that by saving time a worker was doing them a personal favour. But they are there, unremittingly on the back of the foreman, who in turn is on your back; they expect you to show an unheard-of quickness in your movements, as in a speeded-up motion picture."[21]

Capital which is as thirsty as this for every minute, every movement the worker makes, during the whole of the time that "belongs" to it—does this not provide the best illustration of the fact that profit, capitalist surplus-value, is nothing but the unpaid surplus labour of the worker?

We find a striking confirmation of this thirst for surplus labour in the fact that General Motors pays its workers in the United States not by the hour but by the fraction of ten minutes [!] of work they have actually performed.[22]

Daniel Bell sums up admirably the radical revolution that industrial capitalism has carried out in the idea of time: "In the various ways it has been expressed two modes of time have been dominant: time as a function of space, and time as *durée*. Time as a function of space follows the rhythm of the movement of the earth: a year is the curving ellipse around the sun; a day, the spin of the earth on its axis. The clock itself is round; and the hour, the sweep of a line in 360 degrees of space. But time, as the philosophers and novelists—and ordinary people—know it, is also artless. These are the psychological modes which encompass the differing perceptions: the dull moments and the swift moments, the bleak moments and the moments of bliss, the agony of time prolonged and of time eclipsed, of time recalled and time anticipated—in short, time not as a chronological function of space, but time felt as a function of experience.

"Utilitarian rationality [euphemism for industrial capitalism] knows little of time as *durée*. For it, and for modern industrial life, time and effort are hitched only to the clock-like, regular 'metric' beat. The modern factory is fundamentally a place of order in which stimulus and response, the rhythms of work, derive from a *mechanically imposed* sense of time and pace. No wonder, then, that Aldous Huxley can assert: 'Today, every efficient office, every up-to-date factory is a *panoptical prison* in which the workers suffer . . . from the consciousness of being inside a machine."[23] [Emphasis ours.]

In his book *The Anatomy of Work*, Georges Friedmann quotes the example of a British factory in which several operations have been reduced to a duration of less than a minute.[25]* At the Ford works at River Rouge the conveyor-belt allows less than two minutes for most of the workers to carry out their task.[26] Some technicians have begun to question the efficacy of this "speed-up".[27]

The picture of a contemporary factory that G. Friedmann and D. Bell have given us in the passages quoted brings out also the *hierarchical structure* of the organisation of labour. So long as the producer is himself owner of his means of production the question of a "workshop police" does not arise. It is to his own interest to observe a strict economy of raw material. When domestic industry or the *Verlagssystem* become general, we find that complaints become frequent, on the part of the entrepreneurs, that the producers spoil, waste or steal the raw material entrusted to them. This was one of the main reasons for the establishment of manufactories, in which these workers worked under the constant supervision of the entrepreneur.

The latter has become, from being a mere owner of money and head of an enterprise with the aim of putting this capital to fruitful use, at one and the same time the organiser of an exact technical process of production and the *commander of a mass of wage-workers* who have to be supervised. He is no longer master merely of his capital but also of machines and men.

In order to perform this task effectively, he has to perfect the organisation of labour, introduce intermediate rungs, group the workers into teams under leaders, make use of foremen and workshop managers, technicians and engineers. Alongside the purely technical division of labour in the enterprise a *social hierarchic division of labour* develops and becomes ever more thorough, *between those who give orders and those who carry them out*.†

Human labour-power and machine production

Industrial capital finds its *raison d'être* and the essential source of its power to increase surplus-value in the use of machinery. Capitalism does not introduce new machines to increase the productivity of human labour; that is only a by-product of the aims it pursues. The capitalist

* "In time study, work is divided into elements of the order of a second, or a fifth of a second, while in motion study one goes down to one hundredth or one two-hundredth of a second."[24]

† See the striking parallel which Professor P. Sargant Florence has drawn between the hierarchy of the church, the pyramid of military ranks, and the organisation of present-day factories.[28] Vance Packard has subsequently made use of this parallel, too.[29]

introduces machinery to reduce his costs of production, so as to sell cheaper and beat his competitors. And it is not possible to reduce costs of production by means of machines unless the cost of these machines is itself *less* than the wages of the workers whom the machine replaces. The current expression used in English, "labour-saving machines", indicates only imperfectly the function of machines in the capitalist mode of production. To be bought by a capitalist enterprise a machine must *both save human labour and make profit*; it must be "labour-saving" and "profit-increasing". When a machine costs exactly as much as the *saving in wages* that it can achieve, it will doubtless not be bought, despite the fact that, even so, it may represent a substantial *saving in labour-time from the standpoint of society as a whole.* There we see a very important difference between the dynamics of a capitalist industry and those of a planned and socialised industry.

The cigarette industry was born in the United States in the 1860s. At first all the work was done by hand; a skilled worker could roll no more than 3,000 cigarettes in a working day of ten hours. In 1876 the wages cost was 96·4 cents per 1,000 cigarettes of a certain brand. One firm then offered a prize of 75,000 dollars for the invention of a cigarette-making machine. Bonsack came forward in 1881 with a rational machine which produced between 200 and 220 cigarettes a *minute* and cut wages costs from 96·4 to 2 cents [!] per 1,000 cigarettes. A single one of these machines could have produced all the cigarettes made by hand in the United States in 1875.[30]

A machine which saves wages throws producers out of production. The introduction of machines gives rise to unemployment, and does this so directly that the victims tried at first to destroy these machines which were condemning them to poverty (Luddite movement in Britain; similar movement in France, 1816–1825).* Between 1840 and 1843, as a result of the competition of the mechanised linen industry, the number of Flemish women spinning at home fell from 221,000 to 167,000.[32] In 1824–1825 the introduction of mechanical looms caused considerable unemployment in England, and wages were cut by 50 per cent.[33]

If they were to stand up to competition by large scale machinery the manual workers had to accept big reductions in wages. The weekly wages of hand weavers in Bolton fell from 25s. in 1800 to 9s. in 1820 and from 19s. 6d. in 1810 to 5s. 6d. in 1830.[34]

The unemployment of a mass of workers for whom there is no work because of competition by machines becomes a permanent institution

* In the centuries preceding the industrial revolution the public authorities often confiscated machines which condemned labour to unemployment. Thus, a machine for knitting stockings was forbidden, first in Britain and then in France, in the seventeenth century. In 1623 a machine for making needles, and about 1635 a windmill for sawing wood, were banned in England.[31]

of the capitalist mode of production.* This is the *industrial reserve army*, thanks to which the wage-earners are forced to accept as wages the bare cost of reproducing their labour-power. In the first phase of industrial capitalism, whatever the country in which the capitalist mode of production becomes established, the destruction of the crafts by large-scale industry gives rise to an acute problem of unemployment. Subsequently, other phenomena which we describe later on determine the scope and fluctuations of this unemployment.

Industry based on machinery does not merely transform a section of the producers into wretched unemployed. It devalues manual work in general and changes many skilled workers into unskilled or semi-skilled workers. In the epoch of the craft guilds, or that of domestic industry, every producer was in principle a skilled producer, with a thorough knowledge of his craft. The unskilled "hirelings" were a floating mass which lacked great importance, either numerically or economically. The skill of the producers at their trade was the chief condition for the success of any productive enterprise.

But the division of labour effected in manufacture, and then the general introduction of machinery, and finally the progress of semi-automation, simplify and mechanise to the utmost the work of the producers.[35] Their tasks, which no longer require any skill, are henceforth such that anybody can perform them. An apprenticeship of a few months enables anyone today to become a good worker on the conveyor belt. In the Ford works in the U.S.A., 75 to 80 per cent of the personnel in the production workshops can be trained in less than a fortnight; in one of the factories of the Western Electric trust the percentage of skilled workers has fallen to 10 per cent of the labour force.[36]

The sudden formation of great masses of unskilled producers gave rise, at the dawn of industrial capitalism, to the appearance of a mass of *migrant workers*, such as the navvies of Britain who dug canals and built the railways.[37] Capitalist industry, born amid vast human migrations within the modern nations, caused in its turn a series of such migrations on the national and international scale: massive emigration of Europeans to North and South America, Australia, South Africa, etc.; Indian emigration to the countries around the Indian Ocean, and emigration of Japanese and Chinese to the countries around the Pacific, etc.

* Today as previously, official political economy upholds the same view with great candour. The absence of any unemployment would enable the workers to raise wages "excessively" and provoke inflation. See the *Economist* of 20th August, 1955, and *L'Echo de la Bourse* of 15th December, 1959, which quotes these words, ascribed to ex-President Truman: "On the contrary, it is a good thing for economic hygiene that there should always be some spare labour looking for work."

Forms and evolution of wages

In the capitalist mode of production, labour-power has become a commodity.* Like that of any other commodity, the value of this labour-power is determined by the amount of labour socially necessary to produce it. The value of labour-power is thus the cost of reconstituting this labour-power *in a given social setting* (food, clothing, housing, etc.). Because the worker has only his labour-power to sell in order to buy what he and his family need to live, and because of the presence of the industrial reserve army, wages vary around a *subsistence minimum* (an idea we will define later) which maintains the worker in his condition as a proletarian:

"The workers cannot possess the economic means of improving their position. Industry is organised in such a way that, in order to win independence, the workers would need to have money. How could they get it? . . . As regards the wages that the clothier pays to the petty producers, these are obviously fixed and distributed with a view merely to enabling those who receive them to keep themselves alive, so as to go on working under the exploitation of the one who pays them and keeps them alive for his personal and exclusive profit, and not to enriching them so that they may free themselves bit by bit from their former masters, rise to the level of the latter, and eventually compete with them."[38]

This analysis of the wages received by the small craftsmen of the Middle Ages who did work put out to them by the merchant-masters applies to wages in all forms of civilisation. It is an extraordinarily stable phenomenon throughout the ages. Examining the wages of agricultural workers at Eshnuna, in Mesopotamia, at the beginning of the second millennium B.C., Jacques Lacour-Gayet comes to the conclusion that, "reckoned in terms of wheat these wages are very well comparable with those of our day. The amount of wheat they represent is about the same as that represented by a harvest-worker's wages nowadays."[39]

For ancient Greece, Fr. Heichelheim has worked out the vital minimum of a worker at Delos, in the time of Alexander the Great. It is made up of the *sitos* (basic food, bread), the *opsonion* (additional food), clothes and some small extras. In good years the wages rose a little above this minimum; in bad ones, the extra expenses and even the *opsonion* were practically eliminated.[40]

This characteristic situation in ancient Greece already contains potentially the elements of that fluctuation of wages which is to be

* Is it necessary to add, for the benefit of opponents whether ignorant or dishonest, that it is absurd to say that the Marxists degrade labour-power to the level of a commodity? They merely *recognise* that capitalism has carried out this degradation. The term "Labour Exchange" is sufficient evidence of this.

found in country after country and age after age, allowing for differences in customs, manners, traditions and, above all, *relations of strength between sellers and buyers of labour-power*. At certain times, the *opsonion* and the extras may be fairly big and varied: at others they may disappear almost completely. The two elements, the historical and the physical ("absolute minimum"), nevertheless form integral parts of wages.

The evolution of real wages under the capitalist mode of production corresponds to a series of exact and complex laws. Contrary to what was supposed by Malthus, whose ideas were the foundation for the wages theory of Ricardo and Lassalle ("the iron law of wages"), there is no *demographic law* governing fluctuations in the supply and demand of labour-power ("the labour market"). What determine these fluctuations, in the last analysis, are *the laws of capital accumulation.*

This phenomenon is easiest to grasp in the *short-term fluctuations* during the capitalist production cycle,*, which leads industry out of stagnation and depression, through economic recovery and high conjuncture, towards boom and crisis. At the start of the cycle the mass of unemployed available on the "labour market" as a result of the previous crisis, exceeds the demand for labour caused by economic recovery. Wages will thus remain stable at a comparatively low level. (It is indeed the contradiction between these stable wages and an initial rise in selling prices that makes possible an increase in the profit margin. The rate of profit rises and this encourages recovery.) On the other hand, at the peak of the boom, if full employment is actually achieved (which is not at all a certainty, a point to which we shall return), the demand for labour greatly exceeds the supply, and the workers can bring pressure to bear to push wages up, the reduction in the rate of profit which results being one of the causes of the outbreak of crisis.

We find these laws again at work in *long-term fluctuations*. When the accumulation of capital is taking place at a pace slower than the increase in unemployment which it has itself caused, real wages remain stable or even tend to decline. We can say that in these circumstances the accumulation of capital is destroying more jobs (crafts, agricultural work, domestic work, jobs in enterprises which have been put out of business by competition) than it is creating. The industrial reserve army will then tend to grow over a long period, and there will be no full employment even in a boom period, so that the workers will be unable to win wage-increases in that situation (conditions which prevailed in Europe down to 1850–70 and which still prevail in most

* See Chapter 11, devoted to this problem.

colonial and semi-colonial countries).* We can also say that in this case industrial expansion is proceeding at a slower pace than the growth in productivity.

However, when the accumulation of capital is proceeding at a quicker pace than the growth in the unemployment it causes—when the industrial reserve army ceases to grow, and even tends to be absorbed back into employment, e.g. when large scale emigration occurs alongside hindrances to immigration—real wages will tend to rise slowly over a long period. This is likewise what happens when industrial expansion proceeds at a quicker pace than the growth of productivity.

In fact, it is not the *absolute level* of wages that matters to capital. The latter prefers, certainly, that wages should be as low as possible in its own enterprises—but it wants at the same time to see wages as high as possible paid in competing enterprises or by the employers of its customers! What matters to capital is the possibility of extracting more surplus labour, more unpaid labour, more surplus value, more profit from its workers. The growth in the productivity of labour, which makes possible the growth of relative surplus value, implies the possibility of a slow rise in real wages, if the industrial reserve army is limited, on condition that the equivalent of these increased real wages is produced in an ever shorter period of time, i.e. that wages rise less quickly than productivity.

One can indeed observe in history that real wages are generally highest in the countries which have known for some time a substantial growth in the productivity of labour, as compared with countries where this productivity has remained stagnant for a long time or has risen only slowly.

Nevertheless, the rise in real wages does not follow *automatically* from the rise in the productivity of labour. The latter only creates the *possibility* of such a rise, within the capitalist framework, provided profit is not threatened. For this potential increase to become actual, two interlinked conditions are needed: a favourable evolution of "relations of strength on the labour market" (i.e. predominance of the tendencies for the industrial reserve army to shrink over the tendencies for it to expand), and effective organisation (above all, trade union organisation) of the wage workers which enables them to abolish competition among themselves and so to take advantage of these "favourable market conditions".

Statistics and historical studies have shown that any theory that deduces the level of real wages directly from the relative level of productivity of labour, leaving out the two factors we have just mentioned, does not correspond to reality. Here, taken from a study by the International Federation of Metal Workers,[41] is the productivity

* See some concrete examples in Chapter 13.

(annual production of steel per employed worker) and the average wage (in Swiss francs) in a series of steel works in 1957:

	Annual production per worker *tons*	*Annual profits per worker* *frs.*	*Annual cost of labour per worker* *frs.*
U.S. Steel Corp.	110	6,800	30,000
Inland Steel Corp.	170	6,800	29,800
Youngtown Sheet	150	6,100	27,700
Average of 8 American firms	138	6,400	29,500
United Steel Ltd.	96	3,800	10,500
Colvilles Ltd.	115	3,500	8,700
Average of 8 British firms	100	3,400	±9,500
Yawata Iron & Steel	70	2,200	6,000
Nakayama	170	7,000	7,000
Fuji Iron & Steel	82	3,000	6,500
Average of 6 Japanese firms	76	3,100	6,000

The differences are obvious. The physical productivity of the British steel workers is 33 per cent higher than that of the Japanese, yet the financial productivity is only 10 per cent higher. On the other hand, the difference in the respective wages exceeds 50 per cent. Again, the American steel works enjoy a physical productivity 38 per cent higher than that of the British, and a financial productivity 80 per cent higher. But the American wages are more than three times the British. Between the U.S.A. and Japan the difference in productivity is two to one, while the difference in wages is *five* to one! And one Japanese steel works, Nakayama, has the same productivity as the Americans, whereas it pays wages which are only a *quarter* of American wages!

M. Madinier has convincingly shown in a recent work that the persistence of a wage differential of 20 per cent between the French provinces and Paris is explained essentially by the difference in trade union strength between the former and the latter.

It would be wrong, however, to regard trade union strength as an *independent* variable in the fixing of wages. This is because the possibility of overcoming competition among the workers does not exist—outside certain highly-skilled trades which enforce what is practically a *numerus clausus* in apprenticeships or other access to their ranks—unless the reserve army is no longer steadily increasing. Even in this favourable circumstance, the increase of wages comes up against an *institutional* barrier which is not at all a technical or "purely economic" one. Theoretically, a rise in real wages remains possible so long as the total amount paid in wages is less than the net national product. It then implies *a redistribution of incomes and a reallocation of resources* between the consumer goods sector and the production goods sector, two processes which may cause friction but which are nevertheless perfectly possible without giving rise to actual crisis or inflation. They merely require an *institutional* change, i.e. the disappearance of the power of capital, and in particular its power to stop investing when the rate of profit falls too low.

Under the capitalist régime, however, increases in wages come up against a certain barrier well before reaching either the physical or the economic one. When, as a result of full employment, wages increase faster than productivity, the rate of profit and even the rate of surplus value decline. And the risk of such a decline occurring quickly sets in motion the readaptation mechanisms of an economy based on profit: on the one hand, compensatory price increases, inflationary tendencies, fall in investment and reduction in employment; on the other, furious rationalisation and replacement of workers by machines. In both cases, unemployment reappears. As soon as this "barrier" is reached, the rise of real wages becomes impossible under the capitalist régime. This is why the most plain-spoken advocates of capitalism declare that it cannot exist in conditions of "over-employment", i.e. full employment.

How are we to explain, within the framework of the theory of labour-value, the increase in real wages which occurs in the circumstances described above?

The value of labour-power comprises not only the prices of the means of existence needed for its purely physical reconstitution (and the maintenance of the workers' children, i.e. the reproduction of labour-power). It also includes a moral and historical element, i.e. the prices of those commodities (and, later, of certain personal services) which the traditions of the given country have come to include in the subsistence minimum.* These needs depend on the comparative level of (past and present) civilisation, and thus, in the last analysis, on the average level of the productivity of labour over a certain period. So long as the pressure of the industrial reserve army prevents these needs being included in the calculation of the subsistence minimum, *wages, i.e. the price of labour-power, fall in reality below the value of labour-power*. When real wages are increased, the price of labour-power merely catches up with its value, which tends to rise with the overall rise in the level of civilisation.

We thus see that *the growth in the productivity of labour has a contradictory effect on wages*. To the extent that it reduces the value of the means of subsistence it tends to cut down, if not absolute wages then at least relative wages (the part of the working day during which the worker is producing the value-equivalent of his wages), and so to diminish the value of labour-power. To the extent that it reduces the value and price of many luxury products, develops mass produc-

* The influence of the "tradition" factor in the forming of wage-levels is strongly emphasised by Polanyi[42] and Joan Robinson.[43]

tion (often at the expense of quality!) and incorporates a number of new commodities* in the subsistence minimum, it tends, on the contrary, to increase the value of labour-power.

The accumulation of capital also has a contradictory effect on the amount of employment and on the trend of wages. To the extent that machines replace men, the reserve army grows. But to the extent that surplus-value is accumulated, that capital enlarges its spheres of operation, that new enterprises continually arise and existing ones are expanded, the reserve army is reduced and capital sets out to find fresh labour to exploit.†

Taking all these factors into consideration, one can explain the main trends in the evolution of wages since the beginning of capitalism. Two main epochs must be distinguished where the countries of Western Europe are concerned: the epoch that runs from the sixteenth century to the middle of the nineteenth, during which wages fell further and further to the level of the mere *sitos*; and then the epoch that runs from the middle of the nineteenth century to our own day, during which wages first rose, then became stable or declined, then rose once again. The *opsonion* and the extras have increased in quantity and become immensely varied, but have in some instances declined in quality, which is also true of the *sitos*.

The epoch of the primitive accumulation of industrial capital was an epoch of fall in real wages, caused principally by the over-abundance of labour, by the continual increase in the industrial reserve army, and by the lack of effective organisation of the working class resulting from this. Capital increased the production of absolute surplus value by reducing wages to the point at which, in order to meet his need of bread in one year the British worker had to work, in 1495, 10 weeks; in 1533, 14 or 15 weeks; in 1564, 20 weeks; in 1593, 40 weeks; in 1653, 43 weeks; in 1684, 48 weeks, and in 1726, 52 weeks. With the help of the price revolution all "idleness" had been successfully overcome.[45] Recently, E. H. Phelps Brown and Sheila V. Hopkins have fully confirmed these classic data of J. E. Thorold Rogers. They have found that the real wages of British masons fell from index 110–115 in 1475–1480 to 56 in 1528, 45 in 1600, 38 in 1610–1620, 55 in

* "Two centuries ago not one person in a thousand wore stockings; one century ago not one person in five hundred wore them; now not one person in a thousand is without them," triumphantly proclaimed in 1831 the pamphlet "The Results of Machinery", published by the Society for the Diffusion of Useful Knowledge.[44]

† In a country which is already highly industrialised, a sudden large-scale demand for labour can be met only by incorporating millions of housewives, youngsters and retired people in the proletariat, after full employment has been attained. This is what happened during the Second World War, in the United States, in Germany, in Britain, etc. Thereafter, the only thing to do is to import or attract foreign labour.

1700, 65–70 in 1740–1750, 53 in 1765–1770, 47 in 1772 and 38 in 1800. Only around 1880 did the figure again rise above index 100![46]

Nor were matters different in France. The Vicomte d'Avenel has calculated that betwen 1376 and 1525 a carpenter had to work, on the average, 5 days in order to earn the equivalent of a hectolitre of wheat; his daily pay was worth 3 kilogrammes of meat. In 1650 he had to work 16 days to obtain the same equivalent of wheat, and his daily pay was worth no more than 1·8 kilogrammes of meat.[47]

From the middle of the nineteenth century, however, real wages began to rise. In Britain and France they practically doubled between 1850 and 1914.[48] The capitalists succeeded during an entire period (abolition of the Corn Laws in Britain; increasing exports from overseas countries) in bringing about a considerable decline in agricultural prices. The capitalist mode of production experienced a remarkable expansion, conquering enormous international markets. In this way it has to some extent absorbed the industrial reserve army in the countries of Western Europe, only to reproduce it, to "re-export" it on a larger scale, in India, China, Latin America, Africa and the Near East. The mass emigration from Europe to overseas white-settlement countries reduced still further the supply of labour on the European labour market. All these factors, closely interlinked and characteristic of a certain structure of the world market, created conditions favouring the reinforcement of trade-union strength and the rise of real wages in Western Europe.

Competition from female and child labour was for a long time one of the chief means of reducing average wages.*

Another means to the same end from the Middle Ages onward was the *truck system*: payment of wages in kind, i.e. in products of which the employer arbitrarily determined the price or reduced the quality. Opposition by the workers eliminated this form of super-exploitation despite strong resistance from the employers.[50] It continues, however, in a special form, in the institution of shops which belong to industrial concerns, shops in which the workers have to buy the goods they

* Down to 1816, several London parishes were in the habit of "selling" hundreds of poor children to textile mills in Lancashire and Yorkshire, some two hundred miles from London! These children were sent "by wagon loads" and the philanthropist Sir Samuel Romilly declared that they were lost to their parents for ever, no less than if they had been sent to the West Indies. The same writer quotes this particularly frank, cynical and odious passage from a speech made in 1811 in the House of Commons by a Mr. Wortley:

"Mr. Wortley, who spoke on the same side, insisted that, although in the higher ranks of society it was true that to cultivate the affections of children for their family was the source of every virtue, yet it was not so among the lower orders, and that it was a benefit to the children to take them away from their miserable and depraved parents. He said too that it would be highly injurious to the public to put a stop to the binding of so many apprentices to the cotton manufacturers, as it must necessarily raise the price of labour . . ."[49]

need and to which they fall into debt, thus finding themselves tied for life to the same employer (this is one of the forms still prevalent today of *peonage* in the southern states of the U.S.A., e.g. in the turpentine industry).

Leaving aside wages paid in kind, the two most common forms of wages are *time wages* and *piece wages*. Time wages have fewer disadvantages from the standpoint of the interests of the working class. Piece wages, on the other hand, which urge the worker to constant increase in output, to speed-up the pace of production and ceaseless intensification of work, are the ideal tool for the employers to use to increase production of relative surplus value.

A concealed form of piece wages is the *bonus* system, which appeared in the American metal industry about 1870. There are now several different methods of calculating bonus: the Rowan, Halsey, Bedaux, Emerson, Refa and other systems. All these methods have in common that the worker's output increases faster than his wages. Of the mass of value created by the worker, a *smaller and smaller* fraction returns to him, and the relative surplus value increases proportionately. Thus, under the Rowan system, if output increases by 50 per cent, wages rise by 33 per cent; if output increases by 100 per cent, wages rise by 50 per cent; if output rises by 200 per cent, wages rise by 66 per cent, etc.

As for the Bedaux system, it has been estimated in the U.S.A. that it has generally led to an increase in production by 50 per cent, against an increase of 20 per cent in wages.[51]

Writers who are frankly in favour of the bonus system, like Dr. A Perren, admit the advantages that the employers derive from these various systems.[52] The same result is achieved by the various systems of *profit sharing* by which the workers are induced to increase not only their individual output but also that of the entire enterprise.

Additional note on the theory of absolute impoverishment

The "theory of absolute impoverishment" is not to be found in the works of Marx. It was ascribed to him by political opponents, especially what was called the "revisionist" trend in the German Social-Democratic Party. It is to say the least paradoxical that a whole school claiming to be orthodox Marxist has thought it necessary to adopt this "theory of impoverishment" and defend it with persistence and bad faith, bringing discredit on Marxist theory.*

* We will restrict ourselves to two examples:

In the *Textbook of Political Economy* published in August 1954 in the U.S.S.R., it was stated that: "Absolute impoverishment is expressed in the fall in real wages . . . In the twentieth century the real wages of the workers in Britain, the U.S.A., France, Italy and other capitalist countries are lower than in the middle [!] of the nineteenth century."[53] "In the United States . . . real

The idea that the real wages of the workers tend to decline more and more is totally alien to Marx's writings; it was formulated by Malthus and taken up most notably by Lassalle, who wrote of an "iron law" of wages. Marx waged a lifelong fight against this "iron law", a fight which one cannot really dismiss as due to a mere misunderstanding, as John Strachey does.[58] Actually, as we have shown above, he always insisted on the fact that wages are determined by complex laws and that denunciation of the capitalist order must be independent of the relative level of wages.*

What one finds in Marx is an idea of the absolute impoverishment not of the workers, the wage-earners, but of that section of the proletariat which the capitalist system *throws out* of the production process: unemployed, old people, disabled persons, cripples, the sick, etc., *die Lazarusschicht des Proletariats* as he calls it, the poorest stratum "bearing the stigmata of wage labour". This analysis retains its full value, even under the "welfare" capitalism of today.

In the United States poverty has certainly not disappeared, despite the considerable increase in real wages.[61] It is enough to look at the frightful slums that fill entire districts of New York, Chicago, Detroit, San Francisco, New Orleans, and other southern towns, to realise that these victims of an inhuman society, brutalised and dehumanised by this same society, continue to constitute a terrible reproach to the

wages had fallen by 1938 to 74 per cent of what they were in 1900. In France, Italy and Japan . . . real wages fell during the nineteenth and twentieth centuries even more than in the U.S.A."[54] "In France and Italy, real wages amounted in 1952 to less than half of pre-war."[55] "In the U.S.A. 72·2 per cent [!] of all American families had in 1949 incomes which were lower than the excessively modest official subsistence level,"[56] etc.

In the Soviet newspaper *Trud*, Academician A. Leontiev published in July 1955 a series of articles in which the following appeared: "Absolute impoverishment is expressed above all in the fall in the real wages of the bulk of the workers . . . The average real wage of an American worker . . . was in 1947–51 15 per cent less than in 1938–40; in 1951, the real wage of an American worker was 23 per cent less than in 1946 and 21 per cent less than before the war. With their wages the American workers could buy 59 per cent as much food, clothing and other consumer goods [!]."[57]

For amusement's sake one may put these two statements together. Wages in 1951 are 21 per cent less than wages in 1938 which are 74 per cent of wages in 1900. Consequently, from 1900 to 1951 American real wages must have fallen from 100 to 58·5. But in 1900 they were already below the level of the middle of the nineteenth century. One would have to assume then, according to these "statistics", that between 1850 and 1950 American real wages declined by over a half. Is there a single economist capable of really believing such nonsense?

* Roman Rosdolsky[59] has collected all the passages in Marx's economic writings which relate to the theory of wages and has found only one passage that might be found confusing, as to the possibility of an upward trend of real wages when there is a marked increase in productivity. See also Steindl, in his important work *Maturity and Stagnation in American Capitalism.*[60]

richest capitalism in the world.* To this permanent absolute impoverishment of the "infra-proletariat" there must be added the *periodical* absolute impoverishment of the workers hit by conjectural unemployment, the fall in wages during crises, etc.

A more subtle variant of the "absolute impoverishment" school tries to prove that this expression can apply even when real wages are rising. Discussion then gets lost in a semantic maze. Arzumanian declares that "absolute impoverishment" is expressed in intensification of labour, increase in accidents at work, the increase [!] in the value of labour-power and the fact that (rising) real wages fall further and further behind this value.[63] An "absolute impoverishment" which is expressed in an *increase* in the value of labour-power and an *increase* in real wages does violence to logic—formal logic no less than dialectical logic. It seems obvious to us that all these formulations imply a *relative* impoverishment, i.e. an impoverishment *not* in terms of absolute data (in these there is an improvement in status) but *relatively* to social wealth as a whole, to surplus value, to the productive effort contributed by the proletariat, etc.

In fact, the phenomenon of *relative impoverishment* is most typical of the capitalist mode of production. Increase in the rate of surplus value is at once the essential tool of capital for achieving accumulation of capital and also its chief weapon for countering the tendency to a fall in the average rate of profit. It is in this increase in the rate of surplus-value that the exploiting character of capitalist economy is expressed.

Empirical data broadly confirm this tendency to a decline in the relative place of *wages*† in the net product created by labour. John Strachey, though a stern (and unjust) critic of Marx's economic system, states: "In Britain . . . it [the share of wages in the total national income] appears to have been around 50 per cent in Marx's day: to have declined to about 40 per cent in the early years of the twentieth century; to have stayed about there till 1939, and then (including, as you must, the pay of the Forces) to have gone back to around 50 per cent by the end of the Second World War."[64]

By deducting the pay of the Forces, who after all are not producers, we arrive at a percentage of 47 in 1949 and a decline by several points

* Allison Davis has observed that people of this class are so used to living on the brink of disaster and hunger that they do not know what ambition is, or the desire to acquire higher knowledge. "In a sense," he writes, "ambition and the drive to attain the higher skills are a kind of luxury. They require a minimum *physical* security; only when one knows where his next week's or next month's food and shelter will come from can he and his children afford to go in for long-term education and training . . ."[62]

† We shall deal in the next chapter with the question of the extent to which office-workers can be regarded as producing surplus value and whether they are paid out of the surplus value produced by the workers.

after 1951.[65] This slight tendency to decline (or, if preferred, this remarkable stability of labour's share in the national income), has not resulted from the normal functioning of the system, but from a determined struggle by the wage-earners to increase their share. Is it possible now to deny that capitalism shows an inherent tendency to relative impoverishment, to a reduction in labour's share in the net product of industry? "No," replies Mr. Strachey.[66]

These calculations are not completely exact, moreover, since they leave out of account the numerical increase (both absolute and relative) of the proletariat as compared with Marx's time, with the beginning of the twentieth century, or even with the period before the Second World War. Even if "labour's share" in the national income had remained the same as a percentage, it would still have declined from the moment that this 50 per cent of the national income was being shared no longer among 60 per cent but among 80 or even 90 per cent of the population. The most exact mode of calculation would compare income per wage-earner with income per head of population, and study the fluctuations in the relation between these two magnitudes. There is little doubt that the former has declined in relation to the latter as compared with the middle of the nineteenth century, with the beginning of the twentieth century, and with the 1930s, in all the main capitalist countries.

In the United States the tendency is very clear. Here is the share of wages in the net product ("value added") of manufacturing industry:

	%
1880	48·1
1890	45·0
1899	40·7
1909	39·3
1919	40·5
1929	35·5
1939	36·7
1949	38·5
1952	35·0[67]

Still more to the point, here is the evolution of the gross real product per hour of work and gross real time wages, in decade averages:

	Real product per hour, in indices	*Real time wage, in indices*
1891–1900	100	100
1901–1910	122·8	102
1911–1920	146·0	109·1
1921–1930	196·4	137·2
1931–1940	233·5	158 [68]
1941–1950	281·3	209

Periodical absolute impoverishment of the unemployed and other victims of the capitalist production process; more or less general relative impoverishment of the proletariat (i.e. increase in real wages which over a long period is less than the growth in social wealth and the average productivity of labour): these are the laws of development for the working class under the capitalist system.

Dual function of labour-power

In the age of petty commodity production the essential instruments of labour—looms, forges, etc.—were acquired once for all and passed down from generation to generation. Like the peasant's land they did not constitute means of production subject to depreciation out of current production, but merely the conditions, the instruments, of men's livelihood. The clothier sold raw material to the small clothing worker and bought from him his finished product. The difference between these two prices merely represented, in fact, the craftsman's wage. When the entrepreneur took to organising weaving on his own account, his costs of production were confined essentially to costs of raw material and wages. The function of the labour-force whose labour-power he bought was exclusively that of adding to the value of the raw material a newly created value, one part of which (corresponding to wages) increased the entrepreneur's costs of production, while the other part (in exchange for which the workers got nothing) represented surplus-labour, surplus value appropriated by the capitalist.*

Things change with the flowering of industrial capital, of the capitalist mode of production. *The purchase of machines* now becomes the preliminary condition for production intended for a market which is governed by competition. In order to buy these machines, a substantial amount of capital has to be advanced. The machines will not be passed down from generation to generation, nor even used throughout the lifetime of the entrepreneur. They will be used so intensively that after a certain time they will be *physically worn-out*. And not much time will pass before competitors have built more modern machines, producing more cheaply, which will have to be bought if one is not to be overcome in the battle of competition. Thus, the old machines undergo a *moral depreciation* before their physical depreciation properly so called. The capitalist entrepreneur, unlike the petty commodity producer, does not look on them as a mere means of livelihood, but as *capital enabling him to accumulate surplus value*.

The capital advanced for the purchase of machines will thus have

* It was therefore logical that the first classical writers of political economy, especially Adam Smith, reduced the value of commodities to the incomes of the producers and the owners, forgetting the part of this value which reproduced a fraction of the instruments of labour.

to be depreciated within a definite period of time, or else the capitalist will not be in a position to keep up with technical progress and acquire more modern machinery. In the United States it is at present estimated that a machine-tool is physically worn-out after ten years; however, it is morally worn-out after only seven years, and must be replaced by something more up-to-date.[69] Thus, after seven years the capitalist will have to have depreciated the value of his machines, the capital he laid out on their purchase. This "depreciation" can be accomplished in one way only—by transferring to each commodity produced a fraction of the value of the means of production with which it was produced.

In this way labour-power fulfils a dual function from the capitalist's point of view: it conserves the value of the means of production which are used in production; and it creates new value. As part of this new value represents the equivalent of wages, capital advanced by the capitalist, it can be said that labour power *conserves all the value of existing capital and creates all the new value* appropriated by the capitalist.

Every industrialist understands this quite well. He tries to reduce to the utmost possible extent the time during which his machinery, etc., is out of use. Each day, each hour that a machine is not being used to produce is a day, an hour during which it is wearing out physically, and still more morally without a corresponding fraction of its value being conserved by labour power. This is what leads, in many enterprises, to continuous shift work, 24 hours a day.

The capitalist who starts up an industrial enterprise has to divide his capital into two different parts. One part is for acquiring machinery, buildings, raw material, auxiliary products, etc. This part of capital has its value *conserved* in the course of the production process by being incorporated in the value of the finished product. For this reason it is called *constant capital*. The other part of capital goes on the purchase of labour-power. This is the capital that is increased by the surplus-value which the workers produce. For this reason it is called *variable capital*. The ratio between constant and variable capital is called the *organic composition of capital*. The more advanced an enterprise, a branch of industry or a country is, the higher is the organic composition of capital, i.e. the bigger is the share of total capital which is spent on buying machinery and raw material.

The product newly created by labour-power is divided between employers and workers in accordance with the ratio between surplus value and wages. This ratio is called the *rate of surplus-value*: it shows the degree to which the working class is exploited. The higher it is the bigger is the share of the new value created by labour power which is taken by the capitalist. This rate is therefore of the greatest interest to the workers themselves.

But it is of no interest to the employer. *He* is interested in concealing this exact ratio of exploitation, which is hidden behind the exchange of labour-power for wages. What interests the capitalist is the ratio between the mass of surplus value that his business brings him in and the total amount of capital he has advanced: for did he not invest all this capital in order to make a profit on it?

The purchase of machinery is "productive expenditure" for the capitalist only to the extent that the capital laid out for this purpose brings profit, exactly as with the capital laid out for the purchase of labour-power. If it did not, he would not buy a single machine. He therefore looks on the mass of surplus-value produced by his enterprise as a return on his capital as a whole. This ratio is called the *rate of profit*.

If we represent constant capital by c, variable capital by v, and surplus-value by s, we thus obtain the following formulae:

Organic composition of capital: $\frac{c}{v}$

Rate of surplus value: $\frac{s}{v}$

Rate of profit: $\frac{s}{c + v}$

The equalisation of the rate of profit in pre-capitalist society

Under petty commodity production, two kinds of commodities are put on the market: a mass of articles of primary necessity, belonging to producers who work with their own means of production (craftsmen and peasants) and who are thus outside the sphere of operation of capital; and a series of luxury articles and exotic products brought in by merchant capital. In normal times, the articles of primary necessity are sold at their exchange value (determined by the amount of labour socially necessary to produce them); the luxury articles are sold at monopoly prices; i.e. above their value, the merchants accomplishing to their own advantage a transfer of value at the expense of both producers and customers.*

* In mediaeval Europe the price of food was usually fixed in the towns and did not allow big profit margins, except when purchase prices were below value, as was long the case with purchases made by the Hanse towns. In the Islamic Empire, where this fixing of prices was not usual and where the corn trade was more highly capitalised, the alternation of good and bad harvests caused violent fluctuations of prices (and profits). Here are the prices of wheat in Baghdad, in French (Germinal) gold francs per metric quintal and in annual averages: in 960, 29·04 F.; in 970, 12·10 F.; in 993, 163·20 F.; in 1025, 96·81 F.; in 1083, 4·84 F.[70]

For these two commodity circuits to remain separated from each other two conditions were needed. On the one hand, it was necessary that for economic reasons (stability and normal satisfaction of outlets) and also social ones (legislation, defining the conditions of entry into a craft industry) capital should have no access to the sphere of production. On the other, it was necessary that the comparative scarcity of capital and comparative abundance of outlets should make possible the establishing of a series of *parallel monopolies* in the sphere of trade in luxury products. The first condition remained in force right to the end of the Middle Ages. From the sixteenth century, manufacture and domestic industry entered into increasing competition with the crafts, but only with the triumph of the big factory did capitalist industrial enterprise come to produce the bulk of articles of current consumption and so to determine their value.

It was otherwise with the second of these conditions. From the beginning of the fourteenth century, capital engaged in international trade in Western Europe began to outgrow the limits of the outlets to hand. While the big monopoly profits of former days were still to be found in adventurous and distant enterprises (overland trade with India and China), in what Robert Lopez calls "the inner circle" of the international trade of that time, which embraced the whole of Europe and the Near East, fierce competition led on the one hand to increasing costs of purchase at the source, and on the other to considerable reductions in selling prices, and so of profits.[71]

Whereas the Byzantines, at the start, and then the Venetians, had formerly enjoyed real monopolies in the sale of silk and of certain spices, the Genoese, the Catalans, and later the French and Germans, now participated in this trade on an equal footing. Whereas the Flemish master-clothiers had monopolised the trade in cloth, from the fourteenth century the Italians, Brabanters, English, French and Germans broke this monopoly. Whereas the German Hanse had monopolised the trade in herrings, timber and wheat from the Baltic, English, Flemish and especially Dutch merchants were soon to crack open these monopolies.[72]

The fourteenth and fifteenth centuries were thus characterised by a vast ebb and flow of merchant capital, breaking down the monopolist compartments of earlier centuries. This flow of capital made its way towards the sectors in which prices and profits were highest. In this way an *equalisation of the rate of commercial profit* came about, the formation of an average rate of profit which Lopez evaluates at 7 to 12 per cent. Though the sudden increase in profits which accompanied the commercial revolution of the sixteenth century continued for at least a century, commercial competition soon smashed the Spanish and Portuguese monopolies, and the equalisation of prices and profits of luxury articles continued, on a much vaster scale, in the great *entrepôts* and trading centres of the modern world: Antwerp, Amsterdam, London, Venice, Hamburg, Bordeaux, etc.*

The equalisation of the rate of profit in the capitalist mode of production

A similar phenomenon occurred after the advent of the capitalist mode of production. When a new sector of production opens up, capital at first risks itself in this new sector only with circumspection. The first builders of mechanical looms became textile manufacturers and often continued to make their own machines. Capital begins to flow into a branch of industry only from the moment when high profits can be got from it. Thus, during 1820–1830, when the demand for textile machinery was constantly growing, big independent works for making machines were set up in Britain.[74]

In the same way, when, after the Napoleonic Wars, the price of coffee rose steeply in a Europe freed from the Continental blockade, whereas the price of cane sugar declined in face of the competition of beet sugar, many planters in Java, Cuba, Haiti and San Domingo set themselves to replace their plantations of sugar-cane with plantations of coffee. After 1823 a collapse of prices and profits occurred, and the rates of profit on coffee and cane sugar became equal.[75]

The first technician of Portland cement in Germany, M. Bleibtreu, was for ten years the only person to carry on this branch of industry. It needed the boom of 1862–1864 and a profit of 25 per cent per ton to attract other capital, which in turn brought prices down.[76]

The equalisation of the rate of profit in the capitalist mode of production thus results from the ebb and flow of capital, which flows into the sectors where profits are higher than the average and out of the sectors where profits are lowest. The ebbing of capital reduces production, creates a shortage of goods in the given branch, and so leads to an increase in prices and profits. The influx of capital, on the contrary, causes intensified competition in the sectors affected, resulting in a fall of prices and profits. Thus an *average rate of profit* is attained in all the sectors, through competition in capital and commodities.

Under petty commodity production, the producers sell their goods, as a rule, at their actual value (labour time socially necessary to produce them). Under capitalist production, the goods still possess an actual value. It breaks down into value *conserved* by labour-power, the value of the constant capital expended for the production of these

* The Augsburg house of Welser participated in financing the Portuguese expedition to India in 1505, financed another expedition (half-commercial, half-military) to Venezuela in 1527, engaged in the spice trade between Lisbon, Antwerp and South Germany, was a partner in exploiting the silver and copper mines of the Tirol and Hungary, and possessed trading establishments in the chief towns of Germany, Italy and Switzerland.[73] In short, its capital penetrated into every sphere where a high profit was to be obtained.

goods, and value *newly created* by labour-power (variable capital + surplus-value). The value of each capitalist commodity can be represented schematically by the formula $c + v + s$.

Let us imagine three enterprises in different branches of industry: A, B and C. A, let us say, is a *pasta*-making factory, where comparatively few machines are used and a lot of labour; B is a textile mill, where more machinery is used; and C is an engineering works, where even more machinery is used than in A and B. We shall thus have a higher organic composition in B than in A, and in C than in A and B.

Let us now suppose that an average level of productivity and intensity of labour exists and that the rate of surplus-value is the same in the three factories, namely 100 per cent. The value of the production of these three factories could then be expressed like this (each unit representing, say, 1,000 francs).

$$\text{A: } 3{,}000\ c + 1{,}000\ v + 1{,}000\ s = 5{,}000$$

$$\frac{s}{v} = 100\% \quad \frac{s}{c+v} = \frac{1{,}000}{4{,}000} = 25\%$$

$$\text{B: } 4{,}000\ c + 1{,}000\ v + 1{,}000\ s = 6{,}000$$

$$\frac{s}{v} = 100\% \quad \frac{s}{c+v} = \frac{1{,}000}{5{,}000} = 20\%$$

$$\text{C: } 5{,}000\ c + 1{,}000\ v + 1{,}000\ s = 7{,}000$$

$$\frac{s}{v} = 100\% \quad \frac{s}{c+v} = \frac{1{,}000}{6{,}000} = 16.6\%^{*}$$

The rate of profit is thus lowest in the sector with the highest organic composition of capital. This is understandable, since only variable capital produces surplus-value. But the capitalists, as we have seen, are interested only in the rate of profit returned on the whole of their capital. Capital will thus flow towards the sectors with the lowest organic composition of capital, where the rate of profit is highest. And influx of capital means intensified competition, increased use of machinery and rationalisation of work. But these changes lead precisely to an increase in the organic composition of capital. And increase in the organic composition of capital means fall in the rate of profit. The ebb and flow of capital thus tends to equalise the rate of profit in the different branches of production by changing, through competition, the organic composition of their capital.

* This table, like that on page 160, is directly inspired by those used by Marx in *Capital*. Technically speaking, these tables are not quite correct, since they calculate the rate of profit on the basis of the *flow* (in percentage of current production), whereas the capitalists calculate on the basis of the *stock* of capital invested. This distinction between "flow" and "stock" has become current in the contemporary macro-economic techniques: to overlook it would lead to serious mistakes. Nevertheless, it is sufficient to imagine an enterprise which has to renew all its invested capital each year for these examples to become technically correct.

Price of production and value of commodities

Does this mean that a levelling of the organic composition of capital in different branches of industry must actually *precede* the equalisation of the rate of profit? Not at all. Let us look again at our three factories A, B and C, each characteristic of a different branch of industry. The differences in organic composition of capital between these factories broadly correspond to differences in productivity of labour, which we can regard as more or less proportionate to the organic composition of capital.

Let us say that factory B, with its organic composition of capital $\frac{4{,}000\,c}{1{,}000\,v}$ represents exactly the average of the productivity of labour at the given period in the given country. If this is so, then factory A, with a productivity of labour which is lower than B's, is working below the *average* conditions of productivity. From the standpoint of society, *it is wasting labour* (just as a weaver who is too slow wastes labour under petty commodity production). On the other hand, factory C, with a productivity of labour higher than B's, is *saving human labour from the standpoint of society.*

Now, it is the amount of labour *socially* necessary—i.e necessary under *average* conditions of productivity—that determines the social value of a commodity. The social value of A's production will thus be lower than the amount of labour actually expended on producing these commodities, lower than its individual value; the social value of C's production will be higher than the amount of labour actually expended on producing these commodities. Through the competition of capital and commodities a transfer of value and surplus-value thus takes place, from sectors where productivity is low to sectors where productivity is high.

But only what exists can be transferred. The total value of all the commodities cannot exceed the total value conserved and newly created in their production. It is in the redistribution of surplus value between the different sectors that this transfer of value is effected, through the equalisation of the rate of profit. In the example we have taken, the total amount of surplus value produced was 3,000. The total amount of capital advanced (4,000 + 5,000 + 6,000) was 15,000. The average rate of social profit works out thus at $\frac{3{,}000}{15{,}000}$, or 20 per cent. The prices that the commodities A, B and C will fetch on the market will be:

$$\text{A: } 3{,}000\,c + 1{,}000\,v + 800\,s = 4{,}800 \quad \frac{s}{c+v} = \frac{800}{4{,}000} = 20\%$$

$$\text{B: } 4{,}000\,c + 1{,}000\,v + 1{,}000\,s = 6{,}000 \quad \frac{s}{c+v} = \frac{1{,}000}{5{,}000} = 20\%$$

$$\text{C: } 5{,}000\,c + 1{,}000\,v + 1{,}000\,s = 7{,}200 \quad \frac{s}{c+v} = \frac{1{,}200}{10{,}000} = 20\%$$

These prices fetched by the commodities on the capitalist market, consisting of the capital advanced for producing them together with this capital multiplied by the average rate of profit, are called their *prices of production.* The formation of these prices under normal conditions of competition means that each unit of capital appropriates a fraction of the total surplus-values produced by society, a fraction equal to the fraction of social capital represented by the unit of capital in question.

Though the formation of prices of production may cause these to vary considerably from the *individual value* of commodities, this in no way means an impairment of the law of value. It is merely the particular application of this law to a society governed by profit, producing under conditions of competition, with levels of productivity constantly changing. It is precisely through competition that it is discovered whether the amount of labour embodied in a commodity constitutes a *socially necessary* amount *or not*. The fact that, through the competition of capital and the equalisation of rates or profit, a part of the surplus-value produced in branches of industry with a low organic composition of capital is drained off towards the branches with high organic composition corresponds to the waste of social labour that occurs in the former branches. A part of the human labour expended there was expended uselessly, from the standpoint of society, and therefore will not be given equivalent recompense in the process of exchange.*

The operation of the well-known "law of supply and demand" is nothing but an illustration of the same law of value. When the supply of a certain commodity exceeds the demand for it, that means that more human labour has been spent altogether on producing this commodity than was socially necessary at the given period. The market price of these commodities then falls below the price of production.

When, however, supply is less than demand, that means that less human labour has been expended on producing the commodity in question than was socially necessary: the market price will then rise above the price of production.

When market prices fall, profits fall; the capitalists adapt themselves to the situation by improving the average productivity of labour (reducing costs of production), which eliminates enterprises where productivity is too low and brings supply down to the level of demand (which may then rise, when market prices fall to a serious extent). When market prices rise, capital is attracted into the branch concerned,

* Numberless writers, from Böhm-Bawerk to Pareto, have claimed that Marx, after setting out the labour theory of value in Volume I of *Capital*, had to tacitly revise this theory when he tried, later on, in Volume III, to analyse the working of capitalist economy as a whole. It is now known, since the publication of the *Grundrisse*, that Marx had worked out the theory of prices of production not later than 1858, i.e. before he had ever written Volume I![77]

by the high profits obtainable, and production increases until supply exceeds demand and prices start to fall. The working of competition, the variation of market prices around the values (around the prices of production) of commodities, is the only mechanism whereby, in an anarchic society which produces for a blind market, the capitalists can tune in to social needs. But the working of the "law of supply and demand" explains only the *variations* of prices; it does not at all determine the *axis* around which these variations occur, and which remains determined by the labour expended in the production of commodities.

The equalisation of the rate of profit and the distribution of capital and resources between the different branches of the economy in accordance with the needs revealed on the market can take place in classic fashion only if conditions of perfect competition exist at all levels, among buyers, among sellers, and between buyers and sellers.* Such perfect competition has never existed; this is why in the initial period of capitalism there was only an *approximation* to an equalisation of this kind, taking into account the monopoly and semi-monopoly sectors which then survived as vestiges of earlier epochs. Later, when the capitalist mode of production itself reached the stage of monopoly, the equalisation of the rate of profit assumed a new and special form.†

Centralisation and concentration of capital

The equalisation of the rate of profit favours those capitalist enterprises which have the highest degree of productivity. It works against those enterprises that operate with costs of production above the average prices of production. Now, reducing costs of production and increasing the productivity of labour means, first and foremost, improving and adding to the means of production, replacing living labour (labour-force) by dead labour (instruments of labour which are nothing but the crystallisation of unpaid labour). It is therefore the best equipped enterprises, those with the highest organic composition of capital, that come out on top in capitalist competition.

"The industrial employer . . . found himself urged on to new conquests by the pressure of the machine itself. He had to be abreast of his competitors in reducing prices; and this was a perpetual incentive to

* This last condition is *institutionally* put out of the question by the capitalist mode of production so far as the owners of labour-power are concerned.

† The whole problem of the transformation of value into price was examined in great detail, with meticulous calculation, by Natalie Moszkowska: *Das Marxsche System: ein Beitrag zu dessen Aufbau*, a book which appeared in 1929 and which attracted little comment outside Germany. In the next edition of this *Traité* we shall discuss, in a spirit of appreciation and criticism, this contribution of Natalie Moszkowska's to the development of Marxist economic theory.

him both to increase his scale of production and to avail himself of the improved machines that were constantly being produced. There was doubtless . . . an optimum size for any given business beyond which it is could not grow without loss of productive efficiency. But as the optimum was growing larger with very great rapidity, the great majority of businesses were probably well below it and racing to catch up."[78]

The further machine production advances, the higher becomes the organic composition of capital needed for an entrepreneur to secure the average profit. The average capital needed in order to start a new enterprise capable of bringing in this average profit increases in the same proportion. It follows that the average size of enterprises likewise increases in every branch of industry. Those enterprises will be the most likely to succeed in competition which have an organic composition of capital which is above average, which possess the largest reserves and funds for most rapidly advancing along the road of technical progress. Here, as one example among hundreds, is a table showing the increasing size of investments, and so of technical progress, in proportion to the size of enterprises, in West Germany:

Investments in percentages of turnover in 1955.[79]

Enterprises with:	*Chemical industry*	*Engineering*	*Electrical industry*	*Textile industry*
1 to 49 employees	3·4	1·5	—	—
50 to 199 employees	3·8	5·5	5·7	4·2
200 to 999 employees	4·7	6·0	6·1	4·3
Over 1,000 employees	13·6	8·2	7·1	4·8

The evolution of the capitalist mode of production thus inevitably entails a *centralisation* and *concentration* of capital. The average size of enterprises increases uninterruptedly; a large number of small enterprises are beaten in the competitive struggle by a small number of big enterprises which command an increasing share of capital, labour, funds and production in entire branches of industry. A few large enterprises centralise means of production and a number of employees such as were not to be found previously except in dozens or even hundreds of manufactories added together.

In competitive struggle the large enterprises defeat the small ones. These latter produce at prices which are too high, they are unable to continue to dispose of their products at a profit, and they go bankrupt. In periods of crisis and economic depression, failure like this is the fate of hundreds and thousands of small enterprises. Thus, capitalist competition continues that *process of expropriation* with which the capitalist mode of production began. Instead of independent producers as the chief victims, however, it is now the capitalists themselves who have become the object of this process. *The history of capital is the* *history of the destruction of the property of the majority for the benefit of the property of an ever smaller minority.**

What happens to the capitalist entrepreneurs who are crushed by competition? They lose their capital, either directly by bankruptcy or else by the taking over of their property, completely or partially, by the big capitalists. At best, the capitalists who are dispossessed in this way remain as managers, mere employees, of their enterprises. Otherwise, they become under-managers or technicians. If their enterprise was too small, and their connections with the business world were quickly destroyed, they may even become mere workers, in factory or office. This is the *proletarianisation*† of the middle classes, their transformation from owners of capital into mere owners of labour-power. This evolution is evidenced by the following table, which relates to the United States and West Germany:

EVOLUTION OF THE CLASS STRUCTURE‡ IN THE UNITED STATES, IN PERCENTAGES OF THE OCCUPIED POPULATION[80]

	1880	*1890*	*1900*	*1910*	*1920*
Employees of all kinds	62	65	67·9	71·9	73·9
Entrepreneurs of all kinds	36·9	33·8	30·8	26·3	23·5

	1930	*1939*	*1950*	*1960*	*March 1965*
Employees of all kinds	76	78·2	79·8	84·2	86·3
Entrepreneurs of all kinds	20·3	18·8	17·1	14·0	12·4

EVOLUTION OF THE CLASS STRUCTURE IN GERMANY, IN PERCENTAGES OF THE OCCUPIED POPULATION[81]

	All Germany				
	1882	*1895*	*1907*	*1925*	*1933*
Independent (incl. assistants belonging to the family)	48·2	39·1	35	31·2	20·0
Employees	57·2	60·9	65	68·8	70·1

		Territory of Federal Republic only	
	1939	*1950*	*1956*
Independent (incl. assistants belonging to the family)	28·6	26·4	24·8
Employees	71·4	73·6	75·2

* See figures in Chapters 7 and 12.

† This is the scientific meaning of this term, which does not necessarily imply impoverishment in the sense of a lowering of the standard of living.

‡ Strictly speaking, this formulation is not quite correct, as the category of "employees" includes a certain number of managers, engineers, higher executives, etc., who, regardless of their *mode of employment*, belong rather to the bourgeoisie by their way of life, their exact social function, etc.

In France, similarly, employees made up 47 per cent of the occupied population in 1906, 54·3 per cent in 1921, 57·6 per cent in 1931, and 65 per cent in 1953.

When the destruction of medium and small enterprises, especially those of the craft type, is not accompanied by an all-round industrial advance which creates new needs for labour-power, the former owners of means of production, dispossessed through competition, are not transformed into employees but simply thrown out of the production process. They are no longer proletarianised but are completely pauperised. This is what happened at the dawn of industrial capitalism in Western Europe, and later in the backward countries into which capitalist commodities penetrated. A phenomenon of this sort is constantly being repeated on a small scale.

In the United States, the silk industry underwent a remarkable boom during and after the First World War, centred on the small town of Paterson. When overproduction and then the appearance of rayon (synthetic silk) dealt a heavy blow to the silk industry, many workers put out of employment, who had been able to accumulate savings thanks to the high wages they had received in the preceding period, bought second-hand looms and became small entrepreneurs. From 1927 to 1940, however, more than 50 per cent of those enterprises worked continually at a loss. Incomes of six or seven dollars a week were not unusual for these "entrepreneurs".[82] As with peasants owning tiny plots of land, we see here a concealed impoverishment in which the "possession" of means of production conceals the fact that the income obtained is lower even than that of unemployed industrial workers. The "productivity" of this work is so low that this is a phenomenon of *under-employment*, of concealed unemployment.

However, the process of centralisation and concentration of capital is not accompanied by a proportionate disappearance of the middle classes. Many small and medium capitalists withdraw voluntarily from a branch of production when the competition of big enterprises becomes too dangerous, and endeavour to open up new branches. On the other hand, industrial concentration itself gives rise to new activities which are described as "independent". Giant factories surround themselves with numerous repair-shops. They pass on many orders for separate articles or specialised work to small enterprises which can handle this sort of work more profitably.

Finally, the tremendous growth of constant capital engenders a *new hierarchy* in the enterprise, inserted between the old foreman and the general manager: technicians, engineers, chief engineers, production managers, planners, sales chiefs and publicity chiefs, market research staffs, heads of research laboratories, and so on. These are the *new middle classes*, which come into being in this way and whose standard of living broadly corresponds to that of the old middle classes. These new middle classes are distinguished, however, from the old middle bourgeoisie by the *fact that they are no longer owners of their means of production*, but mere employees who are separated from the proletariat in the social sense only by the level of their wages, their traditions, way of life and prejudices.

The tendency of the average rate of profit to fall

The equalisation of the average rate of profit modifies the sharing-out of surplus-value among the enterprises, in favour of the enterprises with the highest organic composition of capital. But if the average organic composition of capital increases for *all* enterprises, the average rate of profit falls, all other things being equal. If, for example, between one decade and the next, the value of annual production grows from 300 million c + 100 million v + 100 million s = £500 million, to 400 million c + 100 million v + 100 million s = 600 million, the increase in the organic composition of capital from 3 to 4 entails a fall in the rate of profit from $\frac{100}{400} = 25\%$ to $\frac{100}{500} = 20\%$. "As a system accumulates more and more productive plant and equipment, the rate of return on new and existing capital becomes depressed."[83]

And increasing organic composition of capital, increase in dead labour as compared with living labour, is the basic tendency of the capitalist mode of production. *The tendency of the average rate of profit to fall* is thus a law of development of the capitalist mode of production.

Here are the rates of profit of American manufacturing industry for successive years.*

	Constant capital		Wages and salaries	Profits	Rate of profit
	Fixed	Circulating			%
1889	350	5,160	1,891	1,869	26·6
1899	512	6,386	2,259	1,876	20·5
1909	997	11,783	4,106	3,056	18.1
1919	2,990	36,229	12,374	8,371	16·2†[84]

Seindl gives the following figures showing the tendency for the pace of capital accumulation to slow down under classical capitalism:[85]

Formation of new business capital in percentages of existing business capital, during a decade:

		%			%
1869–1878	=	3·75	1909–1918	=	2·76
1879–1888	=	4·65	1919–1928	=	2·18
1889–1898	=	4·30	1929–1938	=	0·38
1899–1908	=	3·75			

* Calculated as follows: Value of product-value added = circulating constant capital. Depreciation = fixed constant capital. Value added − (wages + salaries + depreciation) = profit.

† For the evolution of the rate of profit in the epoch of monopoly, see Chapters 12 and 14.

We know that labour power both conserves value and creates new value. When we say that the rate of profit falls we mean that an increasing fraction of the annual product consists merely of the *maintenance* of the value of the existing stock of capital, while a decreasing fraction increases the value of this stock. This fact, established theoretically, is to be found empirically in the following statistics, given by Kuznets, of the annual percentage of American production of equipment which is not destined to replace to existing equipment but to *extend* it:

		%			%
1879–1888	=	57·2	1909–1918	=	43·1
1889–1898	=	57·9	1919–1928	=	36·6
1899–1908	=	54·1			

Kuznets also gives the following figures of the cost of depreciation of existing fixed capital, as a percentage of the gross formation of capital:

		%			%
1879–1888	=	39·7	1919–1928	=	62·4
1889–1898	=	43·0	1929–1938	=	86·7
1899–1908	=	46·5	1939–1948	=	67·8[56]
1909–1918	=	50·1			

However, the tendency of the rate of profit to fall does not work uniformly, from year to year or from decade to decade. Its operation is restricted by a series of factors which work in the opposite direction. *(a) Increase in the rate of surplus-value* = growth in the organic composition of capital means growth in the productivity of labour, which may mean increase in relative surplus-value, and so increase in the rate of surplus-value. If from one decade to another the total value of production grows from: 300 million c + 100 million v + 100 million s = 500 million, to 400 million c + 100 million v + 125 million s = 625 million, the rate of surplus value $\frac{s}{v}$ has grown from 100 to 125 per cent, and in spite of the increase in the organic composition of capital from 3 to 4 the rate of profit has remained the same: $\frac{100}{400} = 25\%$, $\frac{125}{500} = 25\%$.

An *equivalent* increase of the rate of surplus value and of the organic composition of capital is in the long run, however, impossible to achieve, because with the increase in the productivity of labour there often comes an extension of workers' needs and a corresponding increase in the value of labour-power, which in turn encourages the development of the labour movement, thus restricting the growth in the rate of surplus value. We must further mention that the increase in the rate of surplus value comes up against *absolute* limits (the impossibility of reducing necessary labour to zero), whereas there is no limit to the increase in the organic composition of capital.

The breakdown theory (*Zusammenbruchstheorie*) is based ultimately on this incapacity to overcome, in the long run, the tendency of the rate of profit to fall, by way of increasing the rate of surplus value. This incapacity has become a burningly topical question in connection with automation. The inevitability of periodical crises, explained in Chapter 11, also contributes to it.

(b) Reduction in the price of constant capital: The organic composition of capital expresses not the ratio between the *material bulk* of the instruments of labour and the number of workers, but the ratio between the *value* of the means of production and the *price* of the labour power hired. If the over-all productivity of labour increases, the value of each individual commodity declines. This law applies to all commodities, including machinery and other means of production. The growth in the organic composition of capital also works in the direction of a lowering of the prices of machines, and so of the value of constant capital in relation to variable capital, and thus opposes the tendency of the rate of profit to fall.

If, however, all progress in productivity undoubtedly reduces the value of each unit of constant capital, this progress implies at the same time a considerable increase in the number of these units. The value of a machine falls, but the number of machines increases in a bigger proportion, and the value of the total mass of machines thus increases instead of remaining stationary. For example, in the United States the values of producer durables in relation to the national wealth increased from 7·4 per cent in 1900 to 8·3 per cent in 1910, 10 per cent in 1920, 9 per cent in 1930, 8·7 per cent in 1940, 10·9 per cent in 1950 and 11·9 per cent in 1955[87]

(c) The extension of the basis of capitalist production: Through foreign trade, capital brings in raw material and articles of primary necessity at cheaper cost, which reduces both the value of constant capital and that of labour-power, and increases both the rate of surplus-value and the rate of profit. The introducing of the capitalist mode of production into new branches or new countries, where at first a lower organic composition of capital prevails, also counters the fall in the rate of profit.

Nevertheless, the widening of the basis of capitalist production inevitably means an extension of exchange. In exchange for the commodities which the industrial countries import from the backward ones they export thither manufactured goods and capital which end by destroying the indigenous mode of production and introducing the capitalist mode of production. The capitalist mode of production, as it extends and becomes world-wide, reduces the sectors in which a higher rate of profit can be obtained. Though this expansion played a big part throughout a long period in checking or halting the tendency of the rate of profit to fall, its efficacy decreases more and more and it may even produce the opposite effect when the backward countries, industrialised in their turn, compel the advanced countries to undertake a substantial increase in the organic composition of capital in order to stand up to their competition.

(d) Increasing the mass of surplus-value: The steady expansion in the sphere of operation of capitalism, the accumulation of capital, the growth in the number of wage-earners, imply a constant increase in the *mass* of surplus-value. When the fall in the average rate of profit is comparatively modest, this absolute increase is such as to "reconcile" the capitalist to the system. Indeed, the capitalist is not upset by the prospect of making "only" 10 per cent on a billion, instead of 12 per cent on 200 millions. The increase in the mass of profit from 24 to 100 million makes up for the slight fall in the rate of profit. The reduction in the time taken for circulating capital to circulate contributes to a special extent to the growth in the mass of surplus-value.

The value of a commodity under the capitalist mode of production takes the form $c + v + s$. The laws of development of the capitalist mode of production may be represented in the form of relations between the constituent terms of this formula:

(a) The growth of $\frac{c}{v}$ means growth in the organic composition of capital.

(b) The growth of $\frac{s}{c}$ means the growth in the rate of surplus value.

(c) The reduction of $\frac{s}{c + v}$ means fall in the average rate of profit.

But these three tendencies of development appear differently according to whether one considers them from the standpoint of their general historical significance in relation to the development of the productive forces, or else in relation to the *specific form* they assume under the capitalist mode of production.

The increase in the mass of instruments of labour set in motion by living labour in the process of production; the reduction in the part of the working day devoted to the production of mere means of subsistence (production of the necessary product); the reduction of the wealth produced each year as compared with the wealth gradually accumulated by society—these are the general indices of the progress of civilisation, of a high development of the productive forces, in any society at all, including a socialist society.

The specific form in which these tendencies appear under the capitalist order is the *antagonistic form*. The increase in the social surplus product in relation to the necessary product does not lead to a tremendous increase in well-being and comfort for society as a whole, but to an increase *in the surplus labour appropriated by the possessing classes*, in a growth in the degree of exploitation of the working class. The decrease in the ratio between the new wealth created each year and accumulated social wealth does not mean that mankind can live more and more exclusively on this accumulated wealth, it does not mean a constant increase in leisure, but becomes, on the contrary, a periodical source of convulsions, crises and unemployment. The growth in the mass of dead labour in relation to living labour does not mean an ever-greater saving of human labour, but the creation of a vast industrial reserve army, under the pressure of which consumption by the producers remains restricted to the necessary product, and their physical effort is lengthened or intensified. This antagonistic form which is taken by the tendencies of development of the capitalist system is what makes its destruction inevitable.

The supreme contradiction of the capitalist system

All the contradictions of the capitalist mode of production can be summed up in one general and fundamental contradiction, that between *the effective socialisation of production* and the *private, capitalist form of appropriation.*

The socialisation of production under the capitalist system is the most important and most progressive effect of the generalisation of the capitalist mode of production. In place of the fragmentation of patriarchal, slave-owning or feudal society into thousands of little cells of production and consumption, each one independent of every other, with only rudimentary links (particularly exchange links) between them, there has come *the world-wide relationship between men*. The division of labour has become general and advanced not only in a single country but on a world scale. Nobody any longer produces first and foremost the use-values he needs for his own consumption. The work of each is indispensable to the survival of all, so that each can survive only thanks to the work of thousands and thousands of other men. Individual labour survives only as a tiny part of social labour. It is the objectively co-operative labour of all men that makes production under modern capitalism function, or keeps it going. This production is thus objectively socialised, drawing the whole of mankind into its orbit.

The socialisation of production under the capitalist order makes possible an immense development of the productive forces. The growth of constant capital, especially of the mass of machinery and equipment in industry and transport, has been possible only through an extreme development of the division of labour. This prodigious expansion of the productive forces is implicitly contained in the growth of the organic composition of capital, in the concentration of capital, in the increasing extension of the basis of the capitalist mode of production, which tends towards conquest of the entire world. It implies a no less immense development of human needs, a first awareness of the possibility of an all-round development of every man.

But this socialisation of production which transforms the labour of all mankind into objectively co-operative labour is not regulated, directed, managed according to any conscious plan. It is governed by blind forces, the "laws of the market", in fact by the variations in the rate of profit and the working of the equalisation of the rate of profit, the particular form that the law of value takes in the capitalist system. This is why the totality of production, though objectively socialised, develops independently of the human needs it has itself aroused, and is urged onward only by the capitalists' thirst for profit.

The private form of appropriation makes profit the only aim and driving force of production. It causes the development of the productive forces to be uneven and spasmodic. Production develops by leaps and bounds, not in the sectors where the most urgent real needs are to be found, but rather in those where the highest profits can be achieved. The production of alcoholic drinks, of "comic books" and of drugs takes precedence over the struggle against air-pollution, the preservation of natural resources, and even the building of schools and hospitals.[88] In Britain today more money is spent on gambling than on the fight against cancer, poliomyelitis and arteriosclerosis . . . The private form of appropriation of the social surplus product, of surplus value, determines the *anarchy* of capitalist production. Underproduction in one branch regularly coincides with overproduction in another, until general overproduction and crisis bring periodical punishment for the misdeeds of this anarchy. Disequilibrium and disproportion between the different branches of production are the inevitable elements of this anarchy. The distribution of human labour between the different branches of production never corresponds exactly to the distribution of purchasing power for the products of these branches. When this disproportion becomes too extreme, it is resolved by a crisis, which leads to a new equilibrium, itself temporary and ephemeral.

The contradiction between the *de facto* socialisation of capitalist production and the private form of appropriation finds expression as a contradiction between the tendency to unlimited development of the productive forces and the narrow limits in which consumption remains confined. The capitalist mode of production is thus the first one in which production appears to be completely detached from consumption, in which production seems to have become an end in itself. But the periodic crises remind it harshly that production cannot, in the long run, be divorced completely from society's possibilities of effective consumption.

Free labour and alienated labour

The producer in a primitive society does not usually separate his productive activity, "labour", from his other human activities. Thus, this high degree of integration of his whole life is more an expression of the poverty of society and the extreme narrowness of his needs than a conscious effort towards the all-round development of all human potentialities. The tyranny to which he is subjected is that of the forces of nature. It implies a poor knowledge of the natural setting, a degrading subjection to magic, a primitive development of thought. But the effect of this degradation is greatly mitigated by the high level of social solidarity and co-operation. The integration of the individual with society is achieved in a comparatively harmonious way. When the natural setting is not too hostile, labour is combined with pleasure of body and mind. It satisfies needs both physical and social, aesthetic and moral.*

As the productive forces increase, mankind frees itself more and more completely from the tyranny of the forces of nature. It gets to know its natural setting and learns to change this in accordance with its own ends. It subjects these forces to which formerly it was itself doomed to be more or less passively subject. So begins the triumphal march of science and scientific techniques, which will make man the master of nature and the universe.

But mankind pays a heavy price for this emancipating progress. The transition from a society of absolute poverty to a society of relative scarcity is at the same time transition from a society harmoniously united to a society divided into classes. With the appearance of individual leisure for a minority of society there also appears the alienated time, the time devoted to slave labour, the unpaid labour provided for others by the majority of society. As man frees himself from the tyranny of natural forces he falls more and more under the tyranny of blind social forces, the tyranny of other men (slavery, serfdom) or the tyranny of his own products (petty commodity production and capitalist production).

The alienated nature of slave labour does not need to be explained. The slave and the serf are no longer masters of their lives and of the bulk of their time. Not only the free development of their personality but any development at all is closed to them by their social condition. But labour in capitalist society is also alienated labour, it too implies human alienation to an extreme degree.

This alienation appears primarily as a radical separation between labour and all non-"economic" human activities. The overwhelming majority of the citizens of a capitalist society work not because they like their trade, because they fulfil themselves in their work, because

* See, for example, the description of the *dókpwê*, communal labour in Dahomey.[89]

they regard it as a necessary and adequate condition for the development of their physical, intellectual and moral capacities. They work, on the contrary, *from necessity, in order to satisfy their human needs other than labour.* At the beginning of the capitalist system—as still today in a large part of the "third world"— these needs were reduced, moreover, to the almost animal level of subsistence and physical reproduction. As these needs grow bigger and as the duration of working time grows less, the contrast between "time lost" and "time regained" becomes all the more striking and acute.

Alienation is then expressed in the worker's total loss of control over his conditions of labour, over his instruments of labour, over the product of his labour. This loss of control becomes more marked precisely in proportion as the increase of relative surplus-value replaces the increase of absolute surplus-value, as the working day is shortened, but at the cost of a more and more inhuman intensification and mechanisation of this labour.

Shift work, which deprives the workers of the normal rhythm of the succession of day and night, the conveyor belt and semi-automation, the break-up of old skills, the generalisation of detail-work, are so many stages in this process of alienation. At the end of this process the worker is nothing but an insignificant link in two monstrous mechanisms, the machine in the literal sense, i.e. the instruments of labour that crush him,* and the social machine which crushes him no less with its orders, its hierarchy, its commands, its fines and its organised insecurity. With the crushing of the individual is associated the boredom caused by his mechanised work, a boredom which ends by sapping the vitality of the worker at the bench, and to which the office-workers too will be subject in proportion as office work becomes mechanised as well.†

Alienation is, finally, expressed by the all-round commercialisation and atomisation of capitalist society. Everything is bought and sold. The struggle of all against all implies the negation of the most fundamental and most characteristic of human motives: the protection of the weak, of the old and of children; group solidarity; the desire for co-operation and mutual help; love of one's neighbour. All the qualities, aspirations, potentialities of humanity are no longer realisable

* In both the literal (enormous increase in accidents at work) and the metaphorical sense of the word.

† "A hard-working semi-skilled operative learns, after twenty-five years on the job, that the 17-year-old kid next to him, who just quit high school to go to work, is making, within a few pennies, the same hourly wage as he is. And the repetitious arm movement he makes hour after hour is excruciatingly boring. His father, he recalls, was poor, but a craftsman who was proud of the barrels he made. Here the machine has all the brains, all the reasons for pride. Perhaps the rules also forbid him to talk to workers nearby, or to get a drink of water except at the break period."[90]

except by way of acquiring things or services on the market; an acquisition process which capitalism commercialises more and more, thereby levelling and mechanising it. Thus, the shortening of working time is accompanied much less by a growth in humanised and humanising individual leisure than by leisure which is increasingly commercialised and dehumanised.

Recently some Protestant clergymen in West Germany, following the example of the Catholic worker-priests, worked for several months in large factories. On the basis of this experience they have sketched in striking fashion the alienated nature of labour under capitalism:

"The attitude (of the workers) towards labour is usually negative, except for some craftsmen, for whom the skill they have acquired and the experience they are constantly obtaining still play a certain part. As for the rest, they regard work in the factory as a *necessary evil*. His job is the worker's 'enemy', to which he *has to submit* every day for a long stretch, with all that that implies: machines that he must serve; the hierarchy of the enterprise, from the foreman to the management, to which he has been *handed over*, without any possibility of discussion (joint management, i.e. the works council, plays practically no part in our enterprises); but also his fellow-workers, in so far as they themselves are only integral parts of that world which one joins *reluctantly* at the beginning of one's stint and which one leaves *as though escaping* at the end of it . . .

"*The time spent in the factory is regarded as a waste of one's life*.

". . . The mode and form of labour (whether exhausting physical work or merely the watching of mechanical processes) is not so important as its social status, which is likewise expressed, in the workplaces we have come to know, by *the placing of the worker under authority, as the mere object of decisions taken concerning him* . . .

"The worker is undoubtedly, in spite of the trade unions and the works councils, the weakest feature of our economic system: business fluctuations, temporary stoppages and crises find in him their first victim, threatening his job, whereas they can be absorbed without great human damage by the other factors in the production process. *The feeling of insecurity of livelihood* and of *total dependence on an arbitrary process* of evolution of our entrepreneurial economy is nowhere so high as in this social stratum . . . Without any doubt the urgently desirable change in the social consciousness of the workers is conceivable only in conjunction with a real change in their social situation."[91]* [Emphasis ours.]

The class struggle

Never since the division of society into classes has existed have men

* See the analyses, similar in all respects, of the position of the workers in France, in A. Andrieux and J. Lignon: *L'Ouvrier d'aujourd'hui*.

resigned themselves to the reign of social injustice under the pretext that this could be regarded as an inevitable stage in social progress. The producers have never accepted as normal or natural that the surplus product of their labour should be seized by the possessing classes, who thus obtain a monopoly of leisure and culture. Always and unceasingly they have revolted against this order of things. And unceasingly the most generous spirits among the possessing classes have themselves felt compelled to condemn social inequality and join the struggle of the exploited against exploitation. The history of mankind is nothing but a long succession of class struggles.

The dawn of class society was marked by slave revolts. Only the revolt led by Spartacus and the slave revolts in Sicily under Verres are widely known. About the same time, however, there was the revolt of 40,000 slaves working in the mines of Spain, the revolt of the slaves of Macedonia and Delos, and, a half-century later, the great revolt of the miners of Laurium, in Greece.[92] From the third century A.D. a vast uprising of slaves and impoverished peasants spread over the whole western part of the Roman Empire (the movement of the Bagaudae) and North Africa (the Donatist movement). The importance of the part played by these revolts in the collapse of the Roman Empire has usually been underestimated.[93] The spirit that animated them was clearly grasped by the Arab chronicler Abu Zakaria, who wrote as follows about the Donatists:

"They hate the masters and the rich, and when they meet a master riding in his chariot and surrounded by his slaves, they make him get down, put the slaves in the chariot, and oblige the master to run on foot. They boast that they have come to re-establish equality on earth, and they summon the slaves to liberty."[94]

The invasions of the Visigoths in the Byzantine Empire were likewise accompanied by slave revolts, notably those of the miners in Thrace.[95] Later (820–823) a new and terrible revolt broke out in the Byzantine Empire, helped by the poor, which the Emperor Michael II could only crush after three years of fighting.

In the same period, an army of black slaves used by the Arabs to drain the Shatt-el-Arab rose in revolt (868) and held out for fifteen years against the imperial armies. Again, when commercial and manufacturing capital revived slavery overseas in its most abject forms, there were many insurrections, such as that led by Soerapati, in Java (1690–1710), those of the Indians in Bolivia (1686, 1695, 1704, 1742, and 1767) and that of the Black Jacobins of Haiti.[96]

The peasants, crushed by labour-services or land-rent, themselves endeavoured many times to shake off the yoke of exploitation. The entire history of Antiquity—of Egypt, Judaea, Athens and Rome—is filled with peasant revolts against usury, indebtedness and the concentration of property. In the Persian Empire of the Sassanids the fifth and sixth centuries A.D. show the movement of the Mazdakites, who demanded community of goods, abolition of all privileges and prohibition of the killing of any living thing. This is no doubt why historians in the service of the possessing classes call them "barbarians" and "degenerates".

Throughout Chinese history the reigning dynasties were overthrown by revolts of the oppressed peasants. The dynasties of Han and Ming were themselves dynasties established by peasant leaders, who at first strove to combat not only landed property but even usurer's and merchant capital as well.[97] The fourteenth century in Western Europe was marked by "jacqueries" in nearly every country: France, Britain, Flanders, Bohemia, Spain, etc. The sixteenth century saw the development of the great German peasants' war, with comparable social tendencies in the towns, where the boldest revolutionary ideas appeared with Thomas Münzer and the Anabaptists. The history of Japan in the seventeenth and eighteenth centuries was punctuated by a long series of peasant risings against the increased exploitation to which the peasants were subjected as a result of the generalisation of money economy. No less than 1,100 insurrections occurred between 1603 and 1853.[98]

Finally, the small craftsmen, their journeymen and their hirelings, the ancestors of the modern proletariat, rose up against both the lack of political rights in the great towns and their exploitation by merchant capital.* It was not only the craftsmen of the Flemish and Italian cities of the Middle Ages who waged such struggles, but also the craftsmen of the cities of the Islamic Empire, among whom the powerful international movement of the Carmathians had in the ninth century A.D. welded together all the progressive ideas of the age, and which was continued in insurrections by town guilds in Anatolia and Istanbul right down to the seventeenth century.[100] This movement even succeeded in establishing a communist state in Bahrein and the Yemen which survived for over a hundred years (from the eleventh to the twelfth century).

Why did all these movements fail in their attempt to abolish social inequality; either being defeated or else, if victorious, themselves reproducing social conditions similar to those against which they revolted? † Because material conditions were not yet ripe for abolishing social exploitation and inequality.

* The first workers' strike recorded by history was that of Egyptian workers who were working, about 1165 B.C., under Rameses III, at Dehr-el-Medina, on the west bank of the Nile, near Thebes.[99]

† One may quote in this connection the evolution of the Catholic monasteries in which community of goods was at first established, and that of the Czech city of Tabor. When this city was first set up, people had to give up all their possessions, depositing them in "public graves"; but petty commodity production reappeared a few years later.[101]

The absence of classes in man's pre-history is explained by the fact that the social product was there broadly equivalent to the necessary product. The division of society into classes corresponds to a development of the productive forces which already allows of the constitution of a certain surplus, but not yet enough to ensure for the whole of society the leisure needed to exercise functions of social accumulation. On the basis of this inadequate development of the productive forces, the reappearance of social inequality, of the division of society into classes, even where this division had been for a moment abolished, could not in the long run be avoided.

It is the capitalist mode of production that, by the extraordinary advance of the productive forces which it makes possible, creates for the first time in history the economic conditions needed for the abolition of class society altogether. The social surplus product would suffice to reduce extensively the working time of all men, which would ensure an advance of culture that would enable functions of accumulation (and of management) to be exercised by the whole of society. The conscious organisation of labour, already objectively socialised by capitalism, becomes an indispensable condition for a new all-round development of the productive forces.

The development of the capitalist mode of production does not create only the *economic* conditions for the abolition of class society. It likewise creates the *social* conditions. It produces a class which acquires a major interest in abolishing every form of private ownership of the means of production because it possesses none. This class at the same time gathers in its hands all the productive functions of modern society. Through its concentration in big factories it acquires by instinct and experience the conviction that it can defend its lot only by assembling its forces, by exercising its great qualities of *organisation, co-operation* and *solidarity*. To begin with, it uses these qualities to take from the employers a larger share of the new value it creates. It fights for a shorter working day and for higher wages. But soon it learns that this struggle can prove effective in the long run only on condition that the entire domination of Capital and its State is challenged.*

* In *The Town Labourer*, J. L. and B. Hammond describe graphically how in the nineteenth century the State was wholly at the service of Capital. In the areas of Caerphilly and Merthyr Tydfil the only magistrates were two iron-masters who had continually to sit in judgment [!] on their own workers. These same magistrates were responsible for applying the laws which forbade [!] them to employ the truck system. The same writers describe the movements of troops in industrial areas which "came to resemble a country under military occupation . . . ; soldiers were moved about in accordance with fluctuations in wages or employment."[102]

REFERENCES

1. Capt. Elias Joannes: *Staatkundig-godgeleerd onderzoekschrift over de slaverij, als niet strijdig tegen de Christelijke vrijheid*, Leyden, 1742, quoted in R. P. Rinchon: *La traite et l'esclavage des Congolais par les Européens*, p. 139.
2. Jean Yernaux: *Contrats de travail liégeois du XVIIe siècle*, p. 42.
3. R. H. Tawney: *Religion and the Rise of Capitalism*, p. 220.
4. G. Espinas: *Les Origines du capitalisme*, Vol. II, p. 125.
5. Ferdinand Tremel: *Der Frühkapitalismus in Innerösterreich*, pp. 58-59.
6. Espinas: op. cit., Vol. I, pp. 218-19.
7. G. Glotz: *Le Travail dans la Grèce antique*, pp. 104, 223-51.
8. Espinas: op. cit., Vol. IV, p. 263.
9. W. Sombart: *Der moderne Kapitalismus*, Vol. I, p. 37.
10. Otto Hue: *Die Bergarbeiter*, Vol. I, pp. 262-9.
11. Sombart: op. cit., Vol. I, 802-8.
12. J. Dorfman: *The Economic Mind in American Civilization*, Vol. I, pp. 45, 117.
13. Tawney: op. cit., p. 209.
14. Alfred Bonné: *State and Economics in the Middle East*, pp. 155-8.
15. Audrey I. Richards: *Land, Labour and Diet in Northern Rhodesia*, p. 3.
16. J. Kulischer: *Allgemeine Wirtschaftsgeschichte*, Vol. II, p. 186.
17. Ibid., p. 464.
18. E. Levasseur: *Histoire des classes ouvrières de l'industrie en France*, Vol. I, p. 370.
19. A. P. Usher: *An Introduction to the Industrial History of England*, p. 310.
20. 13th Annual Report, U.S.A. Commissioner of Labour, Vol. I, pp. 24 et seq.
21. G. Friedmann: *Où va le travail humain?*, pp. 64-65.
22. Daniel Bell: *Work and Its Discontents*, p. 7.
23. Ibid., pp. 2-3.
24. J. Gouin: in *Revue française du Travail*, January-February 1951.
25. G. Friedmann: *The Anatomy of Work*.
26. Bell: op. cit., p. 17.
27. Friedmann: op. cit., p. 80.
28. P. Sargant-Florence: *The Logic of British and American Industry*, pp. 149-50.
29. Vance Packard: *The Status-Seekers*.
30. R. B. Tennant: *The American Cigarette Industry*, pp. 15-17.
31. W. IJzerman: *De Geboorte van et moderne kapitalisme*, pp. 85-86.
32. G. Jacquemyns: *Histoire de la crise économique en Flandre*, p. 48.
33. A. D. Gayer, W. W. Rostow and A. J. Schwartz: *The Growth and Fluctuation of the British Economy*, p. 239.
34. E. P. Cheyney: *An Introduction to the Industrial and Social History of England*, revised edition, p. 189.

35. Gouin: op. cit.
36. G. Friedmann: *Où va le travail humain?*, pp. 151-3.
37. G. M. Trevelyan: *English Social History.*
38. Espinas: op. cit., Vol. I, p. 165.
39. Jacques Lacour-Gayet: *Le roi Bilalama*, p. 4.
40. F. Heichelheim: *Wirtschaftliche Schwankungen der Zeit von Alexander bis Augustus*, pp. 98-99.
41. International Metal Workers' Federation: *Les plus grandes sociétés sidérurgiques du monde libre*, a study with a preface written for the steel conference held at Vienna between 19th and 21st March, 1959.
42. K. Polanyi: et al., *Trade and Market in the Early Empires*, p. 269.
43. Joan Robinson: *The Accumulation of Capital*, pp. 49, 73.
44. J. L. and Barbara Hammond: *The Rise of Modern Industry*, p. 210.
45. Thorold Rogers: *Six Centuries of Work and Wages.*
46. E. H. Phelps Brown and Sheila V. Hopkins: "Seven Centuries of Prices of Consumables, compared with Builders' Wage-Rates", in *Economica*, New Series, Vol. XXIII, 92, November 1956, pp. 311-14.
47. *Palgrave's Dictionary of Political Economy*, Vol. III, p. 193.
48. J. Kuczynski: *Die Theorie der Lage der Arbeiter*, p. 256.
49. J. L. and Barbara Hammond: op. cit., pp. 199-200.
50. J. L. and Barbara Hammond: *The Town Labourer*, p. 65.
51. M. Dobb: *Wages*, p. 71.
52. A. Perren: *Les primes sur salaires dans les entreprises industrielles*, pp. 38, 43, 73.
53. *Textbook of Political Economy*, German translation of the 1st edition, p. 167
54. Ibid., p. 153.
55. Ibid., p. 330.
56. Ibid., p. 331.
57. *Trud*, 8th July, 1955.
58. John Strachey: *Contemporary Capitalism*, pp. 104-6, *et al.*
59. Roman Rosdolsky: *Der esoterische und der exoterische Marx*, in *Arbeit und Wirtschaft*, November and December 1957 and January 1958.
60. J. Steindl: *Maturity and Stagnation in American Capitalism*, pp. 229-336.
61. J. K. Galbraith: *The Affluent Society*, p. 333.
62. Vance Packard: *The Status Seekers.*
63. Arzumanyan: "*Questions de théorie marxiste-léniniste sur la paupérisation*", in *Economie et Politique*, October 1956, especially pp. 8, 9, 11, 12-13.
64. John Strachey: op. cit., p. 133.
65. Ibid., pp. 144, 146.
66. Ibid., pp. 149-51.
67. U.S. Department of Commerce: *Historical Statistics of the U.S.A., 1789-1939*; *U.S. Statistical Abstract*, 1958.

68. Real product per hour: Frederick C. Mill: *Productivity and Economic Progress*, Occasional Paper 38 of the National Bureau of Economic Research, p. 2. Wages per hour: series published by the *Bureau of Labor Statistics*. Cost of living: series published by Paul Douglas: *Real Wages*, by *Historical Statistics of the U.S.A.*, and by *U.S. Statistical Abstract*, 1958.
69. J. G. Glover and W. B. Cornell: *The Development of American Industries*, p. 659.
70. Aly Mazahéri: *La Vie quotidienne des Musulmans au moyen âge*, p. 213.
71. R. S. Lopez: "The Trade of Medieval Europe: The South", *Cambridge Economic History of Europe*, Vol. II, p. 334.
72. M. M. Postan, "The Trade of Medieval Europe: The North"; *Cambridge Economic History of Europe*, Vol. II, pp. 249-55.
73. Tawney: op. cit., p. 70.
74. Clapham: op. cit., Vol. I, p. 152.
75. Hans Roth: *Die Uebererzeugung in der Welthandelsware Kaffee*, p. 23.
76. Kurt Ehrke: *Die Uebererzeugung in der Zementindustrie*, pp. 16-40.
77. Karl Marx: *Grundrisse der Kritik der politischen Oekonomie*, pp. 338-9, *et al.*
78. G. D. H. Cole: in *Encyclopaedia of Social Sciences*, Vol. VIII, p. 20.
79. *Deutsche Zeitung und Wirtschaftszeitung*, 2nd October, 1957.
80. Figures for 1880–1939, Spurgeon Bell: *Productivity, Wages and National Income*; figures for 1950, *U.S. Statistical Abstract*, 1958. Figures for 1960 and 1965, *U.S. Statistical Abstract*, 1965.
81. *Statistisches Jahrbuch für das Deutsche Reich 1934. Statistik der Bundesrepublik Deutschland*, Vol. XXXVI, section 3, pp. 28 et seq.
82. E. B. Alderer and H. E. Mitchell: *Economics of American Industry*, pp. 431-4.
83. Lawrence R. Klein: *The Keynesian Revolution*, p. 68.
84. U.S. Department of Commerce: *Historical Statistics of U.S.A.*
85. J. Steindl: op. cit., p. 167.
86. Sumner H. Slichter quotes the first figures in *What's Ahead for American Business?*, p. 83. The second series is from S. Kuznets: "International differences in capital formation", in *Capital Formation and Economic Growth*, p. 62.
87. *U.S. Statistical Abstract*, 1958.
88. Galbraith: op. cit., pp. 257-8 *et al.*
89. Melville J. Herskovits: *Dahomey*, Vol. I, p. 64. See the similar description of communal work at Nupe, in Nigeria, in S. F. Nadel: *A Black Byzantium*, pp. 248-9.
90. Vance Packard: *The Status Seekers*.
91. Horst Krockert: in *Die Mitarbeit*, No. 7, 1958.
92. Heichelheim: *Wirtschaftsgeschichte des Altertums*, Vol. I, pp. 630, 642.
93. Robert Latouche: *Les grandes invasions et la crise de l'Occident au Ve siecle*, p. 48.
94. Quoted in E. F. Gautier: *Le passé de l'Afrique du Nord*, p. 259.
95. M. V. Levtchenko: *Byzance, des origines à 1453*, pp. 28-29.

96. Rutgers: *Indonesië*, p. 57; *Handbook of American Indians*, p. 512; C. L. R. James: *The Black Jacobins*, etc.

97. See in *An Outline History of China* the long list of peasant revolts, pp. 44-46, 66-67, 101-3, 122-5, 141-4, 158-60, 166-7, 182-3, etc.

98. Hugh Barton: *Peasant Uprisings in Japan of the Tokugawa Period*, p. 1.

99. Article *"Grèves"* in *Dictionnaire de la civilisation égyptienne.*

100. Louis Massignon: "Islamic Guilds", in *Encyclopedia of the Social Sciences*, Vol. VII, p. 216.

101. Joseph Macek: *Le mouvement hussite en Bohème*, pp. 40-41 and 55-59.

102. J. L. and Barbara Hammond: *The Town Labourer*, pp. 65, 85.

CHAPTER SIX

TRADE

Trade, outcome of uneven economic development

In a society based mainly on production of use-values, merchants' profit arises from buying commodities below their value and selling them above their value. Consequently, at the beginning, trade could not develop between peoples living at a more or less identical level of economic development. In such a case, the approximate amount of labour-time needed to produce the commodities being exchanged is known in both countries. Neither buyers nor sellers would let themselves be drawn into making exchanges which would be extremely unfavourable to them.* Only exceptional circumstances, with the occurrence of sudden shortages of currently needed consumer goods or indispensable raw materials, enable substantial profits to be made through trade under these conditions.

Trade, however, with peoples who are at a lower economic level of development offers ideal conditions for the making of such profits. Raw materials or provisions (metals, timber, wheat, fish, wine) can be bought from them cheap, and finished craft products (pottery, metal utensils, ornaments, textile goods) can be sold them for more than their value. In the uneven economic development between peoples is to be found the origin of the expansion of trade starting with the period marked by the metallurgical revolution and the beginnings of civilisation: *

". . . Inequality and diversity of resources between different societies which are neighbours or which can communicate with each other, the permanent conditions for all exchange, . . . are to be found everywhere on the world's surface, however far back prehistorians go in studying and learning about our ancestors."[1]

Empirically-observed data fully confirm this view. In the first place, they confirm that trade appears in every primitive society in the form of the *foreign trader* come from a more advanced society. The first traders mentioned in the Egyptian sources are foreigners.[2] In ancient Greece, in the archaic period, foreign merchants were the first to appear in the young cities.[3] In the most ancient texts of the *Avesta*, the holy book of Iran, the merchants are foreigners who bring luxury goods

* See Chapters 2 and 3.

for the king and the nobles.[4] In the *Rig-Veda,* the oldest written document of Hindu civilisation, the merchants are foreigners (*pani*) travelling in caravans.[5] Hellenised foreigners were the first traders in Rome.[6] In Byzantium, large-scale trade was at first in the hands of Syrians, Jews and Orientals.[7] In the Islamic empire, the first traders were Christians, Jews and Zoroastrians.[8] Jews and Syrians were likewise the first traders in the Western European Middle Ages,[9] while in the same period the Koreans were the first to introduce trade into Japan.[10] In China, from the Tang to the Ming dynasty, foreigners, principally Indians and Moslems, controlled all foreign trade. The predominance of German traders in Scandinavia, Jewish traders in Poland, Hungary and Rumania, Armenian traders in the Turkish empire in Asia, Arab traders in East Africa, Chinese traders in South-East Asia, continued for centuries this initial phase of large scale trade.

On the other hand, empirically-observed data underline how this same law of uneven economic development implies rapid reversals of the currents of trade as soon as a people acquires the comparatively simple craft technique of petty commodity society, in circumstances where the absence of expensive industrial installations makes it easy to transfer both techniques and technicians. The *metoikoi* from Asia Minor were the first traders in mainland Greece, but soon the Greek colonies came to monopolise trade in Asia Minor, down to the time when, in the Hellenistic epoch, Asia Minor again took its revenge on Greece. Jews, Christians and Persians were the first traders in the Islamic empire; but, soon, Arab traders were playing the chief part in trade in Europe, the Middle East and Persia. In the fifth century A.D. Indian merchants dominated trade in the Arabian Sea; a few centuries later, Arab traders were dominating trade in India;[11] then, under the Mogul Empire, in the seventeenth century, Indian and Persian traders again pushed back the Arab merchants. Jews and Syrians from Byzantium monopolised Italy's large-scale trade in the early Middle Ages; from the eleventh century onward, Venetians and Genoese conquered the dominant place in trade in Byzantium itself.

The history of the Roman empire consists entirely of sharp swings like this. In the second and first centuries B.C., the Roman conquest and the trade which followed in its wake had destroyed the economic preponderance of Asia Minor which had been established since the age of Alexander. But from the first century A.D., Roman trade surrendered the East to the new stratum of Syrian merchants, and withdrew towards Gaul—which, from the second century, pushed back Roman trade in its turn, and shared with the Syrians economic predominance throughout the Empire.[12]

Production and realisation of surplus-value

In the pre-capitalist modes of production, merchant capital is the predominant form of capital. It embodies money economy coming to birth in the midst of an economy essentially based on the production of use values. It makes its appearance in the risky dual form of large scale international trade and local peddling. The more petty commodity production develops, the more producers themselves sell their goods on the market, and no room is left for professional trade except outside this normal circulation of goods.

But the union of production and trade presents technical problems that can be solved only within a restricted framework. The craftsman who himself takes his products to the market has to stop producing while he is travelling; this is why, in a petty commodity society, markets are usually held on holidays. Discussing with Malay fishermen, Raymond Firth noted that as a rule they do not engage in trade on a working day. It is only when not going fishing, for one reason or another, that "one buys fish to sell".[13] To facilitate the petty producer-merchants' journeys to the markets, the Chorti Indians have adopted "the custom of providing food, a bed, and pine torches to anyone, even strangers, who may request them. The giver does not expect to be paid but in turn may request the same hospitality in the future when he needs it . . ."[14] All these customs are effective only if the distance between the place of production and the market is not too big. When the distance increases, the producer finds it too much of a burden to carry his products to the market himself. The craftsmen of Nuremburg in the Middle Ages brought their goods as far as the Frankfurt Fair; but for more distant centres they handed over their products to professional traders.[15]

Professional trade thus appears as the result of a division of labour which spares the producers the losses they would have suffered by interrupting production in order to sell their products directly.[16] Professor Jacquemyns has worked out these losses in the case of the Flemish linen-weavers of the first half of the nineteenth century, who had to go and buy raw material for themselves, in small quantities, in the neighbouring markets, and then to sell their fabric, piece by piece, in these same markets. He estimates them at one-fifth of their small incomes.[17]

Professor Ashton arrives at even more definite conclusions when he studies the situation in the British textile industry in the eighteenth century:

"Generally the [textile] worker had to do his own fetching and carrying [of the products he needed] . . . On the roads of the North large numbers of weavers were to be seen bearing yarn in packs on their backs, or heavy rolls of cloth under their arms. The distances covered were often as great as most men would care to traverse in a day . . . It is said that in the hosiery trade of the east Midlands as much as two and a half days a week might be taken up in getting orders and material, returning finished work, and collecting wages."[18]

Observing a community based on petty commodity production, Professor Sol Tax notes that the producers calculate, in the literal meaning of the expression, the *labour-cost* of the direct selling of their goods to possible customers, and prefer to sell to traders only when the *saving in labour-time* is a real one (when the production which could be carried out during this time lost in selling is worth more than the trader's profit):

"In Panajachel, where merchants come to the farm and bargain for beds of onions even before they are harvested, the farmer calculates his chances of getting more by harvesting the onions, taking them to market, and so selling them at wholesale or retail. In doing so he calculates the value of his time . . ."[19]

The problem arises in the same way when industrial capital takes the place of the independent petty producer, and commercial capital replaces the old merchant. When the production of commodities is completed, the industrial capitalist already possesses the surplus-value produced by his workers. But this surplus-value exists in a particular form; it is still crystallised in commodities, just as the capital advanced by the industrialist is, too. The capitalist can neither reconstitute this capital nor appropriate the surplus-value so long as they retain this form of existence. He must transform them into money. To realise the surplus-value he must sell the commodities produced. But the industrialist does not work for definite customers (except when he carries out orders for the "ultimate consumer"); he works for an anonymous market.

Every time that a production cycle is completed, he would thus have to stop work at the factory, sell his commodities in order to recover his outlay, and only then resume production. By buying what the industrialist produces, the traders relieve him of the trouble of going himself to look for the consumer. They save him the losses and charges involved in interrupting production until the commodities have reached their destination. They, so to speak, advance him the money-capital that allows him to carry on producing without any interruption.

But the traders, who advance to the industrialists the funds they need to reconstitute their capital and realise their surplus-value, must in their turn quickly sell the goods thus bought, so as to begin the operation anew as soon as possible. As the capitalist mode of production spread and commodity production became general, towns and villages were covered with an ever denser network of wholesale and retail shops. Just as the expansion of the luxury trade in the Middle Ages was characterised by the transformation of travelling merchants into sedentary merchants,[20] in the same way the expansion of trade in products of primary necessity, at the dawn of industrial capitalism, was marked by the transformation of the little itinerant hawker into a retailer permanently stationed in the village.[21]*

In the Middle Ages, wholesale and retail trade were not separated so far as products intended for the local market were concerned, and wholesale trade was often completely absent. Specialised retailers begin only with the *mercers*; there were 70 in the whole of France in 1292, 200 in 1570 and 2,800 in 1642.[23] It was after the commercial revolution that the separation of wholesale from retail trade took place as regards luxury products, the big colonial companies keeping only the wholesale trade for themselves.

The industrial capitalist does not only want to *realise* his surplus-value. He further wishes to *capitalise* it, to transform into machines, raw material and wages all that part of it which he does not consume unproductively to meet his own needs. The capitalisation of surplus-value thus itself implies a circulation of commodities in which the industrialist, instead of being a seller, appears as a buyer. In this capacity he is also interested in reducing to the utmost the period of circulation of machinery and raw materials, the waiting period between orders and deliveries. Commercial capital thus does him the twofold service of reducing the circulation-time of his own commodities and also that of the commodities he wishes to buy.

Annual amount of surplus-value and annual rate of profit

The small craftsman who avoids the expenses of waiting and not producing to which he is exposed if he sells the products of his labour himself, thus realises a gain a part of which it is to his interest to hand over to the merchant. The industrial capitalist knows no other gains than the surplus-value produced by his labour-force. Does the reduction in the circulation-periods of the goods he sells and those that he buys increase the amount of surplus-value produced by the workers?

From the standpoint of its circulation, industrial capital comprises two parts. One part of this capital, called *fixed capital*, consists of buildings and machinery which are not replaced until after the lapse of a fairly long period, after a number of production cycles. The value

* In Eastern Europe, in the Balkans and in Russia, these travelling retailers were still to be met right down to the beginning of the twentieth century, together with travelling craftsmen who themselves sold the products of their labour. In the under-developed countries they may still be encountered today, and even in the advanced countries they have not completely disappeared. The *White Book* (1953) of the Belgian Ministry of Economic Affairs shows that the number of travelling merchants who sell from door to door is quite high in the Flemish areas, where the peasants live scattered about the countryside.[22]

of this capital, advanced all at one go by the industrialist, is reconstituted—amortised, or depreciated—little by little. At the end of each production cycle, when the goods produced have been sold, a mere fraction of this fixed capital has been reconstituted. The period needed for reconstituting the whole of this fixed capital, called the rotation period of fixed capital, thus comprises a number of production cycles.

It is otherwise with *circulating capital*, that is, the part of constant capital which consists of raw material and auxiliary products, together with variable capital, the wages advanced by the capitalist. Circulating capital has to be advanced at the beginning of each production cycle. But as soon as the goods produced during this cycle have been sold, the capitalist is back in possession of this circulating capital, and can recommence a fresh production cycle. The rotation period of circulating capital thus breaks down into a production cycle of commodities and a circulation period of these same commodities. Substantially reducing the circulation period of commodities means reducing the rotation period of circulating capital and thus enabling a larger number of production cycles to be accomplished in a given period of time—say, a year.

Let us suppose that in a cotton mill each rotation period of circulating capital comprises two months; one month to produce a given amount of cotton cloth and one month to sell it and buy a fresh stock of raw material. There will thus be six production cycles in a year. By reducing from a month to a week the period needed for selling the cotton goods and buying fresh raw material, the rotation period of circulating capital is reduced to 5·3 weeks, and there will then be ten cycles a year instead of six.

Now, each production cycle brings in the same amount of surplus-value, provided that the capital and the rate of surplus-value remain the same. Increasing the number of production cycles accomplished in one year means increasing the total amount of surplus-value produced in that year. Reducing the circulation time of commodities is thus not only a way of realising surplus-value *more quickly*, it is also a way of *increasing the amount*.

"The quicker the rotation of money-capital in the enterprise the higher is its profitability (its annual rate of profit)."[24]

From the standpoint of the value of the commodities there is no change resulting from the reduction in the rotation period of circulating capital. So long as the production cycle of commodities is not changed, the value of the commodities remains the same. But it is otherwise with the rate of profit on the capital. This rate is not calculated in relation to the production cycle but to the fiscal year. Suppose that the capitalist has installations valued at 1,000 million francs, one per cent of which is depreciated in each production cycle. Further, suppose that in each cycle he has to advance 20 millions, 10 millions to buy raw materials and 10 millions to pay his workers' wages. The value of the production in each cycle will thus emerge as follows, the rate of surplus-value being 100 per cent:

$$20 \text{ millions } c + 10 \text{ millions } v + 10 \text{ millions } s = 40 \text{ millions.}$$

The value of a year's production, after six production cycles, will thus be 240 millions. But when he calculates his annual rate of profit the capitalist does not compare his profit with his *turnover* but rather with his *capital actually expended*: 6 per cent of his fixed capital, i.e. 60 millions, plus his circulating capital of 20 millions, making a total of 80 millions. And as each cycle has brought him 10 millions in profit, his annual rate of profit will be $\frac{60}{80}$, or 75 per cent. If now the number of production cycles in a year is increased from 6 to 10, the capital expended every year increases to ten times 10 million of fixed capital, i.e. 100 millions, plus 20 millions of circulating capital, making 120 millions. The profit will rise to ten times 10 millions, or 100 millions. The annual rate of profit will thus increase to $\frac{100}{120}$, or 83·3 per cent as compared with the previous 75 per cent.

Reducing the circulation period of commodities thus makes it possible to increase the annual rate of profit. Uninterrupted production is an important form of capitalist *rationalisation*; it effectively counters the tendency of the average rate of profit to fall. Japanese manufacturing industry has accomplished a significant rationalisation of this kind since the defeat of 1945 and the American occupation, in order to make up for the loss of the Chinese and Korean markets and the increase in labour-costs (the fall in the rate of surplus-value). The number of rotation periods in a half-year for the whole of the capital invested in Japanese industry (except mining and transport) has increased from 0·66 in the first half of 1936 to 1·54 in the first half of 1950 and 1·84 in the second half of 1951. Whereas, twenty-five years ago, 40 weeks had to pass before the industrial capitalists as a whole had recovered the capital they had advanced, today only 14 weeks are needed.[25]

In order to reduce to the utmost the circulation-time of commodities, this network of shops and businesses is complemented by a dense network of roads, canals and railways. Capital is not merely athirst for surplus-value; it is, further, obsessed with the need to reduce to the utmost the rotation period of circulating capital. This reduction makes it possible *continually to transform circulating capital into fixed capital*, reducing the former in comparison with the latter. This is the very essence of what is called the industrial revolution.[26]

Commercial capital and commercial profit

It is very much to the interest of the industrial entrepreneur that the circulation period of commodities should be reduced as much as possible. This is why he hands over the greater part of all the operations in the distributive sphere (transport, storage, selling and buying at the source, advertisement, etc.) to a specialised branch of capital, commercial capital. For this specialisation to occur, however, it is necessary that capital invested in the sphere of distribution should bring the same rate of profit as the total capital invested in industry. Since commercial businesses need much smaller initial outlay than large-scale industrial concerns, there is much quicker fluctuation as regards entries into and and exits from the sphere of distribution than is the case with that of production. A commercial rate of profit higher than the rate of profit in industry would lead to a flow of capital into trade, a flow which would lower the rate of profit, owing to the increased competition. A rate of profit in trade lower than the industrial rate would lead to an ebbing of capital from the distributive into the productive sphere, an intensification of industrial competition and a corresponding fall in the industrial rate of profit.

Commercial capital thus participates in the general share-out of surplus-value, but without itself producing any part of it. The total amount of surplus-value produced always results exclusively from *production* of commodities, only from the incorporation of unpaid labour in these commodities while they are being produced. Though itself not producing surplus-value, commercial capital shares in the division of the total surplus-value, on an equal footing with industrial capital, because by reducing the circulation-time of commodities it helps the industrialists to increase the total amount and the annual rate of surplus-value. This applies to each branch of commercial capital: wholesale, semi-wholesale, and retail. Commercial profit is thus proportional to the capital invested in trade, on the same basis as industrial profit. Owing to the equalisation of the rate of profit, it constitutes a fraction of the total amount of surplus-value in proportion to that fraction of total social capital constituted by the capital which brings it in.

Suppose that a country's total production is worth 900 billion francs, of which 800 billion represent capital (constant and variable) conserved by labour-power and 100 billion represent surplus-value produced by it. Suppose that commercial capital in this country amounts to 200 billion francs, made up of 100 billion in wholesale trade, 40 billion in semi-wholesale trade and 60 billion in retail trade. The average rate of profit will be $\frac{100}{1,000}$, or 10 per cent. The industrialists will sell the commodities produced to the wholesalers for 880 billion francs, making the average rate of profit, 10 per cent. The wholesalers will sell these commodities to the semi-wholesale traders for 890 billion, so making

10 billion profit, or 10 per cent on their capital of 100 billion. The semi-wholesale traders will re-sell them to the retailers for 894 billion, making a profit of 4 billion, i.e. 10 per cent on their capital of 40 billion. Finally, the retailers will sell the goods to the consumers for 900 billion, making a profit of 6 billion—10 per cent on their capital of 60 billion. At the conclusion of these successive sales, the goods are sold at their exact value: 900 billion francs. No new value has been created in the course of their circulation. Each unit of capital has realised the same average profit, 10 per cent.

It could be claimed that, if commercial capital had not intervened, industrial capial would have made a higher profit, namely, 12·5 per cent. But this would mean forgetting that the total amount of surplus-value, 100 billion, would have been less without the reduction in the circulation-time of commodities which commercial capital ensured, or, what comes to the same thing, that industrial capital would have had to operate with a larger quantity of money-capital, thrown into the production process as the latter went forward continuously, before the commodities of the preceding cycle had been sold to the consumers. In the last analysis, nobody has suffered in the total operation carried out.

In practice, such an *absolute* identity of rates of profit in the different branches of trade and between trade and industry is naturally not found to exist. The variations in commercial profit are many, depending largely on the actual stage of the industrial cycle. In the phases of economic recovery and boom, when prices are rising quickly, stocks can be realised and disposed of with ease, demand exceeds supply, and traders make super-profits in comparison with industry. At such moments, the number of traders rapidly increases. As trade necessitates very much smaller advances of constant capital than industry, many small capitalists can appear, to try their luck in a period of general euphoria. A phenomenon like this was seen in Western Europe after 1945, and in West Germany after the currency reform of summer 1948. But, generally speaking, the rate of commercial profit cannot vary for long from the average rate of profit; otherwise, the industrialists would themselves start to expand their own organisations for direct sale to the public.

Contrariwise, on the eve of and during periods of crisis and depression, the traders are the first to be hit by the fall in sales. Possessing smaller reserves than the big industrialists, and obtaining bank credit less easily, they will be forced to get rid of their stocks at any price, that is, to sell at a loss. The commercial rate of profit then falls below the industrial rate of profit. Through these conjunctural variations the equilisation of the rate of profit in trade and in industry becomes effective.

These conjunctural contractions and expansions in trade can be illustrated by the following figures: in 1929, a year of prosperity, the turnover of the retail shops in the U.S.A. represented 61·3 per cent of the total expenditure of the consumers. In 1933, a year of crisis, it represented no more than 49 per cent. In 1939 it rose to 62·9 per cent, and reached 72·9 per cent in 1945, a boom year.[27]

Commercial capital and labour-power engaged in distribution

At first sight it would seem that commercial capital passes through the same metamorphoses as industrial capital. The large-scale trader launches his enterprise by investing initially a certain amount of money-capital in the form of *fixed capital* (buildings for shops, depots, warehouses) and *circulating capital* (stocks of goods and wages for labour). It would even be possible to talk of the "organic composition" of his capital, since, just as with the industrialist, his fixed and circulating capital have very different rotation-periods.

But there the apparent parallel ends. In reality, the "variable capital" of the trader—the capital needed for the purchase of the labour-power employed in distribution—is not variable at all, since it produces no new value, no surplus-value. The labour-power bought by the commercial capitalist merely enables him to participate in the general share-out of the surplus-value produced by the productive workers.

The concepts of productive and unproductive labour from the standpoint of *production of new value* must not be confused with the concepts of productive and unproductive labour from the standpoint of the general interests of society. When they produce dum-dum bullets, opium or pornographic novels, workers create new value, since these commodities, finding as they do buyers on the market, possess a use-value which enables them to realise their exchange-value. But from the standpoint of the general interests of human society, these workers have done work which is absolutely useless, and even harmful. By recording the arrival and departure of goods in a big shop, or by enabling consumers to choose between different examples of a given commodity, workers employed in the sphere of trade do work which is useful and productive from the standpoint of society's general interests—without, for all that, creating any new value.

Nevertheless, the line separating labour which produces new value and labour which does not is hard to draw. In general, one can say that all labour which creates, modifies or conserves use-values or which is *technically indispensable* for realising them is productive labour, that is, it increases their exchange-value. In this category belong not only the labour of industrial production properly so called, but also the labour of storing, handling and transport without which the use-values cannot be consumed.*

It goes without saying that this does not apply to the storing of goods in the traders' depots, which results from speculation, non-sale, competition, or the trader's mistakes in his estimation of the market. In this case, not only does the commodity not increase in value, it even loses value, because the storage period usually implies a degree of deterioration (real or moral). Similarly the commercial packing of most commodities adds nothing to their value; it represents overhead costs of distribution, included in the outlay of commercial capital on which the latter expects to realise its average profit. But this does not apply to the containers for liquids (milk, syrup, preserved fruit, jam of all kinds) without which these commodities would not reach their consumers. Here it is again a matter of costs which are indispensable for realising the use-value of a commodity, and which therefore add to the value, the price of production, of the latter. Often, these costs actually make up the largest element in the price.

From the trader's point of view, all these outlays, whether used for buying goods or for hiring labour or for renting premises, represent capital on which he has to realise the average profit. The industrialist's position is not the same. He regards as indispensable only those outlays by the traders which make it possible to realise the value of his goods in advance. All the rest constitutes, in his view, extra and useless expense, an increase in distribution charges of which he complains, since it increases the amount of capital which will participate in the share-out of the surplus-value created by his workers. Under the influence of industrial capital, political economy distinguishes the trader's "capital", needed for the purchase of goods, from his "overheads", needed for buying labour, renting shops, etc., "overheads" which are not very flexible and which "uselessly" enhance the price of goods.

It must be added that the "organic composition of capital" is much lower in trade than in industry, and that funds for fixed investments are often lacking. In the United States, insurance companies and building societies often buy sites, build shops on them and then let these to retailers.[29]

The concentration of commercial capital

Like industrial capital, commercial capital is subject to the fundamental tendency towards concentration. In periods of crisis and intensified competition, the big shops which have better reserves and substantial credit resist the blows of bad luck better than the small shop-

* It is interesting to observe that, six centuries before Marx, St. Thomas Aquinas laid down essentially the same distinction between these two forms of "commercial" labour—the one productive and the other not.[28]

keepers who are really working for a modest wage. Similarly, in periods of boom, large-scale traders are able to invest larger amounts, buy bigger stocks of goods and profit to a larger extent from the possibility of realising super-profits. The big shops can sell cheaper because they buy as wholesalers, and are in a position to cut down to a considerable extent the retail profit margin which is added to the wholesale price of commodities where the small shopkeepers are concerned.

"Brokers' fees, wholesalers' commissions, salesmen's salaries, advertising expenditures—all are partially chargeable to the efforts of sellers and manufacturers to find retail outlets for their goods . . . This is the key to much, if not most, of the advantage which the grocery chains have over the independent retailer-wholesaler system. When the function of wholesaling is integrated with that of retailing, it is no longer necessary to 'sell' the retail store."[30]

Other advantages consist in the possibility of using more modern and effective equipment, and of profiting immediately from the creation of new needs for expensive products, in being able to site shops more conveniently, to specialise the staff, standardise goods, rationalise services, and so on.[31] The big shops also received enormous free subsidies for advertisement purposes from the big industrial concerns. For the year 1934 the American "Atlantic and Pacific" chain stores received 6 million dollars for "advertising charges" and 2 million dollars for "advertising commissions", despite the fact that their actual advertising costs did not exceed 6 million dollars![32]

The concentration of capital resulting from commercial competition has taken a variety of forms:

(*a*) *The department stores* which first developed in Paris, through the extension of what were called "novelty" shops (1826: foundation of *La Belle Jardinière*), and then spread in the second half of the nineteenth century throughout all the capitalist countries. In 1852, foundation of the *Bon Marché* in Paris; about 1860, foundation of Whiteley's and Peter Robinson's, then of Selfridge's and Harrods, in Britain; about the same time, foundation of R. J. Macy's in New York (1858), of Marshall Fields in Chicago and of Wanamaker in Philadelphia (1861), in the U.S.A.; in 1881, foundation of Karstadt, and in 1882, of Tietz, in Germany; and so on. Department stores profit especially from an increase in turnover proportionally greater than the increase in capital outlay.[33]

(*b*) *The one-price stores* began in the United States, where Woolworth's was established in 1879. About 1910 a branch of Woolworth's was opened in Britain, about 1925 these one-price stores spread in France and Germany, and in the following decade they spread all over Europe. These stores reduce to the utmost their overheads—less packing, no specialised staff for paying invoices, no delivery to customers' homes, etc.—are able to turn over their capital much more rapidly

(8·4 times a year, compared with 3 or 4 times a year in the French department stores in 1938), and thus realise a higher annual rate of profit.[34]

(c) *The chain stores* are the most characteristic form of concentration of commercial capital. They enable the range of operations to be extended considerably without any increase in the amount of capital tied up in fixed installations. The increase in the rate of profit results in their case mainly from buying cheaper, because on a large scale, and from saving in administration charges.[35]*

The chain stores, which have developed strongly from the end of the last century onwards, have succeeded in absorbing a considerable share of all trade.

In France in 1906 there were 22, with 1,792 branches, in the food sector. In 1936 there were already 120, with over 22,000 branches, or 16 per cent of all the food shops in France.

In Britain the number of chain store firms and the number of their branches has steadily increased since the last quarter of the nineteenth century:

	Number of firms with more than ten branches	*Number of branches*
1875	29	978
1880	48	1,564
1885	88	2,787
1890	135	4,671
1895	201	7,807
1900	257	11,654
1905	322	15,242
1910	395	19,852
1915	433	22,755
1920	471	24,713
1925	552	29,628
1930	633	35,894
1935	668	40,087
1939	680	44,487
1950	638	44,800[37]

Since then, these firms have themselves undergone the process of concentration: their number has declined while the number of branches has gone on increasing.†

* Galbraith, Holton and others point out that in Puerto Rico the turnover per employee increases from 254 dollars a month to 466; 724; 1,061; 1,485 and 1,901 as one proceeds from shops with a monthly turnover of less than 500 dollars to those with one of 500 to 1,000, 1,000 to 2,000, 2,000 to 4,000, 4,000 to 10,000 and 10,000 to 40,000.[36]

† In 1880 there was only one firm which had more than 200 branches; in 1900 there were already 11, in 1920 there were 21, and in 1950 there were 40. The first firm with more than 500 branches had appeared by 1890. In 1910 there were two firms with over 1,000 branches, and in 1950 five firms with over 1,000 (9,695 branches altogether).[38]

In all, the share of chain stores in British retail trade rose from 3 to 4·5 per cent in 1900 and 7 to 10 per cent in 1920, to 14 to 17 per cent in 1935, and 18 to 20·5 per cent in 1950. For certain products, however, this proportion is very much bigger, notably for clothes and footwear, in which it rose from 3·5 to 5 per cent in 1900, to 11·5 to 14 per cent in 1925 and 27 to 30·5 per cent in 1950.[39]

In the United States the chain stores, the most powerful of which is the Atlantic and Pacific Tea Company trust, founded in 1859, accounted in 1929 for 20·8 per cent of the total turnover of retail trade; this percentage rose to 22·7 per cent in 1939 and 30·7 per cent in 1954.[40] The number of branches increased from 8,000 in 1914 to 105,000 in 1950.

We also find in the commercial sector the classical indices of concentration of capital. The number of wage-earners employed in the big shops has increased as compared with the number employed in the small shops. In France the number of wage-earners employed in trading establishments with a staff of more than ten increased from 268,187 in 1906 to 765,293 in 1931, whereas the number of establishments with not more than ten only increased from 517,650 to 631,796. Small and medium shops accounted in 1906 for 66 per cent of all commercial wage-earners, but in 1931 for only 45 per cent.[41] In 1958, 23 per cent of commercial employees were working in enterprises with more than 100 employees—that is, in 0·33 per cent of the total number of shops!

In Germany, commercial enterprises employing more than 50 wage-earners embraced in 1882 2·5 per cent of the total number of commercial employees, in 1895 3·2 per cent, in 1907 8·9 per cent, and in 1925 14·5 per cent.

The turnover of a small number of big stores is equal to that of a very large number of small shops. The census of distribution carried out in England in 1950 showed that in the food sector the 255 largest concerns had a joint turnover of £40 million a year, which was the same as that of 27,000 small shops; 75 per cent of the enterprises accounted for only 35 per cent of the total turnover.[42]

In West Germany, taking retail trade as a whole, 76·7 per cent of small shops (those with an annual turnover less than 100,000 DM) accounted in 1956 for only 22 per cent of the total trade turnover. The 4,447 large or medium-sized firms, 0·85 per cent of the total number of retailers, were responsible for 35 per cent of the total turnover.[43] The tendency towards concentration has been rapid since 1950. It is estimated that in Hanover the share of the big stores in the food trade has risen from 16·2 per cent in 1951 to 19·4 per cent in 1952, 23·6 per cent in 1953, 27·1 per cent in 1954 and 28·6 per cent in 1955.[44]

In the United States in 1954, 65 per cent of the retail shops accounted for only 17·5 per cent of the turnover. One per cent of the retailers (with an annual turnover exceeding a million dollars) accounted for 26 per cent of the total turnover. Among the food shops, 6 per cent of the total, the supermarkets, accounted in 1955 for 60 per cent of the turnover, while the 80 per cent of small shops had only 13·9 per cent of it.[45]

Finally, in Britain, the share of the small retailers in the total amount of retail trade has steadily fallen: from 86·5 to 90 per cent in 1900 to 81·5 to 85·5 per cent in 1910, 77 to 82·5 per cent in 1920, 76 to 80 per cent in 1925, 71 to 76 per cent in 1930, 63·5 to 67·5 per cent in 1939, and 61·5 to 67·5 per cent in 1950.[46]

Though commercial concentration has made enormous progress, especially in this century, the obstacles to such concentration, and especially to complete domination by the big stores, are much greater than in the sphere of production. We have already noted that the small amount of money needed to start a small trading business makes possible the appearance from time to time of new shops, opened by former peasants, craftsmen, or even skilled workers, especially in periods of boom. Sometimes this small-scale trade can be carried on with a tiny return that does not even cover the wages of a worker; the wife, or the pensioned relatives, of a worker seek a modest extra source of income in this field.

Confronted with this tiny profit, the competition of the big store loses its effectiveness, since the use of machines cannot spread in this branch of the economy as it can in industry, to replace human labour-power:

"The highly competitive conditions which prevail in these industries [i.e. the wholesale and retail trades] and the small amount of money which suffices to set up a store result in a rapid influx of new enterprises who just as rapidly drop out again but who have meanwhile operated at a loss, have conducted an inefficient business, and thus contributed toward keeping down the level of productivity in the industry as a whole . . . Some of the persons absorbed must . . . be regarded as having assumed a status of disguised unemployment, judging from the higher rates of mortality of establishments engaged in retail trade and the incomes of large sections of the small businessmen."[47]

The comparative ease of entry into this "capitalist" branch is obviously linked with a frightful mortality rate among the enterprises concerned. Between 1944 and 1945, 21·7 per cent of all the retail shops, 28·9 per cent of all the cinemas and other places of entertainment, 37·2 per cent of all the cafés, bars and restaurants, and 39·2 per cent of all the petrol stations either disappeared or changed ownership, in the U.S.A.[48] About 320,000 enterprises were involved in these two years.

The concentration of capital is accompanied, in trade as in industry, by an increase in fixed costs and, consequently, a tendency for the rate of profit to fall. But whereas in industry this tendency to fall is partly offset by the appearance of *monopoly profit*,* this kind of profit is much harder to realise in the sphere of distribution, where monopolies are rare or non-existent. Thus, the net profits are, in "normal" times, much lower in trade than in monopolised industry. The Harvard Business School estimates them for 1955 at 2·6 per cent in the big stores, 5·1 per cent in the drug-stores, 4·6 per cent in the drapers' shops, 2·5 per cent in the hardware business, and so on.[49] It follows that the expansion of commercial businesses comes up against a profitability barrier, beyond which the concentration of capital leads to a reduction in profit margins. The increase in fixed and overhead costs already obliged the big stores in France to increase their share in selling prices from 25 to 30 per cent towards the end of the nineteenth century to 35 to 40 per cent around 1939.[50] In the U.S.A. this share increased from 27·1 per cent in 1944 to 31·2 per cent in 1948 and 35·2 per cent in 1954.[51] Thereby, the big stores became a factor in relatively raising prices instead of lowering them, and their power to compete with the small shops suffered accordingly.†

On the other hand, the increase in industrial concentration and the appearance of monopolistic trusts in the sphere of production leads to a substantial intervention by these trusts in the sphere of distribution. This intervention takes place not so much by way of establishing big stores as through founding a large number of small dependent businesses (cafés subsidised by the wine, beer and aperitif trusts; petrol stations subsidised by the petrol trusts; motor-car shops, garages and repair shops dependent on the motor-car trusts, etc.). The "heads" of these businesses are really managers appointed by the trusts. But their profit margins are sufficiently small to hinder the concentration of capital. The most striking example is that of the motor-car industry in the U.S.A., where three trusts concentrate over 85 per cent of production, whereas the trade in cars is dispersed among 40,000 enterprises whose profits come, to the extent of 97 per cent from the sale of single items, and 25 per cent of which, on the average, closed down every year before the Second World War.[53] Alderer and Mitchell add judiciously: "The distribution of automobiles is organised so that the burden of competition falls upon the dealers rather than upon the manufacturers."[54]

The ties of dependence which increasingly subject the retailers to

* See Chapter 12.

† This evolution has given rise to a reaction, the appearance of the "supermarkets", which endeavour to reduce their margins by restricting to the minimum the numbers they employ. Nevertheless, these margins remain around 18-20 per cent, and tend to get larger.[52]

the big trusts are also expressed in the spread of resale price maintenance. In Britain, it was estimated in 1938 that 31 per cent of retail sales were made at a price fixed by the manufacturer. In 1955 the percentage was estimated at 55 per cent![55] In West Germany some trusts impose commercial profit-margins so low as 10–15 per cent.[56]

Capital invested in transport

Improvement in the means of transport makes possible a considerable reduction in the circulation period of commodities and at the same time a reduction in their value, as the indispensable costs of transport are embodied in their exchange value. At the beginning of the Middle Ages, bringing back luxury products from the East was a complicated problem and a dangerous business. Transport costs were enormous. Only trade in goods very small in weight and very high in value was profitable.[57] In the sixteenth and seventeenth centuries both sea and land travel was a matter of much time and great risk. This was one of the major obstacles to the development of trade in goods which were both heavy and cheap.

The building of railways and steamships completely changed this situation. Henceforth, every part of the world was more closely linked with the big manufacturing centres than the towns of a single country had formerly been linked together. The establishment of a real international division of labour and a real world market would have been impossible without the prodigious development of means of transport and communication in the nineteenth century.

From the days of itinerant traders, commercial profit and "transport costs" were mixed up together, the latter constituting in fact only a small part of the former and including the subsistence of the merchant himself, his agents and his beasts of burden. Boats, carts, bags were cheap, and their value was replaced in a single expedition. This was no longer so, once the means of transport had undergone their enormous extension, in our own epoch. Railways, vessels that can cross the Atlantic, transport aircraft, all demand substantial outlay. The replacement of this outlay takes effect over a fairly long period. Transport costs thus become fixed charges which are embodied in the prices of commodities, regardless of the stage of the industrial cycle. This compels commercial capital to seek cheaper transport routes for non-perishable goods, even at the cost of considerably prolonging the time these goods spend in transit. In 1933 the cost of transporting grain, per ton-kilometre, varied between 5·50 francs for sea transport to 126 francs for land transport. For coal the figures were respectively, 3·5 francs and 107 francs, and for petrol 4 francs and 210 francs.[58] Commercial competition thus leads capital not to reduce but to extend the circulation period of heavy goods.

Furthermore, the immense investment of capital in the transport sector has given the latter a special dual function in the history of capitalist industry. In the first place, the buiding of means of transport has played a key role in determining the growth of heavy industry; first, railways, and then motor-cars and aircraft soon after, have been its best customers. Consequently, the concentration of capital has been much more radically and rapidly accomplished in the transport sector than in the other sectors of industry. The struggle against the high costs of transport waged by other branches of capital, has generally concluded either with the absorption of the transport sector by monopolistic trusts, whether industrial or financial, or else by the nationalisation of this sector. In the end, the State alone has been shown to be capable of gathering sufficient capital to lower transport costs in the general interest of the capitalist class. Only through the appearance of road haulage on a large scale has medium and even small-scale private capital recently re-entered the transport sector.

International trade

Pre-capitalist large-scale trade was exclusively foreign trade. It drew its strength from the unevenness of economic development as between different parts of the world. With the rise of the capitalist mode of production, international trade attained a volume without precedent. But the nature of this trade changed at the same time as it became general. In former times essentially a trade in luxuries, it now became above all a trade in goods of current consumption, raw materials and means of production. The creation of a unified *world* market cut out, right from the start, fraud and trickery as essential sources of commercial profits. The majority of goods were now sold throughout the world at their actual prices of production. Commercial profits were henceforth deducted from the total amount of surplus-value produced by the workers.

This, however, does not mean that the unevenness of economic development, which continues, and is indeed intensified and worsened by the world development of the capitalist mode of production, has ceased to constitute a source of additional profits, and transfers of wealth from one country to another. The capitalist mode of production, the export of industrial commodities produced by the first great industrial countries, has indeed unified the *world market*. But it is far from having unified *world production*, its technical and social conditions, its average degree of productivity of labour.

On the contrary, the unification of the world market effected by capitalism is a unification of antagonistic and contradictory elements. The gap between the average productivity of labour of an Indian peasant and that of an American or British worker exceeds by far the gap between the productivity of labour in the largest Roman slave enterprise and that of the poorest peasant on the borders of the Empire.

This unevenness of development has become, under the capitalist mode of production, a special source of *super-profits*.

The value of a commodity is the amount of labour socially necessary to produce it. This amount of socially necessary labour depends in turn on the average level of productivity of labour. From the moment that marked differences exist between the average levels of productivity of a number of countries, the value (the price of production) of a commodity may differ markedly as between these countries.

Now, the formation of a world market implies the formation of world prices. As the modern textile industry has not covered from the start, and, in fact, still to this day does not cover, *all* the clothing needs of all the world's inhabitants, part of the human labour expended on making clothes with hand-looms, or by other archaic methods, still constitutes socially-necessary labour on the world market. The value of imported industrial cotton goods will thus be fixed in the backward countries at a higher level than in their countries of origin.

But only *a part*, and a continually shrinking part, of the total human labour expended on making clothes by old-fashioned methods is not socially-wasted labour, that is, actually finds purchasers for its products. This is why the value of cotton goods in the backward countries is fixed well below their local price of production (before the introduction of the most modern production methods).

When they export their goods to backward countries and import from them raw materials, foodstuffs, etc., the industrially advanced countries thus sell goods above their value and buy goods below their value. Behind a seemingly equal exchange "at world market prices", trade between an economically advanced country, possessing an advanced degree of productivity or even a monopoly in the given field, and an economically underdeveloped country, thus represents the exchange of less labour for more labour, or, what comes to the same thing, a transfer of value from the backward country to the advanced country: *

"It has often been said that the European peoples became rich by the impoverishment of other parts of the world, and there is truth in the charge."[60]

International trade is not only a source of super-profits for the advanced capitalist countries. It is also the indispensable safety-valve for the development of capitalist industry. Industrial production expands at a much faster rate than the market in the home countries;

* This explains the enormous profits made by British capital at the beginning of modern capitalism thanks to the notorious "triangular trade"; selling cotton goods in West Africa, where slaves were purchased who were then sold from the same ships in the West Indies, from which in turn these ships fetched sugar and rum to be sold in England itself.[59]

indeed, the contradiction between the tendency to unlimited development of production and the tendency to constant limitation of popular consumption, is one of the essential ways in which the basic contradiction of the capitalist mode of production shows itself. The prodigious development of capitalist industry, above all of British industry, in the first half of the nineteenth century, was possible only because, over and above the national market there was an international market to be conquered which seemed limitless. Exports of British cotton goods expanded with the capitalist mode of production, growing from £300,000 in 1781 to £30 million in 1825.[61] Trade with India grew from 250 million francs in 1820 to over 3 billion in 1880. And the total value of world trade grew from 10 to 30 billion francs between 1830 and 1850.[62]

Costs of distribution

All the expenses of distribution—trade, advertisement, telecommunications, etc.—are undertaken by commercial capital, which shares in the general division of surplus value. So long as this capital is above all ensuring the *increase* in the amount of profit, and the annual rate of profit, by reducing the circulation period of commodities and the rotation period of circulating capital, it contributes, as a whole, to the all-round lowering of prices which is characteristic of the capitalist epoch. The annual amount of surplus value thus increased is in fact transformed into ever more up-to-date industrial plant.

But this role undergoes a profound alteration as the capitalist régime evolves. As the productive forces expand prodigiously, and at more and more frequent intervals come up against the limits of the capitalist market, the essential role of distribution becomes less that of increasing the amount of surplus value than that of *ensuring its realisation.*

This realisation becomes a more and more complicated matter for the total mass of capitalist commodities. It requires longer and longer periods of time. The most frenzied competition dominates it. Stocks of commodities begin to pile up as a regular thing, at all levels, from the manufacturer to the small retailer. They accumulate not just for weeks but for months, and in the case of certain products, for years.*

To the *costs of distribution* which are technically necessary must thus be added the *selling costs* which are determined by the nature of the system, costs which grow unceasingly, making bigger and bigger the price the ultimate consumer has to pay for commodities.†

* Note, however, that these stocks fulfil, *to some extent,* the necessary function of social reserve funds, thanks to which society can face up to a sudden increase in demand, or to the effects of social or natural catastrophes.

† E. H. Chamberlin and Steindl have revealed this difference between distribution costs properly so called and socially determined selling costs.[63]

This increase in distribution costs is expressed first and foremost in the considerable increase in the number of persons employed in the distributive sphere. In the United States trade employed the following percentage of gainfully-occupied persons: in 1880, 10·7 per cent; in 1900, 16·4 per cent; in 1910, 18·9 per cent; in 1920, 21·2 per cent; in 1930, 23·9 per cent; in 1939, 24·4 per cent; in 1950, 24·7 per cent; in 1960, 27·6 per cent.[64]

Harold Barger estimates that 6·1 per cent of the total active population of the United States was engaged in distribution in 1870, 9·9 per cent in 1920, and 16·4 per cent in 1950.[65]

In Germany the proportions engaged in trade were, in 1861 one German in 83, in 1875, one in 65; in 1882 one in 54; in 1895, one in 39; in 1907, one in 30; in 1925, one in 19; in 1939, one in 17·5.[66]

This increase is then manifested in an increase, in the strict sense of the word, in the trade margins in the ultimate selling price. The growth in the general costs and fixed charges of trade is not accompanied by a rationalisation movement such as that which, in industry, accompanies the growth of fixed capital in relation to circulating capital. It is estimated as generally true that distribution costs make up 35 to 40 per cent of the average prices of commodities sold retail in the large capitalist countries.* At the same time, a more and more substantial part of the total available capital is tied up in the various spheres of distribution and in the form of stocks accumulated in the industry itself.

There is no more striking proof of the more and more *parasitic* character that the capitalist mode of production is beginning to assume as it approaches its maximum extension than the more and more limited place occupied by the *producers*, in the strict sense, in certain important branches of industry.

Thus, on 1st July, 1948, there were 2 million wage-earners in the petroleum industry in the United States, of whom only 400,000 were employed in exploration, production, refining and other productive activities; whereas 125,000 were employed in administration and scientific research, 225,000, in transport, 120,000 in supplies and services—in all, about 24 per cent in the spheres intermediate between production and trade. In all forms of distribution and sales, over 1·1 million people were employed, or 55 per cent of all the wage-earners in this branch of industry.[68] Similarly, in the motor-car industry, in the

* For the year 1939 the *Journal of Marketing* estimated at over 50 per cent of the total value added in national production the "value added" by distribution and transport. A recent study carried out in West Germany fixed at 44 per cent (including turnover tax) or 37 per cent (excluding this tax), the element of distribution costs in the prices of all products other than food. For bananas the distribution and transport costs have been estimated in the U.S.A. at 75 per cent [!] of the selling price, the distribution costs alone making up 55 per cent.[67]

same year, there were 978,00 wage-earners in the production sphere, as against 1·5 million in the sale and distribution of cars.[69]

The shift of capital into the struggle not for producing but for realising surplus value becomes a real obsession when capitalism has reached maturity and is entering its declining phase. "The American citizen lives in a state of siege from dawn till bed-time," writes the magazine *Fortune*. "Nearly everything he sees, hears, touches, tastes and smells is an attempt to sell him something . . . To break through his protective shell, the advertisers must continually shock, tease, tickle or irritate him, or wear him down by the drip-drip-drip or Chinese water-torture method of endless repetition."[70]

And a mission from the Belgian Department for Increasing Productivity, made up entirely of executives of capitalist firms, which visited the United States in 1953, summed up admirably the absurd blind-alley of present-day capitalism:

"Production is becoming easier and easier, and perhaps gives cause for alarm [!] by this very ease; it tends to run ahead of effective [!] consumption. Technological unemployment can be avoided only by a continuous extension of consumption, and it is the task of distribution to foster to utmost this increasingly rapid evolution. It is distribution that decides what production will be useful if the consumer buys. 'Why produce if you cannot sell?' It is the last three feet of the course followed by the product on its way to the consumer that decides the success or the failure of the entire production-consumption cycle.

"The great danger at present threatening [!] the economy in several sectors is overproduction. As regards both agricultural and industrial products, the capacity for production is much bigger than needed . . .

". . . The wheels of production nowadays turn at such a rate that the slightest hesitation to buy on the part of the consumer [!] may make the entire economic edifice shake."[71]

Specialists in new techniques, from market study to public relations, including experts in advertising, marketing and motivational research, accordingly strive to avoid or forestall these "hesitations". In 1955 more than 9 billion dollars were assigned to advertising expenses.* This conditioning of the consumer (which makes ridiculous the apology for capitalism as a system which guarantees the freedom of the consumer!) leads to an extreme form of human alienation: the large-scale employment of means of persuasion which mobilise the unconscious, instinctive forces in men so as to cause them to buy, to "choose" and to "act" independently of their own will and their own consciousness! In *The Hidden Persuaders*, Vance Packard has drawn a frightening picture of this conditioning of the masses. He

* In general it is the consumer himself who pays the bill, for advertising costs are included when the cost of production of many products is calculated!

quotes a specialist who declares frankly in *The Public Relations Journal:*

"One of the fundamental considerations involved here is the right to manipulate human personality."[72]

We thus find the contradictions of capitalism pushed to the point of absurdity. Instead of freely distributing the wealth created by the rise in the productivity of labour; instead of making it the foundation for a free development of the human being, capitalism, wishing to keep profit and the market economy under conditions of semi-abundance, is forced to outrage and mutilate people more and more, at the same time the possibilities for their free development are increasing from day to day! The artificial organisation of want amid plenty; the artificial unleashing of passions when the age of reason could be coming to triumph; the dishonest creation of a feeling of dissatisfaction, when all needs could be satisfied; the ever more marked enslavement of man to things (things, moreover, of mediocre quality and dubious value), when man could become the absolute master of matter; this is what the capitalist mode of production has come to, in its most benign, prosperous and ideal form . . .

The Tertiary Sector

Taking up a remark by Sir William Petty, dating from before the industrial revolution, the economist Colin Clark has developed a theory according to which the "tertiary sector" (trade, transport, public services, public administration, insurance, banking, the professions, etc.) is more "productive" than the "secondary", meaning industrial production. According to this theory, the larger the proportion of the active population that is engaged in the "tertiary" sector the higher is the national income.[73] Far from merely serving to realise surplus value, and expressing the increasing difficulties of realising it, the rise in the "tertiary" sector marks an important economic advance by mankind.

We must observe first of all that the definition of this sector (a definition which has been adopted, amplified and modified by the French economist Jean Fourastié, in *Le Grand Espoir du XXe Siècle*, where he writes of the "services" sector) is extremely confused. Colin Clark here lumps together productive activities (transport, public services such as production and distribution of water, gas and electricity) and unproductive ones; useful activities (teaching, health, public administration and accountancy) and others of a much more qualified, or even doubtful, utility (advertising, the armed forces, the police). The militarisation of Nazi Germany, which caused the "tertiary" sector to grow at the expense of the "secondary", was certainly not a sign of economic progress.

The concept of "productivity" is used by Colin Clark in the most vulgar sense, that of "bringing a return". But from the fact that *in a certain social and political context* an expert in motivational research, an admiral of the fleet or a prima ballerina earn more money than an engineer, a miner or a foundry worker it would be mistaken to draw the conclusion that a nation would become richer if all the latter were replaced by the former . . .

Finally, Colin Clark's theory is contradicted by his own statistics. These show that before the Second World War, 34 per cent of the active population were engaged in the "tertiary" sector in Japan, compared with 30·4 per cent of them in Sweden and 33·2 per cent in Switzerland. Yet nobody would deny that Sweden and Switzerland were (and are) more prosperous than Japan. In China 20 per cent of the active population worked in the tertiary sector compared with 16·8 per cent in Bulgaria and 15 per cent in Yugoslavia; yet, despite their backwardness, the latter two countries were nevertheless a lot less poor than China. Egypt and Italy had the same percentage of people employed in the tertiary sector, though an abyss of poverty separated the former from the latter, etc.[74]

Colin Clark's mistake consists precisely in the confusion in his definition of the "tertiary" sector. At least five different phenomena need to be distinguished here, which are moreover *contradictory* in their relation to the economic progress and the average level of productivity of a nation:

1. The *survival* of a mass of small "retailers" and "middlemen" which is merely the manifestation of a degree of under-employment, of disguised unemployment, the absorption of which into manufacturing industry would constitute an enormous step forward economically. This phenomenon explains the inflation of "employment" in the "tertiary" sector in under-developed countries like old China and Egypt.

2. The *specialisation* of certain nations in transport activity (especially maritime) which are in reality productive activities that should be classed in the "secondary" sector. This phenomenon explains the inflation of employment in the "tertiary" sector in countries like Norway, and to some extent Japan.

3. The *backwardness* as regards mechanisation and rationalisation of certain distributive activities and personal services (such as retail trade, insurance and banking, footwear and clothing repairs, hairdressing, beauty parlours, etc.), compared with the mechanisation of industrial production,* which causes employment in the "tertiary" sector

* It is interesting that Alfred Marshall notices the same phenomenon, when he writes of activities in which the use of machinery plays little part,[75] or, still more, when he refers to activities in which the progress of invention has contributed too little to the saving of effort in the attempt to meet a growing demand.[76]

to become inflated as a result of the growth in *industrial* productivity. This inflation of employment, far from expressing the higher productivity of the "services" expresses, rather, their backwardness. But this is, of course, only a *temporary* backwardness; the mechanisation of office work, the appearance of supermarkets, the use of "disposable" napkins and plates, and other phenomena of the same order, make it possible to look forward to a quite different line of development. Further, it must be mentioned, in this connection, that Colin Clark *reverses* the relationship of cause and effect. It is true that the richer a *capitalist* country is, the bigger is the proportion of surplus-value that can be devoted to the purchase of services, the more diversified are the needs of the better-paid workers, and the larger is the proportion of their wages that goes on the purchase of services. It is thus not the development of the services sector that is the *cause* of social enrichment, but social enrichment that is the cause of the development of services.

4. The excessive inflation of the "services" connected with distribution, owing to the increasing difficulty of realising surplus-value in the period of the decline of capitalism. This is an irreversible tendency, but only within the framework of present-day *capitalism*, not that of present-day technique.

5. Finally, the development of creative occupations not linked with the direct production of commodities: pure and applied science, the arts, medicine and public health, education, physical culture, and all the "non-productive" activities connected with leisure. This is the only one of the five phenomena that seems to be definitely and irreversibly linked with economic progress and the rise in the productivity of labour. It means that a larger and larger section of mankind are freed from the obligation of carrying on uncreative work. Here we have not a survival from a dreary past but the harbinger of a wonderful future. When automatic machines will do all the work needed to produce goods for current use, men will all become engineers, scholars, artists, athletes, teachers or doctors. In this sense, but in this sense only, the future is indeed with the "tertiary sector".*

* See Chapter 17.

REFERENCES

1. *Histoire du Commerce*, Vol. III, p. 129.
2. Herman Kees: *Kulturgeschichte des Alten Orients*, Vol. I, *Aegypten*, p. 103.
3. G. Glotz: *Le Travail dans la Grèce antique*, p. 17.
4. F. Heichelheim: *Wirtschaftsgeschichtedes Altertums*, Vol. I, p. 227.
5. S. K. Das: *Economic History of Ancient India*, p. 422.

6. *Histoire du Commerce*, Vol. I, p. 151.
7. G. I. Bratianu; *Etudes byzantines d'histoire économique et sociale*, pp. 137-8.
8. P. K. Hitti: *History of the Arabs*, p. 343.
9. H. Pirenne: *Histoire économique et sociale de l'Occident médiéval*, p. 127.
10. Yoshitomi: *Etudes sur l'histoire économique de l'ancien Japon*, p. 212.
11. N. K. Sinha and A. Ch. Banerjee: *History of India*, p. 193.
12. Rostovtzeff: *Social and Economic History of the Roman Empire*, p. 158.
13. Raymond Firth: *Malay Fishermen*, p. 188.
14. Charles Wisdom: *The Chorti Indians of Guatemala*, p. 25.
15. Alexander Dietz: quoted in J. C. van Dillen: *Het economisch karakter der middeleeuwse stad*, p. 98.
16. J. Kulischer: *Allgemeine Wirtschaftsgeschichte*, Vol. II, p. 113.
17. G. Jacquemyns: *Histoire de la crise économique des Flandres, 1845–50*, pp. 198-200.
18. T. S. Ashton: *An Economic History of England—The 18th Century*, p. 102.
19. Sol Tax: *Penny Capitalism*, pp. 14-15.
20. H. Pirenne: *Périodes d'histoire sociale du capitalisme*, p. 18.
21. J. H. Clapham: *An Economic History of Modern Britain*, Vol. I, p. 220.
22. *L'Economie belge en 1953*.
23. *Histoire du Commerce*, Vol. I, p. 254.
24. W. Steffen: *Die Geldumlaufgeschwindigkeit in der Unternehmung*, p. 42.
25. Japanese Government Economic Stabilization Board: *Economic Survey of Japan, 1951–52*, p. 133.
26. Ashton: op. cit., p. 112.
27. *U.S. Statistical Abstract: Historical Statistics*.
28. Selma Hagenauer: *Das iustum pretium bei Thomas von Aquino*, pp. 28-29; Karl Marx: *Das Kapital*, Vol. III, pt. 1, p. 250.
29. James B. Jefferys: *Retail trading in Britain, 1850–1950*, p. 117.
30. A. C. Hoffmann: Temporary National Economic Committee Monograph No. 35, *Large-Scale Organization in the Food Industry*, p. 67.
31. Jefferys: op. cit., pp. 27-31.
32. Geoffrey M. Lebhar: *Chain Stores in America, 1859–1950*, p. 206.
33. *Histoire du Commerce*, Vol. I, pp. 308-9; J. G. Clover and W. B. Cornell: *The Development of American Industries*, p. 1020.
34. *Histoire du Commerce*, Vol. I, pp. 312-14.
35. Jefferys: op. cit., p. 27.
36. J. K. Galbraith, Holton: et al., *Marketing Efficiency in Puerto Rico*, p. 17.
37. *Histoire du Commerce*, Vol. I, pp. 316-17; Jefferys: op. cit., pp. 22, 61.
38. Jefferys: op. cit., p. 65.
39. Ibid., p. 72.
40. *U.S. Statistical Abstract*, 1958.
41. J. Saint-Germès: *Les Ententes et la concentration de la production industrielle et agricole*, pp. 80-81.

42. *Wörterbuch der Volkswirtschaft*, 1932, Vol. II, p. 285; *The Wholesale Grocer*, September 1954.
43. *Deutsche Zeitung und Wirtschaftszeitung*, 16th April, 1958.
44. Ibid., 30th May, 1956.
45. *U.S. Statistical Abstract*, 1958; S. May and G. Plaza: *The United Fruit Company in Latin America*, p. 63.
46. Jefferys: op. cit., p. 73.
47. Weintraub and Magdoff: in *Econometrica*, October 1940, p. 297.
48. *Survey of Current Business*, December 1945.
49. M. Moreuil: in *Documents de l'Association Française pour l'Accroissement de la Productivité*, No. 109, 15th February, 1957.
50. *Histoire du Commerce*, Vol. I, p. 310.
51. Cornell and Clover: op. cit., p. 1026; Moreuil: art. cit.
52. Moreuil: art. cit.; Mellerowicz: in *Deutsche Zeitung und Wirtschaftszeitung*, 14th December, 1957.
53. E. B. Alderer and H. E. Mitchell: *Economics of American Industry*, p. 157.
54. Ibid., p. 158.
55. Margaret Hall: in *The Listener*, 25th March, 1955.
56. *Deutsche Zeitung und Wirtschaftszeitung*, 14th December, 1957.
57. H. Pirenne: *Le Mouvement économique et social au moyen âge*, p. 38.
58. *Histoire du Commerce*, Vol. I, p. 55.
59. Ibid., p. 55.
60. J. B. Condliffe: *The Commerce of Nations*, p. 204.
61. J. Schumpeter: *Business Cycles*, Vol. I, p. 271.
62. B. Nogaro and W. Oualid: *L'Evolution du Commerce, du Crédit et du Transport depuis 150 ans*, pp. 273, 283.
63. E. H. Chamberlin: *The Theory of Monopolistic Competition*, pp. 117 et seq.; J. Steindl: *Maturity and Stagnation in American Capitalism*, pp. 56 et seq.
64. S. Bell: *Productivity, Wages and National Income: U.S. Statistical Abstract*, 1954, 1962.
65. Harold Barger: *Distribution's Place in the American Economy since 1869*, p. 61.
66. *Wörterbuch der Volkswirtschaft*, article "*Handel*": *W.W.I. Mitteilungen*, 1952, No. 1.
67. *Journal of Marketing*, April 1946; *Bulletin d'Information de l'Institut d'Etude Economique et Sociale des Classes Moyennes de Bruxelles*, August 1959; May and Plaza: op. cit., pp. 40-67.
68. Cornell and Glover: op. cit., p. 265.
69. Ibid., p. 801.
70. Quoted by Daniel Bell in "The Erosion of Work", in *The New Leader*, 13th September, 1954.
71. Report of the Belgian Mission to the U.S.A., 14th October to 26th November, 1953: *Techniques de Vente*, pp. 15-16.
72. Vance Packard: *The Hidden Persuaders*, p. 259.

73. Colin Clark: *The Conditions of Economic Progress*, pp. 397-401.
74. Ibid., pp. 398-9.
75. Alfred Marshall: *Principles of Economics*, p. 276.
76. Alfred Marshall: *Economics of Industry*, p. 155.

CHAPTER SEVEN

CREDIT

Mutual aid and credit

TRADE was born of the uneven development of production in different communities; credit was born of the uneven development of production among different producers within the same community. When cattle breeding or cultivation are carried on as private activities, the differences of aptitude between individuals, the differences of fertility between animals or soils, innumerable accidents of human life or the cycle of nature, bring about this uneven development of production as between different producers. In this way there appear, side by side, farms which accumulate several yearly surpluses and farms which are working at a net deficit, that is, producing less than is needed for current consumption and for seed.

The uneven development of production as between different producers within the same nation does not *automatically* lead to the development of credit. This is not a natural institution but a product of certain social relationships. The private mode of exploitation of flocks and herds, or of the soil, develops within primitive communities which are slowly breaking up. During a long transition period it is combined with labour co-operation. A society based on co-operation does not know credit, but only mutual aid. The better-off members of the community usually come to the help of the less well-off, without expecting to get any material advantages in return for this help. This is still true among several primitive peoples.

Among the Dakotas, a North American Indian tribe, food and hunting equipment are freely lent.[1] In the Indonesian *desa* interest on advances of seed or fruit for planting or loans of cattle, etc., is unknown.[2] The Malay fishermen receive free loans of rice and money from their friends or relations during the monsoon periods, when they cannot go to sea.[3]

When primitive society has been disintegrated to the point where exchange relations and division of labour have become general, the concept of equivalence of values, based on the economy of labour time, replaces the concept of unstinted mutual aid among members of the same community. The more that production of mere use values is ousted by production of exchange-values, the more does the loan charged for replace the free advance made in the spirit of mutual aid.

Among the natives of the New Hebrides it was the custom to advance *food* to members of the same clan without any idea of getting payment in return for such advances. But advances *in the form of shell-money*, or the loan of a canoe to carry on trade with, had to be paid for by gifts.[4] Alonzo de Zurita and Mariano Veytia, two sixteenth-century writers who have left us interesting accounts of the life of the natives of pre-Columbian Mexico, record in the same way that among the Aztecs advances were usually made without any profit being sought. In certain parts of Mexico, however, the custom had developed of obtaining a payment in return for advances in *money* (chocolate-nuts, gold dust, copper discs, jade, etc.). Credit thus separates off from mutual aid at the *periphery* of primitive economic life, in those spheres of activity not directly linked with subsistence in the strict sense.

The ancient custom of mutual aid to ensure the subsistence of all the members of the community was kept up in agricultural societies long after the village community had begun to break up. Lending of wheat without interest went on in China right down to the time of the Chou dynasty.[5] Prohibition of taking interest on loans of corn or cattle is found in the earliest collections of laws: Vedic, Jewish, Persian, Aztec, Moslem.[6] At Susa, in ancient Iran, in the epoch called that of the High Commissaries, interest-free loans continued around 2000 B.C. alongside loans at interest.[7] In the Middle Ages the monasteries gave loans without charging interest.[8] Even in the fully-developed society of petty commodity production in Babylonia which we know from the Code of Hammurabi, "free loans" (mutual aid) for the poor, the sick, peasants hit by harvest-failure, are common alongside business loans at interest.[9]

Today still, "in many indigenous communities (in Latin America) there is a strong tradition of mutual help among independent small landholders and tenants in the granting of small loans without interest."[10] Bauer and Yamey note, similarly, that mutual aid is widespread wherever the "large family system still flourishes, as in India."[11]

The separation of credit from mutual aid thus takes place in the sphere of relations with foreigners sooner than in that of relations within a community. In the Old Testament and in the Koran, this distinction is clearly expressed. The principle of collective payment of taxes by a village, which has survived in all societies where the village community and petty commodity production exist together, represents a special form of mutual aid, preserving the poorest peasants from complete ruin.[12]

The origin of banking

The development of petty commodity production causes the circulation of commodities to be accompanied by circulation of money, and the development of a money economy in the pores of a society based on the production of use values only. This explains the grip secured by *usury* on the producers at this stage of social development. But in a money economy money is not merely the *instrument* of exchange, it also becomes an *object* of exchange. The trade in money separates off from trade in the narrow sense just as the latter previously separated off from the crafts.

At the beginning of money economy, the precious metals were rare and their circulation was limited. They constituted primarily a reserve and security fund for society, and they were hoarded rather than put into circulation. Now, in those disorderly epochs, keeping one's treasure at home meant an excessive risk, especially of confiscation, robbery or destruction. So the custom grew up of entrusting them to the most respected institution of the time, namely, the *temples*. Had not the precious metals, like all objects regarded as precious, had originally a magico-ritual function, which made temples the obvious depositories for important hoards? This concentration of precious metals in the hands of the temples transformed the latter into the *first institutions of occasional credit*, from the first rise of a money economy.

This happened in Mesopotamia, from the first great temple-bank of Uruk (3400 to 3200 B.C.) to the age of Hammurabi (2000 B.C.), when the average rate of interest was fixed by the temple of Samas.[13] In ancient Iran the temples were the first moneylenders,[14] and this was still true in the days of the Sassanids.[15] In Israel, the Temple remained, right to the time of its destruction the chief place for storing movable wealth.[16] In ancient Greece, the temples of Olympia, Delphi, Delos, Miletus, Ephesus, Cos, all the temples of Sicily, functioned as storeplaces for money and as banks.[17] This position remained the same in the Hellenistic epoch.[18] In Rome the Pantheon was the centre of banking.

In the Byzantine Empire the monasteries were, from the fifth century onward, the chief owners of hoards; it took the Iconoclasm of the eighth century to bring these hoards into circulation as money.[19] Something similar happened in China, under the Tang dynasty. The Buddhist temple-banks increasingly monopolised both the stock of monetisable metals and credit operations; the State attacked them, secularised several thousands of temples and monasteries, and had all statues made of precious metal melted down in 843.[20]*

In Japan "the religious establishments . . . were the only places of safety during the Middle Ages, a period marked by civil disturbances . . . People carried on business under the protection of shrines

* Yang Lien-sheng notes that the practice of granting loans on security began, in China and in Japan, in the Buddhist temples. The expression "pawnshops" (*ch'ang-shing k'u*) originally meant "monastery treasuries".[21]

and temples. Some entrusted their precious documents and treasures to these sacred places in order to protect them from the destruction and pillage of warfare. Shrines and temples also acted as financial organs and made loans; organised co-operative credit facilities known by the names of *mujin* and *tanomoshi*; and utilised bills of exchange."[22]

In the period of the Lower Empire, the Buddhist temples were the only banks in the eastern part of Central Asia, where natural economy still prevailed.[23] Finally, in the early Middle Ages in Europe the monasteries likewise appeared as the only credit institutions giving loans *à mort-gage*.[24]* At the beginning of the twelfth century the religious order of the Templars became the first international bank of deposit, clearing and mortgage credit.[25]†

When large-scale trade developed, the precious metals began circulating to a greater extent. Now, as we have seen, large-scale trade was, at the start, above all international trade. This trade thus pre-supposed the simultaneous appearance of a large number of minted coins of different origins and amounts, which had to be exchanged one for another in accordance with their true value. This inevitably led to the appearance of a new technique with money itself as object, the technique of the money-changers. Offering in their turn reliable guarantees to the owners of precious metals who wanted to deposit them somewhere safe, these money-changers and traders in precious metals thus became the first lay guardians of hoards, and then the first *professional bankers*. The word "bank" comes from Italian *banco*, the table on which the money-changers carried out all their operations. Similarly, in ancient Greece, the word for a banker, *trapezites*, comes from *trapeza*, a money-changer's table.

In the ancient world the money-changers were the first professional bankers.[26] This was so in India, too,[27] and in China, where the diversity of coins was not the result of international trade but of the diversity of regional currencies.[28]‡ The money changers became real bankers in Japan in the age of the Tokugawas.[29]

In the Islamic empire of the Abbasids the introduction of a gold standard alongside a silver standard made the money-changers, or

* A loan *à mort-gage* is one where the lender receives as security a piece of land, a house, a mill, etc., from which he draws the revenue until the loan is repaid. This was the chief form of mortgage credit in the Middle Ages, down to the twelfth century, when it was forbidden by a bull of Pope Alexander III, being replaced by the sale of bonds (see Chapter 4). The expression gave rise to the English term "mortgage". It was contrasted with the loan *à vif gage*, in which the revenue from the security (land, or whatever it might be) was set against the debt, gradually reducing it.

† The Templars accumulated their starting capital from the ransoms they extorted from Moslem prisoners.

‡ See Chapter 3.

jahbadh, economically indispensable persons; soon they were fulfilling all the functions of bankers.[30] Kulischer[31] lists the chaotic conditions which determined the appearance of the money-changers in the Middle Ages and favoured their transformation into bankers:

"In the thirteenth and fourteenth centuries there were circulating in France, alongside coins of royal origin, or struck by the great vassals, also Arab, Sicilian, Byzantine and Florentine coins; in southern France, Milanese *libri* and Venetian ducats, in Champagne Spanish *reals*, Burgundian and English *nobili* and crowns from the Low Countries. People everywhere accepted coins minted at Lübeck and Cologne, English *sterling* and French *tournois*. The *grossi* and *ducats* of Venice and the *fiorini* of Florence were the most widespread coins."

The origin of the mediaeval banks has been thus described by R. De Roover:

"The Genoese money-changers specialised first in exchange by hand, but they soon extended their field of action by accepting deposits repayable on demand, carrying out settlements of accounts by transfer in accordance with their clients' instructions, and, finally, advancing loans to their clients on current account. The tables or offices of the money-changers thus gradually became banks of deposit and clearing. In Genoa the evolution was complete before the end of the twelfth century."[32]

The famous Bank of Amsterdam, founded in 1609, owed its formation likewise to the monetary confusion prevailing in those days in the young republic of the United Provinces.[33]

Credit in pre-capitalist society

The first banking operations, money-changing by hand, receiving and guarding hoards, and giving loans on security of land (mortgage loans) were not operations in the "money trade" in the strict sense. Indeed, in the age of the *depositum regolare*, the deposit to be looked after and returned on the mere demand of the depositor, the trustee, far from paying interest to his client, claimed a fee for his services as guardian of the wealth deposited with him.[34] This was still the case with the Bank of Amsterdam in the seventeenth century.[35]*

These operations involved essentially classes of society which were outside the production and circulation of commodities, or only on their periphery. With the development of a money economy, these classes became the classic victims of usury, either large-scale or petty. In the Middle Ages the big international commercial and banking societies practised the loan on security at the expense of kings and

* The practice of charging a small safeguarding rate on hoards deposited reappeared in the second half of the nineteenth century, in the system of safe deposits inaugurated in 1861 by the Safe Deposit Company of New York.

princes, while the more modest Lombards looked after the feudal small fry and the commoners.[36] This was, basically, a form of *consumer's credit*.[37]

The real "trade in money" appeared only in connection with the classes engaged in the circulation of commodities and capital, that is, the young bourgeoisie, usurers and merchants. The development of international trade itself created an inherent need for credit. The separation in time of purchase from delivery;* the separation in space of buyer from seller; the need to transfer substantial sums of money over considerable distances, while the coins concerned were subject to continual fluctuations in value[39] all this gave rise to the need for commercial credit or *circulation credit*. Every society with a developed international trade creates the essential instruments of this credit: bills of exchange and letters of credit. "The negotiation of bills of exchange has its roots in international trade."[40]

We see them appear in 2000 B.C. at Ur in Babylonia, under the Chou dynasty in China (1134–256 B.C.) and at the beginning of the Buddhist epoch in India.[41] In ancient Greece they were in wide use from the fourth century B.C. and subsequently spread throughout the Hellenistic world.[42] From there they passed to Byzantium and the Islamic world from which they made their way back into Europe in the Middle Ages.[43]

The circulation credit provided by these first non-negotiable merchants' bills did not widen the sphere of operation of capital. It only made possible a more rapid turnover and a larger return; when investment credit appeared, that is, the advancing of funds for a business which would bring in surplus value, the sphere of activity of capital was extended; "sterile" money, hoarded money, was transformed into capital and participated in the production of surplus value.

The oldest form of this entrepreneur's credit was the *maritime loan*, the association of a lender with an adventurous captain to carry out an enterprise of maritime trade, a loan which was itself derived from the practices of groups of pirates, as was shown especially in the stipulations regarding the division of profits.[44] From ancient Greece and the Hellenistic world this "loan for a great venture" was passed to the Byzantine and Islamic empires, to reappear from the ninth century in Byzantine Italy and spread from there throughout Europe in the form of *the commenda contract*.[45]

At first, this sort of trading association was confined to a single venture. Later, however, with the transition from itinerant trade to

* "In so far as the Genoese buy wool, paying for it before it is supplied to them, they take care to lower the price they pay . . . They are themselves ready to raise the price by one or two *reals* for each unit of weight, on condition that they pay for it only when they receive the wool, and especially if, for at least half of the bill, there is a further three-months period of grace."[38]

sedentary trade, the *commenda* gave place to *multi-partnership companies* formed for a certain number of years. From the thirteenth century onward, all the big Italian companies (Peruzzi, Bardi, Medici, etc.), were associations of this sort. The Bardi, for instance, were working in 1331 with a capital made up of 58 shares, belonging to 11 partners.[46]

Finally, when international trade became regular and lost its adventurous character, at least in a certain sphere, it attracted a large share of idle capital. This was deposited with the big merchant-banking concerns as *depositum irregolare*, the merchants being authorised to operate with it as they chose, the money not being repayable at short notice, and *fixed interest* being paid on it by the merchants, as a share of the merchants' profit they realised.[47]

The bankers thus became, with petty commodity production, "middlemen between the suppliers of money-capital and the demand for it."[48] Now, at this time, it was not private individuals but the State (kings, princes, communes, etc.) that mainly had need of money. The *public debt* thus developed parallel with circulation credit and investment credit, taking precedence over them.

The oldest known example of public credit is that recorded by the pseudo-Aristotle in the Second Book of the *Economics*: the Ionian colony of Klazomenae, in Asia Minor, lent leaders of mercenaries the means of settling their men's arrears of pay, and covered this loan by a forced loan from its rich citizens, who were obliged to accept iron money in exchange for their gold and silver coins. The annals of Han-chow record that in 154 B.C. a Chinese usurer named Wu Yen-chih had lent 1,000 catties of gold (about 530 lb. or a little under one million gold francs) to the government to enable it to wage war against the "rebellion of the seven kingdoms". He was paid 1,000 per cent interest, or 10 million gold francs.[49]

Public credit soon assumed its classical form by being provided with the *future revenues of the State* as security. In most societies based on petty commodity production, operations of public credit remained rare and risky, and normally ended in the bankrupty of the lenders.

But from the sixteenth century onward, *negotiable bonds based on the public debt** effected a revolution in the history of credit and made it possible to extend considerably the field of operation of capital, by transforming into capital masses of non-capitalised money. Encouraged by the expeditions of the Kings of France into Italy and by the

* "Francis I spent on an enormous scale. In order to have funds, he found himself obliged to resort to a new technique. Turning to the municipality of Paris, he assigned to it 20,000 *livres* of revenue which he collected in the Paris area. The town gave him 200,000 *livres* which it received from its citizens in return for a regular payment of 8 per cent (the twelfth *denier*): these payments were the famous *rentes sur l'Hotel de Ville*."[50]

scattered disposition of the states ruled over by Charles V, public credit became international.

"Credit, after being a mere means of settling accounts, became a value in itself, a negotiable and transmissible object of exchange."[51]

On the Antwerp stock-exchange the obligations of the King of Castile, the letters of credit of the government of the Low Countries and of the Kings of England and Portugal, bonds issued by the great cities of Europe, all were fully negotiable. During the currency upheavals and the disorder of public finances during the sixteenth century, all the old banking houses failed. From this circumstance arose the *modern public banks* which combine the guarantee of the security of deposits which is indispensable for the bourgeois public with the promise to the State that it will be the chief, if not the only beneficiary of these deposits. The *Bank of the Rialto* of Venice, founded in 1587, corresponded above all to the first purpose; the *Bank of Amsterdam*, founded in 1609, added to it the need to regulate the circulation of money. The *Bank of Hamburg*, founded in 1619, united with these functions that of lending to the State. The same applied to the *Bank of Sweden*, founded in 1656, whereas for the *Bank of England*, founded in 1696, it was the last-mentioned function that became predominant.[52]

The remarkable development of international trade after the commercial revolution of the sixteenth century led to a fresh extension of commercial credit. Following the example of the public debt bonds, merchants' bills became negotiable in their turn from the sixteenth century onward, following the practice of endorsement and discounting.[53] At the same time, the development of the colonial joint-stock companies widened the sphere of activity of investment credit. But it was necessary to wait for the development of the capitalist mode of production for credit to pass from the sphere of trade, properly so called, to that of production.

Supply and demand of money capital in the epoch of commercial capital

Thus, with the rise of commercial capital, credit became, from having been an exceptional phenomenon, a regular institution of economic life. The discounting of merchants' bills spread widely from the seventeenth century onward in England, and from the eighteenth century in France and in the big centres of international trade, first for foreign trade purposes, then for internal trade as well.[54] The geographical extension of trade, the long time taken by trading operations with America and the Far East, the concentration of the chief trading concerns in a few big international centres, all favoured this use of trade bills to mobilise capital.

Whereas the bill of exchange had hitherto been only a means of speculating on variations in exchange-rates,[55] it now became a regular means of supplying circulation credit to trade, and also means of short-term investment of "sterile" money capital. In this way a *market for money capital* was developed.

The chief representative of demand on this market was the State, which continued to be, in the epoch of commercial capital, the great, insatiable borrower. Clapham observes that down to the Industrial Revolution the Bank of England carried out the bulk of its credit operations with the King's government.[56] It was the same with the Caisse d'Escompte, founded in 1776, not to mention the ill-starred bank set up by Law, which was sunk by its operations in the sphere of public credit.[57]

Alongside the State, however, other borrowers began to appear. These were, in the first place, the big joint-stock trading companies, whose need for money was enormous for those days and which often had to apply to credit institutions for cover for their needs until a fleet returned to port.

Thus, the Dutch East India Company borrowed money from the Bank of Amsterdam, while, along with the State, the English East India Company was the chief debtor of the Bank of England throughout the eighteenth century.[58]

Next came holders of public bonds (rentiers, nobles, traders and bankers) and the bills of merchants who, needing ready money, discounted this paper. At first the discounting of public bonds predominated, but in the closing decades of the eighteenth century the discounting of private bills began to be more important.

Finally, as in the epoch of petty commodity production, there was demand for money—consumer's credit—on the part of the nobility and the high officials of the State, and this was met by loans on security, the latter taking the form of precious metals, jewellery, deeds, etc.

The supply of money capital came from persons holding liquid capital, principally the large landowners, together with traders who accumulated more money than they could invest in their own businesses. The bankers on the Continent were engaged exclusively in exchange and deposit operations in the seventeenth century and the first part of the eighteenth century, and gave no credit. In England, however, from the seventeenth century onward there appeared the trader who occasionally advanced money to his customers.

With the growth in the circulation of money, the enrichment of society, the parallel development of this demand and this supply of money capital, local private banks began to be formed, about the middle of the eighteenth century, in England first of all, with the function of acting as middlemen between those who were looking for capital and those who were looking for opportunities of transforming into capital their reserves of ready money. These local banks, which normally developed from prosperous trading houses, accepted deposits, issued bank notes and discounted trade bills: this was the birth of the modern banking system.[59]

The Industrial Revolution rapidly expanded this initial network of banks. Whereas in 1750 there were only a dozen local banks, the number had risen to over 200 by the end of the century (even to 350, according to some writers).[60]* The organic way in which these banks developed in the midst of the mode of production of that time is indicated by the example of the house of Gurney, at Norwich, as described in a circular sent by this house itself to bankers on 5th October, 1838:

"The collecting of yarns from . . . manufacturers of the East of England and holding them in stock to supply those who are employed in weaving . . . was a very lucrative business, and we deliberately question whether the Gurneys did not at one time derive from it an annual income greater than is obtained by any bank in the Island of Great Britain . . . In the course of dealing with the worsted spinners for their yarn, this family began to supply them with cash to pay the wages of labour and enable them to carry on their operations in business. Out of these circumstances arose the great banking operations of this family . . ."[62]

This rapid development is explained above all by the uneven development of the different regions of England. The banks in the regions that remained agricultural usually had deposits for which they sought a field of investment,† whereas the banks in the industrial areas were under pressure to furnish credit and were constantly looking for funds. The London money market was born of this situation; it acted as intermediary between the banks with too much in the way of liquid funds and those with too little.

Supply and demand of money capital in the epoch of industrial capitalism

With the Industrial Revolution, however, the market for money capital was greatly enlarged and changed. Alongside supply and demand coming from the pre-capitalist strata of society (landowners,

* On the basis of a study of the records of the private bankers of London at the end of the seventeenth century and during the eighteenth, D. M. Joslin observes that these banks did not as a rule advance funds to traders or entrepreneurs. It was only when, around 1770, some banks were established which included indistrialists among their founders that the first credit operations directed toward industry began.[61]

† Down to the beginning of the nineteenth century rural banks paid commissions to London brokers so that the latter would procure them merchants' bills to discount.[63] This shows how scarce and sought-after were fields for the short-term investment of capital!

traders, craftsmen, civil servants, rentiers, etc.) appeared supply and demand arising from the mechanism of capitalist production itself.

Money capital is the starting point and the finishing point of the rotation of capital. But it does not appear only at the beginning and the end of this process of rotation. Constantly, during the production process itself, money capital is eliminated from the process and turned into money which is "unproductive" from the capitalist's point of view. And, also constantly, a demand for *additional* money capital arises from the entrepreneurs, to enable them to achieve the investment of their own capital in the most profitable way.

The money capital needed to renew the fixed capital of an enterprise is not accumulated until several years and several rotation cycles of circulating capital have passed. This *depreciation fund*, unless it be used meanwhile for other purposes, will lie "unproductive" during this period. The *wages fund* of a big enterprise, advanced at the beginning of each production-cycle, would remain unproductive to the extent that this production-cycle was longer than a month (for employees paid monthly) or even a week (for those paid weekly). The share of the annual profit put aside by the capitalist for his own consumer needs (*unproductive consumption fund*) is expended only during the course of an entire year, so that a large part of it will remain unproductive for a large part of the year. The *accumulation fund* of the enterprise, the share of the profits which is reinvested in the business, is not used in its entirety right from the start of a fresh production-cycle. The capitalist will await the favourable moment, for instance, a good market conjuncture, before investing these profits. There we have four sources of money capital temporarily excluded from the production process and so made unproductive.

On the other hand, the renewal of fixed capital does not take place exactly at the moment when the necessary depreciation funds have been accumulated. Necessitating as it does the involvement of substantial amounts of capital, and entailing very large risks, this renewal will be effected, for preference, at particular moments of the economic cycle, when the capitalists expect a significant expansion of the market.[64] If a certain capitalist has not yet accumulated the depreciation (and accumulation) fund by this precise moment, he will have to try and borrow the capital he needs, so as not to let slip this opportune occasion. The capitalist who has at his disposal a technical invention which would enable him to expand his market at the expense of his competitors is in a similar situation if he lacks the capital needed to exploit this invention.[65]

At certain moments of the economic cycle, the industrialist knows that any increase of production whatsoever can be absorbed by the market. That is the moment when he needs to get his capital together and invest his profits. If he has not yet realised his profits, he will have to borrow so as to be able to invest them in advance.

Finally, the recovery of production, after the close of a production cycle, should in theory begin as soon as the circulation cycle of commodities has concluded. But, as we have seen, the amount and annual rate of profit depend on the number of annual production-cycles, and so on the industrialist's capacity to resume production *before* his circulating capital, invested in commodities which have been produced but not yet sold, has come back to him. For this purpose, too, he will seek to borrow additional money capital, which he will be able to repay as soon as he has received the money from the sale of his goods.

The function of credit institutions under capitalism is to fulfil the same role of intermediary between those who hold unproductive sums of money and those who are looking for opportunities to increase their own capital with the aid of borrowed capital. The pre-capitalist relationship between bank capital and the other forms of capital is thus reversed; in the capitalist mode of production, bank capital begins as a subordinate servant of industrial capital. But whereas the separation of the modern capitalist trader from the capitalist industrialist is only a question of functional division of labour, the separation of the capitalist banker from the capitalist industrialist or trader is inevitable from the very first appearance of the capitalist mode of production.

Contrary to the industrialist and the trader, the banker has in fact to play a social role *directly*. He is useful to the capitalist mode of production only to the extent that he can overcome the fragmentation of social capital into a multitude of individual properties. It is in this function of *mobiliser and centraliser of social capital* that his whole importance to society consists. This function goes beyond the class limits of the bourgeoisie in the strict sense and embraces the centralisation of the funds saved by landowners, rich and middle peasants, craftsmen, civil servants, technicians, and even skilled workers in prosperous periods.

"[By about 1875] the organisation by which all free British capital was sucked into the London money market was functioning almost perfectly. Compared with other national organisations, or lacks of organisation, it had been highly efficient even twenty years earlier. In the interval, Scottish and provincial branch banking had drawn in almost the last of those rustic hoards which country folk had kept 'in their desks and cupboards'; and a smooth open channel had been cut, down which the northern surpluses flowed South. The channels from East Anglia, the South-West, and rural England generally, had been cut long before . . . From Town, what was not used there ran out into the industrial districts, by way of the discount or re-discount of manufacturers and merchants' bills. These were the greatest days of the London bill-brokers, the Lombard Street houses."[66]

At the same time the market for money capital became more and more specialised, and two distinct markets came into being:

(1) The money market, the supply and demand of *short-term credit*, dominated by the banks, except in England, where the bill brokers have long played a predominant part, and (2) The finance market, the supply and demand of *long-term credit*, at first dominated by the banks and the stock-exchange, joined in the twentieth century by the insurance companies, the savings banks, the building societies and other organisations of institutional saving (pension funds, health insurance funds, semi-public institutions, etc.), which seek to transform into capital (often without any profit to the owner)* all money income not immediately spent. The centralisation of money capital thus attains its highest, perfected phase; the banks "allow no sum of money to remain unproductive".

Interest and rate of interest

Like the profit on usurer's capital with which it is identified in its beginnings, interest is at the time of its first appearance in the economy only a *displacement* of value from debtor to creditor. When a peasant has to borrow X amount of wheat in order to survive till the next harvest, and when he then has to deduct from this harvest X + Y amount of wheat in order to repay his creditor, the total amount of wheat in the possession of these two people will not have increased owing to the loan. An amount Y will merely have been transferred from the debtor to the creditor. This form of usury, which is far from having disappeared, permanently impoverishes its victims and enslaves them to their creditors:

"In Cochin-China the farmer, or *ta dien*, borrows from his landowner the means of feeding himself and his family until the harvest; when the harvest is in it is usually not big enough to release him from his debt, and the *ta dien* remains tied to the land by his debt no less surely than a mediaeval serf was tied by custom."[67]

This is no longer true with circulation and investment credit in capitalist society. The advancing of funds no longer has for its aim the survival of the debtor, but is intended to *enable him to realise a profit*:

"Business will pay a positive interest if a present sum can be so used in commerce and industry as to yield a greater sum in future" [i.e. the sum borrowed, plus a surplus value, a profit.][68]

"It is a well-recognised principle . . . that in the last analysis the

* This is in particular the case with the funds of the savings banks and the social insurance funds, which are used to finance the State's expenditure. See Chapter 13, section "War Economy".

money rate of interest depends upon the supply of and demand for *real capital* . . . that the rate of interest is regulated by the profits from the employment of capital itself . . ."[69]

Circulation credit is intended to realise in advance the value of commodities already produced: investment credit has for its purpose to increase the capital of an enterprise. In both cases the amount of surplus value increases, either by reduction in the rotation-time or by growth in the amount of capital. The interest is thus nothing but *a fraction of the extra surplus-value obtained through the borrowing of capital*. It is lower than the profit,* because if it were equal to the latter there would normally be no advantage in borrowing, since the capital borrowed is expected itself to bring in the average profit. The creditor is satisfied, because before he lent his capital it was "lying idle" and bringing no return. And the debtor is also satisfied because, though he has to surrender interest to the creditor, he still makes more than if he had borrowed nothing.

The interest paid by a capitalist entrepreneur for the borrowing of capital is a fraction of the total surplus value produced by his workers, a fraction surrendered by the entrepreneur because the loan has enabled him to increase this total surplus-value by an amount greater than the interest due. But with the generalisation of the capitalist mode of production every entrepreneur is on the look-out for additional capital. At the same time, the socially-centralising function of the banks enables *every* sum of money to be transformed into additional money-capital. Thus, by the working of supply and demand in relation to money capital the *average rate of interest* is constituted, the "normal return" on every sum of money which is not "lying idle". This, needless to say, has nothing to do with the "intrinsic qualities" of the money, but represents the outcome of definite relations of production, which enable this sum of money to be *capitalised*, so that it may appropriate a fraction of the surplus value produced by the totality of workers in the given society. From this basis the habit spreads in bourgeois society of regarding all income as the income on an imaginary capital, capitalised at the average rate of interest: † "With the growth of capitalist mentality an obviously useful habit has developed, the beginnings of which are in Germany, for instance, observable since the fourteenth century, of expressing any returns,

* Except in the backward countries, where the rate of interest also includes part of the ground rent. It thus exceeds the rate of profit on merchant capital, which is what explains the predominance of usurer's capital in these countries. The *New York Times* reported in 1955 the case of a laundryman of Karachi (Pakistan) who paid 3,925 rupees in interest on a loan of 100 rupees, at the rate of 25 per cent a month, or 300 per cent a year, for 13 years and one month.[70]

† An income of £500, when the average rate of interest is 5 per cent, would be regarded as the return on an assumed capital of £10,000.

except returns to personal services, as a percentage of a capital value."[71]

This habit has led bourgeois economists to the idea of similarly separating, in the case of a capitalist entrepreneur who operates with his own capital only, the interest on his capital and the entrepreneur's profit (called "a sort of rent" by some writers, such as Marshall) which is left when this interest is deducted from the total profit. This is obviously an "ideological" operation, that is, a fictitious one, since any entrepreneur expects to obtain on his capital not the average rate of interest but the average rate of profit. This practice is all the more useful for bourgeois economists in that it enables them to dodge the problem of profit, that is, of exploitation, and replace in their systems all theory of profit by a simple theory of interest.*

The credit organisations do not fulfil their function, as intermediaries between those who have money capital to offer and those who want it, out of pure altruism. They, too, operate with a capital of their own which must bring in the average rate of profit. Their profit appears in the form of *banker's profit*, which consists mainly in the difference between the rate of interest paid by these institutions for money entrusted to them on deposit and the rate of interest they exact from those to whom they grant credit. To this must be added other income derived from, e.g. commission and brokerage for making investments, carrying out exchange transactions, etc.

As credit institutions, the banks especially, pay interest (even though very little) on every sum of money deposited with them, even for a few days (current accounts), it is to their advantage to lend out in their turn all the money at their disposal, so that these transactions may end in a profitable balance for them. Thus there appears on the money market, alongside circulation credit in the strict sense, *day-to-day credit* ("call money"). It began in England in 1830, when, on the eve of the quarterly payments of interest on government stock, large sums of money accumulated in the Treasury's accounts in the Bank of England, which caused a shortage of money on the money market. To offset this shortage, and so as not to let these sums remain "unproductive", they were advanced for a period of a few weeks, or even a few days, to clients desirous of this sort of credit, especially to the discount houses, which used them to increase the volume of their rediscounting operations. These advances made on security of deeds and bonds deposited could be recalled merely on demand. The deposit banks, too, adopted the practice of lending available funds from day to day.[72]

In this way a whole scale of rates of interest has been established,

* With Keynes the bourgeois economists rediscovered that interest relates only to the demand for *liquid* capital, that is, money capital, and so cannot determine the profit brought in by productive capital.

rising higher and higher, from the rate paid on long-term deposits and demanded for investment loans. At each level there is a difference between the rates paid by the banks and credit institutions and the rates they in turn demand from their clients.

The difference between these different rates arises in the first place from the degree in which the credits contribute to increasing directly the amount of surplus value produced by society. Clearly the rate of long-term interest, that which governs investment credit, which means especially the purchase on credit of means of production, is the highest, closest to the average rate of profit, and governs *ultimately* all the variations in the different rates of interest. The rate of short-term interest, which mainly governs circulation credit, is lower than the rate of long-term interest to the extent that circulation credit, by reducing the rotation-period of capital, makes *possible* but does not ensure the increase in the amount of surplus value. The short-term rate of interest may, however, sometimes exceed the long-term rate, for instance when there is a shortage of money on the money market which threatens not merely to extend the rotation period of capital but to destroy capital itself (danger of bankruptcy).

Also to be taken into account is an insurance and risk premium which is contained in interest and which varies according to the duration of the loan and the particular moment in the industrial cycle and also according to the particular conditions of supply and demand of money capital at the various levels, which (given a free market) subject the different rates of interest to daily fluctuations.* But these fluctuations occur around an average figure determined in the last resort by the level of the average rate of profit.

This is why, apart from the regular fluctuations resulting from the phases of the industrial cycle, it is hard to establish laws of long-term evolution applicable to the rate of interest. The latter depends in the last analysis on the *relative* shortage or plenty of money capital, in relation to the relative level of the rate of profit.

Thus, the rate of interest goes down in a society of petty commodity economy which has unified a vast international market within which the unevenness of economic development between different regions is increasingly reduced. This is what happened in Antiquity from the time of Caesar,† and in mediaeval Europe (Western and Southern Europe) from the second half of the fourteenth century.[73] The rate of interest goes down also when money economy becomes general in an agricultural country, and when in consequence the agricultural

* For the reciprocal effect of variations in long and short-term interest during the industrial cycle, see Chapter 11.

† At this moment it becomes more profitable to make *loans in kind* to the peasants, loans which continue to bring in very high interest. These loans in kind became the main form of usury in the Roman Empire.

classes free themselves a little from the oppression of usurer's capital; interest then no longer includes as heretofore a part of the ground rent.

On the eve of the great imperialist expansion of the last quarter of the nineteenth century, the industrialised countries all experienced a marked lowering of the average rate of interest, owing to the lack of fresh fields of investment for capital. On the morrow of the Second World War, in the United States and in Switzerland, the plentiful supply of capital and the lack of fields for investment offering the average profit severely reduced the rate of interest, whereas it was rising in the other capitalist countries, where a shortage of capital prevailed as a result of war damage and general impoverishment (Germany, France, Italy).

Circulation credit

All credit granted so as to make possible the realisation in advance (i.e. before actual sale) of the *value of commodities* is a circulation credit.[74] This is a short-term credit, rarely for longer than three months, which is granted by banks, both specialised and other.

With the generalisation of the capitalist mode of production, production becomes increasingly separated from the market, and the realisation of the value of commodities and surplus-value becomes more and more complicated, with risk of prolonging the rotation period of capital, even taking into account the intervention of commercial capital. But it is precisely at this epoch that, in order to react against the tendency of the rate of profit to fall which results from the immobilisation of an ever-growing fraction of capital as fixed capital, the capitalist seeks to *shorten* the rotation time of circulating capital. This is the essential function of circulation credit, which makes it possible to cut down to the minimum the entrepreneur's own circulating capital.

"The Bullion Report, referring to the increased operations of brokers in the four or five years before 1810, pointed out that the improved discount facilities available in London had tended to increase the business of the country manufacturer, by enabling him to turn over his capital more quickly."[75]

Macrae estimates that 30–40 per cent of the circulating capital of the whole of British industry is provided by credit.[76]

In the nineteenth century, circulation credit functioned mainly in the form of *discounting merchants' bills*. The producer of cotton goods does not pay his supplier in cash, but gives him a draft or promissory note. The supplier goes to a banker who takes over this merchant's bill, paying him the sum due, less an interest called discount. When the promissory note falls due to be paid, the cotton manufacturer pays the amount stated on it to the banker. The latter has thus in reality lent this sum for three months to the supplier of raw cotton, so enabling him to reduce by three months the rotation time of his capital (and also that of the cotton manufacturer, who receives credit from his supplier only because the latter in his turn receives credit from his banker).

Since the Middle Ages, however, another form of circulation credit has existed.[77]* Each capitalist has a current account with the local banker which enables him to make payments and receive sums of money by way of mere written orders (transfers from one account to another). All the payments in and out thus pass through the hands of the banker, who becomes a sort of central book-keeper. At a given moment a manufacturer has in his bank only a current account of one million francs to his credit. To continue production, however, he needs immediately two million francs, so as to be able to pay wages. The banker knows that, a few weeks later, the manufacturer will make large payments-in of money arising from the sale of his commodities. He therefore allows him to draw out of his account more money than he possesses (to have an overdraft); in fact, he advances him one million francs. Naturally, the manufacturer will pay interest for such an "advance on current account", normally not less than 5 per cent, except when very large firms are involved.†

From the last quarter of the nineteenth century, the advance on current account has more and more taken the place of the discounting of merchants' bills as the main form of circulation credit.[79] The concentration of capital leads to the formation of enterprises so big that they possess sufficient credit with their banks to obtain by way of advances on current account all the short-term credit they need. Small enterprises, however, are more and more embarrassed by the need to settle the discounted merchants' bill at *a fixed date*, and fear the discredit attached to the non-payment (protesting) of drafts when this becomes known. Finally, the integration of big enterprises with their suppliers of raw material and their selling organisations in trusts, financial groups, etc., abolishes the classical partnerships that made use of merchants' bills.[80] Thus, in Great Britain, the volume of ordinary merchants' bills discounted fell from £250 million in 1913 to £100 million in 1937, whereas advances on current account to industry reached £850 million in 1929 and £1 billion in 1938.[81]

Nevertheless, since the great crisis of 1929, especially in the United States, advances on current account to large-scale industry have begun to decline in their turn, owing to the accumulation of huge reserves of ready money by monopoly capital,‡ the relative decline of the

* Polanyi declares that a system of advances on current account was already practised by the bankers of ancient Assyria.[78]

† On the *monetary* consequences of this form of credit, see Chapter 8.

‡ See Chapter 14, section "Overcapitalisation".

industries especially dependent on bank credit, the extension of cash payments in retail trade, and the development of specialised credit institutions. It is above all the small and medium entrepreneurs who are responsible for the bulk of requests for advances on current account.[82] Along with this, in the last few years there has been a growth in the amount of discounting in some European countries, such as Switzerland, France and Belgium, as a result of an attractive policy of rediscounting on the part of the currency authorities, who expect to be able to influence more directly the fluctuations in the volume of money if circulation credit takes the form of discounting rather than of credit on current account.[83]

Investment credit and the finance market

All credit given in order to increase the *amount of capital* of an industrial or commercial entrepreneur is an investment credit. It is a *long-term credit* involving comparatively substantial sums, and is given, from the creditor's point of view, with the purpose of bringing in *a lasting income*.

The immediate origins of this form of credit are to be found in the purchase of ground-rent in the Middle Ages, in the constitution of the mediaeval trading companies, in the depositing of sums of money at fixed interest with the great trading associations of the fourteenth century, and in the long-term loans granted to kings, princes and cities by merchants and usurers in the Middle Ages.* It did not assume its modern character until the sixteenth century, with the appearance of the stock-exchange and negotiable instruments. From then onwards there was a social class which sought to dedicate its wealth—its capital—to investment in long-term credit operations, so as to increase this capital by the product of these investments. These people furnished the *supply* of capital on the embryonic finance market. The *demand* for capital was provided above all by the State, and then, to an ever-increasing extent, by the joint-stock companies. The predominance of government stock on the finance markets of Western Europe continued throughout the whole epoch of commercial capital, that is, in the majority of countries, down to the beginning or even the middle of the nineteenth century.

The public debt quickly took on the form of *fixed-income* stock payable from the future receipts of the State;† private stock was and remained above all *variable-income stock*, the actual return depending

* See Chapter 4, where also described are the origins of the stock-exchange, the public debt and joint-stock companies.

† Governments unable to pay the interest on their public debts experienced the seizure by foreign powers of their customs administration, this being the principal source of their income! This happened to China in the nineteenth century and to Venezuela in the twentieth.

on the yearly (or half-yearly, etc.) profits of the companies issuing the stock. In both cases the purchase of a share represented for the capitalist the purchase of a *claim to income*, a right to participate in the future share-out of society's surplus-value. The social nature of investment credit became more and more marked as stock-exchange operations widened their scope and numerous bourgeois built up portfolios containing shares in a growing number of companies, together with stock issued by many States, provinces, communes and other public entities.

The risk run in lending substantial sums to an enterprise for a lengthy period of time logically implies that additional guarantees are sought: the right to supervise the management of the money lent and the general administration of the business. This is why direct share-holding in the enterprises being aided, that is, the formation of multiple-partnership companies, has always been the most usual form of investment credit.

The old companies of the Ancient World, of China, of the Middle Ages, of the Arab and Byzantine civilisations, and so on, were all companies of *unlimited liability*: the partners were liable for the company's debts to the full extent of their possessions, whether these were invested in the company or not. This brought about the rapid collapse of all the mediaeval banks which granted investment credit. In Venice, of the 103 banks set up in the fourteenth century, 96 went bankrupt.[84] The development of the capitalist mode of production ended by *depersonalising* credit, a process which reached its stage of perfection in the joint-stock company and limited liability company of modern times. The purchase of shares and debentures in a business has become the normal way of giving investment credit.

Though the joint-stock company began to appear in the sixteenth century, it was not until the nineteenth century that it finally became dominant. Two shattering bankruptcies which occurred at the opening of the eighteenth century, that of the South Sea Company in Britain and that of the Mississippi Company in France, had developed in the bourgeoisie a holy terror of the risk implicit in this form of credit.[85] Actually, the manufacturing epoch was not yet propitious to such an extension of credit as the later rise of industrial capitalism demanded.

Thus, the investment credit given to private businesses increased little between the sixteenth century and the end of the eighteenth. While joint-stock companies developed but slowly, the deposit banks, remembering the lessons of the end of the Middle Ages,[86] turned away from investment operations, which, moreover, were forbidden them if they were chartered as public banks. The banks confined their long-term operations to the State and a few rare privileged customers.

Only when the British merchant bankers and the Continental "*haute banque*" establishments appeared, towards the end of the eighteenth century, did bankers begin afresh to interest themselves in private business, commercial and industrial. In 1822 the *Société Générale de Belgique* was the first business bank in the true sense, which, by at first granting short-term advances to industrial enterprises, soon found itself suffering from excessive tying-up of capital and was thus led to acquire shares and to take the initiative in founding joint-stock companies.[87]

The example of the *Société Générale* was followed in France, but the resounding downfall of the Pereira brothers' *Crédit Mobilier* set back the expansion of business banking in most European countries until after 1872.[88] Several countries then saw the rise of mixed banks, that is, banks which accept deposits and which also give investment credit.

In the twentieth century the finance market has become transformed under the influence of the development of insurance companies, savings banks, social insurance funds, etc., which, while assembling huge amounts of capital, cannot use them to buy securities with variable income. Several countries have passed laws defining these limitations or even extending them to the deposit banks. As a result, government stock has assumed the preponderant place on the contemporary finance market in most countries, just as used to be the case before the nineteenth century.[89] This phenomenon has accompanied that of *self-financing* of big concerns.*

It would be wrong to regard the sums deposited in the social security funds, the savings banks, etc., as an *accumulation of money-capital* more or less equivalent to the accumulation of capitalist funds in the banks. In reality, workers' savings constitute a *deferred consumption fund* which will be mostly spent during the depositor's own lifetime. In a global figure of the incomes of *the class of wage and salary earners*, there must be set off against these workers' savings the debts of sick, disabled and pensioned workers, the aid they have to seek from public assistance, or from family or other private sources, the reductions in level of consumption by these sections falling below the subsistence minimum, etc. The overall balance, which these figures confirm, shows that one generation of workers accumulates practically nothing in the way of transferable securities in the course of its lifetime taken as a whole.

The Stock Exchange

The capitalists and credit institutions who invest their available money capital in the form of shares and debentures in joint-stock

* See Chapter 14, section "Self-financing".

companies expect to obtain for these loans the *average rate of interest*. With debentures and fixed-income shares this is guaranteed them in advance. With the mass of shares in the proper sense of the word, the interest obtained fluctuates with the profit realised; it is called the *dividend*.

But shares, debentures and other transferable securities, as claims to income, become negotiable and are bought and sold on the stock-exchange. Their price is then simply *the capitalisation of the annual dividend (income) at the average rate of interest*. This price is the share's quotation on the stock-exchange.* Since the dividend paid by a company varies from year to year, and as estimates of probable dividend likewise vary throughout the year, these quotations may fluctuate violently. Real speculation on a rise or a fall is organised, often causing artificial changes in quotations; false rumours are circulated, or imminent sharp changes affecting the profitability of the business are concealed.

In some countries this speculation is carried on to a large extent on credit; thus, in New York, credits to speculators on Wall Street constitute the chief operations of the money market.[90]

Holders of shares and debentures receive the *average interest*; joint-stock companies in industry, trade and finance realise the *average profit*. Where does the difference go? In so far as it is not reinvested in the business and transformed into reserves, it is *capitalised in advance* in the form of *founder's profit*: additional shares, special preference shares, etc., are assigned to the founders of the company.

Let us suppose that an industrial enterprise has a capital of 100 million francs, and it wishes to obtain a further 200 million francs from the public to expand its business. Let us suppose that the average rate of profit is 10 per cent and the average rate of interest 5 per cent. If shares were issued for the sum of 300 million francs, they would be expected to bring in every year, on the average, 15 million francs in dividends. But the founders of the joint-stock company anticipate an annual profit of 30 million francs. The difference between the average interest and the average profit, or 15 million francs, will be capitalised at the average rate of interest of 5 per cent thus forming an additional capital of 300 million francs, which the founders take for themselves. The founder's profit thus materialises in the fact that the total capital for which shares have been issued will be 600 million francs, whereas only 300 million francs will have actually been paid in. The 300 million francs of additional shares will constitute merely *claims to income*, enabling their holders—the founders of the busi-

* This is not absolutely true. Also to be taken into account is possible reimbursement in the event of the winding-up of the company. This factor does not enter into calculations, however, except when such winding-up is in actual prospect.

ness—to take every year the difference between the average profit and the interest (the dividend), or entrepreneur's profit. Thus, when the great British chemical trust, Imperial Chemical Industries, was formed in 1926, its nominal capital was £56,803,000, whereas the aggregate of enterprises merged together to form it had capital totalling only £39 million.[91]

The capitalisation of founder's profit explains the remarkably rapid enrichment of "captains of industry" in the great periods of foundation of joint-stock companies (*Gründerjahre*). But in fact it capitalises *in advance* the *future* difference between the average profit and the interest, and so includes a large speculative element. Many joint-stock companies, overcapitalised in this way, prove unable to pay for long dividends equivalent to the average interest, precisely as a result of this overcapitalisation, while others even go bankrupt.

Another way of appropriating founder's profit is to boost the quotations of shares on the stock-exchange. Take a company founded with a capital of 10 million francs, divided into 1,000 shares each of 10,000 frances. This company is expected to earn an annual profit determined by the average rate of profit, say, 15 per cent, or an annual profit of 1·5 million francs, or 1,500 francs per share. Now, the average interest being 5 per cent, a sum of money lent is not expected to bring in more than 5 per cent, and 1,500 francs is regarded as the normal annual income on 30,000 francs. The founders will therefore succeed in selling their shares on the stock exchange for 30,000 francs each instead of 10,000 francs, and thus appropriate the difference, which is again the capitalisation of a difference between *future* average profit and the present average interest. When Dunlop, the British rubber trust, was refloated in 1896, shares issued at £3 million were sold six weeks after issue for £5 million.[92]

A good example of a combination of these two forms of founder's profit is provided by Harrods, the large British department store, established as a joint-stock company in 1889. The company had a capital of £1 million, of which £1,400 was preference shares for the founders, who assured themselves a large and increasing participation in the profits. Despite the fact that Harrods' ordinary shares paid annual dividends of 10 per cent at first, and later 20 per cent, on the average, during over 20 years, the founders' shares were immediately capitalised at £140,000 and were worth on the stock-exchange in 1911 not less than £1,470,000, ten times their nominal capital and 1,000 times the capital actually paid in . . .[93]

While shares and debentures continue their independent circulation on the stock-exchange, among brokers, the real values they represent may have long since disappeared. The warships built with capital borrowed by a government may long since have gone to the bottom of the sea, just as the machines bought with the money raised by the sale of shares may have been transformed into so much old iron. The divorce between real capital and the mass of negotiable claims, already marked as a result of the overcapitalisation of many joint-stock companies, thenceforth becomes complete. The mass of claims no longer represents anything but a *fictitious capital* which, under the appearance of a fraction of the total capital of society, hides its true nature, that of a mere claim to income, which confers a right to participate in the share-out of society's surplus-value.

Joint-stock companies and the evolution of capitalism

For a long time some people have wanted to see in the development of joint-stock companies a proof that capital, far from becoming concentrated, is "democratising" itself. Are there not millions of shareholders in some countries, for instance, in the United States? Is it not possible for any skilled worker to use his savings to buy shares in big industrial companies?

This notion is based on a twofold confusion. First, not everybody is a capitalist who claims an income from the sharing-out of society's surplus-value; if that were so, every disabled ex-Serviceman would be a "capitalist". Only those shareholders who, thanks to the income on their capital, can live without selling their labour-power, and live at a standard which corresponds at least to that of a small industrialist, can be classed in this category.

Investigations carried out by the Brookings Institute in the U.S.A. in 1952 showed that out of more than 30 million American workers only 2 per cent held shares. Out of a total of 6·5 million shareholders, 4·5 million held fewer than 100 shares each and received from them an *annual* income of less than 200 dollars, or less than the *monthly* wage of an average worker. It would therefore be absurd to regard them as being "capitalists".

Consequently, though the joint-stock companies appear formally as institutions which *diffuse* ownership of the means of production, in reality they constitute an important stage in the *concentration* of capital. It is a mere legal fiction to regard a small shareholder as being "co-proprietor" of a giant trust like General Motors, for instance. In return for this title he has in practice handed over his savings to the big industrialists and bankers to do what they like with them. The joint-stock company is therefore rather a disguised form of *expropriation* of small savers, not for the benefit of a nameless force but for that of the *big capitalists*, who thus succeed in getting control of a mass of capital which greatly exceeds their own property.

"In effect, when an individual invests capital in the large corporation, he grants to the corporate management all power to use that capital to create, produce and develop, and he abandons all control over the product. He keeps a modified right to receive a portion of the profits, usually in the form of money, and a highly enhanced right to sell his participation for cash. He is an almost completely inactive recipient."[94]

It is interesting to note that the decision of a British court has confirmed this view. Lord Evershed declared in 1949: "Shareholders are not, in the eye of the law, part owners of the undertaking. The undertaking is something different from the totality of shareholdings." And the *Economist* adds: "In other words, an ordinary stockholder does not own an aliquot part of the company's assets. He is entitled to an aliquot part of the profits that the directors recommend for distribution . . ."[95]

Before the rise of the joint-stock company one had to own the greater part of the capital of a business in order to control it effectively. Gardiner C. Means has shown how, thanks to the development of these companies and the dispersal of their shares among small shareholders, a few big shareholders can be sure of controlling the trusts with shareholdings which give them only a minor part of the capital.[96] In the American Telegraph and Telephone Company, for instance, 43 big shareholders held in 1935 more shares than 242,500 small shareholders. In one of the chief American cigarette trusts, the Reynolds Tobacco Company, there were in 1939 66,357 shareholders; but 20 of these held 59·7 per cent of the "A" ordinary shares and 22·5 per cent of the "B" ordinary shares.[97] The British Bowaters trust had 42,866 shareholders on 1st June, 1959; but the 26,000 smallest shareholders held altogether £2·8 million ordinary shares, compared with £4·3 million in the hands of 151 big shareholders—63 of whom held £3·4 million worth!

The Brookings Institute investigation already mentioned showed that 2 per cent of the total number of shareholders, or less than 0·1 per cent of the American people, or 130,000 persons, each one holding 1,000 shares or more, together account for 56 per cent of the stock-exchange value of all American shares, and so control the bulk of American capital.

Professor Sargant Florence has examined in detail the distribution of shares among the small and large shareholders of the chief joint-stock companies of Britain and the U.S.A. The result is significant. In 1,429 American companies 98·7 per cent of the shareholders—the mass of small shareholders—hold only 38·9 per cent of the shares, whereas 0·3 per cent of the shareholders—those who each hold more than 5,000 shares—concentrate 46·7 per cent of the shares in their hands. If we take only the big companies with a capital exceeding 100 million dollars, these percentages remain practically the same. (These figures relate to the situation in the years 1935–37.)

In Britain, in the case of the 30 largest companies, 96·4 per cent of the shareholders—the small ones—hold 40·1 per cent of the shares, while 0·5 per cent of the shareholders—the big ones—hold 35·9 per cent of the shares.

Of the 126 largest joint-stock companies in the U.S.A., the 20 principal shareholders hold over half the shares in one quarter, from 30 to 50 per cent in another quarter, and from 20 to 30 per cent in a fifth. In Great Britain, out of the 82 largest joint-stock companies, the 20 principal shareholders hold over half the shares in 40 per cent, from 30 to 50 per cent of the shares in 17 per cent, and from 20 to 30 per cent of the shares in 21 per cent.

Finally, analysing the way all these companies are run, one finds that 58 per cent of the British and American companies are clearly dominated by the principal shareholders, while 33 per cent of the British and 15 per cent of the American companies are "marginal" cases.

And Professor Sargant Florence concludes: "Proceeding thus from the known to the unknown there is certainly evidence for believing that the managerial revolution has not proceeded as far as is sometimes thought (or stated without thought) and that leadership and the ultimate decision on top policy may remain in many companies or corporations with the larger capitalist shareholders."[98]

Norman Macrae estimates that in Britain 2 per cent of the population holds over 90 per cent of all the shares, and that between 100,000 and 150,000 people (0·2 to 0·3 per cent of the population) hold more than 50 per cent of these.[99]

It is the same in India, where the shares of some of the biggest companies are distributed like this: [100]

	Advance Mill		*Tata Mills*		*Tata Hydro-Electric*	
Category holding	*share-holders* %	*shares* %	*share-holders* %	*shares* %	*share-holders* %	*shares* %
From 1 to 25 shares	93·6	40·0	79·0	14·1	82·0	24·2
Over 150 shares	0·9	36·5	2·4	64·0	2·2	48·33

In each case, a small number of large shareholders hold as many shares as or more shares than the great mass of small shareholders and thereby control the joint-stock companies. In reality, a still narrower group wields a preponderant influence on the joint-stock companies: *

"The company form favours the creation of a real aristocracy or oligarchy. It gives rise to professional administrators whose role consists exclusively of undertaking the administration of the big capitalist companies . . . By multiplying the links which connect them with numerous companies they form among themselves a sort of personal dynasty. An entire system of interlocking relationships comes into being, to which a great variety of names are given: 'communities of interest', 'inter-directorates' . . . this dual fact of personal freedom from

* See Chapter 12.

responsibility and possession of administrative authority favours the making of alliances and agreements (i.e. monopoly)."[101]

The generalisation of joint-stock companies (limited liability companies, corporations, etc.), constitutes an important stage in the *de facto* socialisation of credit and of the economy as a whole. When the bank lends an industrialist the money that a small rentier has deposited with it, the industrialist remains the owner of most of the capital with which he operates. With the formation of joint-stock companies we see a more and more marked separation of the entrepreneur from the *rentier*-owner. The entrepreneur's capital becomes a means of control over capital many times larger than his own.

Consumer's credit

Circulation credit and investment credit essentially remain within the circle of the bourgeoisie, big and small. But the capitalist epoch also sees the reappearance of consumer's credit, whether provided by way of usury or otherwise. Falling into debt in the shops where they have to buy goods of primary necessity, the workers, office-workers, unemployed, and declassed people may soon find themselves chained for life to a pitiless creditor who seizes a large part of their meagre incomes as interest on a debt which they will never be able to shake off. This form of usury is particularly hateful when it is practised by shops which belong to the very enterprise to which the worker sells his labour-power.

With the mass production of what are called consumer *durables* (cookers, sewing-machines, refrigerators, washing-machines, radios and television sets, motor-cycles and cars, etc.) there appeared, around 1915, another modern form of consumer's credit.[102] Usually, the wages of workers and office-workers, even skilled ones, are inadequate for them to buy such goods for cash. The payment of a fraction of their weekly or monthly wage enables them, however, to acquire the goods as their own property, after a certain time. Industrialists and traders are interested in fostering this *hire-purchase* method of selling because it constitutes the only way to expand the market for these consumer durables, and because as a rule they receive considerable interest on this credit (difference between the cash price and the hire purchase price).* Also the traders' overheads (storage and handling) are substantially reduced, since the purchasers take responsibility for these charges. But even apart from the exploitation which is implicit —return to the company of articles on which an instalment has not been paid—the excessive development of the hire-purchase system is a factor of instability in the capitalist system, especially

* This interest is often usurious, since it continues to be calculated on the total price of the article, even after 50 per cent or 75 per cent of the price has already been paid.

towards the end of the boom and on the eve of the slump in each economic cycle.[103]

The close link between this modern consumer's credit and the mass production of consumer durables is clear from the fact that, almost non-existent before 1914, these credits developed in the U.S.A. after the First World War—6·3 billion dollars in 1929, 25 billion in 1952—and in Great Britain, West Germany, Belgium, Sweden, France, etc., after the Second World War, at the very moment when the motor car, motor-cycle, refrigerator and T.V. industries were expanding in these countries.[104]

Credit and the contradictions of capitalism

Credit has thus deeply marked the history and development of capital. It has mightily extended the field of operations of capital, by making possible the capitalisation of every available reserve of money. It has facilitated, accelerated, generalised the circulation of commodities. It has stimulated capitalist production, competition, the concentration of capital, in short, all the developmental tendencies of capitalism. Credit appears as an instrument no less indispensable to the capitalist mode of production than trade, making possible a substantial reaction against the tendency of the average rate of profit to fall.

Credit has likewise transformed the bourgeois class itself. The separation of interest from profit, of a class of rentiers from the mass of the bourgeoisie, marks at the same time both the logical culmination of capitalist development and the first definite sign of its decay. Here, indeed, is a fraction of the bourgeoisie who live merely on their *ownership* of capital, and who, by doing this, are placed completely outside the production process, without any direct contact with the machines or the workers. The *private* character of capitalist appropriation, which remains personal and tangible in the capitalist enterprise which is family property, becomes more and more objective, abstract, in the joint-stock company. The rule of capital assumes its most general and anonymous form. Apparently it is no longer men of flesh and blood who embody exploitation, but "companies", synonyms of objective, blind economic forces.

Like trade, credit makes possible a considerable reduction in the rotation-time of capital, *an ever greater mobility of circulating capital, in contrast to the tying-up of a growing share of capital* in gigantic fixed installations.* It thus mitigates for the immediate future the

* At the beginning of the crisis, credit even makes it possible to absorb the first shock of a sudden fall in prices. In so far as the entrepreneur is operating with borrowed capital, he can sell *below the price of production*. The price obtained need only be sufficient to pay the interest, which is less than the average profit.

contradictions resulting from the evolution of capitalism. At the same time, however, it intensifies these contradictions in the long run. At the beginning of industrial capitalism, each capitalist was able to check very quickly whether the labour-time expended to produce his commodities was socially-necessary labour-time or not. It was enough to go to the market-place and there look for buyers of these goods at their price of production. When trade and credit insert themselves between the industrialist and the consumer, the former begins by realising automatically the value of his commodities. But thereafter he is unaware whether or not they will find a real outlet, whether they will find an "ultimate consumer". Long after he has already spent the money representing the value of the commodities produced, it may turn out that the latter are unsaleable, not really representing *socially necessary* labour-time. The slump is then unavoidable. Credit tends to postpone the slump while making it the more violent when at last it comes.

By making possible an expansion of production without any direct relation to the absorption capacity of the market, by concealing for a whole period the real relationships between the production potential and the possibilities of effective consumption; by stimulating the circulation and consumption of commodities over and beyond the real purchasing power available, credit puts off the date of the periodical crises, aggravates the factors of disequilibrium, and thereby makes the crisis the more violent when it breaks. Credit merely develops the basic divorce between the two essential functions of money—means of circulation and means of payment—and between the circulation of commodities and the circulation of the money which realises their exchange value, contradictions which are the primary and general sources of capitalist crises.

REFERENCES

1. Ruth Bunzel: *The Economic Organization of Primitive Peoples*, p. 346.
2. J. H. Boeke: *De Theorie der Indische Economie*, p. 49.
3. Raymond Firth: *Malay Fishermen*, p. 162.
4. H. Cunow: *Allgemeine Wirtschaftsgeschichte*, Vol. I, p. 241.
5. Kin Wei-Shan: *Democracy and Finance in China*, p. 66.
6. Cunow: op. cit., Vol. I, p. 240; R. Thurwald: article *"Wirtschaft"* in *Reallexicon der Vorgeschichte*, Vol. XIV, p. 408.
7. C. Huart and L. Delaporte: *L'Iran antique*, pp. 138-9.
8. H. Pirenne: *Le Mouvement économique et social au moyen âge*, p. 17.
9. E. Cuq: *Les Nouveaux fragments du Code de Hammourabi sur le prêt à intérêt*, pp. 21-28; W. Eilers: *Die Gesetzgebung Hammurabis*, p. 23.
10. International Labour Office: *Les populations aborigènes*, p. 407.
11. P. T. Bauer and B. S. Yamey: *The Economics of Under-developed Countries*, p. 65.

12. For Byzantium, G. Ostrogorsky: *Geschichte des byzantinischen Staates*, pp. 88, 217; for India, *Cambridge History of India*, Vol. IV, pp. 451-4; for China, K. A. Wittfogel: *Wirtschaft and Gesellschaft Chinas*, pp. 349-50; for Japan, M. Takizawa: *The Penetration of Money Economy in Japan*, pp. 21-22, etc.
13. A. Dauphin-Meunier: *Histoire de la Banque*, p. 5; E. Cuq: op. cit., pp. 26-32.
14. Huart and Delaporte: op. cit., p. 141.
15. A. Christensen: *L'Iran sous les Sassanides*, pp. 166-7.
16. A. Dauphin-Meunier: *La Banque à Travers les âges*, Vol. I, pp. 30-31.
17. F. Heichelheim: *Wirtschaftsgeschichte des Altertums*, pp. 351-2.
18. M. Rostovtzeff: *Social and Economic History of the Hellenistic World*, pp. 1278-80.
19. Steven Runciman: *La Civilisation byzantine*, p. 90-92.
20. Jacques Gernet: *Les Aspects économiques du bouddhisme dans la société chinoise du Ve au Xe siècle*, pp. 167-8, 20, *et al.*
21. Lien-sheng Yang: "Buddhist Monasteries and Four Money-Raising Institutions", in *Harvard Journal of Asiatic Studies*, Vol. XIII, June, 1950, Nos. 1-2, pp. 174-6.
22. Eijiro Honjo: *The Social and Economic History of Japan*, pp. 72-73.
23. Aly Mazahéri: *La Vie quotidienne des Musulmans au moyen âge*, p. 302.
24. G. Génestat: *Le Rôle des monastères comme établissements de crédit*, p. 19, for Normandy; Karl Lamprecht: *Deutsches Wirtschaftsleben in Mittelalter*, Vol. I, p. 1446, for Germany; G. G. Coulton: *The Mediaeval Village*, pp. 284-6, for Italy; Mackinnon: *Social and Industrial History of Scotland*, p. 74, for Scotland; H. van Werveke: in *Annales*, Vol. IV, pp. 459-60, for the Netherlands, etc.
25. A. Dauphin-Meunier: op. cit., Vol. I, pp. 86-89.
26. Heichelheim: op. cit., Vol. I, p. 342.
27. G. B. Jathar and S. G. Beri: *Indian Economics*, Vol. II, p. 329.
28. Ki Fein-Shen: *Essai sur l'origine et l'évolution des banques en Chine*, pp. 4-5.
29. Paul E. Eckel: *The Far East since 1500*, p. 105.
30. Walter J. Fischel: *Jews in the Economic and Political Life of Mediaeval Islam*, pp. 3, 7, 13-14, 26-28.
31. J. Kulischer: *Allgemeine Wirtschaftsgeschichte*, Vol. I, p. 330.
32. R. De Roover: *L'Evolution de la lettre de change, xive-xviiie siècle*, p. 24.
33. J. C. Van Dillen: *History of the Principal Public Banks*, pp. 81-84.
34. R. G. Rodkey: article "*Deposits*" in *Encyclopaedia of Social Sciences*, Vol. II, p. 416.
35. A. E. Sayous: *Les Banques de dépôt, les banques de crédit et les sociétés financières*, p. 12.
36. G. Bigwood: *Le Régime juridique et économique du commerce de l'argent dans la Belgique du moyen âge*, pp. 362-7 et passim; R. De Roover; *Money, Banking and Credit in Mediaeval Bruges*, pp. 117-20.
37. J. Schumpeter: *Business Cycles*, Vol. II, p. 614.
38. R. P. L. Molina: *De Iustitia et Iure*, Vol. II, 1597-359: 15.
39. R. De Roover: *L'Evolution de la lettre de change*, Vol. II, p. 26.

40. Ibid., p. 23.
41. Dauphin-Meunier: op. cit., Vol. I, p. 9; Ki Fein-Shen: op. cit., pp. 144-5; *Cambridge History of India*, Vol. I, pp. 218-19.
42. G. Glotz: *Le Travail dans la Grèce antique*, p. 73.
43. Boissonnadex: *Le Travail dans l'Europe chrétienne du moyen âge*, pp. 65-66; Fischel: *Jews in the Economic and Political Life of Medieval Islam*, pp. 17-24; N. S. B. Gras: article "Bill of Exchange" in *Encyclopedia of Social Sciences*, II, p. 450.
44. G. Glotz: op. cit., p. 73.
45. Glotz: op. cit., p. 142; R. S. Lopez: "Trade in Mediaeval Europe: The South", in *Cambridge Economic History of Europe*, Vol. II, p. 267.
46. A. Sapori: *La Crisi delle compagnie*, p. 249.
47. R. De Roover: *Money, Banking and Credit in Mediaeval Bruges*, p. 40.
48. Fischel: op. cit., pp. 28-29.
49. Nancy Lee Swann: *Food and Money in Ancient China*, p. 393.
50. Robert Bigo: *Les Bases historiques de la finance moderne*, p. 100.
51. H. Hauser and A. Renaudet: *Les Débuts de l'âge moderne (Peuples et Civilisations, Vol. VIII)*, p. 346.
52. Van Dillen: op. cit., passim.
53. R. De Roover: *L'Evolution de la lettre de change*, Vol. I, p. 350, Vol. II, p. 83.
54. W. T. C. King: *History of the London Discount Market*, p. 5; R. Bigo: *La Caisse d'Escompte et les origines de la Banque de France*, p. 16; J. H. Clapham: *The Bank of England*, pp. 6, 18, 27, 123.
55. R. De Roover: *L'Evolution de la lettre de change*, Vol. I, p. 119.
56. Clapham: op. cit., p. 153.
57. Bigo: *La Caisse d'Escompte* . . ., passim.
58. Clapham: op. cit., p. 118.
59. Schumpeter: op. cit., Vol. I, p. 292.
60. King: op. cit., pp. 7-8.
61. D. K. Joslin: "London private bankers, 1720–1785", in *Economic History Review*, Vol. VIII, No. 2, 1954, pp. 171-2, 182.
62. King: op. cit., p. 18.
63. Ibid., p. 11.
64. G. Von Haberler: *Prospérité et Dépression*, Vol. II, p. 333.
65. Schumpeter: op. cit., Vol. I, p. 124.
66. J. H. Clapham: *An Economic History of Modern Britain*, Vol. II, pp. 352-3.
67. René Dumont: *Le Problème agricole français*, p. 334.
68. Schumpeter: op. cit., Vol. I, p. 124.
69. J. G. K. Wicksell: *Lectures on Political Economy*, Vol. II, p. 190.
70. *New York Times*, 17th January, 1955.
71. Schumpeter: op. cit., Vol. II, p. 608.
72. King: op. cit., pp. 83, 270-1.
73. Heichelheim: op. cit., Vol. I, p. 687; Lopez: art. cit., pp. 309-10; De Roover; *L'Evolution de la lettre de change*, Vol. II, p. 35.
74. S. Schweizer: in *Evolution récente du rôle des banques*, p. 79.

75. King: op. cit., p. 16.
76. Norman Macrae: *The London Capital Market*, p. 130.
77. R. De Roover: *Money, Banking and Credit in Medieval Bruges*, pp. 294-7.
78. K. Polanyi: et al., *Trade and Market in the Early Empires*, p. 14.
79. Clapham: *An Economic History of Modern Britain*, Vol. II, p. 336.
80. Fernand Baudhuin: *Crédit et Banque*, pp. 47-49.
81. M. Compton and E. H. Bott: *British Industry*, pp. 170, 178.
82. R. S. Sayers: *Modern Banking*, p. 44.
83. S. Schweizer: in *Evolution récente du rôle des banques*, p. 95.
84. J. Kulischer: *Allgemeine Wirtschaftsgeschichte*, Vol. I, p. 343.
85. J. B. Condliffe: *The Commerce of Nations*, p. 96.
86. R. De Roover: *L'Evolution de la lettre de change*, Vol. I, p. 16.
87. F. Baudhuin, op. cit., p. 188; Paul H. Emden: *Money Powers of Europe*, passim.
88. Clapham: *An Economic History of Modern Britain*, Vol. II, p. 355.
89. Macrae: op. cit., pp. 88, 177.
90. Sayers: op. cit., p. 65.
91. Patrick Fitzgerald: *Industrial Combination in England*, p. 101.
92. Clapham: *An Economic History of Modern Britain*, Vol. III, p. 234.
93. Ibid., p. 242.
94. A. A. Berle: *The XXth Century Capitalist Revolution*, p. 30.
95. *The Economist*, 14th February, 1959, p. 613.
96. Gardiner C. Means: *The Structure of American Economy*, p. 153.
97. Richard B. Tennant: *The American Cigarette Industry*, p. 101; *Manchester Guardian*, 5th June, 1959.
98. Sargant Florence: *The Logic of British and American Industry*, pp. 183, 189, 203, 193.
99. Macrae: op. cit., pp. 386-9, 104.
100. A. Mehta: *Democratic Socialism*, p. 105.
101. Oualid: *Répétitions écrites de législation industrielle*, pp. 184-5.
102. Seligman: *Instalment Credit*, Vol. I, pp. 13 et seq.
103. F. Baudhuin, op. cit., pp. 16-17.
104. Schweizer: op. cit., pp. 92-93.

CHAPTER EIGHT

MONEY

The two functions of money

MONEY, the universal equivalent, is above all a commodity in the value of which all other commodities express their own exchange value.[1] The equation: 25 sacks of wheat are worth 1 pound of gold expresses an equivalence in exchange value, that is, in socially-necessary labour-time. As a common measure of value money possesses no mysterious quality. It can fulfil this function because it is itself a product of human labour and itself possesses a definite value.

When exchanges are simple, and buying and selling are gradually replacing barter, this basic quality of money is obvious. At the beginning of petty commodity economy there are usually two or three universal equivalents, which are used together as measures of value: wheat and gold or copper in Egypt and Mesopotamia; wheat, rice and silver in China, etc. Under these circumstances, nobody could regard money as being merely a conventional instrument of exchange.

The social division of labour is still relatively simple and transparent. When 25 sacks of wheat, 5 cows and a pound of silver are exchanged, the respective labour of the cultivator, the cattle-breeder and the miner appear reduced to a common measure, a common fraction of the total labour-time available to the given society based on accounting in labour-time.

But when exchanges become numerous and more and more common, this simple and quite transparent relation vanishes. Money is no longer merely the common measure of values, it has also become the means of exchange.[2] A large number of commodities come together on the market, in the possession of their respective owners. These commodities will pass from hand to hand until they reach those purchasers who wish to realise their use value. The latter take them finally off the market. Money facilitates these successive exchanges and makes them possible in the conditions of a unified market.[3] For it to carry out this function, however, its own intrinsic value is only of secondary importance. If the value of 25 sacks of wheat is equal to that 5 cows, it matters little to the cultivators and the cattle breeders that they have exchanged these two commodities after having first received and then paid one pound of fine silver, or ten pounds of crude-alloy silver. Because the entire circulation of commodities looks like a succession of exchange transactions in which money plays only the part of an *intermediary*, the illusion may arise that the value of the universal equivalent itself is of no importance for the proper functioning of the economy.

This is indeed an illusion. In so far as the circulation of commodities develops into a circulation of commodities and a circulation of money, money itself develops simultaneously into a means of circulation and a *means of deferred payment*. In a society which is essentially commodity-producing, a mass of commodities is in circulation thanks to credit. The money equivalent of these commodities will not be received until later.[4] Every fluctuation in the intrinsic value of money, the universal equivalent, immediately gives rise to disturbances in the relations between debtors and creditors, harming the former when the value of money rises (as happened with copper in the days of the Roman Republic) and ruining the latter when the value of money collapses.

The value of metallic money and price movements

Since the moment when the precious metals were more or less universally adopted as universal equivalents, fluctuations in their intrinsic value have always caused great upheavals in commodity prices, that is, in the expression of the value of these commodities in money terms. A rise in the value of metallic money causes a fall in prices expressed in this money, whereas a fall in the value of metallic money causes prices to rise.

The first great revolution in the value of money occurred when, as a result of the use of iron tools, the conditions of production of silver were much improved, and this led to a fall in the value of the metal, about 900 B.C. This decline in value caused a marked rise in prices expressed in silver: the price of a "qur" of wheat rose from two silver shekels under Hammurabi (2,000 B.C.) to 15 shekels about 950 B.C.[5] Six centuries later, Alexander the Great seized huge amounts of precious metals accumulated in the Persian imperial treasury, and this loot had the same effect as very cheap production—it led to a fall of about 50 per cent in the value of gold and silver, and a corresponding rise in prices.[6]

From the second century A.D. the reverse process occurred. The increase in the price of slaves, the decline in their output, the closing of numerous mines, the ebbing of the plundered treasure back towards India, increased the value of gold and silver, and caused a fall in prices expressed in precious metal (though this was obscured by the debasement of the coinage by successive Emperors).[7] This movement reached its culmination about the eighth and ninth centuries A.D. Then the trend was again reversed. From the fourteenth and fifteenth centuries onward, a real technical revolution in silver mining brought about a fall in the value of this metal and an all-round rise in prices. This became general in the second half of the sixteenth century, following the opening up of the silver mines of Potosi in Bolivia, and those of Mexico, by means of slave labour, which greatly reduced the costs of production and led to the closing of many mines in Europe.

When comparing the fluctuations in value of metallic money with the fluctuations in prices, one must not lose sight of the fact that the same technical upheavals that, by increasing productivity, cause a fall in the value of the metal, may likewise bring about a fall in the value of *all* commodities. In these circumstances, a fall in the value of gold and silver may be accompanied by stability or even decline in the prices of commodities. Thus, the same revolutionary technique of the iron age which lowered the value of silver in the tenth century B.C. made possible a considerable extension of agricultural production at lower costs, and led to a collapse of agricultural prices between the tenth and seventh centuries B.C. (the price of wheat, for instance, fell from 15 shekels to half a shekel per "qur").[8]

So long as the world market was fragmented into thousands of regional markets whose mutual relations were infrequent and slight, the coexistence of numerous universal equivalents in the world was not felt as any special difficulty in the way of exchanges. When the Portuguese, and later the Dutch, began trading in Indonesia, they found there various currency standards in force side by side. Gold and silver money has been able to coexist with shell money in aboriginal communities.[9] Only when industrial capitalism has effectively unified the world market, when nothing but exchange values are being produced, does the need for a universal equivalent for all countries make itself felt. The attempt made by several countries to base the universal equivalent simultaneously on gold and on silver (bimetallism) was doomed to defeat. These two metals having each their own exchange-value, which is subject to many variations in the capitalist epoch, constant disturbances were inevitable in the expression of the price of one metal in terms of the other and in the expression of the prices of commodities in either of them.[10] Finally, towards the end of the nineteenth century, nearly all countries were obliged to come round to accepting the gold standard; gold became the universal measure of gold for all countries. Resistance was prolonged, however, in the Far East, where, from the sixteenth century, silver had been used as the universal equivalent, first in China and later in India and Japan.

The circulation of metallic money

The precious metals serve as instruments of exchange by themselves representing a definite exchange-value. Equal values exchanging for equal values, it seems obvious that with the use of metallic money a precise ratio is established between the total price of all the commodities in circulation and the amount of currency needed for the exchange value of these commodities to be realised. To determine this ratio, account has to be taken of the fact that one unit of currency can effect several successive exchanges.

A peasant has brought a coin to market in order to buy some cloth. With the same coin the cloth merchant buys a supply of flour from the miller. The miller in his turn buys some wheat from a peasant, still using the same coin. The latter will thus have effected in one day three exchange transactions, each being equal to the value of the coin itself. If we represent by v this velocity of circulation of the currency—the number of exchange transactions carried out by one coin in a certain period of time—by Q the number of commodities in circulation, and by p the average index of prices, we get the following formula which defines the amount of currency in circulation, M:

$$M \times v = Q \times p$$ [11]

The total amount of currency in circulation, multiplied by the velocity of circulation of the currency, must be equal to the total amount of commodities in circulation multiplied by the average index of prices. From this we get the following formula for the amount of currency needed for exchanging all the commodities in circulation:

$$M = \frac{Q \times p}{v}$$

Finally, by replacing $Q \times v$ by P, the total sum of the prices of all the commodities in circulation, we get the following formula:

$$M = \frac{P}{v}$$

The total amount of currency in circulation must be equal to *the sum of the prices of all the commodities exchanged*, divided by the velocity of circulation of the currency.

This formula must not be regarded as reversible. Nor must it be considered as an algebraic formula in which the knowledge of three factors enables one automatically to deduce the fourth.[12] It is P that must be seen as being normally the *only independent variable* of the formula. The prices of production of the commodities may fluctuate with their value; technical progress may cause a more or less radical fall in prices. In that case, some of the metallic money may be withdrawn from circulation, and perhaps hoarded. If the quantity of commodities in circulation increases markedly, without any corresponding increase in productivity (i.e. a corresponding decrease in the value of each commodity), an extra amount of metallic money will be needed to make exchanges possible. There will therefore be a drive to increase by all possible means the production of precious metals (reopening of closed mines, search for new mines, etc.). This is what happened from the end of the fourteenth century down to the sixteenth. But the velocity of circulation of currency is not an autonomous factor. "The velocity with which currency circulates tends to vary with production itself, and, in this sense, variations in currency circulation do not affect prices."[13]

Origins of private fiduciary currency

From the rise of petty commodity economy, however, the use of metallic money alone could put a brake on the rapid settlement of exchanges. A sharp expansion in international trade could cause a shortage of coin and so hinder economic growth. This happened not only in Western Europe in the fourteenth and fifteenth centuries but also in the Islamic Empire in the days of the Abbasids,[14] in Egypt in the Hellenistic epoch,[15] in ancient Greece before the discovery of the mines of Laurium,[16] in China in the ninth century A.D.[17] Periods of shortage of currency are usually characterised by an ever more rapid circulation of coins, which wear out more quickly and so deteriorate in weight and value.

Moreover, the use of metallic money alone entails a number of difficulties in the setting of fully developed petty commodity production. The departure of maritime expeditions and caravans which have to carry their means of exchange for a long period may cause sudden shortages of currency. R. de Roover quotes a fifteenth-century treatise on trade,[18] written by Uzzano, which shows that in Venice, every year, in the months of June and July, there was a shortage of currency owing to the departure of the galleys for Constantinople. This "tension" on the mediaeval "money market" regularly continued until after the departure of the galleys for Alexandria at the beginning of September, and was repeated between 15th December and 15th January, after the departure of the galleys sent to fetch cotton. On the other hand, in October and November there was plenty of currency around, because at that time the German merchants who had come to buy spices brought a lot of money to Venice.[19]

The simple need to transport often substantial amounts of coin in order to make payments shows that the use of metallic money could become very cumbersome.

"[Under Louis XVI] the transport of coin undertaken by the stage-coach service was very burdensome . . . On the 10th, 20th and 30th of every month, Mercier tells us in his *Tableau de Paris*, between ten o'clock and mid-day one encountered porters lugging bags full of money, and bending under their weight, running as though an enemy army was about to surprise the town . . ."[20]

These transport difficulties were found particularly troublesome in countries like China, where the metals used for coinage were baser than gold and silver, namely, copper and even iron.

To this must be added the great monetary insecurity that usually prevailed in those days, as a result of the simultaneous circulation of a wide variety of coins,* and also of fraudulent operations such as clipping, etc., especially on the part of the royal exchequers. In the sixteenth and seventeenth centuries this phenomenon existed on so large a scale in England that in 1695 50 per cent of the value of the country's tax receipts was lost through the inadequate weight of the coins paid in.[21]

All these reasons explain why, at a certain stage of development of petty commodity production, the growth of trade leads merchants to invent *tokens for money* by means of which exchanges can be accelerated and their settlement simplified. The two classical forms of these tokens, which appear more or less generally in every society with a developed merchant capital, are bills of exchange and transfers of bank deposits (bank money).

We have seen how the bill of exchange was born of the separation in time between purchase and delivery and in space between the buyer and the seller.* In mediaeval Europe these bills were, at first, exchange contracts and credit instruments. In other societies, they were mere credit instruments, like the "rice bonds" of Japan,[22] or cheques payable in metallic money or in specific commodities, like the "tea bonds" in China under the Sung dynasty.[23] What is characteristic of these documents, leaving aside the part they play as credit instruments, is that when their use has become general it is possible for them to serve as tokens for money. All that is needed is that they be capable of circulating, that is, be accepted by persons other than those named on the given document. In Western Europe this circulation was ensured though the practice of *endorsement of bills of exchange* which became widespread there in the sixteenth century.[24] At the beginning of the nineteenth century, in Scotland and Lancashire, bills of exchange still circulated as means of exchange, each being covered with many signatures.[25]

The technique of transfers of bank deposits by writing was more extensively used to make up for the inadequacy of metallic money, at least in Western Europe from the Middle Ages onward. The majority of merchants opened accounts with the big merchant banker houses. When they bought goods they instructed their banker to enter in his books the sum to be paid, on the debit side of their account and on the credit side of their supplier's account. Similarly, when they sold products, they had entered on the credit side of their account the sum due

* See Chapter 7.

to them, while the same sum was entered on the debit side of their customer's. At certain intervals, the net balances of the debit and credit accounts of each merchant were settled by means of deposits which they placed with the bankers, and possible extra payments of cash which had become necessary. This clearing system, which developed mainly through the fairs of the thirteenth century, enabled mediaeval society to make a tremendous saving in currency.

"These great fairs, where the trade in the spices of the Levant and the cloth of the West was centralised, were familiar with payments by setting-off one deal against another. Very little money was actually handled at Troyes or Provins; what was exchanged was chiefly bills, and at the end of the fair the money-changers' shops became a real clearing-house. The unpaid bills could, moreover, on payment of a commission, be carried forward from one fair to another."[26]

De Roover found in Bruges thousands and thousands of clearing entries in the books of the Bruges bankers of the fourteenth and fifteenth centuries; he estimates that, at that time, bank deposits had become a real currency.[27] Bank clearings used as means of exchange and payment are called bank money because the transfer of funds is carried by mere written entries in the bankers' books.

Bills of exchange, like bank money, can be used instead of metallic money to carry out a series of money transactions. But these money-tokens constitute a fiduciary currency, because they are accepted in payment only to the extent that the people concerned have confidence in the issuer, or in the banker who carries out the clearing. This is a *private fiduciary currency*, because it is issued by private persons.

Tokens for metallic money can serve as means of exchange and payment of commodities only provided they are *ultimately convertible into metallic money*, the universal equivalent. The circulation of private fiduciary currency always implies an ultimate settlement in public currency which is universally acceptable. Each merchant is naturally alone responsible for the convertibility of his own bills. If these are ultimately not paid, the merchant goes bankrupt, and those who are left holding his bills have lost the money they advanced. Private fiduciary currency is thus, by definition, a form of credit, a *credit currency* the solidity of which—the degree of its equivalence with the metallic money of nominally the same value—depends on the solvency of those who issue it.

Origins of public fiduciary currency

There is, however, something odd in the *private* effort to make up for the inadequacy of metallic currency. Money, the universal equivalent, is by definition a *social* instrument which has to neutralise precisely that which is purely private in commodities so as to make possible a development of exchange with the minimum of restrictions in time and space. Currency tokens the use of which depends on the solvency of individual bourgeois cannot in the long run fulfil such a social function. This is why the development of merchant capital demands the creation of *public currency tokens*, that is, the creation of a public fiduciary currency. Historically, public fiduciary currency derives from a third form of private fiduciary currency, deposit receipts functioning as bank notes. This originated in China.

The merchant's bill was known there from the time of the Chou dynasty (1134–256 B.C.).[28] In the ninth century A.D., which was marked by a severe shortage of metallic currency, the merchants arriving in provincial capitals adopted the habit of depositing their precious metals with private persons and circulating the *deposit receipts* they obtained from them.[29] This private fiduciary currency was called *fei-ch'ien*, or "flying money". The central government forbade this practice because it feared that the precious metals might disappear from circulation. As, however, the shortage of currency was genuine, the State was obliged, in the year 812, to open deposit offices itself, in the capital. With the receipts given them by the central government, the owners of these deposits could have metal coins paid to them in any of the provincial branches of the imperial offices. Later, in the tenth century, a "Bank for Easy Currency" was set up to regulate the system as a whole.

The deposit receipts issued by this bank were still made out to named individuals. But at the beginning of the eleventh century the metal coins of Szechwan province, made of iron, were hindering the circulation of commodities by their excessive weight. The merchants then decided to stop the circulation of coins completely. Sixteen rich merchant houses assembled all their metal coins and issued letters of credit, no longer by name, but *to the bearer*, covered by this stock, and replacing all the metal currency in circulation. The issue of these notes was undertaken rashly and the merchants were ruined. But the central government now intervened again and set up, in 1021, a Bank in Szechwan for the issue of *public bank-notes*. Two years later, these notes began to circulate throughout the Empire. A special bank was then set up to issue and convert this paper money. In 1161 the latter was already circulating to the value of 41,470,000 *kwan*, whereas there were only 700,000 *kwan* of metal coins. Under the following dynasties of Yang (the Tatars) and Ming, paper money remained preponderant, with many phases of depreciation and inflation. The fall of the Ming dynasty was partly due to a galloping inflation of paper money.* After this disaster, the Manchu dynasty, in the seventeenth century, abolished paper money, which was not re-established in China until the middle of the nineteenth century.

Public fiduciary currency was born in Europe in exactly the same

* See later in this Chapter, page 254.

fashion. From the fifteenth century onward, private banks in Venice and Barcelona had adopted the custom of giving deposit receipts to their depositors. When they crashed, towards the end of the sixteenth century, the *Banco di Rialto*, later the Bank of Venice, both public institutions, issued deposit certificates "to bearer", which circulated as paper money, but which soon became depreciated. The Bank of Amsterdam, founded in 1609, issued only certificates of equivalent of the metal coins deposited with it to the currency of the United Provinces. These notes remained remarkably stable down to the end of the eighteenth century. The first issues of bank notes in the strict sense were made by the Bank of Sweden in 1661.[30]

Creation of public fiduciary currency. First source: discounting

It was in Britain that public fiduciary currency, the bank note, received its classical form. In this country, too, it originated from private fiduciary currency, the *goldsmith notes*. The English merchants at first deposited their jewels and private hoards with the King. But in 1640, Charles I, struggling with ever more serious financial difficulties, confiscated their wealth. Thereafter the merchants adopted the custom of depositing their riches with goldsmiths who, in exchange, issued deposit receipts called "goldsmith notes", and then, when the goldsmiths began calling themselves bankers, "banker's notes".[31]

At first, these notes were issued for the total amount of the deposit; if the depositor withdrew part of this deposit, the note was given an additional inscription recording this withdrawal. Later, the bills were drawn up in fixed sums, and a depositor received a number of notes, the total value of which was equal to that of his deposit. Private bankers in Scotland, and the Bank of England, founded in 1697, issued notes which likewise went through these two successive stages.[32]

Now, from a certain moment onward, the Scottish bankers and the goldsmiths began lending to third parties the stock of metal currency which did not belong to them. In exchange for these loans they were given acknowledgements of debt. From that time, the fiduciary currency circulating among the public was covered not only by a stock of metal coins but also by acknowledgements of debt from third parties (one of these covering another). When the Bank of England was founded, in 1697, it issued notes covered by its stock of metal coins and by a State debt owed to it.[33]

Experience taught the bankers that bank-notes covered by third parties' acknowledgements of debt can be issued up to a definite limit (for example, three or four times the value of the stock of metal currency), because the public never all try at once to convert their bank notes into metal coins. Slowly, during the course of the eighteenth century, the Bank of England established a procedure by which the issue of bank notes was regulated both by the stock of metal currency in its possession, and by the discounting, first, of government bonds only, and later also of merchants' bills.[34] The discounting, and later above all the re-discounting, of merchants' bills, was during the nineteenth century the chief source of the creation of bank notes, of public fiduciary currency, not only in Britain but in all the capitalist countries.

When the bank of issue discounts (or re-discounts) a merchant's bill, it pays the owner of the bill (or his bank) the face value less the interest; it thus puts into circulation bank notes for a value equal to this amount. When the time comes for the bill to be paid, it receives this sum back; the same amount in bank notes is withdrawn from circulation. The fluctuations in the volume of its collection of bills will thus determine the amount of paper money in circulation. As the volume of merchants' bills presented for discounting increases in periods of good conjuncture and declines in periods of crisis and depression, the issue of paper money covered by the discounted bills constitute a very flexible currency instrument, which makes it possible to adapt the stock of currency to the economy's need of means of exchange.[35]

Creation of public fiduciary currency. Second source: advances on current account (overdrafts)

So long as the discounting of merchants' bills was the chief form of circulation credit, the bulk of the fiduciary currency in circulation originated from the discounting and re-discounting transactions of the central banks of issue. But from the moment that advances on current account (overdrafts) replaced discounting as the main form of short-term credit—from the end of the nineteenth century in Britain, at the beginning of the twentieth century in the rest of the capitalist world, it was the circulation of bank deposits (of bank money) that became the principal element in currency circulation.

The capitalists do not in fact keep more than a small part of their circulating capital in the form of ready money. Most of it is deposited in the banks. The bankers function as their cashiers, paying out the amounts they owe and taking in the sums paid to them. All these payments are effected by cheques* or by clearing, and are thus completed without cash playing any part, through mere comparison of entries.

* The word cheque comes from the English "to check", i.e. to compare, to verify, and relates to the practice of tearing bills payable to order in such a way as to make an irregular edge which can be compared with the corresponding edge of the other half.[36] In Antiquity the same method was used with potsherds. The first paper cheques were used in Barcelona and Venice in the fourteenth century, but they were then forbidden.[37] The custom of tearing bills payable to order in such a way as to make an irregular edge was kept up in the Middle Ages for recognizances of debt, such as those which Des Marez discovered at Ypres.[38] The first English cheque that has been preserved dates from 1675.

One might suppose that this bank money originates from payments in of cash by the depositors, but this is only partly true. A large share of bank deposits do not originate from payments in actually made by the bank's clients but from advances on current account (overdrafts) granted by the bank to capitalists. These are the "loans that make deposits":

"The bulk of the deposits arise out of the action of the banks themselves; for by granting loans, allowing money to be drawn on overdraft, or purchasing securities, a bank creates a credit in its books which is equivalent to a deposit."[39]

The bank deposits thus created—or at least the current accounts—really represent *currency,* since they can be used for any transaction of purchase or payment within the country. They represent a *fiduciary currency,* because in the last resort their circulation depends on the good management and solvency of the banks, and not on the intrinsic value of the universal equivalent. And they represent a *public fiduciary currency,* because in all the advanced countries all the important deposit banks are linked to the central bank of issue by a special system which ensures that the bank money is covered by the bank notes of the central bank.

The credits given by the banks to the capitalists and which are at the origin of many current accounts, are intended for use. The banks create deposits so that these may circulate. If a bank, by granting a loan on current account to Mr. X, increases his deposit from 4 to 6 million francs, Mr. X will use these 6 millions to pay a debt to Mr. Y or buy goods from Mr. Z. These other capitalists also have bank accounts. If their accounts are with the same bank, all these transactions will take place by comparison of entries and will not require any transfer of bank notes. The deposit of 6 millions will merely be transferred from the account of Mr. X to that of Mr. Z. If their accounts are with other banks, the transfers in question will require a transfer of cash only to the extent that these other banks do not have to transfer an equal amount to Mr. X's bank. Actually, clearing houses specially set up for this purpose reduce to the absolute minimum any transfer of cash from one bank to another.*

Banks, finally, are able to increase their loans on current account

* The cashiers of the London banks, who had the task of transporting the amounts of money needed for settlements between these banks, adopted the custom, in the second half of the eighteenth century, of meeting together over drinks in order to compare their accounts and hand over only the difference between the amounts due and the amounts to be received, and vice versa. Starting in 1775 the bankers themselves imitated their example, which gave rise to the Clearing House. Clearing houses have developed in all the big cities of the world. Their transactions involve huge sums. In 1945, for instance, the Federal Reserve Banks carried out in the U.S.A. clearing operations for a total of 688 billion dollars.[40]

and thus create bank money, to the extent that other banks grant them credit or the central bank allows them to increase their debit accounts with it.[41] Experience has shown bankers that in normal times the public does not withdraw its cash from the banks in excess of a relatively small fraction of the total amount deposited.* It is thus sufficient that these deposits should not exceed a definite relationship with the liquid assets, called the cash ratio, or liquidity ratio (i.e. minimum cash in hand, expressed as a percentage of the total assets) for the banks to be able in normal circumstances to give loans on current account and create bank money. At exceptional moments the central bank has to step in to prevent the collapse of this credit system from entailing the collapse of the entire currency system. In order to avoid rashness, the majority of advanced countries lay down a "cover ratio" fixed by the government.†

In Britain this has been 8 per cent since 1946.[43] In the U.S.A. it is 24 per cent for current accounts in the big banks, in Belgium 4 per cent for short-term deposits, in Sweden and Italy 25 per cent, etc. Furthermore, in Belgium 65 per cent of the total of current accounts have to be covered by public bonds.[44]

It is thus apparent that bank money makes up a large share of the stock of currency, that is, of the totality of means of exchange and payment circulating in a particular country. In 1952, bank money constituted 78·6 per cent of this stock in the U.S.A., 74 per cent of it in Britain, 65 per cent in Australia, 51 per cent in Italy, etc.[45] To this must be added that bank money usually circulates more rapidly than bank notes.[46]

Creation of public fiduciary currency. Third source: public expenditure

The public fiduciary currency created by discounting or by overdrafts corresponds to needs—for credit, exchange, payment—inherent in the economic system. The fact that the State regulates the creation of this fiduciary currency corresponds to the social character of money, which becomes more and more marked as exchange-relations become increasingly interlocked and complex in modern capitalism. But this regulation, which is indispensable for the proper functioning of the economy, can at the same time give rise to many disturbances.

The State which regulates the issue of paper money and ultimately determines the volume of the stock of currency as a whole is actually itself both buyer and seller, and so needs means of exchange

* These withdrawals are mainly made in order to pay wages and salaries or to meet the needs for unproductive consumption of the capitalists and other savers.

† Distinction is made between the *cash ratio* (ratio between cash in hand and total deposits) and the *liquidity ratio* (ratio between holdings of cash, money at call or short notice, and bills discounted on the one hand, and total assets on the other).[42]

and payment. From the beginnings of public fiduciary currency, the governments which regulate its issue have been subjected to the temptation to use it at the same time to meet their own needs. The first experiments in issuing paper money have invariably led to inflationary disasters. This happened with China's paper money which, under the Tatar emperor Kublai Khan, attained the circulation, fantastic for those days, of 249,652,290 *kwan* issued.[47] It was the same with the first experiments in others continents, such as the "card money" in the British and French colonies in America in the seventeenth century, the "Continental money" issued during the American War of Independence, the *assignats* issued during the French Revolution, etc.[48]

Even in a bourgeois state conducted according to principles of strictest monetary orthodoxy, it is inevitable that a certain seasonal and cyclic movement of increased need for disposable funds (e.g. on the eve of the dates for payment of civil servants' salaries) should lead the Treasury to increase its debts to the central bank which in turn will increase the stock of currency. This extra mass of currency is usually re-absorbed in time. But when the State increases the circulation of currency in order to finance its long-term expenses or, still worse, its budgetary deficit, risks of loss of value of the currency arise in so far as no extra mass of commodities corresponds to this extra mass of currency in circulation.[49]

Socially-necessary stock of currency

The whole pyramid of bank money is thus built up on a basis of paper money. It is the same with private fiduciary currency, as we have already shown. All credit money needs, as means of final settlement, a definite amount of currency. In reality, it is a question of a mass of bills which, after clearing, have to be honoured financially. The mass of currency thrown into circulation in a capitalist society thus has to fulfil a dual role, that of constituting the equivalent of the *commodities* which enter into this circulation (money acting as means of circulation), and that of representing the value of the *bills* which fall due, taking into account those which neutralise each other (money acting as means of payment). Here we meet again the two functions of money already described.

Money as means of payment, effecting the payment of bills, like money as means of circulation, has a definite velocity of circulation: the same sum of money may, passing from hand to hand and from firm to firm, effect a successive series of payments in a given period of time. We thus obtain the following formula for the amount of currency needed to settle all payments due (e.g. during one month):

$$\frac{\textit{Total of payments due, minus total of payments which cancel each other out}}{\textit{Velocity of circulation of means of payment}}$$

By adding the stock of currency needed for the circulation of commodities and the stock needed for the payment of bills, one can determine the total stock of currency which is essential for the proper functioning of the capitalist economy. It must be remembered that the same bank note may be used successively to purchase a commodity, and then to enable the seller of this commodity to pay a bill. The stock of currency needed by the economy for a certain period of time must therefore be equal to:

$$\frac{\textit{The sum of the prices of the commodities in circulation}}{\textit{The velocity of circulation of money as means of circulation}}$$

$$+\ \frac{\textit{The sum of payments due, minus the sum of mutually-cancelling payments}}{\textit{The velocity of circulation of money as means of payment}}$$

$$-\ \textit{The sum functioning successively as means of circulation and means of payment.}$$

It follows directly from this formula that the *stock of currency necessary* for the proper working of the economy is a very elastic quantity, which varies uninterruptedly during the course of a month. On the eve and at the moment of the first day of each month, for instance, very much more currency, as means of payment, is needed than eight days later. The stock of currency necessary likewise fluctuates in accordance with the ups and downs of the conjuncture. It also follows that a currency instrument of a *very flexible* kind is needed in order that it may be rapidly adapted to the constantly changing needs of the economy.

In the nineteenth century a series of credit crises were caused in Britain by the fact that the Bank of England was obliged by the Peel Act to keep within a rigid maximum in its issuing of banknotes. This act had to be suspended on each occasion.[50]

In the twentieth century bank money has proved a currency instrument even more flexible than paper money. When the mass of bank notes and current accounts remains stationary, while the demand for circulation credit and means of payment is increasing, the increase in the *velocity of circulation of bank money*—that is, the use of the same deposit for the increased number of transfers in a given period of time—offers a solution to the difficulty. This is what happened in Belgium in 1950 and at the start of 1951, when this velocity of circulation increased by 20 per cent.[51]

The circulation of inconvertible paper money

Bank money is based on public paper money. So long as the latter is convertible and remains based on the stock of metal currency in the bank of issue, the use of token currency does not present any problems regarding the nature of currency. The latter is continuing to serve as universal equivalent by virtue of its own intrinsic value. The fact that only a fraction of the banknotes are covered by the metal in hand (just as only part of the bank money is covered by banknotes) merely represents a social saving in circulation devices, a saving made possible by the laws of behaviour on the part of the public which have been discovered empirically.

These laws reflect in their turn *the increasing socialisation of the capitalist economy, the more and more objective nature of money*. In order that the working of the currency mechanism be not hindered it is sufficient to keep the use of convertible fiduciary currency within the limits of the socially necessary stock of currency. Any issue which went substantially beyond this would cause an outflow of precious metals and a stoppage of convertibility which would doom the currency to devaluation.

By starting from this more and more objective nature of modern capitalist money it is possible to grasp the problem of the circulation of inconvertible paper money. This does not necessarily entail a fall in purchasing power, an obvious depreciation. Experience showed this already in the nineteenth century. The French franc was made inconvertible between 1870 and 1877, but it lost hardly 1·5 per cent of its value in relation to gold and to convertible currency.

In fact it is enough to restrict severely the issue of inconvertible paper money (and the creation of bank money) to the currency stock which is socially necessary, in order to avoid in the main any manifestation of fall in the value of money. All the currency thrown into circulation being absorbed by current economic transactions—exchanges and payments—an inconvertible paper currency of this kind circulates representing only the same amount as a convertible paper currency would have represented in its place, and *within the limits of the national market* no disturbance can occur.

Some writers have seen in this phenomenon proof that money has never been a commodity with its own value, but has always had a "rate" determined by the public authorities.[52] However, nineteenth century experience, especially in countries with bimetallic currency, showed that currency fluctuations were caused by fluctuations in the intrinsic value of gold and silver: "After the great gold discoveries in California and Australia [in the 1850s], silver was an expensive metal and hard to keep in circulation . . . Soon, however, an abrupt reversal took place. From 1842 on, metallurgical processes were discovered which improved the recovery of silver from lead ones. These were widely used after what are now the Rocky Mountain States were taken over by the United States from Mexico in 1848 and 1853. A flood of silver cheapened the metal in relation to gold, and silver was progressively demonetised."[53]

In reality, the transition from the money based on the gold (or silver) standard of the nineteenth century to *partly inconvertible* money after the First World War corresponded to two quite different phenomena. On the one hand, a real currency depreciation caused by the huge expenditure on arms and war, together with the burden of a constantly growing public debt. This currency depreciation even hit the U.S.A., the country possessing a big share of all the world's gold reserves, since in purchasing power a dollar in 1958 was worth less than 50 cents before the war (of 1939). On the other hand, the increasing intervention of the State in economic life, the growing organisation of certain sectors of the economy by the State in the interests of the bourgeois class as a whole, and thereby the elimination of the "pure" conditions of a market economy, an elimination also achieved through the intervention of other "organising" and "conscious" forces, the cartels, trusts, holding companies and monopolistic groupings in general.* A currency with an intrinsic value is essential to a pure market economy based on exchange. The more elements of "economic organisation" are introduced into the economy, the more completely can an "abstract" currency, a money of account, be substituted for this currency of intrinsic value.[54]

But the elements of organisation that capitalism introduces into the economy during its period of decline are disparate and contradictory. They abolish the anarchy and automatic working of the market at one level, only to reproduce them at higher level. In the days of currencies based on the gold standard, many of the payments made, not only on the national market but also on the international market, were carried out without the use of precious metals. In the days of inconvertible or only partly convertible national currencies, international settlements are more complicated; gold (or currency convertible into gold) is insisted on more than before for payments on the international market.

Consequently, even under the régime of inconvertible paper money, the precious metals, commodities with intrinsic value, remain ultimately the only universal equivalent on the world market. A "managed" world currency, the only one which would finally sever the instrument of circulation from its metallic base, cannot be created in a capitalist economy. It can result only from a world-wide planning of the economy, the outcome of the world-wide victory of socialism.

This is why modern currencies are not in reality completely severed from a metallic base, even when the law lays down that no quantity of gold may be obtained in exchange for a banknote (become paper money).† Through foreign trade and the movement of international

* See Chapters 12 and 14.

† It is interesting to observe that this duality has been given curious applications in the courts. French law normally recognises only the "nominal" franc in all disputes that arise between persons resident in France. But as soon as it

payments, every national currency is linked at once to gold and to other national currencies, and the fluctuations in its relative purchasing power, the fluctuations in its rate on the free or black market, are indices of the extent to which it is or is not depreciated. This depreciation results from a property which is peculiar to public fiduciary currency alone: *the solidarity, the collective equivalence, of all the banknotes printed by the State.*

Metallic currency, a product of human labour, possesses an intrinsic value. The increase in its circulation, over and above the stock of currency socially necessary, does not lead to its becoming depreciated but to its being hoarded. It is the same with convertible banknotes, the excessive issue of which may furthermore lead to a flight of gold. *Private* fiduciary currency, issued by insolvent capitalists, brings about its own complete depreciation along with the bankruptcy of the issuer, but does not automatically depreciate the private fiduciary currency issued by other private persons.

Public inconvertible paper money, on the contrary, is subject to depreciation as soon as an excess issue takes place, not accompanied by an equivalent increase in the commodities in circulation. All the banknotes being depreciated together, the increase in the currency in circulation, far from leading to their being hoarded, causes, on the contrary, their de-hoarding. Their value thenceforth depends on their declining purchasing power. The quantity theory of money here applies with a certain amount of validity.*

As this currency is now depreciated, people try to get rid of it and instead to hoard precious metals, metallic money or other, non-depreciated paper money.† Private hoarding of gold between 1946 and 1951 was estimated at an annual average of 250 million dollars. In this way Gresham's Law made itself felt: "bad" money (more or less depreciated) drove good money out of circulation.

The automatic rise of prices as a result of the depreciation of paper money occurs only in a country where price-formation is more or less "free", i.e. determined by economic forces alone. The inconvertible

is a question of international disputes, only the gold value counts, whether this be to the advantage of the French parties to the dispute (dispute about Serbian and Brazilian loans before the Hague Court in 1929, and about the Norwegian loans in 1957) or to their disadvantage (loan issued by the *Messageries Maritimes*).[55]

* On the quantity theory of money, see Chapter 18.

† The depreciation of paper money is a very relative notion. Between 1938 and the end of 1946 the bank notes in circulation in the U.S.A. increased by 400 per cent, whereas industrial production barely doubled. The dollar lost nearly 40 per cent of its purchasing power. This was an obvious case of depreciation. Nevertheless it was not so serious as the depreciation of other paper currencies, such as the French franc and the lira, so that dollar bills were hoarded in France and Italy.

banknotes can be imposed on a country for a certain time, along with strict regulation of the exchanges, which makes it possible to limit to the minimum the increase of prices, in spite of a substantial issue of paper money, shown only on the free currency market abroad and the "parallel", illegal markets in the country itself. This was the case in Nazi Germany.[56] However, a system like this of "deferred inflation" implies other contradictions which need to be studied separately, within the framework of the "managed" economy and the economy of rearmament and war.

The balance of payments

Even when a paper currency is "solid", i.e. when it has not been issued in excess of the socially *necessary stock of currency,* and when it possesses a gold cover traditionally regarded as adequate, it may lose its convertibility into gold. This happened to the pound sterling after 1931. The cause of this inconvertibility lies in the *dual function of gold,* at once cover for paper money and also sole international means of payment. Just as private fiduciary currency circulates within a country only to the extent of the private issuer's solvency (i.e. his capacity to pay a bill when it falls due), public fiduciary currency circulates internationally only to the extent that the issuing country is solvent, that it has the capacity to settle in gold (or in currency convertible into gold) its debts to other countries.

This does not mean that every purchase made abroad entails a transfer of gold to the selling country. On the international plane as on the national and local plane a clearing system operates which implies the transfer of the *net balances* only between the amounts due to the foreign country and the amounts due from it to the country in question. These net amounts appear in the balance of payments, which is mainly made up of the following entries:

(*a*) The trade balance, i.e. the difference between exports to a given country and imports from it. If exports exceed imports in value, there is a credit entry in the balance of payments, if the opposite, there is a debit entry.

(*b*) The movement of capital, i.e. the difference between the outflow and inflow of capital. Into the first of these categories go the purchase of shares, factories and bonds abroad, and foreign landed property, together with the placing of capital in foreign banks, and the sending abroad of dividends, interest, assurance premiums or insurance for foreigners who own property in the country in question. Into the second go the purchase of shares, bonds, factories, land in the country in question by foreigners who bring in their capital, the placing of foreign capital in national banks, the repatriation of dividends, interest, assurance premiums, etc., by residents of the country, and the sending of gifts, public and private, from abroad to the country in question. If the import of capital exceeds the export, this will mean a credit entry in the balance of payments; if the reverse, a debit entry.

(*c*) Maritime traffic. Ships of the given nation which carry goods abroad are paid for the freight in foreign currency which they bring into the country. Contrariwise, foreign ships which bring goods into the country are paid in currency which they take out of the country. If the first total is greater than the second, there will be a credit entry in the balance sheet; if the other way round, a debit entry.

(*d*) Tourist traffic. If the tourists of the country in question spend more money abroad than foreign tourists spend when they visit this country, the entry will be on the debit side. If the opposite is true, it will be on the credit side.

(*e*) The movement of immigration and emigration. If immigrants bring more funds with them than emigrants take out, the entry will be on the credit side; if the contrary, there will be a debit entry. Etc.

So long as a country has normally a credit balance of payments, the convertibility of its paper currency is secured by a relatively modest stock of metal. But as soon as the balance of payments begins to become regularly a debit balance, only a substantial stock of metal can, as a rule, maintain the convertibility of the paper currency. Otherwise, the outflow of gold risks causing speculation and panic.[57] Finally, if the majority of the commercially important countries abandon the gold standard, as happened during the 1930s, the other countries are compelled to follow suit, since otherwise their national currencies become the object of international speculation and are systematically withdrawn from circulation.

The balance of payments affects the volume of money in circulation, and thereby, when the paper currency is partly or totally inconvertible, the purchasing power of money. A permanent deficit in the balance of payments is the product of inflationary tendencies, a surplus is the product of deflationary tendencies.* However, in the short run, when the Central Bank pays exporters the equivalent of the currency surplus it accumulates, a surplus in the balance of payments may provoke an inflationary tendency, because this extra purchasing power finds no counterpart on the market.[58] To avoid these effects, the surplus in the balance of payments would have to be neutralised by an increase in domestic saving.[59]

* A credit balance of payments over a long period corresponds in fact to a *sterilisation of purchasing power*; the gold which is accumulating in the vaults of the central bank could have been used to import various goods, that is, to create extra income. In the same way, a persistently deficitary balance of payments expresses the fact that *surplus purchasing power*—inflation!—has been created in the country, in exchange for which more and more goods and services have to be imported from abroad.

Central banks and bank credit

So long as a currency is based on the gold standard, the role of the issuing institution consists in safe-guarding first and foremost the convertibility of the currency. The restriction of credit that it can bring about by raising the discount rate is conceived in the first place as a means of restricting the fiduciary circulation, and only indirectly as a means of correcting the excesses of a boom. In the age of inconvertible paper money, however, the tasks of the central bank extend to become a function of supervising the entire economy. It has in fact to regulate the credit policy of the commercial banks, which, in their turn, influence the whole progress of the economy.[60]

The central banks of the nineteenth century had as cover the banknotes which they issued, their supply of gold (or silver), and the bills they discounted. They influenced the volume of credit by means of the discount rate.

The economic and financial instability characteristic of the epoch of decline of capitalism, after the First World War, compelled the central banks to resort to extra cover and to different methods of influencing credit. On the one hand the large private banks possess considerable reserves which render them largely independent of the discounting policy of the central bank. On the other, in a period of marked depression, the mere lowering of the discount rate is no longer an adequate stimulus to increase the volume of credit, exchanges and circulation of money. In these conditions, the central bank resorts to an old technique, which was already in extensive use by the public banks of the seventeenth and eighteenth centuries: the policy called that of the "open market".

This policy had always been permitted in the U.S.A. but was practised on a large scale particularly after 1933. It was authorised by a special act in Britain in 1931, and in France and Belgium in 1936. It provides that the central bank may buy and sell government stock (loans, treasury bonds, etc.) on the open market. When the government wants to effect a contraction in the volume of money in circulation (credit), it can sell government stock, which results in an ingathering (and so a sterilisation) of banknotes, or, what comes to the same thing, a reduction in the current credit accounts of the private banks with the central bank, and a reduction in the amount of bank money that these banks can henceforth create.[61] Contrariwise, when the government wants to enlarge the volume of money in circulation (credit) it must buy up government stock, which results in an issue of new banknotes or an increase in the credit accounts of the private banks with the central bank. The open market system can, however, easily degenerate into a means of covering state expenditure due to a budget deficit.[62]

It is in the U.S.A., where the depreciation of the currency has nevertheless gone less far than in Europe, that government stock today represents the chief corresponding value to the bank money of the private banks, and a far more important entry in the assets of the central bank than the private obligations:

"Until 1933, the principal way in which money came into existence was through short-term borrowing by business concerns. In 1929, the loans of commercial banks accounted for nearly two-thirds of the country's supply of money . . . At the end of 1950, they accounted for less than one-third . . . The largest single source of money supply is borrowing by the government. The holdings of government obligations by commercial banks are half again as large as their short-term loans."[63]

However, the supervisory function that the central bank can exercise in its capacity as ultimate source of cash is not absolute. It can either rigidly determine the amount of currency or else rigidly determine the cost of money-capital (cash), that is, the rate of interest. The first path was followed in the nineteenth century, the second is being followed now.[64] But to regulate simultaneously and rigidly *both* the amount of currency *and* the rate of interest is impossible in a capitalist economy.

Currency manipulations

The dual function of gold, that of serving as metallic basis to paper money and that of acting as international means of payment, makes this precious metal an instrument of economic and commercial policy. When the national currencies are freely convertible into gold, their respective value is determined directly either by the metal content of the coinage or else by the gold cover of the banknotes, which are mere tokens for the precious metals. When the convertibility of paper currencies is more or less abolished, these currencies acquire a *forced rate* in relation to foreign currencies. This rate is usually determined by international conventions, but it can be modified unilaterally. If it corresponds to the actual relationship between the purchasing power of the two currencies, it will usually be respected and will undergo only slight ups and downs, caused by temporary fluctuations in the balance of payments between two countries, in the reciprocal supply and demand of their respective currencies.[65]

If this rate is, on the contrary, an artificial one, a "parallel", "free" or "black" market will appear, on which the currency thus officially over-valued will be depreciated in exchange for other currencies.

A government may attempt to bring about internationally such a depreciation, with the aim of favouring its exports, either in order to improve the balance of payments or to help the general state of business. As the rate of exchange of an inconvertible currency is a forced rate, the government can lower it by mere decree. It can announce arbitrarily that henceforth there will correspond to the unit of currency a gold equivalent devalued, say, by 20 per cent, and that consequently, foreign currencies will henceforth be quoted at a rate 25 per cent higher than before. A depreciation of the currency effected like this, called devaluation, causes the prices of a country's products in foreign markets to fall.

American and British cars are competing on the Australian market. Let us suppose that the current selling price of the American car most frequently sold in Australia is 3,000 dollars, which is worth £A750, at the rate of £A1 = 4 dollars. The British cars, which cost £600 sterling will be sold at £A750 too, if £1 sterling is worth £A1·25. But if the pound sterling is devalued by 20 per cent, this same car will be sold at £A600, without any reduction in the cost of production or the manufacturers' profit.

The use of devaluation as a weapon in competition comes up against two obstacles, however:

(a) It risks starting a snowball, with all countries trying to improve their trade balance in the same way. This is what happened after the devaluation of the pound sterling in 1931, which entailed the devaluation of 34 other national currencies between 1931 and 1935. The same phenomenon recurred after the devaluation of sterling in 1949.

(b) Every country has not only to export but to import as well. If devaluation reduces export prices, it increases the prices of imports. It thus favours the industries working for the export trade using home-produced raw materials, as against the industries working for the home market using imported raw material, and so leads to a redistribution of the national income. These effects can be mitigated if substantial stocks of foreign raw material have been accumulated before devaluation, or if a fall in the price of these goods is expected, a favourable change in the "terms of trade".* In the end, the elasticity of the foreign demand for the products exported by the country devaluing its currency will prove decisive.[66]

A currency policy opposite to devaluation can likewise tend to bring about an increase in exports. Without modifying the backing of the country's paper money in gold or currency, it is possible to cause a fall in prices on the home market by restricting credit and the amount of money in circulation, lowering nominal wages, etc. This fall will then react on export prices. As a rule, however, this policy of *deflation* increases the stagnation of business and the degree of unemployment within the country,[67] so destroying all the advantages to be expected from an increase in exports, which, moreover, are neutralised, as with devaluation, by international chain reactions:

"If pressure on money wage rates improves a country's balance

* The expression "terms of trade" is used to mean the relationship between the price index of exported goods and the price index of imported goods.

[of payments], it becomes possible for home producers to gain advantages at the expense of foreign producers, and thus to shift the incidence of unemployment on to other countries. These other countries who find their exports declining and their imports rising will react to the resulting unemployment by putting pressure on their own wages. If, however, wage cuts in country A are followed or outpaced by wage cuts in country B the former does not obtain a net advantage."[68]

In fact, after the outbreak of the economic crisis of 1929, there followed one after the other two international chain reactions, first a deflationary one, then one of devaluation.

The manipulations of paper currency by governments who try to use it as a weapon against the trade cycle have created illusions as to the possibility of correcting serious excesses in the conjuncture by means of a "managed currency". By increasing the amount of fiduciary money in circulation and lowering the rate of interest, the banks of issue can in fact encourage an expansion of credit by the commercial banks, which is expected to favour economic recovery when there is depression.

However, the influence of the rate of interest on economic conjuncture should not be exaggerated. An investigation undertaken in the U.S.A. shows that the interest paid by the entrepreneur represents there a very small element in the cost of production: 0·4 per cent of the cost of production of manufactured goods: 0·2 per cent of the cost of production in the building trade; 0·8 per cent of that of mineral products; and 0·2 per cent of distribution costs.[69]

It is an illusion to suppose that the banks can ensure on their own (with the aid of the central bank) an expansion of credit and of the stock of currency. They can at most grant loans more easily and at lower cost. But for the stock of currency to increase effectively by way of credits on current account, it is further necessary that the entrepreneurs should *effectively use* the facilities thus provided. It is the entrepreneurs and not the banks who are really the initiators of the expansion of bank money at the start of recovery.[70] Now: "In a [deep] depression things look so gloomy that no conceivable drop in the rate of interest is likely to induce [a businessman] to embark upon any but the most blatantly desirable adventures."[71]

It is then, in the last analysis, the factors that determine the economic conjuncture as a whole that explain the transition from a depression to an economic recovery—and among these factors the manipulation of the stock of currency and the rate of interest play only a subordinate role.*

Three forms of inflation

Depreciation of the currency is as old as public currency itself. It is

* See Chapter 11.

engendered by the needs of the State which mints the coins or issues the notes. Its oldest form is the falsification of the alloy, base metals being substituted for precious ones. Owing to the sharp oscillations in prices to which it gives rise, it disorganises the economy of any society based on petty commodity economy. The Czech chronicler Cosmas, who died about 1125, called it "worse than the plague, more disastrous than an enemy invasion, than famine or other calamities."[72]

Paper money, which seems to free itself from its metallic basis, offers by its very nature a strong temptation to depreciation, either intermittent or continuous.

Accordingly, in the imperialist epoch, this depreciation or inflation has become a quasi-universal phenomenon. Several degrees of gravity need, however, to be distinguished.

Moderate inflation corresponds to an issue of fiduciary currency (or an increase in the stock of currency by other means) without any immediate equivalent increase in goods or services, but in circumstances in which the volume of employment and production increases. For this to happen a certain amount of unemployment and a reserve of unemployed means of production are needed, among other things.[73]* When the State uses the increased stock of currency to buy goods and labour-power which serve to make means of destruction—i.e. goods which do not come back into the reproduction process—it can, by imposing a strict control of prices, *conceal* the inflation for the time being, until the disproportion between the amount of money in circulation and the actual circulation of commodities breaks the ephemeral equilibrium. The balancing equivalent to this price-control has in these conditions to be the sterilisation of a part of the public's income in the form of forced saving.[74] In this case, *concealed* or "deferred" *inflation* represents a promise to increase the circulation of goods some time in the future through an increase in home production converted back to normal uses, or else by the plundering of foreign countries. If this reabsorption of purchasing power without any counterpart does not take place, the inflation effected will eventually bring about a rise in prices.

When a substantial issue of inflationary paper money is accompanied by a stagnation or a diminution in the circulation of purchasable commodities over a prolonged period—notably, when full employment has already been achieved, or in the setting of a war economy—the rise in prices takes place at once, and starts a vicious circle. *Inflation feeds on itself*. Depreciation of the currency leads to a rise in prices, this increases the budget deficit, which in turn is covered by a fresh inflationary issue of paper money, and that entails a new

* See Chapter 10, section "War Economy", and Chapter 14, section "A crisis-free capitalism?"

wave of price increases. The depreciated fiduciary currency does not go out of circulation any more. Everybody who can tries to get rid as soon as possible of this depreciated currency and hoards *real values*: gold, foreign currency, jewels, works of art, industrial shares, property in land and buildings, etc. The wage-earning classes are hardest hit.[75]

When the State's expenditure begins to exceed its income by a big margin, as the result of a lost war, occupation costs, reparations to be paid, etc., what appears is *galloping inflation*. The depreciation of the currency goes from bad to worse every day, if not every hour. Bank-notes are issued with astronomical face-values, and depreciate faster than they can be printed. Exchanges by means of money grow fewer and fewer, and people go back to barter. Industry risks being unable to reconstitute its capital and no longer realising surplus-value if it exchanges commodities for such depreciated currency. Its products are therefore withdrawn from the market and stored, which brings about a stoppage in the economy and the complete collapse of the currency. These phenomena occurred in Germany in 1922–23 and in 1945–48, in China in 1945–49, in Rumania and Hungary in 1945–47, etc.*

Purchasing power, circulation of currency, and rate of interest

When interest is seen as "the rent for money" and it is thought to depend on the supply and demand of *cash*, there is a temptation to seek some ratio between the amount of currency in circulation and the rate of interest. But this is to forget that the rate depends on the supply and demand of *liquid money capital* and that definite *social* conditions are needed if the currency in circulation is to be transformed into *capital*. In fact, this mass of currency is divided socially into two major categories:

(a) The amount corresponding to the wages and salaries of workers and other employees, together with that part of the capitalists' funds earmarked for their expenditure as private consumers.

(b) The amount corresponding to the circulating capital of enterprises, profits not yet reinvested, depreciation funds of fixed capital not yet used, and "savings" from all sources.

The first category does not represent in any way a supply of liquid money-capital, but is instead a *demand for consumer goods*. The second category may represent both a *demand for means of production* and a *supply of liquid money-capital*.[76] It is only through the quantity of this second category of currency in circulation that the rate of interest may effectively influence the proportion of money-capital that will be hoarded, the proportion that will be lent to banks or to industrial and commercial firms, and the proportion that will be directly used by the owner for buying means of production. But this

* On the inflationary tendencies inherent in declining capitalism, see Chapter 14.

allocation of the mass of money-capital between different destinations will not depend exclusively, or even primarily, on the rate of interest but on the general state of business (the exact stage in the industrial cycle, the rate of profit, the ratio between rate of profit and rate of interest, etc.). "It cannot be asserted that an increase in the stock of money causes the rate of interest to fall and a diminution of the stock of money causes it to rise. Whether the one or the other consequence occurs always depends on whether the new distribution of property is more or less favourable to the accumulation of capital."

"There is no direct connection between the rate of interest and the amount of money held by the individuals who participate in the transactions of the market; there is only an indirect connection operating in a roundabout way through the displacements in the social distribution of income and wealth which occur as a consequence of variations in the objective exchange value of money."[77]

This does not mean that expansion of the volume of currency plays only a secondary role in the evolution of capitalism. On the contrary, its expansion is an essential condition for this evolution, for two reasons.

On the one hand, the tremendous increase in production and productivity which is characteristic of capitalism would have been impossible without a corresponding increase in the stock of currency, independently of the ups and downs of the exploitation of mines of precious metals.[78]

On the other hand, given the influence it exercises on the level of prices, the expansion of the stock of fiduciary and bank money determines the particular form taken by the redistribution of the national income, i.e. the *increase in the rate of profit* which occurs at the beginning of every economic recovery and without which this recovery would not be possible in a capitalist economy.

Economists such as Von Mises and Schumpeter have sufficiently described the phenomenon they call *forced saving*.[79] Forced saving, i.e. the reduction in the purchasing power of wages through depreciation of the currency, is indicated by Von Mises as a source of the formation of capital. And in this indirect way these writers, who reject any theory of surplus-value based on exploitation, recognise that capital is not the product of the thrift and self-sacrifice of the capitalists, but of the forced saving and sacrifices *imposed on the wage-earners by the way capitalism works*:

"One class has, for a time, robbed another class of part of their incomes; and has saved the plunder. When the robbery comes to an end, it is clear that the victims cannot possibly consume the capital which is now well out of their reach. If they are wage-earners, who have all the time consumed every penny of their income, they have no wherewithal to expand consumption. And if they are capitalists, who have not shared in the plunder, they may indeed be induced to consume now a part of their capital by the fall in the rate of interest; but not more so than if the rate had been lowered by the 'voluntary savings' of other people."[80]

In other words, and paradoxically, only a fall in the rate of interest *accompanied by a rise in the rate of profit* at the expense of the wage-earners (i.e. of their purchasing power) constitutes a real stimulus to capitalist production.

REFERENCES

1. B. Nogaro: *Cours d'économie politique*, Vol. I, p. 323.
2. R. P. Kent: *Money and Banking*, pp. 6-7.
3. B. Nogaro: *La Monnaie et les systèmes monétaires*, p. 6.
4. R. P. Kent: op. cit., p. 9.
5. F. Heichelheim: *Wirtschaftsgeschichte des Altertums*, pp. 202-4.
6. Ibid., pp. 421, 428.
7. Ibid., pp. 684-6.
8. Ibid., p. 204.
9. P. Bakker: *Eenige Beschouwingen over het Geldwezen in de inheemsche Samenleving van Nederlandsch-Indië*, pp. 1-3.
10. B. Nogaro: *La Monnaie et les systèmes monétaires*, pp. 87-88.
11. Irving Fisher: *Purchasing Power of Money*, (1911), p. 24.
12. B. Nogaro: *Cours d'économie politique*, Vol. I, pp. 391-2.
13. B. Nogaro: *La Monnaie et les systèmes monétaires*, p. 218.
14. F. Løkkegaard: *Islamic Taxation in the Classic Period*, p. 94.
15. Heichelheim: op. cit.
16. G. Glotz: *Le Travail dans la Grèce antique*, p. 278.
17. Chen Huan-Chang: *The Economic Principles of Confucius and His School*, Vol. II, p. 432.
18. *Pratica della Mercatura*, pp. 152-5.
19. R. De Roover: *L'Evolution de la lettre de change*, Vol. II, p. 52.
20. R. Bigo: *La Caisse d'Escompte et les origines de la Banque de France*, p. 19.
21. J. Kulischer: *Allgemeine Wirtschaftsgeschichte*, Vol. II, p. 346.
22. *Histoire du Commerce*, Vol. III, p. 445.
23. Ibid., Vol. III, p. 303.
24. R. De Roover: op. cit., Vol. II., p. 83.
25. R. Bigo: *Les Bases historiques de la finance moderne*, p. 22.
26. H. Hauser: *Les Débuts du capitalisme*, pp. 21-22.
27. R. De Roover: op. cit., Vol. I, p. 115; id., *Money, Banking and Credit in Mediaeval Bruges*, p. 283.
28. Ki Fein-chen: *Essai sur l'origine et l'evolution des banques en Chine*, pp. 144-5.
29. Chen Huan-Chang: op. cit., Vol. II, p. 433.
30. J. C. Van Dillen: *History of the Principal Public Banks*, pp. 40-41, 81-82 et seq., 336, *et al.*

31. Kulischer, op. cit., Vol. II, p. 346.
32. Ibid., p. 348.
33. A. Dauphin-Meunier: *La Banque à travers les âges*, Vol. I, p. 318.
34. J. H. Clapham: *History of the Bank of England*, pp. 122-31.
35. Kent: op. cit., pp. 104-6; Jean Marchal: quoted by L. Camu in *Evolution récente du rôle des banques*, p. 23.
36. R. Eisler: *Das Geld*, p. 204.
37. A. P. Usher: *The Early History of Deposit Banking in Mediterranean Europe*, pp. 21-22.
38. Kulischer: op. cit., Vol. I, p. 332.
39. MacMillan Report, quoted in John Strachey, *A Programme for Progress*, p. 106.
40. Kent: op. cit., p. 125.
41. B. Nogaro: *La Monnaie et les systèmes monétaires*, p. 23.
42. N. Macrae: *The London Capital Market*, p. 239.
43. R. S. Sayers: *Modern Banking*, pp. 35-36.
44. L. Camu: in *Evolution récente du rôle des banques*, pp. 29-31.
45. Ibid., pp. 21-22.
46. Macrae: op. cit., p. 195.
47. H. J. Laurence Laughlin: *A New Exposition of Money, Credit and Prices*, Vol. II, p. 35.
48. Nogaro and Oualid: *Evolution du Commerce, du Crédit et des Transports depuis 150 ans*, pp. 59-60, 143-50.
49. *Palgrave's Dictionary of Political Economy*, Vol. II, p. 792.
50. F. Baudhuin: *Crédit et Banque*, p. 112.
51. *Problèmes Economiques*, 21st August, 1951.
52. Mossé: *La Monnaie*, pp. 30-37.
53. J. B. Condliffe: *The Commerce of Nations*, pp. 186-9.
54. J. Strachey: op. cit., pp. 120-2.
55. L. A. Rabinovitch: in *Le Monde*, 19th-20th May, 1957.
56. B. Nogaro: *La Monnaie et les systèmes monétaires*, pp. 68-70.
57. Baudhuin: op. cit., pp. 152-3.
58. Sayers: op. cit., p. 179.
59. Ibid., p. 83.
60. G. D. H. Cole: *Money, its Present and Future*, pp. 40-41.
61. Baudhuin: op. cit., p. 58.
62. Ibid., p. 58.
63. Sumner H. Slichter: *What's Ahead for American Business?*, pp. 6-7.
64. Sayers: op. cit., p. 131.
65. B. Nogaro: *La Monnaie et les systèmes monétaires*, pp. 48-59; *Rapport de la Banque Internationale des Payements*, 1952, pp. 145-6.
66. T. Balogh: in *The Economics of Full Employment*, p. 142.
67. Ibid., p. 136.
68. F. A. Burchardt: in *The Economics of Full Employment*, pp. 9-10.
69. H. G. Moulton: *Controlling Factors in Economic Development*, p. 306.
70. Strachey: op. cit., p. 112.

71. Sayers: op. cit., p. 196; Balogh: op. cit., p. 129.
72. Eisler: op. cit., p. 178.
73. J. M. Keynes: *General Theory*, pp. 311 et seq.; Hawtrey: in *La Monnaie*, p. 18; F. A. Burchardt: in *The Economics of Full Employment*, p. 21.
74. J. M. Keynes: *How to Pay For The War.*
75. R. Lewinsohn: *Histoire de l'inflation*, pp. 27-29.
76. B. Nogaro: *La Monnaie èt les systèmes monétaires*, pp. 215-16.
77. L. von Mises: *Theory of Money and Credit*, pp. 346-8.
78. Strachey, op. cit., pp. 108-9.
79. J. Schumpeter: *Sozialprodukt und Rechenpfennige.*
80. Piero Sraffa: in *Economic Journal*, March 1932, p. 48.

CHAPTER NINE

AGRICULTURE

Agriculture and commodity production

THE development of agriculture lays the foundation for a real division of labour, the separation of town from country, and for generalising exchange-relations.* But agriculture long remains outside the mode of production which it has engendered. Long after petty commodity production has appeared in large towns, centres of international trade, production of use-values continues to predominate in the countryside, only a few leagues from these metropolises. Only the surplus of the production of a few farms is sent to market.

When the Roman Empire undertook to ensure the feeding of the Roman proletariat, together with its numerous Legions, the trade in wheat, oil, wine and olives experienced a great expansion. The oscillations in the trade in these commodities have even been regarded by some authors as the decisive index of the decline of the Empire.[1] But this was actually a matter of providing supplies not for an anonymous market but for the State,[2] and, furthermore, supplies which were unpaid for or paid for at a very low price,[3] and thus a direct or concealed form of taxation. It was only in the centralising and transport of these masses of agricultural produce that merchant capital played a big part. The State in its turn distributed this produce free to the population of big centres such as Rome and Byzantium and to the Legions. In this way the entire cycle of supply remained outside the realm of commodity production. The latter appeared, so far as agricultural produce was concerned, only in the sale on the local markets of the surpluses of the peasants and nobles, and in the sale to the State of the produce of the slave plantations in Sicily. It was, generally speaking, the same in all pre-capitalist societies.

When, from the sixteenth century onward, money economy became general in Western Europe, commodity production extended more and more in the countryside. At the same time, the development of capital gave rise to a new social class, the farmers. These men did not want land as a means of obtaining their subsistence; they wanted it as a basis for producing agricultural *commodities*, the sale of which would bring in a *profit*.

Domestic industry and rural crafts, heavily attacked by the products

* See Chapter 1.

of large-scale factory industry from the eighteenth century onward, began to fade away. This evolution was fully completed in Western Europe only during the nineteenth century. In Eastern Europe and other economically backward parts of the world, the corresponding evolution took place only at the end of the nineteenth and the beginning of the twentieth centuries. It is today far from complete in all countries. Nowhere, moreover, has the production of agricultural commodities completely done away with the production of use-values, since even in highly-industrialized countries like the U.S.A., Germany and Belgium, subsistence farmers still exist to this day—i.e. peasants who sell on the market only the surplus of their production (their numbers were estimated, in the U.S.A., at 1,250,000 families in 1939).[4]

Pre-capitalist rent and capitalist ground-rent

In civilised pre-capitalist society agriculture constitutes man's chief economic activity. Ground rent is therefore the essential form of society's surplus-product. It is produced by agricultural producers who, in practice, dispose of their own means of production and possess at least a customary right to their land, in exchange for which they surrender part of their labour-time (labour-service) or of their production (rent in kind) to the property-owning classes. This division of the peasant's product into necessary product and surplus-product (ground rent) takes place wholly outside the market, in the sphere of the production of use-values.

In pre-capitalist society, the transformation of ground-rent from rent in kind into money rent is already in itself a sign of social decomposition. It presupposes an extensive development of the production and circulation of commodities, and also of the circulation of money. It is by selling part of their production that the peasants obtain the money they need to pay this new form of rent that they owe to their feudal lords. Although, however, commodity production is necessary for money rent to appear, the latter remains quantitatively independent of market conditions. What is typical of it, and situates it at the end of the evolution of *pre-capitalist rent*, which always has this characteristic, in all its previous forms, is that it is *fixed*, and, thereby, independent of the movement of prices and of the total money income of the producer.[5]* It was precisely to the extent that rent remained fixed that the peasants were the great beneficiaries of every period which saw a marked rise in agricultural prices (notably the period between the beginning of the thirteenth and the middle of the fourteenth centuries).[6]

Moreover, in the epoch of pre-capitalist rent, the land itself is only

* This naturally does not mean that pre-capitalist rent remains fixed during entire centuries. But it does not fluctuate from one harvest to another.

by way of exception regarded as an investment for money-capital which is expected to bring in an income proportional to this capital: "In the barbarian period and the first part of the feudal period, only a small part of the land was freely negotiable: immense areas, left as forest and grassland, were royal domain; other huge areas were the inalienable property of the Church and the monasteries; and even the secular possessions were mostly tied up with a whole hierarchy of relations between those who granted land and those to whom it was granted, whereby their alienation, though not completely impossible, was nevertheless hindered in a thousand ways. No less fixed were the relations between owners and cultivators. As regards the latter, the tie of custom took the place of the bond of contract, reducing the great majority of the workers on the land to the condition of *coloni* tied to the soil, who could not freely leave the land and yet could not be evicted from it, either."[7]

Capitalist ground rent is quite different from this. It appears in a society in which the land itself and its main products have become commodities. It results from the investment in agriculture of capital which has to bring in the average profit. Like capitalist industry it thus presupposes a separation of the producers from their means of production. It further implies a separation between the basic means of production and the farmer-entrepreneur, between the owner of the land and the owner of capital. It is in this circumstance that it is distinguished and is separated from capitalist profit.

Origins of capitalist ground-rent

The origin of a *market for agricultural produce* in Europe is intimately linked with the development of the towns in the Middle Ages. An initial development of trade disorganised the manorial supply system, and favoured the appearance of these first local territorial markets:

"The lord's manorial marketing system was giving way to the organisation of a local territorial market slowly being worked out. It was found unprofitable to cart corn long distances to a home manor for consumption, or to a market centre within the manorial group, when good market places had to be passed on the way, and when, perhaps, the corn was finally deposited in a district of a large surplus, and therefore low price. In other words, the territorial market gradually cut in upon the manorial corn supply system, and ultimately supplanted it."[8]

This evolution was a slow one, however; it was only in the second half of the fifteenth century that real local markets became predominant in Britain.[9] Moreover, the formation of territorial markets was hindered by the supply policy of the towns, which endeavoured by all means to prevent an increase in the price of foodstuffs.[10] In these conditions the unification of the national market was not possible, and in each country a series of regional markets were established with markedly different price-levels, reflecting the particular regional conditions of comparative plenty or want. In mediaeval England the region with the highest price for wheat and that with the lowest were only 50 miles apart; in April 1308 there was a difference of 40 per cent in the price of wheat between the towns of Oxford and Cuxham, separated by only 12 miles![11]

It is in the evolution, from the sixteenth century onward, of these local markets supplied essentially out of the surpluses of producers of use-values, into great metropolitan markets, that we must look for the origin of agricultural capitalism. The prodigious development of urban centres like London, Paris, Antwerp, Amsterdam, Hamburg, etc., upset the relations of supply and demand as regards agricultural produce.[12] These great cities concentrated within their boundaries a considerable proportion of the national population—in the case of London, 10 per cent of the British population from the end of the seventeenth century and 20 per cent by the nineteenth century. The supply of foodstuffs to these populations depended no longer merely on the neighbouring agricultural areas, but on a large proportion of the entire agricultural production of the whole country.[13] This tended to level out agricultural prices on the national scale, and this in the sense that the prices paid in the metropolitan area became the basis for the national price of wheat.

Thereby, contrariwise to what happened in the local markets of the Middle Ages, the areas with big wheat surpluses which were near the capital could sell their wheat dearer than remote areas where there was a shortage (allowing for transport costs).[14] After the metropolitan market the next stage, achieved in a single century, was the *world grain market*: London attracted not only the wheat needed for its own feeding but also all the wheat intended for export, for maximum valorisation on the markets of the world.[15]

The appearance of vast metropolitan markets from the sixteenth and seventeenth centuries onward was accompanied by a complete reversal of the food-supply policy of the big towns. For these it was no longer a question, as in the Middle Ages, of restricting the price of foodstuffs by every means. On the contrary, it was a question of ensuring by every means an adequate supply of foodstuffs for the town *at any price*.[16] It was in this sense that the metropolises played the part of an apparently unlimited market, thus fostering the introduction of capitalism in agriculture. No longer were only the surpluses of rural production sent to the town; the maximum possible amount of wheat was sent, so that often the country people were reduced to subsistence level.[17]

The movement for the enclosure of common land was stimulated not only by attractive prospects for sheep-raising but also by very high prices of wheat. The appearance of the metropolitan market and the ending, for the agricultural producers, of free use of the soil (i.e., the introduction of capitalism in agriculture), were intimately linked together.[18] The importance of this stimulus can be judged if one considers that, from 1500 to 1800, the price of wheat in Britain rose from index 100 to index 275, and in France from index 100 to index 572, whereas the prices of metals and textiles rose by only 30 per cent during the same period.[19]

In the same epoch, the rationalisation of agriculture, the transition from the three-field system to the planting of crops which restore the soil's fertility, and the growing use of chemical fertilisers, increased, first in Flanders, Holland and some parts of Germany, then later in Britain and France, the minimum funds needed by a farmer if he were to take advantage of this miraculous manna of rising agricultural prices. From the end of the eighteenth century one needed, in England, to dispose of a minimum capital of £5 an acre in order to exploit an arable farm, £8 an acre for a mixed farm, and £20 an acre for a cattle or sheep farm.[20] The ownership of *capital* thus became the condition for any viable agricultural enterprise, however modest. In this way all the conditions for the penetration of capital into agriculture were realised.

Now, as it penetrated into agriculture in the old countries of Western and Central Europe, this capital was confronted by two circumstances which were utterly different from those existing in industry and trade. Whereas in industry all the material factors of production—machinery, raw materials, labour—could be produced and reproduced by capitalism itself, and produced at a price relatively or absolutely lower and lower (in the case of labour, thanks to the industrial reserve army!), in agriculture, the basic material element of production, the land, is given, in *limited* quantity, once for all. It constitutes a natural monopoly, marked for ever with the stamp of shortage.[21] Whereas capital could freely enter and leave every sphere of industry, it could not freely enter agriculture. There, the ownership of the land had been seized by a class of *landowners* who forbade access to it unless a rent was paid.

The land thus constituted a twofold monopoly at the beginning of the capitalist mode of production: a natural monopoly and a property monopoly. So long as agricultural productivity lags behind the increase of the population and the productivity of industry, a dual differentiation of prices will exist. Since the whole of agricultural production is absorbed by the market, the selling price of wheat will be determined by the conditions of production prevailing on the plots of land which are *least profitable* (through their degree of fertility, the way they are cultivated or their geographical position), so that this price will greatly exceed the price of production on the more profitable farms, which will thus realise a *super-profit*. Since, furthermore, agriculture does not participate in the general equalisation of the rate of profit, owing to the existence of the monopolies mentioned, even the wheat produced under the least profitable conditions is not sold at its price of production but at its *value*, which is higher than the price of production just because of the technical backwardness of agriculture as compared with industry, the lower organic composition of capital in the agricultural sphere. *Capitalist ground rent originates in this dual differentiation, and exists only to the extent that this differentiation exists.*

Differential ground-rent

In industry, superprofits are realised when the productivity of an enterprise is higher than the average. Even if this higher productivity makes it possible to sell commodities above their price of production, it leads to a *lowering* in the average market prices. In agriculture too, big differences in productivity enable certain enterprises and the owners of certain pieces of land to realise a surplus profit. But this profit does not coincide with a reduction but with an *increase* in the market price. So long as, through increase in population and a lag in agricultural productivity, the demand for agricultural produce exceeds the supply, this price will remain determined by the value of the agricultural commodities produced under the worst conditions of profitability. If all the human labour expended for the production of foodstuffs is socially necessary labour—so long as all the products of agriculture find purchasers!—even those agricultural commodities which are produced under the least profitable conditions will find an equivalent for their value; it will thus be this value that will determine the average selling price of wheat. The difference between this price and the price of production of the wheat produced on land with a higher productivity represents a *differential* rent which is taken by the landowner.

This differential rent may arise in two different ways: from the difference in natural fertility, or geographical situation, between different plots of land, or from the investment of different amounts of capital. We call these two cases differential rent of the first type and differential rent of the second type.

Take three plots of land of the same area, on which three farmers are working, each with capital identical in amount and organic composition. This capital, for one million francs expended in a year, produces 80 quintals of wheat from plot A, 100 from plot B, and 120 from plot C. If the average rate of profit is 20 per cent, the selling price of the wheat will be $\frac{1{,}200{,}000}{80}$ francs, or 15,000 francs per quintal, the price of production of the wheat on the least fertile of the plots.

Plot A will thus bring in no differential rent. The product of plot B will be worth 1·5 millions; if this plot be let, the owner will receive a differential rent of 300,000 francs; the farmer who actually cultivates it will have to be content with the average profit of 200,000 francs. The product of plot C will be worth 1·8 millions; if this plot be let, the owner will receive a differential rent of 600,000 francs, the farmer who actually cultivates it having, once more, to be content with the average profit of 200,000 francs.

As transport charges are incorporated in the selling prices of agricultural products, the plots nearest to a metropolitan centre will bring in a substantial differential rent. Here is an example taken from the United States:

Distance from Louisville (Kentucky) in miles	*Rent of land per acre dollars*	*Price of land per acre dollars*
8 or less	11·85	312
9 to 11	5·59	110
12 to 14	5·37	106
15 or over	4·66	95[22]*

From 0 to 5 miles from an urban centre: dairying zone: average rent, 15 dollars.

From 5 to 17 miles from an urban centre: maize zone: average rent, 8 dollars.

From 17 to 27 miles from an urban centre: wheat zone: average rent, 5 dollars.

From 27 to 50 miles from an urban centre: ranching zone: average rent, 2 dollars.

So long as agricultural prices tend to rise, the capitalists are interested in investing in agriculture, so as to extend cultivation to uncultivated land or to get higher production from land already under cultivation. In the first case, it is not necessarily a matter of less fertile land: it may involve land which is less accessible, more remote, land which needs considerable drainage or irrigation if it is to produce more than land already under cultivation. But these investments of capital have to be depreciated over a certain period; during that period they therefore increase the cost of production, and, thereby, the price of production.

The same is true when production is increased on land already cultivated, through the use of additional quantities of fertiliser, a better

* Though all these plots are not suitable for the same crops, their relative distance from the urban markets determines to a large extent the profitability of the different kinds of agriculture, taking into account the costs and the relative speed of transport, the perishable nature of the produce, etc. Ely and Wehrwein[23] give the following table of average rent per acre in the United States:

selection of seed, the introduction of agricultural machinery, the employment of agronomists—in short, through further investment of capital.

Experiments in the U.S.A. have shown that in the fifties an average of 12·33 bushels of wheat per acre could be got there when wheat is grown without a break and without using fertiliser; 23·58 bushels when a certain optimum amount of fertiliser is used, but without any break in the growing of wheat; and 32 bushels when an optimum quantity of fertiliser is used and a four-year rotation system followed.[24]

Let us go back to our example of the three plots of land, A, B and C. Assume that an extra investment of one million francs in plot C results in an increase in production from 120 to 220 quintals. On the two million francs thus invested, the capitalist has to realise an average profit of 20 per cent, or 400,000 francs. But the 220 quintals will be sold for 3·3 million francs, if the selling price continues to be determined by the price of production of wheat on the least fertile plot, or 15,000 francs per quintal. Of these 1·3 million francs of surplus value, 400,000 francs will go to the capitalist as average profit, 600,000 francs will go to the landowner, as differential rent of the first type; and 300,000 francs represent the differential rent of the second type which the farmer will endeavour to keep but which the landowner will try to get included in the rent, when the lease is renewed.* Unlike differential rent of the first type, rent of the second type is less obvious and therefore less directly seizable by the landowner.

Absolute ground-rent

Up to now we have encountered rent, super-profit, only on land where, through better fertility or geographical position, or through additional investment of capital, the price of production is lower than it is on less profitable land, so long as the latter price determines the price at which agricultural products are sold. What will happen, though, to land of this latter category? Where the cultivator and the owner are the same person, there is no problem, since the capitalist will, in principle, be content with the average profit alone. It will not be the same, however, where the owners of these plots of land do not cultivate them themselves. In this case, the payment of a rent to these landowners remains a pre-condition for the plots concerned to be opened to cultivation. So long as the selling price of wheat is less than or equal to the price of production of wheat on these plots, they will

* This is not grasped by a number of critics of Marx, who, like Arthur Wauters, reproach him with mixing up interest and differential rent of the second type. Interest goes to the owner of *capital*; differential rent goes to the owner of the *land*, even if he has not invested a single centime in his land. At least, it goes to him after the renewal of a tenancy. It must be noted that Marx himself answered this criticism, when it was levelled at Ricardo.[25]

remain uncultivated, because farmers would not be able to pay the rent without encroaching on their own average profit. Why should they, when, by transferring their capital to industry and trade, they can realise this average profit? But from the moment that the selling price rises sufficiently to bring in a rent even on these least fertile plots of land, their exploitation will be undertaken.* And throughout the first period of the capitalist mode of production, the lagging behind of agricultural productivity, as compared with industrial productivity and the increase of population, actually did create such a situation.

Where does this rent come from which appears on the least fertile land? Its source lies in the fact that the wheat produced under these conditions is not sold at its price of production but at its value, and that the latter exceeds the price of production because the organic composition of capital is lower in agriculture than in industry, whereas the monopoly of landed property prevents the free flow of capital in and out of agriculture, so that agricultural capital is thus prevented from "sharing" in the social equalisation of the rate of profit, giving up part of the surplus-value created in "its" sphere to the general share-out of this surplus-value.

Suppose that the annual production of industry amounts to: 400 billion c + 100 billion v + 100 billion s = 600 billion.

Agricultural production might be determined somewhat like this: † 20 billion c + 100 billion v + 105 billion s = 405 billion.

The average rate of profit in industry would be $\frac{100}{500}$ = 20 per cent.

In agriculture, the products will not be sold at their price of production, embodying a profit of 25 per cent (i.e. at 375 billion),‡ but at their value, or 405 billion, i.e. with 30 billion super-profit. This will be the *absolute ground rent* which appears by way of this super-profit. The rate of profit in agriculture will be $\frac{105}{300}$, or 35 per cent.

Let us now go back to the three plots of land, A, B and C, which we quoted as examples in connection with differential rent of the first type:

Plot	*Capital*	*Production*	*Selling price per quintal*	*Total received*	*Average profit*
A	1 million	80 q.	16,875	1,350,000	200,000
B	1 million	100 q.	16,875	1,687,500	200,000
C	1 million	120 q.	16,875	2,025,000	200,000

* This does not mean that these plots are necessarily the last to be cultivated. The spread of cultivation to more fertile land may cause cultivation to be given up on less fertile land, if the selling price of wheat goes down.

† The rate of surplus-value is usually higher in agriculture than in industry because agricultural wages, as is well-known, are lower than wages in industry.

‡ Total social surplus-value of 205 billion gives an average rate of profit of 25,625 per cent on a social capital of 800 billion.

	Absolute rent	*Differential rent*
A:	150,000	—
B:	150,000	337,500
C:	150,000	675,000

The selling price is equal to the *value* of a quintal of wheat produced on the least profitable of the plots, A, that is, to the capital invested, 12,500 francs, plus 35 per cent profit, 4,375 francs, or, altogether, 16,875 francs. The absolute rent arises from this difference between the value of a quintal of wheat produced on plot A and its price of production, 15,000 francs (12,500 francs + 20 per cent average profit).

Ground rent, needless to say, is not "produced" by the land. A piece of waste land does not "produce" an atom of rent. Ground rent is produced by labour-power engaged in cultivation. It is thus surplus-value, unpaid labour, exactly like industrial profit. But it is a special kind of surplus-value, *which does not participate in the general equalisation of the rate of profit*, owing to private property in land, and which thus provides a super-profit as a result of the lower organic composition of capital in agriculture as compared with industry (absolute rent). This super-profit is further increased by a super-profit which arises from the fact that all the labour engaged in agriculture is socially necessary, even if it is engaged under conditions of productivity lower than in industry.

Ground-rent and the capitalist mode of production

Ground rent thus represents a *twofold loss* for the bourgeoisie as a whole. On the one hand, a certain amount of surplus-value does not participate in the equalisation of the rate of profit, and as this amount is produced by capital with an organic composition lower than in industry it could have increased the average rate of profit. On the other hand, the prices of agricultural products are increased, since they are sold according to the value of the products coming from the least profitable plots. This makes necessary a minimum level for wages which is higher than would be the case if rent were abolished, and thus means to some extent a transfer of value from industry to agriculture.

This is why the most logical representatives of the liberal industrial bourgeoisie, notably Ricardo and John Stuart Mill, fought for the abolition of private ownership of land. In newly settled countries like the United States, Australia or Canada, where enormous expanses of virgin land were at the disposal of the settlers, absolute rent could disappear completely: the land was distributed free, on payment of a purely nominal tax due to the state. In the U.S.A., under the Homestead Act of 1862, it was possible to become the owner of 160 acres of uncultivated land after five years of effective occupation. In Canada,

90 per cent of the 58 million acres occupied by the settlers were distributed in the same way.[26] The source of absolute ground rent, namely, the private monopoly of ownership of land, was thus proved, by a negative experiment. Where this monopoly is not found, neither does absolute rent exist.

The existence of ground rent is not only an obstacle to the optimum development of the capitalist mode of production in general. It especially hinders the development of capitalist relations in the countryside. The rent taken by the non-cultivating landowners is withdrawn from agriculture and not reinvested. It reduces the investment fund available and slows down the accumulation of capital in agriculture. Thus, in Switzerland, between the eve of the First World War and the eve of the Second, the farmer's total capital increased from 1,160 to 1,673 Swiss francs per hectare, whereas the landowner's capital increased from 4,280 to 6,167. Only a small fraction of this latter increase, 52 Swiss francs to be exact, came from improvements in the land![27] The rate of accumulation of capital in agriculture is thus lower than in industry. This determines a productivity of labour in agriculture which is much lower than in industry, as may be seen from the following table:

Occupational distribution of the population, and contribution of industry and agriculture respectively to the formation of the national product, in percentages, in 1950-51:

Country	*Industry*		*Agriculture*	
	Pop.	*Gross national product*	*Pop.*	*Gross national product*
Italy	23	34	49	29
France	29	40	36	29
Denmark	32	36	28	22
Netherlands	32	39	19	12
Norway	32	46	31	15
West Germany	44	55	22	12[28]

For 1956 the "Report on the Economic Situation in the Countries of the Community" of the Common Market Commission shows that the agricultural product per head of active population amounts to no more than 76 per cent of non-agricultural income in the Netherlands, 58 per cent in Belgium, 57 per cent in France, 56 per cent in West Germany and 38 per cent in Italy.[29]

The fact that a great part of farmers' capital is tied up in the renting or purchase of land* entails a period of *rotation of capital* which is longer in agriculture and building than in industry: a rotation cycle takes 4 to 5 years, on the average, in agriculture, and 8 to 10 years in the building trade in the towns in the United States.[31]

* "Nearly two-thirds of investment in agriculture is accounted for by investment in (the price of) land."[30]

But the appropriation of differential ground rent by the landowner presents above all a major obstacle to *land improvement*. Farmers have little interest in working to achieve an improvement which will inevitably cause the landowners to increase the leasehold charge they have to pay! Landowners try to make tenancies renewable as frequently as possible (annually, if they can), so as to ensure a correspondingly regular increase in differential rent. Farmers, for their part, are interested in securing long leases, so as to be able to benefit by the improvements due to their capital (or their labour, in the case of small farms).

Nineteenth-century Ireland offers the classic example of the injustice resulting from the appropriation of differential rent by the landowner:

"In the year 1870 there were 682,237 farms in Ireland, of which 135,392 were leasehold and 526,628 belonged to the class of yearly tenancies. A yearly tenancy was terminable at six months' notice without compensation. Only in the case of about twenty estates were the buildings and standing farm equipment provided by the landlords . . . In all other cases the tenant had to supply the fixed capital as well as every other form of capital required on his farm. The termination of the tenancy thus enabled the landlord to confiscate the capital invested by the tenant. Between 1849 and 1880 nearly 70,000 families were evicted and dispossessed. The alternative to eviction was willingness and ability to pay a higher rent, and this in fact enabled the landlord to confiscate by another method the capital as well as the industry of an industrious tenant."[32]

Such an unjust system inevitably leads to a defensive reflex by the farmer which is detrimental to land improvement:

"Even with [a lease of] nine years . . . the farmer had too often to spend the first three-year rotation reconstituting the fertility impaired by his predecessor; he cultivated the land normally during the second three-year period, and then spent the last three years exhausting the land in one way or another. A friend of mine who is familiar with agricultural problems estimates at 20 per cent the resulting underproduction."[33]

Certain crops, such as orchards, which require constant attention over many years, are incompatible with leasehold and the separation of landownership from the actual cultivation of the land.[34]

The price of land and the evolution of ground rent

With the world-wide extension of the capitalist mode of production, all income is conventionally regarded as being a return on capital, real or imaginary, invested at the average rate of interest.* Ground rent is a real economic category, with its source in the surplus value produced by all the workers on the land. But the "value of land" is

* See Chapter 7.

an expression which in itself is meaningless. Land has no value, any more than air, light, or the wind that moves a sailing-ship. It is a "factor of production" provided by nature, not a commodity produced by human labour.* Where the monopoly of private ownership of land has not been established, land has neither "value" nor price. So recently as the present century, the white settlers in Rhodesia obtained their land for the token price of a penny an acre!

Only where private appropriation of land has transformed it into monopoly property does land acquire a *price*. This price is nothing but *ground rent capitalised* at the average rate of interest:

"The price of land is determined by the price of the products [of the soil] and not the reverse."[35]

Buying a piece of land is not buying a "value" but a *claim to income*, future income being calculated on the basis of present income:[36]

"The buyer of land is actually buying the right to receive a series of annual incomes, and the most tangible basis for judging what these annual incomes will be in the future is what they have been in the immediate past. Studies show that income received from land for a seven-year or ten-year period preceding sale is a most effective gauge of the price the purchaser will agree to pay."[37]

This origin of the price of land is confirmed by the way this price has evolved since the end of the eighteenth century. The price of land does not vary around a "real value", but follows the oscillations, often sharp and violent, of the agricultural conjuncture.

The increase of population, the bringing under cultivation of less fertile land which required considerable investment of capital if it was to be cultivated, brought about a marked rise in agricultural prices in the second half of the eighteenth century, followed immediately by a corresponding rise in rents. Between 1750 and 1800 the price of wheat increased on the average by 60 per cent in England, 65 per cent in France, 60 per cent in North Italy, and 40 per cent in Germany. In the same period d'Avenel estimates that average rent per hectare rose in France by 50 per cent. In England and Germany an even bigger increase in rent was observed, owing to a marked fall in the rate of interest.[38] The rise in agricultural prices on the Continent between 1820 and 1870 was likewise accompanied by a notable rise in rents.

The average value of all agricultural land in the U.S.A. has for a century followed the movement of agricultural prices: from 1860 to 1890, a rise of 16·32 dollars per acre, to 21·31 dollars; from 1890 to 1900, a decline to 19·81; from 1910 to 1920 [war boom!], a rise of 39·60, to 69·38; between 1920 and 1935, decline [the great crisis!] to 31·16, etc.[39]

* This does not apply to land which, like the *polders* of Flanders and Holland, has been literally "produced" by human labour, which has reclaimed it from the sea.

For differential ground rent to appear, the selling price of agricultural products must ensure the average profit even on capital invested in the least profitable land. For absolute ground rent to appear, this same selling price must ensure the sale of wheat produced under the worst conditions of productivity, not at its price of production but at its value. When the prices of agricultural products fall, these conditions, or one of them, may be eliminated, temporarily or for good. At that moment rent vanishes from certain plots of land. They cease to be cultivated unless they are exploited directly by their owners. If they are, the owners have to be satisfied with an income lower than the average profit, perhaps merely equivalent to a wage.

This phenomenon, which occurred already during all the pre-capitalist crises of agriculture,* made itself vigorously felt in the last quarter of the nineteenth century. At that time, vast expanses of prairies and pampas were beginning to be brought under cultivation in overseas countries, with the aid of mechanical methods, which reduced the cost of production by 50 per cent.[40] At the same time, the improvement in means of transport made possible a reduction in freight charges, which, for wheat despatched from New York to Liverpool, fell from 0·60 gold francs per bushel in 1860 to 0·25 in 1866 and 0·05 in 1910.[41] These two developments together brought to Europe quantities of agricultural produce from overseas, often without any ground-rent entering into their prices, and thus caused a collapse of agricultural prices.

This collapse led both to a fall in the price of land and to the abandonment of all cultivation on the less profitable plots of land. In France between 1875 and 1900 the "value" of rural property was reduced by 35 per cent, on the average.[42] The area of land under the plough shrank from 25 million hectares in the middle of the nineteenth century to 18 million in the middle of the twentieth.[43] Clapham notes that after the fall in agricultural prices at the end of the nineteenth century the fate of some land was to " 'tumble-down' to third-rate pasture, as on the Essex 'three-horse' clays."[44]

True, the agriculturists of Europe strove by various reactions to reverse this current. In some countries, such as France, Italy and Germany, there was an attempt, by means of *protective tariffs*, artificially to maintain high agricultural prices. These prices thus ensured the difference between the average price on the world market and the price on the least profitable plots of "national" land—that is, precisely, the differential rent of the best-endowed landowners! * In

* In France "the purchase price of wheat is calculated on the basis of the cost of production on the most old-fashioned farms of Ariège and Rouergue... The big capitalist agriculturists of the Paris basin, whose real costs of production are almost 60 per cent lower than those of these small peasants, pocket the difference!"[45]

* See Chapter 11.

other countries, such as Denmark, Holland, Belgium, etc., attempts were made to consolidate ground rent and the price of land by a considerable investment of capital, large-scale use of fertilisers—per hectare-year, 30 kilogrammes of nitrogenised fertiliser were used in 1938 (49 kilogrammes in 1956) in Belgium, as against 6·7 (9·7 in 1956) in France; 35 kilogrammes of phosphates (51 in 1956) in Belgium, as against 13 in France (18 in 1956); 46 kilogrammes of potash in Holland (68 in 1956; 76 in this same year in Belgium) as against 8·7 in France (14·5 in 1956)[46]—and above all by transforming cultivated land into meadows, the animal products of which (meat, butter, milk, etc.) serve as basis for a more stable rent, because a substantial section of the population of the big towns prefers to consume fresh animal products, even at a higher price.[47]

In the 1920s this new equilibrium of Europe's agriculture was upset by a violent shock: the world agricultural crisis which went on down to the Second World War, and reasserted itself from 1949 onward. The expansion of agriculture in overseas countries creates a permanent "surplus" of agricultural produce, despite the state of chronic undernourishment in which hundreds of millions of human beings live in China, in India, in the rest of Asia, and in most of Africa and Latin America.[48]

It has now been shown that, within the setting of the capitalist mode of production, the relative stability (inelasticity) of the demand for agricultural produce, once a certain degree of industrialisation has been attained* (the same inelasticity which has been the source of agricultural super-profit through several centuries), may become a source of permanent crisis as soon as agriculture experiences, belatedly, upheavals in productivity comparable to those in industry.[51]† In the

* This stability is only relative. For the U.S.A., Renne declares: "If all consumers in the United States were to have diets considered adequate by nutritional experts, vegetable consumption would probably be increased at least 50 per cent, and consumption of dairy products at least 15 or 25 per cent."[49] Statistics show, moreover, that in 1939 the industrial workers in England and Germany consumed, per head, half the amount of milk consumed in Sweden and Switzerland, a third of the amount of butter consumed in Canada, Germany and Holland, half of the amount of sugar and meat consumed in Australia, etc.[50]

† Here is a striking summary of the advance in the productivity of agricultural labour:[52]

To reap and bind one hectare of wheat in one hour, there were needed in France:

About 1750, using sickles, 40 to 50 men About 1830, using scythes, 25 to 30 men About 1870, using reaping machines, 8 to 10 men	Productivity increased by 500 per cent
About 1905, using reapers and binders, 1 to 2 men In 1950, using reaper-binder-threshers, less than one man—and the harvest is threshed at the same time.	Productivity increased by over 1,000 per cent

period 1930–1955 agricultural productivity increased by over 100 per cent in the U.S.A. As regards the cultivation of grain, productivity has *trebled* in 30 years! [53]

Between 1930 and 1950, the increase in productivity in American agriculture was almost equal to that in industry. The same increase took place in Great Britain.* In its turn, the U.S.A. experienced the shrinkage of the area sown to wheat and the transformation of cultivated fields into meadows, if not the disappearance of all agricultural use of the least fertile land.

Thus, between 1919 and 1929, cultivation was abandoned on 20 per cent of the land in the South and West of the U.S.A., where, in spite of mechanisation, the cost of production of a bushel of wheat did not fall below one dollar, whereas in the plains of Montana, Kansas, Nebraska, etc., it fell to 60 cents.[56] As for the old countries of Europe, rent could vanish or become insignificant for a large part of the least fertile land, as happened in France on the eve of the Second World War.[57] Recently Baron Snoy, secretary-general of the Belgian Ministry of Economic Affairs, has stated that the abandonment of the policy of agricultural protection in Western Europe would make it possible to reforest very large areas where agriculture had been given up.

Landed property and the capitalist mode of production

Private property in land, far from being a condition for the penetration of the capitalist mode of production *into agriculture*, is a hindrance and brake upon it. The private appropriation of *all cultivable land*, which prevents free settlement of new peasants on the land, nevertheless remains an absolutely indispensable condition for the rise of *industrial capitalism*. So long as there are vast expanses of land available, urban labour-power has a refuge from the factory prison, there is practically no industrial reserve army, and wages may well rise in consequence of competition between industrial and agricultural employment. The high wages which existed in the U.S.A. before the disappearance of the Western "frontier", which definitely established a

* In Great Britain, since 1950, 40 per cent of the farms of 5 to 10 hectares, 60 per cent of those between 10 and 20 hectares, and practically all the larger farms have possessed at least a tractor. Between 1944 and 1952 the number of tractors per 100 farms increased from 10·4 to 28 in Sweden. It grew from 8·9 to 23·7 between May 1949 and April 1952 in West Germany. It doubled between 1949 and 1951 in Denmark, and between 1949 and 1952 in Austria and Belgium. In 14 countries of Western Europe (including Great Britain) there were about a million tractors in 1951 and their number was increasing by 15 per cent per year.[54] What is typical of the countries with the most highly mechanised agriculture, namely, Britain, West Germany and Sweden, is that the increase in the number of tractors concerns more and more the middle-sized and small farms, the big ones having already been mechanised nearly 100 per cent.[55]

wage scale higher than any in Europe, are to be explained to a large extent by this factor.

From the middle of the eighteenth century, American politicians frankly recognised this fact and demanded, like Benjamin Pale, of Connecticut, that migration westward be stopped. And Samuel Blodget, one of the first American economists, observed in 1806 that cheap land makes labour dear.

"No freeman will work for another if he can buy good land sufficiently cheap to provide him comfortable subsistence with two days' labour a week."[58]

Private appropriation, by robbery and legal or illegal violence, of the greater part of the virgin land in the countries with reserves of land accompanied the entire progress of the capitalist mode of production outside Western Europe, where, moreover, a similar phenomenon occurred in the form of the private appropriation of the common lands. The idea of private ownership of land has become to such an extent a fundamental idea of bourgeois society that the courts even recognised as a transfer of property the gift of a 600-acre forest by the State of Pennsylvania to God, and subsequently "expropriated" this "owner" for non-payment of tax![59]

From the end of the eighteenth century the East India Company transformed into landlords of entire provinces the *zamindari* or tax-farmers of the Mogul Empire.[60] In the Argentine, between 1875 and 1900, 30 million hectares of land were sold for insignificant sums: most of it has been left waste to this very day, but the whole of the public domain was alienated in this way. In Canada nearly a third of the entire public domain was taken over by the railway companies.[61] In the U.S.A., while 96 million acres were distributed under the Homestead Act and other laws of the same kind (a considerable part of this land, moreover, going to capitalist companies, for whom farmer applicants acted as men of straw), 183 million acres were left to the railway companies.[62]

In North Africa, French colonisation led to large-scale alienation of native land: 3 million hectares appropriated by the French settlers in Algeria, under specific laws;[63] 1·4 million hectares in Tunisia, or half of all the arable land in that country;[64] 1 million hectares appropriated in Morocco by 4,700 European settlers, while 8 million Moroccans have to subsist on 3·8 million hectares of less fertile land.[65]

Also in Africa the British settlers seized 50 million acres in Southern Rhodesia, on which live 100,000 whites, while 1·6 million Africans have only 29 million acres to live on. The settlers have taken 12,750 square kilometres in Kenya, which are at the disposal of 29,000 Europeans, leaving 43,500 square miles for 5 million Africans!

Thanks to this system, the "native reserves" as they are cynically called by the whites, furnish abundant labour-power both to the settlers and to the European mining and industrial companies. Many forms of serfdom, forced labour either open or concealed,* ground rent paid in the form of labour service, are imposed on the wretched Africans who have been brutally torn from the land, that is, from their customary means of existence.[67] This system has been carried to an extreme in South Africa, where 2 million whites have appropriated 88 per cent of the land, leaving 12 per cent, much of it useless, for the subsistence of 8 million Africans, herded into "reserves" and ferociously exploited: the total annual wages of the 400,000 Africans working in the South African gold mines amount to £30 million, if one estimates very generously the value of the meagre food-rations given these workers, whereas the annual profits of the gold-mining companies amount to £50 million.[68]

Striking the balance of the agrarian laws introduced by Britain in Ceylon, an official Ceylon Government commission remarks that they served to deprive the villages of their common forests and meadows, together with some of their land used for secondary crops, and this exclusively in the interests of capitalists coming, in the first place, directly from Europe, and later, from the coastal provinces of the island.[69]

Production-relations and property-relations in the countryside

The special relations which, by the creation of the industrial reserve army and by the economic role of ground rent, link agriculture with industry in the capitalist epoch, gave rise to the special forms of development in agriculture itself. The introduction of slavery in the American colonies between the sixteenth and nineteenth centuries, the introduction of forced labour in the African and Oceanian colonies at the end of the nineteenth and in the twentieth century† were, in the special conditions of the countries in question, necessary conditions for creating *capitalist property-relations* in these countries. They none the less hindered for a long time the penetration of capitalist *production-relations* in the country.

A similar and still more important phenomenon appeared in Eastern Europe, and in the Middle East and Far East at the end of the nineteenth century and in the first part of the twentieth. The penetration of capitalist products into these countries, their inclusion in the world market, brought about the destruction of the age-old equilibrium of village economy, based on the combination of crafts with agriculture.[70] The land itself not being capable of supporting the whole of the non-

* See the chapters dealing with the Belgian, British, French and Portuguese colonies in the publication of the United Nations International Labour Office, "Report of the *Ad Hoc* Committee on Forced Labour".[66]

† The sugar industry of Queensland was based exclusively on the semi-slave labour of the Kanakas from 1860 until about 1900.

urban population, and no substantial increase in employment being forthcoming in the towns, *chronic overpopulation of the countryside* made its appearance—a mere concealed form of chronic unemployment.*

This overpopulation of the countryside gives rise to a fierce competitive struggle among the peasants for the tenancy of little plots of land, not so much as means of acquiring the average profit as mere means of livelihood. It is to the interest of the landowner to let out his land in small lots rather than to exploit it as a large-scale capitalist enterprise. *The bourgeois property-relations prove an obstacle to the introduction of the capitalist mode of production in agriculture.* The extreme fragmentation of units of production which results from this is especially marked in India, where the average area of a farm is 4·5 acres, while in the highly-populated state of West Bengal, one-third of the farms are less than 2 acres in size. The same phenomenon leads to a formidable increase in ground-rent and to *overcapitalisation* of the land.[71] The peasants impoverished in this way eventually lose their little holdings and become proletarianised, either obviously or in some disguised way. The small farmers, clinging desperately to their little plot of land, pay a *usurious rent* which expresses their super-exploitation, their income often being less than that of an agricultural worker. When they have not even the minimum capital and have to exploit the land they have leased in the form of share-cropping,† they transform themselves into real proletarians, working for a wretched wage:

"In Arabic, share-cropper is *mraba*, that is, one who has a quarter share. This is, in fact, the usual arrangement. In grain-growing villages the landowner provides the fellah with a house, land, seed and the means of ploughing. The latter is pretty sketchy: two oxen—sometimes only two cows—and the sort of plough used in the region. The share-cropper, it will be seen, contributes nothing but his labour, together, of course, with that of his whole family. Having nothing that belongs to him, except his wife and children [this is the literal translation of 'proletarian'! E. M.] . . . he is wholly dependent on the landlord, who can, in theory, evict him at the end of each agricultural year. As reward for this year of labour, he receives a quarter of the harvest . . ."[72]

The extreme forms that this usurious rent can take was shown by the example of pre-war Korea. H. K. Lee observed there in 1936 that rent amounted in such extreme cases to 90 per cent of the harvest.[73]

And as share-croppers reduced to such a level of poverty invariably

* See Chapter 13, "Imperialism", section "The economic structure of the underdeveloped countries."

† Share-cropping is a transitional form between pre-capitalist and capitalist rent.

end by falling into debt, the usurer being most often the landlord himself (or the big farmer standing between the share-croppers and the landlord), they easily pass from the status of proletarian to that of serf: "In Iraq (there is) . . . a law which forbids the sharecropper to leave the land as long as he is indebted to his landlord, which is generally the case."[74]

Alfred Bonné has further shown that this system, like the similar system introduced in Eastern Europe in the sixteenth century, represents the landlord's response to a dangerous shortage of labour-power when this makes itself felt on his broad estates.[75]

Concentration and centralisation of capital in agriculture

Because in agriculture, in contrast to industry, bourgeois property relations and capitalist production relations do not necessarily coincide,* the problem of the concentration of capital presents itself in a special way. The law of the concentration of capital is a law which springs from the *capitalist mode of production*; it is not a universal law springing from the mere existence of private ownership of the land.

Where the capitalist mode of production is merely *beginning* to penetrate agriculture, where we are still confronted with old semi-feudal estates in process of disintegration, it would be as absurd to look for agricultural concentration as it would be to study industry as it was at the end of the eighteenth century from the stand-point of the concentration of capital. *It is only when agriculture as a whole has been subjected to the technical upheavals inherent in the capitalist mode of production that the problem of concentration can arise.* Such phenomena as the remarkable concentration of landed property in Eastern Europe before the Second World War, in Spain, or in most of the countries of Latin America, have nothing to do with this category: in these cases it is a matter either of survivals of pre-capitalist property or else of investment of capital in land owing to the lack of industrial outlets for it (in Chile, for example, 2,300 landowners possessed in 1952 31 per cent of the cultivable land and 60 per cent of all the land in the country, whereas 150,000 small enterprises covered only 16·5 per cent of the cultivable land and 6 per cent of the total).[77]

Once given the capitalist mode of production in agriculture, two

* For this same reason, present-day agriculture conserves in one way or another all possible forms of pre-capitalist society. Thus, there are parts of South Africa, especially in the Transvaal and Natal, where the black farmers have to pay their rent in the form of 90 to 180 days of labour-service (unpaid work) on the white landowner's farm. These forms of mediaeval exploitation can also be found in a number of countries of Latin America: "This form of tenancy is often met with in Bolivia, Chile, Colombia, Ecuador, Peru and Venezuela, among the agricultural workers of the plantations, to whom the landowner assigns a small plot of land, in return for which they have to work without payment a certain number of days every week."[76]

factors hinder the manifestation in it of the concentration and centralisation of capital. We know that ground rent arises from the fact that the least profitable enterprise determines the price of production of agricultural products. But the concentration of capital operates precisely through the elimination of the least profitable enterprises! So long as the latter have a guaranteed market in spite of their technical backwardness, the centralisation of capital cannot show itself in agriculture. Concentration will nevertheless show itself by way of the enormous difference which emerges between the price of the least profitable land and that of the most profitable, that is, by way of the capitalisation of a huge differential rent.

Similarly, plots of land which are below the threshold of profitability can nevertheless be exploited, not to produce the average profit but to provide a mere subsistence-basis for a small farmer who in this way sacrifices his standard of living in order to cling to "his" farm.[78]* Working with little or no capital, doing without rent and profit, he remains notwithstanding at the mercy of bad harvests and conjuncture fluctuations. This is what accounts for the very high mortality of these small agricultural enterprises. In the U.S.A. in 1935, 25 per cent of all the heads of agricultural enterprises had been in occupation of their farm for only one year or less; 47 per cent of all the farmers and 57 per cent of all the sharecroppers had been in occupation for less than two years.[80] It is estimated that 100,000 family farms have vanished each year during the decade beginning in 1950.[81]

When this guaranteed market disappears, in practice from the last quarter of the nineteenth century, small enterprises can continue to compete with big ones by going over to *intensive cultivation,*† which makes possible an output higher than that given by the extensive cultivation of the big estates.

For this reason, even though the amount of capital invested has increased enormously‡—an indirect form of concentration of

* Thus, in Belgium it has been calculated in the 'fifties that the income per hour of the small farmers is only 14·5 francs in the case of farms of 5 hectares, whereas the minimum hourly wage in industry was 25 francs. In West Germany several inquiries have led to the finding that on small farms the monthly income per worker can be as low as 150 DM, far below the lowest wages paid in industry.[79]

† The difference between extensive and intensive cultivation relates to *output per unit of area.* In 1935–39, Denmark, Holland and Belgium produced, respectively, 45, 45 and 40 quintals of wheat per hectare, as against 10 in the U.S.A. and 12 in Canada, Argentine and U.S.S.R.[82] Intensive cultivation is the result either of a higher investment of capital per hectare, as in the above-mentioned countries, or of a tremendous extra expenditure of highly-skilled labour, as in the cases of Japan, China, Thailand, etc.

‡ In the U.S.A. in 1940 the investment needed for a profitable farm was estimated at 29,000 dollars for maize-growing, 25,000 dollars for sheep-raising, and 17,000 dollars for wheat-growing. By 1958 these figures had risen to 97,000, 84,000 and 81,000 respectively.[83]

capital—enterprises of intensive agriculture have not been able to increase in area, and there have been no obvious manifestations of centralisation.

Wherever these two restrictive factors have not operated, and where, in fact, capitalist agriculture in the strict sense has been able to develop in the pure state, the tendency towards concentration and centralisation of capital has, however, clearly shown itself in agriculture. This is especially true of the U.S.A., and to a smaller extent of Germany.

Agricultural concentration in the United States[84]

Type of farm	*1920*	*1925*	*1930*	*1935*	*1940*	*1945*	*1954*	*1959*
1. Less than 50 acres:								
% of total number	35·7	37·9	36·5	39·5	37·5	38·4	36·5	28·4
% of total area	6·0	6·1	5·7	5·6	4·7	4·1	2·9	2·0
2. Between 50 and 500 acres:								
% of total number	61·0	58·8	58·7	56·7	58·2	56·8	57·8	62·5
% of total area	60·4	59·0	55·3	54·2	50·4	45·2	39·8	36·5
3. Between 500 and 1,000 acres:								
% of total number	2·3	2·3	2·5	2·5	2·7	3·0	4·0	5·4
% of total area	10·6	10·5	11·0	10·8	10·8	10·6	11·4	12·3
4. Over 1,000 acres:								
% of total number	1·0	1·0	1·3	1·3	1·6	1·9	2·7	3·7
% of total area	23·1	24·3	28·0	29·4	34·3	40·3	45·9	49·2

In other words, the largest farms (categories 3 and 4), which in 1920 occupied only a *third* of American agricultural land (33·7 per cent), by 1959 already occupied more than *three fifths* of it (61·5 per cent). This growth was moreover nearly entirely accomplished by the largest farms, those exceeding 1,000 acres.

In Italy, where the penetration of capitalism into the countryside has been going on at a rapid rate for over a century, comparative statistics are not available, but the result is extremely eloquent. Here is the division of landed property and income from land among private persons in 1948, as given in publications of the I.N.E.A. (National Institute of Agrarian Economy):

Type of property	*Percentage of total number*	*Percentage of total area*
Up to 0·5 hectares	53·9	4·1
From 0·5 to 2 hectares	29·4	13·3
From 2 to 5 hectares	10·1	13·6
From 5 to 25 hectares	5·5	24·2
From 25 to 50 hectares	0·6	9·7
Over 50 hectares	0·5	35·1

This means that the 0·5 per cent of large landowners possess more land than the 95 per cent of small landowners. 502 very large landowners, owning more than 1,000 hectares each, possess more land than 5,135,851 small landowners, each of whose properties is no larger than 0·5 hectares.

Bracket of taxable income	*Percentage of No. of taxpayers*	*Percentage of total taxable income*
Up to 100 lire	49·1	2·2
From 100 to 400 lire	27·8	8·5
From 400 to 1,000 lire	12·5	11·3
From 1,000 to 5,000 lire	8·5	25·1
From 5,000 to 10,000 lire	1·1	11·0
Over 10,000 lire	1·0	41·9

We find here an income structure fully corresponding to the structure of property. One per cent of the landed taxpayers have a total income which is *double* the income obtained by 30 per cent of the landowners; 3,531 very large landowners who declare more than 100,000 lire of taxable income possess the same share of the total income declared for taxation as 7,030,397 small landowners who declare less than 400 lire each.*

The wretched lot of the agricultural worker

It is the constant pressure brought to bear on the wages of the agricultural workers by the thousands of small peasants clinging to their little bit of land and ruthlessly sacrificing their own standard of living and that of their family, that basically explains the poverty of these workers, and their pay which is much lower than that of the workers in industry and trade. Country life, the absence of the new needs created by urban existence, the payment of wages partly, or even wholly, in kind, are factors which still further bring down the wages of the agricultural worker. The latter is often a seasonal worker, or even a migrant; if he has another job during the dead season he may be able just to reach subsistence level. If, however, this second job is not to be had, especially in the under-developed countries, he sinks to the lowest depths of human misery.

In the long run, however, the evolution of the agricultural worker's lot depends less on the special conditions of agriculture than on the general rate of expansion of industry. When this rate is such that it results in reducing the industrial reserve army, the exodus from the countryside will become bigger and bigger. An all-round shortage of agricultural labour will appear in the countryside, entailing a rise

* In Mexico, thirty years after the agrarian reform of 1910 which distributed part of the old semi-feudal estates among the landless peasantry, for cultivation in the form of agrarian communities, or *ejidos*, 63·87 per cent of the peasants had been again reduced to the lot of landless agricultural workers, 26·42 per cent of the peasants lived in the *ejidos*, and 4·25 per cent of the peasants, the landowners, had acquired the best land and the rich farms. Since 1946 this tendency has become still more marked.[63]

in agricultural wages, though these will not reach the same level as wages in industry.

When the long-term tendency is, on the contrary, for the industrial reserve army to grow, the agricultural workers, competing fiercely among themselves in order to find some work for a few months of the year at least, put up with the lowest possible wage, often a mere pittance. Their ranks are swollen, moreover, by the mass of small landowners and small farmers whose incomes from their "enterprises" are insufficient for them to make ends meet. Under these conditions there can be no question of a long-term rise in agricultural wages:

"When there is a surplus of agricultural labour and, consequently, unemployment and under-employment exist, each worker is probably more concerned with finding work than with getting a high wage . . ." writes the official report of the United Nations Organisation on *Problems of Agrarian Reform.*[86] It should be added that the big farmers in many countries endeavour to create artificially this plentiful supply of agricultural labour by organising large-scale *immigration of seasonal workers*. This was notoriously the case in Germany before the Second World War (Polish workers). It remains so in the U.S.A., where nearly half a million *braceros* (Mexican seasonal workers, often recruited on a more or less compulsory basis), working for wages as low as 16 to 25 cents an hour, bring about a fall in the wages of agricultural workers, which are as a rule *less than half* the average wages paid in non-agricultural employment.[87]

From the theories of Malthus to agricultural Malthusianism

In 1798 the British clergyman Robert Malthus published anonymously a pamphlet entitled: *Essay on the Principle of Population*, in which he sounded the alarm for mankind by outlining an extremely gloomy prospect: observing that the increase in population was taking place in geometrical progression (2, 4, 8, 16, 32, 64, etc.) whereas, so he claimed, agricultural production could increase only in arithmetical progression (2, 4, 6, 8, 10, 12, etc.), he concluded that mankind was threatened with overpopulation unless it managed to restrict its own procreation. One should therefore applaud the efforts of industrialists to keep workers' wages down to the minimum, as this would set a natural limit to procreation by the workers. As, however, the risk of overproduction of goods might arise in this way, it was necessary to increase the share of the national product which served unproductive consumption by landowners, that is, ground rent. Malthus thus appeared as the defender of the landowners, in face of the agitation for the abolition of ground rent.

The experience of the nineteenth century has shown that Malthus was wrong on two counts. On the one hand, the increase in population fell off with the subsequent progress of technique and culture in the advanced countries.* On the other, the mechanical revolution, belatedly taking hold of agriculture, has increased production in this sphere to a degree much greater than "arithmetical progression". As a result, since the last quarter of the nineteenth century, it has no longer been overpopulation but *overproduction of agricultural products* that has seemed to threaten society.[89] Instead of restricting births, it is agricultural production that men have tried to restrict by all possible means: agricultural Malthusianism had appeared.

In the same period, however, serious scientists, notably the German Liebig, had drawn attention to a really disturbing phenomenon, the increased exhaustion of the soil, the *Raubbau*, resulting from greedy capitalist methods of exploitation aimed at getting the highest profit in the shortest time. Whereas agricultural societies like China, Japan, ancient Egypt, etc., had known a rational method of carrying on agriculture which conserved and even increased the fertility of the soil over several thousand years, the capitalist *Raubbau* had been able, in certain parts of the world, to exhaust the fertile layer of soil, the humus, in half a century, and thereby to cause erosion on a large scale, with all its harmful consequences.

These warnings were not listened to. The great agricultural crisis at the end of the nineteenth century attracted attention more and more to the problem of overproduction. The agricultural crisis which prevailed between 1925 and 1934 created a permanent psychosis of agricultural overproduction in the bourgeois world. Agricultural Malthusianism triumphed. Huge bonuses were given to peasants for them *not* to cultivate their land or grow certain crops. Eight million head of cattle were slaughtered in the U.S.A. in 1934. The area planted with cotton was reduced by nearly a half in that country—from 17·3 million hectares, on the average, between 1923 and 1929, to 9·8 million in 1938. In Brazil, 20 million bags of coffee were burnt between 1932 and 1936, or an amount sufficient to meet *the whole world's needs for eighteen months*. Nobody was then worrying about a threatened overpopulation of the world.

The Second World War, the great setback to agricultural production which it caused in some countries, the beginning of the industrialisation of backward countries, accompanied by a great increase in population, the rise of the revolutionary movement in the Far East, driven forward by the waves of famine which swept over that region, made the ideas of Malthus topical again. An old British writer, a precursor of Utopian socialism, Robert Wallace (1679–1771), had

* Defending a bold thesis, Joshua De Castro declares that, in our age, it is not overpopulation that causes famine, but famine (or, more precisely, chronic undernourishment) that causes overpopulation. He endeavours to prove this thesis by examining the influence of undernourishment (especially in animal protein) on the index of human fertility.[88]

already maintained, in his work *Various Prospects*, that, though socialism was good in itself, it would nevertheless lead to a great misfortune, namely, the overpopulation of the world and the danger of mankind's extinction. Prophets of doom who have appeared since the Second World War have tried to show that it is much more urgent to combat the increase of population than to raise the standard of living of the colonial masses, which would entail the risk of causing still greater over-population.

Two important works especially, *The Road to Survival*, by William Vogt, and *Our Plundered Planet*, by Fairfield Osborne, have seemed to reach these conclusions. Both of them describe a real evil: the irrational methods of agriculture inherent in the frenzied search for profit have exposed a large part of Asia, Africa, and both Americas, to a rapid erosion of the soil. There has followed from this a chain reaction which increasingly restricts the extent of land normally cultivable. To check this evil it is above all necessary to check the erosion process, through a vigorous intervention by the public anthorities. Beyond this first conclusion, which he himself regards as cautious, Osborne sees no long-term solution of the problem. Indeed, he declares that there is no such solution. Vogt suggests vigorous measures to restrict the growth of the population, and welcomes disasters such as wars, epidemics, etc., because they operate radically in this direction.

Though the danger indicated by Vogt and Osborne is a real one, it is from the very start wrongly defined. Several of their assertions, such as that it is impossible to reconstitute the layer of humus which gives the soil its fertility, do not correspond to reality. Again, it is wrong to calculate the possibilities of feeding mankind on the basis of the land surface *at present cultivated*. U.N.O. statistics estimate at 440 million hectares the world's reserves of cultivable land, an amount equivalent to all the land under cultivation in the U.S.A., India, China, France, Australia and Canada, or an area capable of feeding 1·5 billion people, given a rational system of agriculture.* Over and above these immediate reserves, it is possible to improve a huge area of land which is regarded by Vogt and Osborne as finally lost to agriculture.

* "According to Kellogg (*Food, Soil and People*) it may be assumed that at least 20 per cent of the unused tropical soils of the Americas, Africa and the great islands, such as New Guinea, Madagascar and Borneo, are cultivable; this would add one billion additional acres to the 300–400 million acres [of reserves] in the temperate zones. This area of 1300–1400 million additional acres would indeed be a tremendous reserve for increasing food production. To translate this potential into reality will mean a complex and difficult job which is bound to employ humanity for years. It will require careful planning and in particular simultaneous development of transportation and secondary industries."[90]

New chemical products such as *krilium** or liquid ammonia fertiliser, make possible a considerable increase in the fertility of the soil. The transition to intensive agriculture in countries like the U.S.A., Canada, Australia, the Argentine, and the improvement of agricultural technique in the backward countries would make it easily possible to double the output per hectare and greatly increase the world's production of agricultural produce. If modern agricultural science were used throughout the world, it would be possible to produce sufficient foodstuffs to feed four billion people, so claimed the Finnish Professor Arturi I. Virtanen, recipient of the Nobel Prize for chemistry, at the 12th international conference of pure and applied chemistry, held in New York between 10th and 13th September, 1951.[91]

Outside agriculture in the strict sense of the word, the first experiments in food production otherwise than from the soil have already proved satisfactory. In Jamaica a factory is at work producing food from yeast; the cultivation of algae offers unlimited prospects of food supply; and cultivation without land (hydroponics) would make possible a purely "industrial" solution of the food problem.

It is true than an effective struggle against erosion, a rational organisation of agriculture, a transition to intensive cultivation in overseas countries, a development of food production otherwise than from the soil "would bring with them a social revolution of such magnitude that the whole structure of human society would be torn apart."[92]

But when mankind is confronted with the choice between perishing and reorganising society on a more rational basis, it is not possible to doubt which decision is dictated by both reason and feeling. This is all the more so because at the very moment when erosion threatens to destroy the material foundation of all agriculture, and when hundreds of millions of human beings are terribly undernourished —the daily intake of calories in India was 1700 in 1952, or *half* the normal level!—agricultural Malthusianism is manifesting itself again in the most scandalous way, foodstuffs (including 3·5 billion bushels of grain) to the value of 10 billion dollars (4,500,000,000,000 French francs!) being put in store in the U.S.A. and vast destructive operations being carried out on crops of maize, potatoes, and vines,† etc. At the end of 1957 the United States authorities boasted that they had "saved" a billion dollars by . . . *preventing* the cultivation

* *Krilium* increases the growth of plants and prevents the soil from being carried off by water or wind, through increasing its capacity for retaining water and air. It is considered that *krilium* is between 100 and 1,000 times more effective than humus, natural fertilisers or compost.

† *Le Monde*[94] reported that 17 million hectolitres of wine were "denatured" in France in 1951–53 and that an unsaleable surplus of more than 15 million hectolitres was expected at the end of August 1953.

of some nine million hectares![93] More than ever is it obvious that the problem does not lie in the absolute increase in population but in the capitalist condition of production and distribution which creates a situation of plenty and poverty side by side.

Ground-rent and the marginal theory of value

The theory of ground rent worked out by Ricardo and perfected by Marx was the point of departure of the marginal theories of value which, in the second half of the nineteenth century, challenged the labour theory of value.* According to Marx's theory of ground rent, it is in fact the *demand for agricultural products* which in the last resort determines the price of these products. This price is based on the value of the unit produced on the plot of land with the worst conditions of productivity (marginal price) where products find a buyer. According to the fluctuations of demand it either will or will not embody the absolute ground rent (in those countries where there is no more unoccupied land, i.e. where the monopoly of landownership is complete) and it either will or will not embody a differential rent (depending on whether the less profitable plots of land are cultivated or given up).

The transformation of this theory of ground rent into a general theory of value is based on two mistakes of analysis. In the first place, it leaves out the *special conditions of property in land* which give rise to ground rent. Further, it leaves out the different institutional conditions that govern ownership of land, ownership of capital and "ownership of labour-power", respectively, under the capitalist system.

Ground rent does not arise because the land is a fundamental factor in the process of production. It arises only because there inserts himself between the land and this production process a landowner who *arbitararily demands* his share of the amount of income created in this production process. To proceed from the way in which this share is obtained in order to construct from it a general theory of the division of *income created in the production process* creates a serious error of logic. In a "pure" capitalist society from which ground rent was banished, for example, by nationalisation of the land (and the economy of certain overseas countries in the second half of the nineteenth century was somewhat like that), it would be difficult to proceed from . . . nothing to explain the whole mechanism of the division of income and the production of value within the capitalist mode of production!

A generalisation from the special case of ground rent would be justified, theoretically, only in a society in which the "capitalist" entrepreneurs were faced simultaneously with landowners, slave-

* Other aspects of these theories, their subjectivist nature, etc., will be dealt with in Chapter 18.

owners and owners of machines. The laws determining the share taken by these three categories of owner from the current income created by "capitalist" production would doubtless be similar to those which determine the appearance and fluctuations of ground rent. But we have been careful to put the word "capitalist" between inverted commas because such a society, in which there existed neither monopoly of the means of production by the bourgeois class nor free labour (free from serfdom or slavery), would, of course, not be a capitalist society.

For ground rent to appear it is necessary not only that ownership of land be a monopoly* which the bourgeoisie has not managed to break, so that the landowners are able to prevent the capital invested in agriculture from participating in the general equalisation of the rate of profit, and thus to collect their share of the value created in agriculture; it is further necessary that the production of agricultural commodities be carried on under special conditions which escape from control by capital.

According to the supporters of the marginal theory of value, three kinds of "owner" appear on the market, in order to "exchange" on an equal footing, three different "commodities", the prices of which will thus be determined, in complete equity, by the "marginal product, or income", that is, by the last, that is the least profitable, unit sold—owners of land, owners of capital, and owners of labour-power.

Now, there is a fundamental qualitative difference—through the very functioning of the capitalist mode of production—between these three categories of "owner". In the classical capitalism of the nineteenth century in Western Europe (the very capitalism in which ground rent appears in its complete and classical form!) there is *an absolute shortage of land*; total potential agricultural production hardly covers society's need for food. It is for this reason, and for this reason alone—because capital cannot extend at will the area of cultivable land, at least in Western Europe—that ground rent can appear and continue for a long period. As Marx observes, the importation of food plays only a regulatory role, preventing the prices of agricultural products from exceeding even their value, and the landowners from securing for themselves part of the surplus value *produced in industry*.†

Capital, for its part, comes on to the market in conditions of *relative shortage*. By its very logic it prevents an abundance of capital from undermining the profitability of capital: this is the objective

* We shall see later on (Chapter 12) that a mechanism comparable to that of ground rent regulates *monopoly profit* in the present phase of capitalism (cartel rent, etc.).

† Comparable conditions exist today in countries like India, where a "secular shortage" of foodstuffs prevails.

function of the cyclical crises.* But the "owners of labour-power" are weakened in advance by the conditions of *relative abundance* in which they have to offer their commodity on the market. This abundance (industrial reserve army) is not only the result of the historical conditions in which capitalism was born. It is also a result of the mechanism of capitalist production itself, which continually replaces men by machines and periodically "releases" masses of unemployed from the production process.

It will now be seen that there can be no question of negotiation on the market "on an equal footing" between these three classes. The dice are loaded. The rules of the game are such that one class lays down conditions dictatorially (the class of owners of land) whereas another class *has to accept* what is offered it (the proletariat).

These rules of the game operate all the more in a sense which reduces to absurdity the idea of an exchange of "marginal products", as the capitalist class does not "work" for subsistence but in order to accumulate capital. Its subsistence is guaranteed. When the wages demanded by the workers seem to it to be too high, it may prefer to close the gates of its factories rather than "work" for an insufficient profit, or at a loss.

In their turn, the landowners may prefer to leave some of their land to lie waste rather than let it at a price such that the total rent they draw is too low. By withdrawing this land from cultivation they contribute, moreover, to reducing agricultural production and so to reconstituting their rent at a later stage.

In contrast to this, the proletariat is in a special situation: that of not possessing any reserves beyond its two hands, which it *must* hire out if it is not to die of hunger. Not being in a position to "await a more propitious moment of the conjuncture", it is thus compelled to accept a wage which is not determined by the "marginal productivity of labour" but merely by the average subsistence needs in the given country and period. Once again, the dice are loaded.

To resume our imaginary description of a society in which this "negotiation on an equal footing" might be established, it would be necessary that, on the one hand, the bourgeois should possess reserves of foodstuffs, say, for several years (or that there should be large tracts of land without an owner), and that, on the other hand, the workers should likewise possess reserves of foodstuffs, or money, that would enable them to supply their needs and those of their families, for several years. In such conditions as these, "negotiations" between landowners, capitalists and producers would be placed on a relatively equal footing, and the division of income that would result would be quite different from that which governs the capitalist mode of production. But it is obvious that in a society like this there would neither

* See Chapter 11.

exist a monopoly of capital in the hands of the bourgeoisie nor a proletariat as a class, so that it would not be capitalist society.

A critic of Marx whom recently there have been mistaken efforts to rehabilitate, L. von Bortkiewicz,* does not grasp why the owners of land are able to *compel* the capitalist farmers to pay absolute ground rent, even on the least profitable land.[96] He approaches this question logically instead of historically.† Seen in this way the answer is simple: they can compel the farmers to pay absolute rent, and avoid the giving-up of the least fertile land, so long as there is a permanent shortage of foodstuffs, that is, so long as, owing to the delay in revolutionary technical changes in agriculture, the whole of a country's agricultural production is hardly adequate to meet its needs.

When this condition disappears, especially as the result of the opening up of the vast uncultivated lands of the two Americas and Australia, absolute rent may indeed tend to disappear, over large areas, as Marx foresaw. In fact it would already have vanished over a large part of Western Europe, but for the protectionist policy by which it is artificially maintained (or re-established). Under these conditions, it is only through exceptional circumstances of shortage (notably during world wars) that prices suddenly flare up, re-establishing absolute ground rent in its former grandeur.

* This is attempted by Sweezy in *The Theory of Capitalist Development.*[95]

† Von Bortkiewicz shows a similar lack of historical sense when, following Lexis, Böhm-Bawerk, Sombart, Stolzmann, Cornélissen and others, he declares that the transformation of value into price of production does not reflect any real historical process[97] Today it has become almost commonplace to stress that this transformation reflects the transition from petty commodity production (based on *stable* technological conditions) to capitalist society, based on technological conditions which are in *perpetual revolution.*

REFERENCES

1. F. Heichelheim: *Wirtschaftsgeschichte des Altertums*, pp. 691-2, 704.
2. M. Rostovtzeff: *Social and Economic History of the Roman Empire*, pp. 148-9.
3. G. I. Bratianu: *Etudes byzantines d'histoire économique et sociale*, p. 139.
4. E. O. Heady: *Economics of Agricultural Production*, p. 418.
5. Diehl: in *Schmollers Jahrbuch*, Sonderheft, 1932, p. 28.
6. W. Abel: *Agrarkrisen und Agrarkonjunktur in Mitteleuropa*, pp. 15-16.
7. Gino Luzzato: *Storia Economica d'Italia*, Vol. I, p. 211.
8. N. S. B. Gras: *The Evolution of the English Corn Market*, p. 28.
9. Ibid., p. 45.
10. Luzzato: op. cit., Vol. I, pp. 246-7.
11. Gras: op. cit., pp. 47-56.
12. Abel: op. cit., p. 54.

13. Gras: op. cit., p. 123; F. J. Fisher: "The Development of the London Food Market", in *Economic History Review*, Vol. V, No. 2, p. 50; A. P. Usher: *History of the Grain Trade in France*, pp. 61-62, 56.
14. Gras: op. cit., p. 218.
15. Ibid., pp. 123, 144-9, 220.
16. Ibid., pp. 76-77; Usher: op. cit., p. 60.
17. Usher: op. cit, pp. 6-8, *et al.*; Fisher: art. cit., p. 64.
18. Gras: op. cit., p. 218.
19. Abel: op. cit., p. 61.
20. N. S. B. Gras: *A History of Agriculture*, p. 218.
21. R. T. Ely and G. S. Wehrwein: *Land Economics*, p. 119; article "*Grundrente*" in Conrad's *Handwörterbuch der Staatswissenschaften*, Vol. V, p. 167.
22. Ely and Wehrwein: op. cit., p. 137.
23. Ibid., pp. 134-5.
24. I.B.R.D Mission Report: *The Economic Development of Iraq*, p. 235.
25. A. Wauters: "*Les sources doctrinales du marxisme*", in *Revue des sciences économiques*, A. L. D. Lg., 33rd year, No. 116, December, 1958, p. 232; Karl Marx: *Das Kapital*, 1st edition, Vol. III, pt. 2, pp. 278-9.
26. N. S. B. Gras: *A History of Agriculture*, p. 274.
27. F. Baudhuin: *Economique agraire*, p. 89.
28. *Bank of International Settlements*, 22nd annual report, 1952, p. 41.
29. *Rapport sur la situation économique dans les pays de la Communauté*, September 1958, p. 35.
30. U.S. Dept. of Agriculture, *Changing Technology*, p. 37.
31. R. R. Renne: *Land Economics*, p. 421.
32. J. Johnston: *Irish Agriculture in Transition*, p. 5.
33. René Dumont: *Le Problème agricóle français*, p. 329.
34. N. S. B. Gras: *A History of Agriculture*, p. 148.
35. Ely and Wehrwein: op. cit., p. 121.
36. Ibid., p. 120
37. Renne: op. cit., p. 215.
38. Abel: op. cit., pp. 103, 118-22.
39. Ely and Wehrwein: op. cit., p. 172.
40. F. A. Shannon: *The Farmer's Last Frontier*, pp. 126-7.
41. Nogaro and Oualid: *Evolution du Commerce, du Crédit et du Transport depuis 150 ans*, p. 194.
42. A. Garigou-Lagrange: *Production agricole et économie rurale*, p. 66.
43. René Dumont: op. cit., preface.
44. J. H. Clapham: *An Economic History of Modern Britain*, Vol. III, pp. 83-84. See also Conrad's *Handwörterbuch der Staatswissenschaften*, Vol. I, article "*Agrargeschichte*", p. 218.
45. Serge Mallet: in *France-Observateur*, 10th December, 1959.
46. René Dumont: op. cit., p. 317, and *Rapport sur la situation économique dans les pays de la Communauté*, September 1958, p. 35.
47. Baudhuin: op. cit., p. 91.
48. J. de Castro: *Géopolitique de la faim*, passim.

49. Renne: op. cit., p. 268.
50. G. D. H. Cole: *World in Transition*, p. 89.
51. Heady: op. cit., p. 701.
52. Henri Brousse: in *Revue économique*, September 1953.
53. Gilbert Burck: in *Fortune*, June 1955.
54. Food and Agriculture Organisation: *Annuaire de Statistiques*, 1952.
55. *Bulletin du Comité National belge de la FAO*, Vol. VIII, No. 3, 1954.
56. J. Schumpeter: *Business Cycles*, p. 739.
57. René Dumont: op. cit., pp. 324-5.
58. J. Dorfman: *The Economic Mind in American Civilization*, pp. 118, 338.
59. Ely and Wehrwein: op. cit., p. 76.
60. Palme Dutt: *India Today*, pp. 243-8, German edition, 1951.
61. Ely and Wehrwein: op. cit., p. 97.
62. Shannon: op. cit., p. 64.
63. *Cahiers algériens*, No. 3, pp. 17-18.
64. *La Question tunisienne*, No. 2, p. 25.
65. *Morocco*, pp. 73-74.
66. *Report of the Ad Hoc Committee on Forced Labour, U.N.O.*, p. 621.
67. George Padmore: *Britain's Third Empire*, pp. 38-40, 50, 59-60.
68. Ibid., pp. 17-18, 28.
69. *Kandyan Peasantry Report*, pp. 71-73.
70. Condliffe: *The Commerce of Nations*, p. 316.
71. For Egypt, Hans Briner: in *Basler Nationalzeitung*, 8th May, 1953.
72. Weulersse: *Le Pays des Alaouites*, p. 225.
73. H. K. Lee: *Land Utilisation and Rural Economy in Korea*, p. 163.
74. I.B.R.D. Report, *The Economic Development of Iraq*, p. 6.
75. Alfred Bonné: *State and Economics in the Middle East*, p. 132.
76. *La Réforme agraire*, U.N. publication, 1951, p. 18.
77. *Panorama Economico*, 1953, No. 1, p. 34.
78. Fleddérus and Van Kleeck: *Technology and Livelihood*, p. 92.
79. Institut d'Economie Agricole de Gand: *Berichte über Landwirtschaft*, 1, p. 43, Hamburg
80. Ely and Wehrwein: op. cit., p. 207.
81. *Socialist Call*, April-May 1957.
82. G. D. H. Cole: *World in Transition*, pp. 26-27.
83. *La Libre Belgique*, 12th December, 1959.
84. *U.S. Statistical Abstract, 1958 and 1965* and *Historical Statistics*.
85. Jacques Séverin: *"Démocratie mexicaine"*, in *Esprit*, May 1952, p. 791.
86. *Progrès de la Réforme agraire*, published in 1954 by the U.N., p. 181.
87. *New York Times*, 10th September, 1959, and *Socialist Call*, April-May 1957.
88. J. de Castro: *Géopolitique de la faim*, pp. 47, 90-93.
89. Nogaro and Oualid: *Evolution du Commerce, du Crédit et du Transport depuis 150 ans*, p. 165.
90. Alfred Bonné: *Studies in Economic Development*, p. 146.

91. *Facts on File*, September 1951.
92. Fairfield Osborn: *Our Plundered Planet*, pp. 74-75; *New York Times*, 20th February, 1959.
93. *New York Times*, 27th December, 1959.
94. *Le Monde*, 24th July, 1953.
95. Paul M. Sweezy: *The Theory of Capitalist Development*, pp. 115-25, *et al.*
96. L. Von Bortkiewicz: *Die Rodbertus'sche Grundrententheorie und die Marx'sche Lehre von der absoluten Grundrente*, in *Archiv für die Geschichte des Sozialismus und der Arbeiterbewegung*, by Karl Grünberg, Vol. I, 1911, pp. 426-9.
97. Ibid., pp. 423-4.

CHAPTER TEN

REPRODUCTION AND GROWTH OF THE NATIONAL INCOME

New value, new income and tranferred income

In a society where there was no economic activity other than the capitalist production of commodities there would be no income other than that created by this production. Labour-power, as we know, has the dual function of conserving the value of constant capital (the stock of machinery, raw materials, buildings) by transferring part of this value to currently produced commodities*, and of producing all the new value available to society. The first-mentioned property of labour-power makes it possible to conserve the accumulated stock of social wealth and instruments of labour, which determines the average level of the productivity of labour and the material civilisation of the given society. The second makes it possible to create an income—a "value added"—which in capitalist society is divided between income of labour (wages) and income of capital (surplus-value).

In practice, however, bourgeois society—the only form of society which makes the production of commodities universal—does include other economic activities and other sources of income besides this capitalist commodity production. One can in fact distinguish:

(a) The sector of petty commodity production which survives in capitalist society (craftsmen and small peasants working for the market without employment wage-labour);

(b) The sphere of distribution and that of transport which is *not* indispensable for the consumption of commodities. The wages paid in this sphere come out of society's capital; the capitalists obtain part of the surplus-value of society.†

(c) The sector of private services, the enterprises in which capitalist entrepreneurs and wage-earners provide specialised labour services to the consumers;

(d) The sector of public services, in which the employees are paid by the State (and subordinate public authorities), and which sell

* "The raw material is considered as receiving an increment of cost . . . from the machine; the machine gives off, so to speak, a part of its value, which becomes embodied in the finished product."[1] But the machine cannot "give off" any part of its value unless it be used, set in motion, by living labour. Without the application of the latter it purely and simply depreciates.

† See Chapter 6, sections "Commercial capital and commercial profit", and "Commercial capital and labour-power engaged in distribution".

services to the consumers (the sale of piped water, gas and electricity by public enterprises must be included in the commodity production branch, since here it is material goods that are being sold, not specialised labour);

(e) The public services provided free by the State or by public enterprises (free primary education, etc.);

(f) The production of use-values which do not appear on the market: production by subsistence farms, household production, "do-it-yourself", etc.

Of these six sectors which are outside the realms of capitalist commodity production in the strict sense, the first four retain the outward form of buying and selling. Except in the first case, that of the production of value which is not accompanied by production of surplus-value,* what is involved is the buying and selling not of material goods but of labour-time, specialised labour, etc. As for the last two sectors, they are outside commodity production as such.

The circulation of commodities in capitalist society results in their consumption, whether productive or unproductive; the intermediate phases that these commodities pass through before being consumed do not create new value. The enterprises which have charge of them during these phases cannot make profit from them except by appropriating part of the surplus-value already produced during the production-process. But distributive activity creates *new incomes*—the incomes of the wage and salary earners who work in the distributive sector. *These incomes do not constitute a part of the surplus-value currently produced by the productive workers, but a part of the social capital invested in this sector.*

Do these incomes tend to reduce the wages of the industrial workers? This view can be maintained only on the basis of the theory of the "wages fund", which regards the total amount of wages paid out during a given period as pre-determined. In reality, that would be so only if all the social capital available were wholly invested—if, in other words, every sum not invested in trade, or in the service sector, were automatically invested in industry, and if the organic composition of capital were rigid and stable.

* In so far as the peasants and craftsmen produce commodities *in competition* with the capitalist sector, three cases may present themselves. Either the productivity of their labour is equal to the average, in which case their products are sold at their exact value; or their productivity is lower than the average (this is the usual situation), in which case part of the value they have created is transferred to certain capitalist sectors; or else their productivity is, by way of exception, higher than the average (or, what comes to the same thing, the total production of a craft sector is not adequate to meet the effective demand), in which case, the petty commodity producers appropriate a small quantity of the surplus value produced in the capitalist sector of the economy. This last case occurs especially in periods of sudden shortage, during or just after wars, etc.

Actually this does not happen. The division of social capital between the different branches of the economy; the division of income between surplus-value (potential new capital) and wages, and of capitalised surplus-value between new constant capital and new wages (variable capital); the division of savings (new potential capital) between investment and hoarding—all depend on a number of different relations and many different mechanisms, which are much more complicated than is supposed by the supporters of the "wages fund" theory.*

The production of commodities and the allocation of available social capital thus create essentially the incomes of the workers (both productive and unproductive) and those of the capitalists (in the different spheres of capital investment). But the *circulation* of incomes complicates the picture; when these incomes buy a commodity they merely realise their value and create no new incomes, but when they buy services,† they create the illusion of giving rise to new incomes. Actually, they are only transferred.

It is not easy to draw the line between new and transferred incomes. This must be done, however, if we are to estimate economic growth adequately and make comparisons of national income, in time and space. The problem may be regarded as a purely conventional one when it is a matter of calculating this income in one country during a very short period; but it becomes vital when this calculation is extended over a long period and international comparisons are brought in.

If we neglect the distinction between new value, social income newly created, and incomes which are merely transferred, we inevitably land ourselves in obvious contradictions, for instance, *Pigou's paradox*. If we add to the national income of a nation the wages of its domestic servants, we come to the conclusion that the national income declines, the nation becomes poorer, when bachelors marry their housekeepers, who thenceforth no longer receive wages for doing the same work as they were doing before they married.[3] The transformation of a million beggars into producers (e.g. agricultural producers, as a result of

* Jean Marchal and Jacques Lecaillon[2] have undertaken a somewhat Byzantine exegesis of the writings of present-day Marxists in order to show that, according to Marx, the payment of the unproductive wage-earners takes place at the expense of the productive ones. True, they do quote other writings which maintain a different point of view. The whole of their study is fundamentally mistaken, however, because it does not proceed from *the real conditions in which the accumulation of capital takes place*. In a period in which there is a lack of fields for investment where more than the average profit can be obtained, when it is more and more difficult to realise surplus value, the development of the unproductive sectors tends notably to limit the scope of chronic unemployment, and thereby to make possible a greater stability (or even growth) of real wages.

† A service is the useful effect of a use-value—essentially of a contribution of skilled labour—the production and consumption of which coincide, because it is not embodied in a material product.

internal colonisation) would in no way increase the national wealth, if the money incomes of these peasants did not exceed the money incomes they received when they were beggars.*

The attitude of academic economics is contradictory in this respect. It eliminates from the calculation of the national income a whole series of paid activities, or incomes regarded as transferred incomes (notably the payments made to unemployed persons, policemen, firemen, etc.).[5]† But it includes most of these activities as soon as they become private instead of public. It eliminates from the national income every addition to prices which results from indirect taxes, but on the other hand it includes increases—usually quite arbitrary ones—in the case of services, which nevertheless do not create any new value but merely increase the incomes *transferred* from other sectors to the services sector.

Of course, the two series of additions each serve different purposes. The total amount of *incomes of all the households, private enterprises and public organisations* provides the data needed for various analyses, for example, in order to determine at what total of money incomes danger of inflation will arise, given a certain productive capacity. The total amount of net value newly *produced* in society is, however, the essential concept for measuring the possibilities and successive staging-points of economic growth. The way national income is nowadays calculated by official Western economics is a hybrid compromise between these two principles, and leads to serious mistakes in both directions.

Certain writers implicitly accept the soundness of this view. In *The Organisation Man,*[6] William H. Whyte, Jnr., correctly observes, for example: "The great majority of small business firms cannot be placed on any continuum with the corporation. For one thing, they are rarely engaged in primary industry; for the most part they are the laundries, the insurance agencies, the restaurants, the drugstores, the bottling plants, the lumber yards, the automobile dealers. They are vital, to be sure, but essentially they service an economy; they do not create new money within their area and they are dependent ultimately on the business and agriculture that does."‡

* Bauer and Yamey point out that in a number of under-developed countries the incomes of the beggars are not at all inconsiderable.[4]

† On the grounds that these activities are paid for out of the product of indirect taxation.

‡ See in Chapter 18 a surprising application of this idea. This quotation has all the greater value in that it relates to the most advanced capitalist country in the world. Some writers, such as J. Markovitch,[7] have declared that while the purchase of services may properly be regarded as transfer expenditure in backward countries, this is not so in advanced countries. Above all, the *exchange of services for services* ought not to be overlooked. All the same, even according to the present academic method, the purchase of a service by an unemployed person must be left out of account. Transfers at the third stage do not modify the problem at all.

Carl Shoup writes, from his standpoint: "National income analysis is interested in production, and it reserves the term 'investment' for the kinds of things that imply production, either current or past. The purchase of a share of stock, even if it is newly issued stock, is not an act of investment, in national income terminology."[8]*

Again, Simon Kuznets argues in favour of the exclusion from the national income of what he calls the "negative consequences of large-scale urbanisation" in the case of *international* comparisons between national incomes (but why include them, then, in estimates on the national scale?):

"A clear case is the transportation of employees to and from work—an activity that can hardly be said to constitute direct welfare to ultimate consumers and is merely an offset to the inconvenience that large-scale industrial production imposes upon the active participants in it . . . Payments to banks, employment agencies, unions, brokerage houses, etc., including such matters as technical education, are payments not for final goods flowing to ultimate consumers, but libations of oil on the machinery of industrial society—activities intended to eliminate friction in the productive system, not net contributions to ultimate consumption."[10]

Nevertheless, these fragmentary opinions have not yet made it possible to re-examine objectively, using precise scientific criteria, the way of calculating the national income, which, consequently, is overestimated by some 20 to 30 per cent, according to Kuznets.[11]

In order to determine the *value of (gross) production* in a country during one year, it is not enough merely to add up the values of all the commodities that issue from any enterprise in the course of this year. Otherwise one would inevitably include duplicated entries, since some of the finished products of one enterprise reappear in the form of raw material in the ultimate value of the products of another. It is necessary either to set aside altogether all the unfinished products, and add to the value of the finished products manufactured during

* The same writer nevertheless falls immediately into the error of mixing up productive and unproductive labour, when he goes on: "In a country where household services have come to be performed largely outside the home, or inside the home for pay, and the housewives use the time thus freed to work in paid occupations, the national income as at present computed will be larger than in a country where most of these services are performed by the family itself. The production of the former country is not actually as much greater as the difference in national income figures would indicate."[9]

The author forgets that during "the time thus freed", the housewives, having become working-women, produce new commodities and create new value, something which, for once, is faithfully reflected in the calculations of national income. And even from the standpoint of national accounting in hours of work, the saving accomplished by the carrying out of domestic work in specialised enterprises is enormous.

the year merely the fluctuation in the stocks of raw materials, or else to add up merely the value added in each enterprise.[12]

No different method should be employed when the *new social income* of a country during the same period is to be established. Just as one cannot merely add up the value of all the commodities, one cannot merely add up all the individual incomes. It is necessary to determine exactly which incomes—created by *production*—represent a net addition to the national income, and which are merely the result of transfers, whether private or public. Otherwise, the total amount of income will contain duplicated entries, exactly as would happen with the total amount of the prices of all the commodities.

The State, surplus-value and social income

Up to now we have brought into our model of a "pure" society of commodity producers only persons engaged in distributive activities, together with persons selling personal services to the consumers. We must now add the totality of the economic relationships characteristic of the activities of what are called the "public authorities", in the widest sense of the expression.

In so far as the State is itself a commodity producer, the incomes created by this production are naturally added to the income of the entire community under consideration. It is of little significance, in this case, that the "profit" (or the "loss"), that is, the surplus value created, is annexed not by a group of capitalists but by the State budget. Similarly, it makes little difference that the producers are public employees.

But in all the capitalist countries the bulk of the State's income, and of the income it distributes, does not originate in the production and sale of commodities by the State itself. This income originates in four main ways:

(a) Direct Taxes: these represent part of the income created by commodity production, and so part of the wages and the surplus value produced during the period under consideration.

(b) Public Loans: these transfer part of the accumulated wealth of the nation from individuals to the State. To this can be added a small part of the wages of the most highly skilled workers, which is used for the purchase of bonds. The income thus obtained by the State comes, accordingly, from the surplus value actually or potentially accumulated, and from the saved income of the middle classes, which is thus transformed into capital. In exchange, the State transfers to subscribers to public loans a part of its own current income.

(c) Indirect taxes: turnover tax, customs duties, excise, purchase tax, etc. What is involved here is not a share of already created income which is thereby redistributed, but *a general addition to the selling price of commodities*, which, through an all-round increase in prices,

brings about a reduction in the real income of all consumers. This reduction is not proportional to *total* income but only to income spent on goods subject to these taxes. In fact, almost the whole of wages is spent on these goods, whereas the bourgeois classes do not need to spend a considerable share of their income in this way. Indirect taxation thus affects the workers much more severely than the capitalists, and is the fiscal device preferred by every reactionary capitalist government, to the extent at least that goods in current consumption are not systematically relieved of tax-burdens and the latter shifted on to luxury goods.

(d) Inflationary issue of bank notes: this, provided it remains within certain limits, is a source of real income for the State, since it enables the State to purchase commodities and pay salaries with these depreciated notes. It has the same effect as an increase in indirect taxes: an all-round increase in prices which hits the wage-earners and lower income-groups much harder than the well-to-do classes, who can transform a substantial part of their income into "stable values" (gold, foreign currency, real estate, industrial shares, works of art, etc.).

These four kinds of public income thus constitute only an appropriation by the State—whether directly, or indirectly in the form of the reduction of real income resulting from the rise in prices—of income created by the production of commodities, or subsequently redistributed by the circulation of income and commodities. They cannot be taken into account when it is a question of determining the growth (or the reduction) of the newly-created value, that is, the net social income, of a community. In calculating this income one can start from the gross income of the wage-earners and the gross surplus value, or one can start from net incomes, adding to these the total of direct taxation and deducting the consequences of currency inflation, using stable price indices.[13]

If the State merely annexes incomes which result from production, in so far as it is not itself a producer, the way in which it makes use of this income may have decisive effects on the volume of net social income, that is, on the level of production itself. Its expenditure consists, in fact, of purchases of commodities, investments, wage and salary payments and gifts of various kinds, together with the payment of interest on the public debt. When the State budget absorbs a substantial share of social income, the allocation of this expenditure between the different sectors mentioned above can modify the "spontaneous" allocation of demand as between different commodities, and thus influence the general progress of business, or even modify the way the industrial cycle evolves.*

* These problems are dealt with in more detail in the last section of this chapter, and also in the following chapter and in Chapter 14, section "A crisis-free capitalism?"

The sharing-out of surplus-value

An official Japanese publication shows, for the year 1951, the following share-out of "value added", i.e. newly-created value, in Japanese industry as a whole:

	billion yen
Wages and salaries	706·8
Interest	111·8
Taxes	317·2
Dividends	40·3
Undistributed profits	150·9
	1,327·0[14]

The apparent rate of surplus value (without taking into account the surplus-value appropriated by the capitalists operating outside the sphere of production) is thus around 100 per cent. Actually, the category of *wages and salaries* includes the income of all the higher managerial personnel (managers and business executives) who belong sociologically to the bourgeois class rather than to the working class. Their incomes should be regarded as taken from surplus-value: "But although part of the salaries and other emoluments, of managers and executives should, by the economist, be included in wages, another part is a rough contractual equivalent for, or share in profits in our sense" states Schumpeter.[15]

And Woytinsky[16] justifiably criticises the official statistics which include in "income of labour" "the fees of directors of limited companies, the salaries of higher civil servants and many other officials . . . The statistics of national income almost always tend to over-estimate the income of labour, while underestimating other forms of income."

To go back to our Japanese table: the total of wages in the strict sense will thus be lower than 700 billion yen, and probably lower even than 663·5 billion yen, that is, half of the "value added" in industry. Let us, however, stick to the hypothesis of an amount of wages exactly equal to half of this "value added" of 1,327 billion, i.e. 663·5 billion yen. In this case, the apparent surplus-value also amounts to 663·5 billion yen, shared out as follows:

	billion yen
Factory managers, company directors, etc.	43·3
Banks, rentiers and landowners	111·8
Shareholders	40·3
Undistributed profits (accumulation funds of businesses)	150·9
The State (taxes)	317·2
	663·5

In the case of Japan, as with most large industrialised countries, the State takes a substantial share of the "value added" (the surplus value which arises in industry). It is not without point, however, to make clear that this means, very largely, a *redistribution of surplus value* among the various sectors of the bourgeoisie. The latter, in fact, profits from the national debt, State contracts and the salaries of the high dignitaries and officials of the State, the Army, the Church, the Judiciary, etc.

The total *surplus-value* produced *exceeds*, moreover, the figure which results from the above sum. The Japanese statisticians, in calculating the value "added", i.e. "newly created" by labour-power, went no further than the factory gates. But, as we know, *commercial profits*, which are not included in these figures, together with the share of these profits which, in their turn, the traders have to surrender to the banks, the landowners, the State, etc., likewise make up part of the total surplus value produced by the worker-producers. Re-examining the share-out of this surplus value from a functional standpoint, we can define the following categories of income:

(i) entrepreneur's and founder's profit, partly represented by the salaries of directors and executives, partly by dividends (on preference shares, founders' shares, etc.), and partly by undistributed profits, which are *available* to the entrepreneurs even if they do not use them as income in the strict sense of the word;

(ii) commercial profit, represented by the incomes of large and medium-scale traders, the dividends and undistributed profits of commercial joint-stock companies;

(iii) interest (income of individuals, companies and institutions advancing money-capital);

(iv) bank profits, which appear partly as interest and partly as undistributed profits or dividends of the banks;

(v) ground rent, the income of landowners (or of building societies), likewise deducted from the total amount of social surplus-value.

In so far as there is no longer a landlord class separate from the bourgeoisie, at least in the chief capitalist countries, the total of these incomes can be regarded as *income of the bourgeoisie*, the sharing-out of which involves only a struggle (competitive, in one way or another) between different sectors of this one class.

The ultimate origin of all the incomes distributed in capitalist society is shown more clearly still in the following table of national income in the United States in 1947[17] (in millions of dollars):

Wages and salaries	121,913
Social security payments	5,588
Income of unincorporated enterprises	45,997

Net Interest	4,293
Dividends	6,880
Undistributed profits	11,195
Corporate profits taxes	11,709

The only entry in this table that presents any problem is that of the profits of individual (unincorporated) enterprises. This includes the income of peasant producers, craftsmen, etc., which cannot, as a whole, be regarded as surplus-value. But, allowing for this qualification, the total amount of surplus value is determined by the total amount of all the entries except wages and social security payments.

The entry "wages", in the strict sense (which moreover includes the income of wage-earners in trade, banking, transport, etc.) constitutes only a part, often remarkably small, of the entry "wages and salaries". Thus, in Great Britain in 1951, out of a total of £8·4 billion shown as "income of labour", only £5 billion or 60 per cent was wages. Salaries—defined by the British blue book as the income of non-manual personnel, namely, managers, supervisors, foremen, technicians, office-workers, researchers, etc.—came to £2·5 billion. Employers' contributions to the national insurance fund amounted to £500 million, the pay of the armed forces to £300 million, etc.[18]

Social product and social income

The value of all the finished commodities produced by a society (a country) during a certain period (a year, for instance) represents the value of the *gross social (or national) product.*[19]

The value of this gross product is made up of newly-created value and conserved value. If we regard the raw material *additionally* produced during the year as finished products, the conserved value contained in that of the gross (national) product is that of the fixed capital used up (machinery, industrial plant and buildings, etc.) together with that of the stock of raw materials. The newly created value, called the *net (national) product* is equal to the value of all the commodities produced, less the value of the constant capital conserved. Or, put another way: the value of the net annual product is equal to the value of all the consumer goods produced together with that of all the *new* means of production.[20] We here find again the distinction between the *value of the annual product* ($c + v + s$) and the value newly-created each year ($v + s$). This new value can be rediscovered more easily by simply adding the new value (the value added) created in all the enterprises.

Assuming that all the commodities produced in the year have been effectively sold, the production of these commodities has created the following incomes: v, the total wages of all the workers; and s, the total surplus-value of the entire bourgeoisie (broken down as shown above). When the calculation is made on the basis of prices, the indirect taxes added to the selling prices of the commodities, and absorbed by the State, must be added,[21] while taking into account the fact that among the commodities produced (and the incomes distributed) we must also include those produced by the State. *The (national) income is thus equal to the net (national) product*, at market prices, less the indirect taxes, or rather, to the total value of all the finished products, less the conserved value of the constant capital (indirect taxes being regarded as an arbitrary addition to the value).*

Ruggles[22] offers the following table (in millions of dollars) of the *gross national product* of the United States in 1947, which enables us to rediscover with ease our fundamental categories: †

Fixed constant capital used up	Capital consumption allowances (Depreciation charges)	13,299			Gross national product at market prices
Variable capital	Wages and salaries	121,913	National income at factor prices	Net national product at market prices	
	Social insurance contributions	5,588			
Surplus-value‡	Income of unincorporated enterprises	45,997			
	Net interest	4,293			
	Dividends	6,880			
	Corporate profits taxes	11,709			
	Undistributed profits	11,195			
Arbitrary addition to commodity prices	Indirect taxes	18,488			

In the equation between *incomes* and *values of commodities produced*, the word "income" is used, however, in a quite special sense.

* The following problem could be discussed *ad infinitum*—should indirect taxes be regarded as an integral part of the surplus-value produced, and the national income be evaluated at market prices? Or should the national income be estimated on the basis of factor prices, re-evaluating the constituents and deducting the share taken by the State in indirect taxes? The result is practically the same.

† The price of circulating constant capital renewed during the year, the stock of raw materials reproduced, has been similarly broken down in this table into its constituent elements: c (fixed) $+ v + s +$ indirect taxes. From the Marxist standpoint this operation is valid, in so far as the value of this stock has been conserved. For, while the raw material embodied in the production of finished products does not represent a new value but only a conserved value, nevertheless the *production* of this raw material obviously gives rise to new value.

‡ Except for part of the income of the independent petty commodity producing producers.

It simply means *potential purchasing power*. Let us study these incomes more closely.

The incomes of the workers, wages, are usually spent, being quickly exchanged for commodities. The working class cannot go on living without realising its wages in commodities. The incomes of the capitalists, however, are divided into two parts:

(i) a part which is *consumed unproductively*, being usually transformed into consumer goods in order to keep the bourgeois class alive, and

(ii) a part which is *saved*, that is, not transformed into consumer goods. This part of bourgeois income is further divided into a part which is *invested* (serving to buy additional means of production, including fresh supplies of raw materials, goods or values, which bring in an income etc.) and a part which is *hoarded*, i.e. kept for a longer or shorter time in the form of money capital.[23]

For all the commodities produced in a given period to be effectively bought, the incomes distributed in the course of this same period must all be effectively spent. If some of the bourgeoisie's income (surplus-value) is hoarded, some of the commodities produced will not immediately find buyers. In the calculation of the national product, as it is normally carried out, the entry "stocks" will become larger for a time. If, however, this process goes on to the point where a crisis of overproduction occurs, the reduction in prices following the slump will reduce the absolute value of this entry, and of the gross product, bringing it down to the level of the value of the raw material, etc., effectively replaced as a result of production.

The above is, of course, only a crude approximation. To find a more exact formula one would have to take a large number of other factors into account. The sale of a commodity does not merely produce income: it also brings in the counter-value of the constant capital used up (sums serving to renew the stock of raw material and depreciate the fixed capital). And this counter-value can for a moment serve as additional purchasing power for commodities which are unrelated to this renewal of constant capital. In this case, the sale of all the commodities currently produced can disguise the reduction of the social capital available in the country concerned.

The stocks of raw material may fluctuate in both directions. If they increase, it has been possible to use part of their counter-value to buy other commodities, which again means that, despite the hoarding of part of the surplus-value, all the commodities produced during this period will have been effectively sold.

Also needing to be taken into account is the movement of prices. If, between the moment when commodities are produced and that when they are sold, prices fall, then the incomes distributed at the time of production will be capable of buying all the commodities produced, even if some of them have been hoarded.

Finally, there is the effect of relations with other countries. A net export of capital has, in principle, the same effect as the hoarding of a part of surplus-value, while a net import of capital, on the other hand, creates an additional demand for the commodities produced in the country. Similarly, a balance of trade surplus reduces, in principle, the amount of commodities available in relation to the incomes created by producing them. A trade balance deficit however, increases the amount of commodities circulating in the country, in relation to the incomes created by national production.

Despite all these qualifications, and many others, the establishment of a comparatively simple relation between national income (distributed during a year) and the value of the commodities produced during this same period makes it possible to determine the primary origin of the cyclical movement of capitalist production and of crises: the separation in time between the *production* of commodities—and the distribution of incomes which it implies—and the *realisation* of their value by their owners. It is as a result of this lack of an automatic coincidence between purchasing power distributed and commodities produced that the problem of realisation of surplus value can arise for the capitalist owners of commodities.

Distribution of income and realisation of commodities

The relation between incomes distributed in the course of production and commodities produced and offered on the market as counter-value to these incomes is further expressed in qualitative terms:

"Most commodities and services are purchased by two classes of users: consumers and business firms . . . Consumers buy goods to satisfy some physical or psychological need. Businessmen buy goods in order to increase the profits of their companies. The second are aptly called investment goods, the first, consumer goods."[24]

We shall retain, from this definition, first of all this division of the mass of commodities into two broad categories: consumer goods, which are "bought in order to satisfy physical or psychological needs", and investment goods (capital goods), bought in order to enable capitalists to increase their profits. Businessmen are also consumers, and as such they buy consumer goods in order to meet their own needs and those of their families. They devote to this purpose the part of surplus value which is not accumulated. The workers, however, are consumers only, they are not purchasers of investment goods, since their wages are usually inadequate to meet all their "physical and psychological" needs. The total of commodities produced and incomes (purchasing power) distributed, thus corresponds to the following diagram:

Supply	*Demand*
Consumer goods	Wages. Unaccumulated surplus value. Surplus value accumulated in order to hire more workers.
Investment goods	Depreciated constant capital. Accumulated surplus value.

The dynamics of capitalist production depend essentially on the relations of equilibrium (or disequilibrium) between these different categories.

The value of the consumer goods offered on the market—produced during a certain period of time, say a year—can be broken down into its constituent elements: $c + v + s$. The income created by the production (and sale) of these commodities is obviously inadequate to create the purchasing power needed to constitute their counter-value.

In fact, only the wages (v) of the workers who have participated in producing them, and the part of the profits not accumulated in c (s minus s in c) represent purchasing power relevant to consumer goods. The *conserved* value comprised in the value of these consumer goods, along with the part of surplus value accumulated in constant capital, represent purchasing power for capital goods (machinery, raw materials, etc.). If, in the course of a given year, all production consisted of consumer goods, there would be an inevitable disequilibrium, a supply of consumer goods equal to $c + v + s$, but a demand equal only to v + (s minus s accumulated in c). The *phenomenon of overproduction*, that is, of a quantity of commodities not finding on the market any counter-value in purchasing-power to realise their value, and thus remaining unsaleable or having to be sold off at a loss, would make its appearance.

Alongside consumer goods, however, capital goods are also produced in the course of each year. *And the production of capital goods gives rise to purchasing power for consumer goods.* The workers who work in factories where machines are made receive wages with which they buy, not machines, but consumer goods. The capitalists who own these factories likewise devote part of their surplus value to buying consumer goods. It is thus the total purchasing power created by the production of the two categories of commodities that must be studied in order to determine whether or not there is overproduction of consumer goods.

Furthermore, we have already seen that the production of consumer goods, in its turn, gives rise to purchasing power for capital goods, needed to replace the constant capital used up in production and perhaps to make possible the purchase of additional constant capital with the aid of the accumulated part of surplus value.

If we represent the value of capital goods by $\mathrm{I}c + \mathrm{I}v + \mathrm{I}s$ and that of the consumer goods by $\mathrm{II}c + \mathrm{II}v + \mathrm{II}s$, we can thus reconstruct as follows the overall diagram of supply and demand on the capitalist market.

Supply	*Demand*
Consumer goods: $\mathrm{II}c + \mathrm{II}v + \mathrm{II}s$	$\mathrm{I}v + \mathrm{I}$ (s minus s accumulated in c): demand for consumer goods on the part of workers and capitalists in the capital goods sector. $\mathrm{II}v + \mathrm{II}$ (s minus s accumulated in c): demand for consumer goods on the part of the workers and capitalists in the consumer goods sector.
Capital goods: $\mathrm{I}c + \mathrm{I}v + \mathrm{I}s$	$\mathrm{I}c + \mathrm{I}s$ accumulated in c: demand for capital goods on the part of the capitalists working in this sector. $\mathrm{II}c + \mathrm{II}s$ accumulated in c: demand for capital goods by the capitalists working in the other sector.

For the system to be in equilibrium, both equations must be effective, supply and demand must balance for the two categories of commodity:

$$\mathrm{I}c + \mathrm{I}v + \mathrm{I}s = \mathrm{I}c + \mathrm{I}s \text{ acc. in } c + \mathrm{II}c + \mathrm{II}s \text{ acc. in } c.$$
$$\mathrm{II}c + \mathrm{II}v + \mathrm{II}s = \mathrm{I}v + \mathrm{I}\,(s \text{ minus } s \text{ acc. in } c) + \mathrm{II}v + \mathrm{II}\,(s - s \text{ acc. in } c).$$

By eliminating in the two equations the terms common to both sides we twice obtain *the same equation, the conditions for general equilibrium of capitalist production:*

$$\mathrm{I}v + \mathrm{I}\,(s \text{ minus } s \text{ acc. in } c) = \mathrm{II}c + \mathrm{II}s \text{ acc. in } c.$$

This equation of equilibrium of the capitalist market does not represent a fiction. $\mathrm{I}v + \mathrm{I}$ (s minus s acc. in c), i.e. the wages paid and the part of surplus value not accumulated in constant capital in the capital goods sector, *is the total demand for consumer goods created by the production of capital goods.* $\mathrm{II}c + \mathrm{II}s$ acc. in c, i.e. the constant capital to be replaced and the constant capital to be accumulated in the sector of consumer goods, is the *total demand for capital goods created by the production of consumer goods.* The equation between these two magnitudes, as the equation of equilibrium of the capitalist market, signifies simply this: *capitalist economy is in equilibrium when the production of capital goods gives rise to a demand for consumer goods equal to the demand for capital goods to which the production of consumer goods gives rise.* Or, in other words, the capitalist market is in equilibrium when reciprocal supply and demand is equal as between the two sectors of capitalist production.

Production and reproduction

The equation of equilibrium establishes a relation between the value of the commodities produced and the purchasing power which serves as counter-value to these commodities from a *static* point of view, in the setting of a specific, well-defined period. But the reality of capitalist production is that of a process which unfolds in time, one cycle of production succeeding another. The question of the *continuity* of capitalist production presents problems of both a social and an economic character which can be called problems of reproduction.

For capitalist production to be continuous in time, it must reproduce, first and foremost, the fundamental conditions of the capitalist mode of production: the monopoly of the means of production (of capital) in the hands of one class of society; and the existence of another social class which is obliged to sell its labour-power in order to get the money it needs to acquire the means of life. It is thus necessary, first, that wages be "obviously determined and distributed so as to enable those who receive them merely to keep themselves alive, so as to be able to go on working in the service of whoever pays them and keeps them alive for his own personal and exclusive profit, but not so as to enrich them to the extent that they may gradually free themselves from their former masters, attain equality with them and enter into competition with them."[25]

St. Thomas Aquinas had already described the condition of the wage-earners as that of persons unable to accumulate any wealth: "Because they are poor they become wage-earners, and because they are wage-earners they are poor."[26]

Statistics of savings show quite plainly that the overwhelming majority of the working population of the capitalist countries consume in the course of their lives everything that they have earned, and thus cannot accumulate any capital. Their savings are only *deferred consumption*, in the literal meaning of the term: their "accumulations" relate only to consumer durables—or, at most, to houses.

Thus, in the period 1946–1950, 62·4 per cent of the British population possessed only 3 per cent [!] of British capital, or a "capital" per head of some £44.[27] In Belgium, during the same period, 27·5 per cent of the families possessed only 2·2 per cent of the privately owned *wealth* (less than 50,000 francs per family) and 48·8 per cent of the families possessed 20 per cent of it (less than 250,000 francs per family, or the value of a small working-class house). In the United States, in 1935–36, 90 [!] per cent of the households possessed only 19 per cent of the savings; in 1947–48 90 per cent of the households still had only 22·5 per cent of the savings. It should be stressed that, in these same years, 40 to 50 per cent of households had no savings at all![28]

It is further necessary that the sale of the commodities produced should enable the capitalists to reconstitute the capital they have expended in production, and to acquire newly-produced means of production. The analysis of the capitalist mode of production has shown us that it fulfils these two conditions.

This was not so in the societies which preceded capitalism. Herkovits relates the following about the Chuckchee tribe, who live as reindeer-herdsmen in the north-east of Siberia:

"Some Chuckchee families are so poor . . . that they own almost no herds at all, and such people enter the service of the more wealthy for extended periods. For the hard work they do, they receive supplies of meat and skins, though they must furnish their own pack-animals, when they move from one camp to another. A family working under this arrangement receive about ten fawns annually in addition to the subsistence return mentioned, if their employer is pleased with their work. In the course of five favourable years these animals and their increase give such a family a herd of some hundred reindeer, sufficient to permit them to attain independence."[29]

Similarly, the journeymen of the Middle Ages normally became master-craftsmen, or could at least nurse a legitimate hope of becoming such. Capitalist society is, on the contrary, characterised by this special feature that it constantly reproduces a proletarian class.

The continuity of capitalist production further demands a certain qualitative breakdown of the commodities produced. For it to exist, the capital used up in production must, in the course of a series of production cycles, at least be reconstituted. It is necessary therefore that it be possible at least to reproduce the machinery and raw material used up in the course of successive production processes and to produce at least sufficient consumer goods to reconstitute the labour-power needed.

We know that every society is in the last analysis based on an economy of labour-time. A certain proportion of the social labour-time totally available has to be devoted to the maintenance, repair and reproduction of the instruments of labour and to the upkeep of the fields and buildings, or otherwise, after a certain time, production can no longer be resumed on the same scale as before: society will be impoverished in the absolute sense of the word.

What in societies which produce use-values is a simple problem of allocating the social labour-time totally available is complicated in capitalist society by the fact that it is a mode of producing *commodities*. For the continuity of capitalist production to be guaranteed, it is necessary that during a series of production cycles:

1. The capital goods needed to replace those used up in the course of production, and the consumer goods needed to reconstitute labour-power, be materially produced;

2. Purchasing power capable of realising the value of these capital goods and consumer goods be created and actually spent; and

3. This purchasing power be distributed in such a way that supply and demand balance as regards both capital goods and consumer goods.

The study of the economic problems of reproduction in capitalist society is essentially the study of the questions raised by these three conditions, without which the continuity of capitalist production is broken.

Simple reproduction

Simple reproduction appears as a succession of production cycles which makes possible the *maintenance* of social wealth but not its increase. In a society which produces use values, simple reproduction means that the annual amount of products is sufficient to support a stable population and to replace the instruments of labour used up during this year. In a society which produces commodities, simple reproduction means that the value of the annual product (gross national product) suffices exactly to reproduce labour-power, the instruments of labour and the stock of raw material used up during the year, and to support the possessing classes. In a capitalist society simple reproduction means that the annual surplus value is wholly consumed unproductively by the bourgeois class and that there is no accumulation of capital.*

While the pre-capitalist modes of production passed through long periods of simple reproduction, they mostly ended by attaining at a certain moment in their evolution a stage of *expanded reproduction*, that is, a certain development of the instruments of labour, a certain accumulation of social wealth in the form of stocks of products and above all of stocks of additional tools. The mere accumulation of food reserves was already a primitive form of expanded reproduction.

As for the capitalist mode of production, it is distinguished from all previous modes of production precisely by the fact that it is not unproductive consumption but productive consumption, the capitalisation of the social surplus product, that represents the driving force of action and exploitation on the part of the possessing classes. In this case, expanded reproduction is the normal form of reproduction under

* Since she starts from the assumption that the capitalists use no part of their profits for their own unproductive consumption, Joan Robinson has described simple reproduction in its state of bliss, when "all labour is . . . employed on producing consumption goods and maintaining capital . . ."[80]

the capitalist régime, simple reproduction being possible only at exceptional moments in the capitalist production cycle.

How will the three conditions for the continuity of capitalist production present themselves in the setting of simple reproduction? Let us assume, for instance, that the total value of the annual production of all the commodities is 9,000 (millions of currency units). For continuity of production to be ensured, one part of these commodities must represent capital goods—machinery, raw materials, industrial buildings, auxiliary products, power, etc.—and the other must represent consumer goods. Let us suppose that, in value, two-thirds of production, or 6,000, represent capital goods, while the remaining third, or 3,000, represent consumer goods. Annual social production can then be defined as follows, assuming the rate of surplus value and the rate of profit to be the same in the two broad sectors of production:

$$\text{I}: 4{,}000\,c + 1{,}000\,v + 1{,}000\,s = 6{,}000 \text{ capital goods}$$
$$\text{II}: 2{,}000\,c + 500\,v + 500\,s = 3{,}000 \text{ consumer goods.}$$

In the course of production, capital goods to a total value of 6,000 have been used up (4,000 in the sector I and 2,000 in sector II). These goods can be replaced, since in the same period capital goods to the value of 6,000 have been produced. The social labour power needed requires consumer goods to the value of 1,500 in order to reconstitute itself. This can be done, because consumer goods to the value of 3,000 have been produced.

The sale of all the commodities brings the capitalists 9,000. Of this 9,000, 6,000 is needed to reconstitute constant capital (capital goods) and 1,500 to reconstitute variable capital (money capital with which labour power will be bought in the following year). The remaining 1,500 represents profit, the year's surplus-value. As, by definition, surplus value is wholly consumed unproductively in a case of simple reproduction, this 1,500 will be used to buy consumer goods. These consumer goods will actually be available, since they have been produced to the value of 3,000, and 1,500 have sufficed to reproduce the labour-power used up during the year.

Finally, supply and demand balance in the two sectors, since we have:

CAPITAL GOODS

Supply: 6,000, total production. *Demand:* { 4,000 capitalists I; 2,000 capitalists II }

CONSUMER GOODS

Supply: 3,000, total production. *Demand:* { 1,000 workers I; 500 workers II; 1,000 capitalists I; 500 capitalists II }

The purchasing power created by production has been distributed in such a way as to make possible the purchasing of all the commodities produced. These have thus vanished from the market, and we begin a new annual production cycle with a constant capital of 4,000 in sector I and 2,000 in sector II; money-capital, available as variable capital, to the value of 1,000 in sector I and 500 in sector II; a labour force of the same size as at the beginning of the previous cycle, and completely reconstituted. In other words: the new cycle starts from exactly the same level of production as the previous one. Simple reproduction has been achieved.

Expanded reproduction

Expanded reproduction takes the form of a succession of production cycles which makes possible an increase in social wealth. In a society which produces use values, expanded reproduction means that the yearly amount of products is greater than is needed for the support of the whole population and the conservation of the stock of instruments of labour. Social wealth grows in the form of an increased stock of instruments of labour, increased reserves of food, etc. Such an expanded reproduction is the indispensable condition for a more or less sustained increase in population.

In a commodity-producing society, expanded reproduction means that the value of the annual product (gross national product) is greater than the value of the labour-power, the instruments of labour, and the stock of raw material used up during the year, together with the goods needed for the upkeep of the possessing classes.

In a capitalist society, expanded reproduction means that surplus value is divided into two parts: one part consumed unproductively by the capitalists, their families and their hangers-on, and another consumed productively, i.e. accumulated and invested, capitalised in the form of machinery, raw materials, *additional* wages, which make it possible to start a new production cycle with a larger capital—capital of a greater value—than in the previous cycle.

How will the three conditions for the continuity of capitalist production appear in the setting of expanded reproduction? In the case of simple reproduction, the value of all the capital goods produced in a single cycle must be equal to the value of the constant capital used up in the course of this production cycle. In the case of expanded reproduction this will not do, for the capital goods needed to start the next cycle with an increased constant capital will be lacking. The first condition for expanded reproduction is thus the production of an *additional amount* of capital goods, over and above what have been used up in the previous production cycle (an additional amount does not mean a *larger number* but a higher *value*). The equivalent of this additional amount of capital goods is precisely the part of surplus value destined to be accumulated as additional constant capital.

Similarly, the production of an additional amount of consumer goods, over and above those bought during the previous cycle by the workers and the capitalists, is necessary, since these consumer goods are to provide the counter-value of the additional variable capital (wages) which part of the accumulated surplus value represents, and which is destined to purchase an additional quantity of labour power.

Let us assume that the total gross product of a year has a value of 11,400 (million currency units), divided between 7,000 worth of capital goods and 4,400 worth of consumer goods. The value of the gross product may, let us imagine, be analysed like this, if we assume an equal rate of surplus value in the two sectors but a higher rate of profit in sector II, where the organic composition of capital is lower:

1st cycle
- I: $4{,}000\,c + 1{,}500\,v + 1{,}500\,s = 7{,}000$ capital goods
- II: $2{,}000\,c + 1{,}200\,v + 1{,}200\,s = 4{,}400$ consumer goods

Total: 11,400

Let us assume, again, that the capitalists in sector I allocate their surplus-value like this: 500 consumed unproductively and 1,000 accumulated, of which 700 as constant capital and 300 as variable capital. As for the capitalists in sector II, they allocate their surplus-value, let us suppose, like this: 700 consumed unproductively, 500 accumulated, of which 300 as constant capital and 200 as variable capital.

During the previous production cycle 6,000 had been used up as constant capital in the two sectors together. Total production of capital goods exceeds this 6,000—it amounts to 7,000. The 1,000 additional capital goods enable the capitalists of sector I to accumulate constant capital to the value of 70 and the capitalists in sector II to do the same to the value of 300. During the same previous cycle 3,900 consumer goods had been used up (2,700 for the workers in both sectors, 500 for the capitalists of sector I, and 700 for the capitalists of sector II). But the production of consumer goods attains a value of 4,400. These 500 extra consumer goods will enable the extra workers hired under expanded reproduction to find the counter-value of their wages, the surplus value accumulated as variable capital, namely, 300 in sector I and 200 in sector II.

Thus, both the commodities and the purchasing power needed for expanded reproduction have been supplied by the previous cycle. The continuity of production is assured because the allocation of this purchasing power makes it possible to balance supply and demand in the two sectors:

CAPITAL GOODS

Supply: 7,000, total production.

Demand:
- 4,000, capitalists I: reconstitution of *c*.
- 2,000, capitalists II: reconstitution of *c*.
- 700, capitalists I: accumulation of *c*.
- 300, capitalists II: accumulation of *c*.

CONSUMER GOODS

Supply: 4,400, total production.

Demand:
- 1,500, workers I.
- 1,200, workers II.
- 500, capitalists I.
- 700, capitalists II.
- 300, counter-value of accumulation of *v* by capitalists I.
- 200, counter-value of accumulation of *v* by capitalists II.

The new production cycle will thus begin with the following capital:

I: (4,000 + 700) *c* + (1,500 + 300) *v*.
II: (2,000 + 300) *c* + (1,200 + 200) *v*.

Still assuming a rate of surplus value stable at 100 per cent, production in this second cycle of enlarged reproduction will have the following value:

2nd cycle	I: 4,700 *c* + 1,800 *v* + 1,800 *s* = 8,300 capital goods II: 2,300 *c* + 1,400 *v* + 1,400 *s* = 5,100 consumer goods	13,400

Assuming that the surplus-value of capitalists I is allocated like this: 600 consumed unproductively and 1,200 accumulated, of which 800 as *c* and 400 as *v*; that the surplus value of capitalists II is allocated like this: 700 consumed unproductively and 700 accumulated, of which 500 as *c* and 20 as *v*, we can, as indicated above, deduce a third cycle of expanded reproduction, production in which will have the following value:

3rd cycle	I: 5,500 *c* + 2,200 *v* + 2,200 *s* = 9,900 II: 2,800 *c* + 1,600 *v* + 1,600 *s* = 6,000 consumer goods	15,900

and so forth . . .

It will be seen that expanded reproduction is expressed in the increase, between one cycle and the next, in the total value of the commodities in each sector, as also in the increase of surplus-value in each sector. Under simple reproduction these values remain stable from one cycle to another.

Expanded reproduction and the laws of development of capitalism

In the diagrams of expanded reproduction set out above, each sector realised the whole of the surplus-value produced by the workers in that sector. This is in contradiction to the actual development of the capitalist mode of production, in which an equalisation of the rate of profit occurs whereby the sectors with a higher organic composition of capital—sector I—annex a share of the surplus value produced by the workers of the other sectors. The diagram can easily be corrected, however, by calculating the average rate of profit on the whole of capital, then transforming the value of commodities I and II into their prices of production.* In this way the following succession of cycles of expanded reproduction would be obtained:

1st cycle

I: 4,000 c + 1,500 v + 1,705 profit = 7,205 capital goods
II: 2,000 c + 1,200 v + 995 profit = 4,195 consumer goods } 11,400

2nd cycle

I: 4,905 c + 1,800 v + 2,060 profit = 8,765 capital goods
II: 2,300 c + 1,400 v + 1,140 profit = 4,840 consumer goods } 13,605

3rd cycle

I: 6,005 c + 2,160 v + 2,450 profit = 10,615 capital goods
II: 2,760 c + 1,600 v + 1,310 profit = 5,670 consumer goods } 16,285

etc.

At the same time we also observe in these diagrams the tendency of the rate of profit to fall, with 31 per cent in the first cycle, 30·75 per cent in the second and 30 per cent in the third.†

* In the first cycle, 1,500 s + 1,200 s give a total surplus value of 2,700, or 31 per cent of profit on a total capital of 8,700. The price of production of I and II is calculated by adding 31 per cent of profit to the respective capitals. In the second cycle, 1,800 s + 1,400 s give a total surplus value of 3,200, or 30·75 per cent profit on a total capital of 10,405. In the third cycle, 2,160 s + 1,600 s give a total surplus value of 3,760 on a total capital of 12,525, or 30 per cent profit. We assume an unproductive consumption of profit of 500 in I and 495 in II during the first cycle, and of 600 in I and 480 in II during the second.

† Some writers[31] declare that calculation carried out in this way must inevitably lead to mistakes and contradictions because the value of c and v in each cycle is not itself transformed into price of production. This view is unfounded. The price of production of c results from the equalisation of the rate of profit *during the previous cycle*. It is a constant because, independently of the gains or losses of a capitalist in competition with others, he has paid (or owes) a *previously determined price* for the machines, raw material, etc., he has bought. As for the transformation of values into prices of production, as applied to the diagrams of simple reproduction, this is indeed incorrect, but not for the reason alleged by the writers mentioned above. This transformation results from *capitalist competition*, which is just what is missing in the

Nevertheless, one must be careful not to ascribe to these formulae a significance they do not possess. By arbitrarily choosing one's starting figures, or the initial relations between the different terms in the formula, one may succeed in "discovering" laws of capitalist reproduction, including its "inevitable collapse" (as the Marxist economist Henryk Grossman has done), after a certain number of cycles. This is a perfectly useless and sterile game.

In reality, reproduction formulae merely indicate the conditions of continuity of *capitalist production as a whole*, leaving aside all the *concrete conditions* under which the capitalist mode of production progresses: birth in a non-capitalist setting; transfers of capital from one sector to another; role played by credit; fluctuation of money prices, etc. In so far as capitalist production is production for the market, a production of commodities and not a conscious allocation of society's resources between different branches of production, it is these *concrete conditions* in which the capitalist mode of production operates that determine both the laws of development of capital—without the whip of competition, for instance, the increase in the organic composition of capital and the tendency of the rate of profit to fall which is implicit in it would be inexplicable—and the cyclical form taken by economic life under capitalism.

The reproduction formulae which leave out all these concrete conditions therefore cannot and should not be expected to "reveal" these laws of development, or the causes of this cyclical movement. They can at most indicate how, *despite* the operation of thousands of individual capitalists fiercely competing one with another and thereby determining the actual progress of the capitalist mode of production, the continuity of production is maintained *in the long run*, notwithstanding frequent periodical interruptions. The usefulness of these formulae is appreciated when one asks this question: how can it happen that the continuity of production is maintained, when the value and the proportions of this production seem to result from individual decisions by thousands of businessmen who hide their intentions from each other? The reproduction formulae show the conditions that must be fulfilled if this continuity is to be safeguarded.

In the real life of capitalism, these conditions of continuity are achieved *through the breaks in continuity. Capitalist economy is seen as a unity of continuity and discontinuity in its economic activities.* "Progress . . . not only proceeds by jerks and rushes but also by one-sided rushes productive of consequences other than those which

diagram of simple reproduction and in an economy based on petty commodity production such as this formula reflects. It is to be observed, incidentally, that these writers confuse price of production and market prices expressed in money terms, since they bring the conditions of the gold-producing industry into their argument.

would ensue in the case of co-ordinated rushes . . . The history of capitalism is studded with violent bursts and catastrophes . . . Evolution is a disturbance of existing structures and more like a series of explosions than a gentle, though incessant transformation."[32]

In this sense, the formulae represent, so to speak, *averages* over a *decade* or over a cycle, reciprocal proportions between the different elements in capitalist production. They imply precisely the *elimination* from the abstract formula of all the factors which determine the cyclical progress of production. They cannot therefore explain concretely either capitalist expansion or the reason why crises break out.

Expanded reproduction, economic growth and social accounting

The analysis of the different conditions of expanded reproduction is at the same time the analysis of the factors which ultimately determine the economic growth of the capitalist mode of production.

In any society, the two conditions which are necessary and sufficient for economic growth are:

(1) that *per capita* production be greater than the necessary product, that is, that the society produce more than it consumes (including in consumption the wearing out of its instruments of labour);

(2) that this net surplus assume, at least in part, the form of extra instruments of labour, that is, that it be consumed productively. A borderline case is that in which this net surplus is used to support a larger number of *producers*, and in which it makes possible, thanks to better feeding of these producers, an immediate increase in their output. In this case, however, one merely puts off for a stage the need to see a net product of additional instruments of labour appear as a necessary condition for economic growth.

In capitalist society, these two conditions appear precisely as the conditions for expanded reproduction:

1. There is a surplus value which is not wholly consumed by the capitalists.
2. Its unconsumed residue is partly invested in fresh constant capital.

Generally speaking, three proportions are thus fundamental in determining the rate of growth of a capitalist society:

(*a*) The absolute amount of profit (s) and its ratio to the gross national product;

(*b*) The absolute amount of profit not consumed unproductively (s minus s cons.) and its ratio to the gross national product (and the total quantity of surplus value);

(*c*) The absolute amount of these accumulated profits which is invested in capital goods (s minus s cons. minus s acc. in v minus s hoarded) and its ratio to the gross national product and to the total quantity of surplus value.

Because these three proportions are intertwined, it is not possible to isolate a single one of them in order to determine the source of the relative slowness (or the speed) of economic growth.

Thus, a country may have a very low rate of productive investment not because the amount (or the rate) of profit or of surplus value is low, but because a very high proportion of this surplus value is consumed unproductively or accumulated in ways other than productive investment (for instance, speculation in land, hoarding of precious metals, export of capital for non-productive purposes, etc.). This is particularly the case in a number of under-developed countries.*

It would similarly be quite wrong to assume that a considerable rise in real wages, bringing about a fall in the rate of profit, must automatically slow down economic growth. This hypothesis is correct only if, during the previous phase, nearly all the surplus value was invested productively. Given any other conditions, such a rise in wages may, on the contrary, stimulate economic growth, by compelling the possessing classes to reduce their unproductive consumption and their accumulation outside productive spheres, so as to neutralise the monetary fall in the rate of surplus value by an increase in relative surplus value (an increase in the productivity of labour).

Calculations of the national accounts which are based on the hybrid, and purely descriptive, criteria of the theory of income cannot enable us to distinguish the *potential sources of accumulation of productive capital*, or in other words the total amount of surplus value or of social surplus product. They do not distinguish between the productive consumption of workers' households, the unproductive consumption of the possessing classes, the easily reducible consumption of luxuries, and pure waste. In the same way the building of houses for the people, which corresponds to a pressing need, is included in the same entry with the building of luxurious banking and office premises which are often ways of evading taxation and not "productive investments" in any sense. In the category of public investments, productive investments are mixed up with the purchase of military equipment, a typical form of unproductive expenditure!

It is thus urgent to modify the way of calculating the national accounts, in accordance with the social structure, so that abstract (or purely monetary) concepts of saving may be replaced by the concept of total surplus value and of the available potential accumulation fund.†

In the foregoing we have assumed that the existing enterprises and labour force were already fully employed. This assumption does not correspond to a permanent reality. Consequently, economic growth

* See Chapter 13.

† In Chapter 16 we endeavour to show that the *maximum* rate of accumulation *never gives* the highest rate of growth, is never the *optimum* rate.

may result not only from an additional creation of means of production, but from a better (more rational, uninterrupted, etc.) use of those which already exist. It is not so much the increase in productive investment as the better use of the existing productive forces (human and mechanical) that matters in this case. Nevertheless, though such a possibility is very important in the short run (especially in crises!) it constitutes only an intermediate phase in longer term views. As soon as full employment of the existing means of production has been attained, economic growth is again identified with their expansion.

Contracted reproduction

Contracted reproduction occurs as a succession of production cycles which no longer allow social wealth to maintain itself but instead cause it to shrink. In a society producing use-values, contracted reproduction means that the annual amount produced is not sufficient to support the whole population or to maintain the existing stock of tools of labour, or both. In a commodity-producing society, contracted reproduction means that the value of the gross annual product is less than the total amount received in payment by the working classes, the value of the instruments of labour and raw materials used up in the course of production, and the value of the commodities serving to support the ruling classes. In capitalist society contracted reproduction means that for various reasons the capitalists are unable to renew the constant capital used up and that the wages paid out do not enable the producers completely to reconstitute their labour-power.

In pre-capitalist societies, contracted reproduction might result from two different combinations of circumstances. First, a *sudden decline in production*, owing to natural or social calamities, drought, floods, earthquakes, invasions, epidemics, wars, civil wars, etc.

Let us suppose that the total needs of an agricultural community amount to 1,000 tons of wheat a year, of which 750 are for consumption and 250 for seed and for use in exchange for other articles of prime necessity. If during several consecutive years the harvest declines to 500 tons and no external help is received, there will be contracted reproduction all along the line. The amount of seed will be inadequate; some of the land will remain uncultivated; part of the population will perish; the number of producers (the labour force) will shrink. Even when a good harvest does come, a smaller number of producers working on a smaller sown area will produce less wheat than before.

Contracted reproduction could also result from a *change in the distribution of available social resources*. For production to ensure the continuity of economic life at a certain level, it must in fact produce use values which are such as to *reconstitute the material elements of production*: labour power and instruments of labour. However, it is possible to use these elements *for purpses which are sterile as far as reproduction is concerned*, i.e. for producing goods which do not make possible renewal either of the labour force or of the instruments of labour used up during the given period of production. In this case there will inevitably be contracted reproduction, since part of the productive resources used will not have been reconstituted and work will therefore be continuing with smaller resources.

Thus, during the reign of the Mongol emperors in China, says the historian Eberhard, a large number of poor peasants subject to labour service were concentrated for the purpose of building luxurious imperial establishments.[33] These peasants were obliged to abandon their fields while they were carrying out this work; these fields therefore remained uncultivated. A series of cycles of contracted reproduction was thus started, the distribution of the labour-power totally available to society having been carried out in such a way that production in the basic sector, that of agriculture, had to be contracted.

In the capitalist mode of production we encounter both of these forms of contracted reproduction. First, that which is caused by a sudden fall in production, by an economic crisis. Contrary to what happened in pre-capitalist society, it is not the decline in the *amount* produced but in its *value* that brings about the break in continuity, the economic crisis. But the cumulative effect of the shrinking of economic life remains no less characteristic in the case of capitalist economic crises. A fall in the value of production leads to the closing of factories and dismissing of workers. This then causes a sudden fall in the total purchasing power, which further accentuates the piling up of unsold goods, the fall in prices and the closing of businesses. From one month to the next—and during prolonged crises, from one year to the next—less and less is produced, with less capital and fewer workers; the basis of production shrinks.

Similarly, capitalism can experience contracted reproduction due to a change in the distribution of available productive resources. If part of constant capital and labour power is used to produce commodities the use value of which does not make possible either the reconstitution of this constant capital or the reconstitution of this labour-power, at the end of a certain time contracted reproduction will prevail, that is, production carried on with a reduced amount of constant capital and labour-power.

War economy

War economy is the typical example of contracted reproduction under capitalism. War economy implies that part of the productive resources of constant capital and labour-power are devoted to the making of *means of destruction*, the use-value of which does not make possible either the reconstruction of machinery, or of stocks of raw material, or of the labour force, but tends, on the contrary, to bring about the destruction of these resources. For this reason, war economy can reach a point at which either the maintenance (depreciation from the financial standpoint, replacement from the physical) of the constant capital is no longer guaranteed,* or the labour force is not completely reconstituted, because consumption by the workers falls to too low a level, and the productivity of labour declines, to which may be further added the effect of an absolute reduction in the number of workers.

Thus, the British national income during the last war assumed this form, compared with peacetime (in millions of £):

	1938	*1943*
	(figures in 1938 pounds)	
Government expenditure	837	3,840
Private consumption	4,138	3,270
Private investment at home	305	−95
Foreign investment	−55	−485[35]
National income:	5,225	6,530

It will be seen that a war economy can be accompanied by an *increase* in real national income and the value of the gross national product, as it is at present calculated: ". . . an increase in any one type of product must be accompanied either by a decrease in other kinds of product or an increase in total production. If the goods and services that government uses in time of war are counted as a final product, as is the custom in current computations, the record might be expected to show some increase in total output, but also a decrease in non-war products, during the war period."[36]

The production of tanks, aircraft and shells, sold by the capitalists engaged in the sector of means of destruction, is a production of commodities the value of which is realised on the market. But as these commodities do not enter into the process of *reproduction*, this increase in national income is accompanied by an absolute reduction in the amount of existing constant capital and a very big reduction in the productivity of labour.

The British example during the last war was, moreover, a relatively benign one. In Japan, the textile industry had, in the same world war,

* This point of *contracted reproduction* was actually reached in the United States during the Second World War. The production of new fixed capital (durable equipment) declined from 7·3 billion dollars in 1929 and 6·9 billion in 1940 to 5·1 billion in 1942, 3·1 million in 1943 and 4 billion in 1944, while the annual wearing-out of existing fixed capital was estimated at 8 billion dollars during the same period. The net formation of new capital declined to less than 1 per cent of the national income in 1943. During the same period, war expenditure absorbed in 1942 32 per cent, in 1943 43 per cent and in 1944 43 per cent of the gross national product of the United States.[34]

to transform into scrap-iron two-thirds of all the cotton spindles.[37] The fixed capital of sector II became circulating capital for sector I. In Germany and elsewhere the average productivity of labour fell to a point at which it was again possible to use forced labour on a large scale.

This contracted reproduction can be presented diagramatically by introducing a third sector into a reproduction formula, that of destruction goods:

1st cycle

I: 4,000 c + 1,500 v + 1,500 s = 7,000 capital goods
II: 2,000 c + 1,200 v + 1,200 s = 4,400 consumer goods } 11,400

2nd cycle

I: 4,000 c + 1,500 v + 1,500 s = 7,000 capital goods
II: 2,000 c + 1,200 v + 1,200 s = 4,400 consumer goods
III: 1,000 c + 500 v + 500 s = 2,000 destruction goods } 13,400

3rd cycle

I: 3,900 c + 1,200 v + 1,100 s = 6,200 capital goods
II: 1,800 c + 900 v + 800 s = 3,500 consumer goods
III: 1,300 c + 600 v + 500 s = 2,400 destruction goods } 12,100

This diagram is based on the assumption that, after the first cycle, the capitalists of categories I and II invest all their surplus value in the arms industry. As a result, production in these two sectors does not increase in the second cycle. It would, of course, be possible to introduce several intermediate cycles during which a decreasing fraction of the accumulated surplus value would continue to be invested in sectors I and II.

The 7,000 capital goods produced during the second cycle are to be divided in the third cycle between categories I, II and III, which means a reduction in the capital goods available for sectors I and II, where the phenomenon of contracted reproduction starts to appear. Part of the surplus value of capitalists I and II can no longer be invested in these sectors, for lack of any counter-value on the market; it is transformed into means of financing the third sector, or else is hoarded (forced loan, company reserves, etc.). The value of the consumer goods available to the workers similarly contracts, which causes a fall in output and a shrinkage in the rate of surplus value.*

* During the Second World War the U.S.A. reached approximately this second cycle of contracted reproduction, at least so far as stagnation of the sector of capital goods was concerned. Towards the end of the war, Great Britain, Germany and, still more, Japan, experienced the third cycle, with reduction of production in I and II. Professor Jacquemyns was able to analyse the state of health of some 500 Belgian miners and metal-workers in May—June 1941, after a year of rationing which had reduced by 25 per cent the normal consumption of bread, by 60 per cent that of fats, meat and potatoes,

The contracted reproduction of consumer goods and of certain capital goods, under the influence of the production of destruction goods, in the setting of a war economy, is revealed very clearly in the following table: [39]

Value of the production of the different branches of industry in percentage of the value of Germany's total industrial production

	1936	*1939*	*1944*
Raw material industries;	34·4	31·4	33·3
of which, coal and other mines	7·5	7·4	6·3
Industries producing capital goods;	39·5	34·9	41·4
of which, metal-work, incl. production of destruction goods	15·3	21·8	25·5
Consumer goods industries;	30·5	27·6	19·0
of which, textiles	7·5	5·0	3·7
of which, foodstuffs	11·4	11·9	7·0

Redistribution of the national income by the State

The rise of the labour movement and the increasing popular antipathy to the inequality of income characteristic of modern capitalism have led to defensive reactions on the part of the possessing classes. Since income tax was introduced in Great Britain, and above all since the New Deal experiences in the U.S.A., many economists have stressed the fact that, through its budget, the State—especially in the Western countries of bourgeois democracy—redistributes a large proportion of the national income at the expense of the possessing classes and for the benefit of the working classes.

Progressive income tax and death duties, they say, reduce the inequality of incomes and wealth. The services which the State places freely at the disposal of all its citizens—compulsory education, upkeep of roads, public health, with free medicine in Great Britain, etc.—are above all advantageous to the poorest classes of the population, and tend to equalise citizens' incomes still further. The evolution of present-day capitalism is said to be not towards a concentration but, on the contrary, a dispersion, an ever-greater levelling of incomes.

So far as wealth and property are concerned, especially the ownership of industry and property in capitalists' savings, these allegations are a crude untruth: all the facts we have point to an increasing concentration of this ownership.* But as regards income it is usually accepted that the action of the public authorities has served effectively to reduce the inequality of income. Is this really so, and, if it is, what

and by 75 per cent that of eggs and fish. The result was a loss of weight of at least 4 kilogrammes—and in some cases as much as 15 kilogrammes—below the normal in the case of 64 per cent of the workers, leading to decline in arterial tension, permanent fatigue and a rapid falling-off in output.[38]

* See Chapter 7, section dealing with the "scattering" of shares, and Chapter 12.

place must be given to this phenomenon in the recent evolution of the capitalist mode of production?

The State's income, as we have already said, normally comes from two different sources—direct taxes on income, and indirect taxes, increasing the selling prices of goods (the issue of paper money by the State having the same effect as indirect taxation). If progressive income taxation hits the well-to-do classes harder than the poorer ones, this is not at all true of indirect taxes.

"In general, taxation of consumption will fall more heavily upon the lower income brackets than upon the higher, and accordingly it will to a certain extent make up for the income-levelling effects of the taxation of income."[40]

In fact we observe that in France the wage-earners paid in 1949 450·5 milliard francs in indirect taxes, as against 271·5 milliard paid by businessmen and professional men. In Great Britain the total taxation of all kinds paid by the poorest class of taxpayers (those earning less than £500 a year) increased from £499 million in 1937 to £1,791 million in 1949, because indirect taxes increased five-fold in this period. In Denmark, indirect taxes reduced the income of the poorer classes of taxpayers by 11·2 per cent, whereas their incidence on the incomes of the middle classes is only 9·1 per cent.[41]

It is true that in the U.S.A. indirect taxes are responsible for only a small part of public revenue. But in that country it is necessary to take into account the effect of direct taxation on wages and salaries, a factor which is indeed playing an even greater role in other capitalist countries. Actually, in France the wage-earners pay more in direct taxes than the businessmen and professional men! In Belgium the wage-earners, who receive barely 50 per cent of the national income, paid, in 1959, 57·5 per cent of the income tax.[42]*

If we draw up the overall balance-sheet of the taxes paid by the working people and the benefits they receive from social security, etc., we usually reach the conclusion that the redistribution of income in their favour is slight or even non-existent. Thus, for France, Rottier and Albert remark:

"Limiting ourselves . . . to the group of non-agricultural wage and salary earners, we have not been able to obtain precise results on the vertical redistribution of income within this group. However, it is probably not very large . . . [The] relative increase in the share of the social wage has not been accompanied by a growth in the total share of wages and salaries in the national income. There has thus been a marked decrease in the share of this income which a wage or salary earner can spend as he likes."[43]

* In West Germany indirect taxation brought in 27·5 billion DM in 1960, as against 3·8 billion RM in 1928–29 for the entire Weimar Republic. In the same period, wages and salaries increased by 150 per cent only.

And for Great Britain F. Weaver reaches similar conclusions: "A primary feature of the increase in post-war redistribution in the United Kingdom is that it occurs mainly within different income classes on the basis of consumption habits rather than between classes . . . Most of the post-war increase in personal taxes has been levied indirectly on consumption and has fallen on those who smoke and drink or consume non-utility clothing and household goods. The incidence of regressive taxes is mainly on the working class who are also the chief recipients of the benefits of redistributive governmental expenditures. Generally, the low income group pays for its benefits . . ."[44]

It may be objected that this purely monetary calculation does not take into account such free material benefits as the general improvement on the level of health and education, the lengthening of life which has resulted, a certain change in the structure of consumption, an increase in what workers spend on culture and leisure in the industrially advanced countries, etc. This is a pertinent argument.

But, as the Danish economists Lemberg, Ussing and Leuthen observe, the "services" rendered to the workers by the State in this way are to be explained less by a desire to redistribute income than by a desire to "qualify the recipients as fully as possible for productive work."[45] In the same way, the lengthening of the average expectation of life also means the lengthening of the workers' productive life; instead of producing surplus value for 25 years for the capitalists, the worker now produces for 40 or 45 years. In so far as the price of labour power includes a relative element,* namely the average needs determined by the average level of civilisation in a country at a certain epoch, the State, by guaranteeing to the wage-earners certain services which they do not have to purchase with their money wage, *merely guarantees, on behalf of the bourgeoisie as a whole, the payment of an integral part of wages*. The State does not transform surplus value into wages; it merely plays the role of central cashier for the bourgeoisie, *paying part of wages in a collective form, so as to socialise certain needs*.

There are situations in which the redistribution of the national income benefits the working class on a larger scale. But this is not, paradoxically, the case with "social capitalism"; rather does it apply in the case of society's great penances.

When a capitalist country is hit by the cataclysm of a serious economic crisis, or a lost war, the redistribution of the national income does indeed take place in favour of the poorest strata—the unemployed, in the first instance, the victims of war in the second. These sections of the population must be included in the proletariat; they constitute precisely that "Lazarus stratum" of which Karl Marx speaks.

* See Chapter 5.

In Western Germany, where there are millions of cripples and badly wounded war-victims, together with victims of fascist and racial repressions, war veterans and people who are sick as a result of wartime privations, this "Lazarus stratum" receives nearly 10 per cent of the national income, by way of redistribution through the State. It will be agreed, however, that the workers cannot derive much satisfaction from the conclusion that they do not "profit" from the redistribution of national income except in so far as they become unemployed or war-cripples.

It is obvious that what we have here is a measure with political and social aims, a lubrication of the social mechanism intended to avoid an explosion, and not an *economic* evolution which in some way or other contradicts the relative impoverishment of the proletariat.

A study by Simon Kuznets[46] which appeared in 1953 tried to work out in figures the effects of the redistribution of national income in the U.S.A. He came to the conclusion that the net share taken by the rich (after paying direct taxes)—and by the rich he meant the richest one per cent of the taxpayers—of the national income had been reduced to a striking extent, from 14·3 per cent, on the average, in 1919–38 to 7·9 per cent in 1948.

This study suffers, however, from grave methodological weaknesses. In the first place, it is based exclusively on the taxpayers' own declarations, which in the case of self-employed people, and especially of the rich, are notoriously underestimates aimed at dodging taxation.*

It takes account of direct taxation but not of the rise in the cost of living, which is particularly unfavourable to the lower income groups. It employs arbitrary categories ("the one per cent richest taxpayers", "the seven per cent richest taxpayers," etc.) and not *concrete social* categories.

If we re-examine the official statistics, without even taking into account undeclared income, we observe nevertheless that the share of the lower income group has not increased at all, as may be seen from these figures:

	Percentage of households	*Percentage of personal family income received*
In 1910	50	26·8
In 1918	50	26·6
In 1929	50	22·0
In 1937	50	21·2
In 1944	51·9	24·9
In 1956	51·7	25·2

* Dr. Selma Goldsmith, of the National Bureau of Economic Research, estimates that in the U.S.A. 24 per cent of dividends, 29 per cent of businessmen's income and 63 per cent of interest payments were not declared in 1946.[47]

It is hard to interpret these figures in the sense of an historical improvement on the part of the lower income groups, especially if we note that 51·7 per cent of families quoted for 1956 earned less than 5,000 dollars a year; that the 51·9 per cent of families quoted for 1944 earned less than 3,000 dollars a year; and that between 1944 and 1956 the purchasing power of the dollar fell by 40 per cent, so that the 5,000 dollars of 1956 were exactly equivalent to the 3,000 dollars of 1944.[48]

According to Kuznets, in 1929 the 7 per cent of the taxpayers with the highest incomes received 30·3 per cent of personal income; in 1956 the 10 per cent highest-paid taxpayers received 31 per cent of personal income. The "redistribution" consisted merely of a certain *enlargement of the upper middle classes*, a phenomenon characteristic of every period of boom (and "exaggerated" in these figures owing to tax-dodging). This impression is further reinforced when one observes that the 3·8 per cent of all families who receive more than 15,000 dollars a year received in 1956 altogether 17·3 per cent of family income, whereas in 1929 the same percentage was received by some 2 per cent of the families.* The share of the "rich" has not changed at all; they have merely become somewhat more numerous.†

But if we know that 40 per cent of the taxpayers together receive less than this 3·8 per cent of the population (their share was reduced from 20 per cent in 1916 to some 13 per cent in 1950!) it is impossible to find in these figures any pointer to a reversal of the classical tendencies to concentration of capital and income in the capitalist mode of production.[51]

* The German official statistics show that in 1928 88·84 per cent of the taxpayers received 61·1 per cent of the private incomes; in 1950, 86·05 per cent of West German taxpayers received 59·7 per cent of the private incomes. At the other end of the pyramid, in 1928 0·45 per cent of the taxpayers received 11·1 per cent of private incomes; in 1950 1·24 per cent of the taxpayers received 10 per cent of private incomes. In 1928 the share of the 4·3 per cent most prosperous was 24·7 per cent; in 1950 the share of the 4·4 per cent most prosperous was 23 per cent.[49]

† "Despite the laments about high taxes, the number of American families with a net worth of a half-million dollars has doubled since 1945. Most of the very rich manage, one way or another, to hold on to the bulk of their new incomes each year. Meanwhile, corporate lawyers have applied their ingenuity to find non-taxable benefits for key executives. These range from deferred payments in the form of high incomes for declining years and free medical check-ups at mountain spas, to hidden hunting lodges, corporate yachts, payment of country-club dues (according to one survey, three-quarters of all companies sampled did this), and lush expense accounts."[50]

REFERENCES

1. Carl Shoup: *Principles of National Income Analysis*, p. 27.
2. Jean Marchal and Jacques Lecaillon: *La Répartition du revenu national*, Vol. III, pp. 141-53.
3. Carl Shoup: op. cit., p. 85.
4. P. T. Bauer and B. S. Yamey: *The Economics of Underdeveloped Countries*, p. 20.
5. Simon Kuznets: *Government Product and National Income* in *Income and Wealth Series*, Vol. I, pp. 193-4.
6. William H. Whyte, Jnr.: *The Organization Man*, p. 19.
7. F. J. Markovitch: *Le problème des services et le revenu national*, *Bulletin S.E.D.E.I.S.*, No. 699, 1st June, 1958, pp. 44 et seq.
8. Carl Shoup: op. cit., p. 24.
9. Ibid., p. 85.
10. Simon Kuznets: *Economic Change*, pp. 161-2.
11. Ibid., p. 196.
12. *National Income Statistics, Sources and Methods*, published by the (British) Central Statistical Office, pp. 3, 10, 31-32.
13. Alvin Hansen: *Business Cycles and National Income*, p. 96.
14. *Economic Stabilisation Board of Japan: Economic Survey of Japan 1951–1952*, p. 272.
15. J. Schumpeter: *Business Cycles*, Vol. II., p. 566.
16. W. Woytinsky: *Les conséquences sociales de la crise*, publication of the International Labour Office, pp. 139-40.
17. R. Ruggles: *An Introduction to National Income and Income Analysis*, p. 68.
18. *National Income Statistics, Sources and Methods*, p. 72.
19. Hansen: op. cit., p. 94.
20. Ibid., p. 96.
21. Ibid., p. 96.
22. Ruggles: op. cit., p. 68.
23. Rudolf Eckert: *Les théories modernes de l'expansion économique*, p. 42.
24. M. Abramovitz: *Inventories and Business Cycles*, p. 329.
25. G. Espinas: *Les Origines du capitalisme*, Vol. I, p. 165.
26. Quoted in Pitirim A. Sorokin: *Society, Culture and Personality*, p. 274.
27. A. Carr-Saunders, D. Caradog Jones and C. A. Moser: *A Survey of Social Conditions in England and Wales*, p. 176.
28. Shoup: op. cit., p. 326; Kuznets: *Shares of Upper Income Groups in Income and Savings*, p. 216; Shoup: op. cit., pp. 326-30; *Federal Reserve Board and Michigan Survey Research Centre: 1950, Survey of Consumer Finances.*
29. M. Herskovits: *Economic Life of Primitive Peoples*, p. 93.
30. Joan Robinson: *The Accumulation of Capital*, pp. 82-83.
31. L. Von Bortkiewicz: *Zur Berechtigung der Grundlagen der theoretischen Konstruktion von Marx in 3. Band des Kapitals*, in *Jahrbücher für Nat. Oekonomie und Statistik*, July 1907; Paul Sweezy: *The Theory of Capitalist Development*, pp. 114-28.

32. Schumpeter: op. cit., Vol. I, p. 102.
33. Wolfram Eberhard: *Chinas Geschichte*, p. 264.
34. Shoup: op. cit., pp. 179, 194, 216.
35. *Economist*, 6th May, 1944.
36. Shoup: op. cit., p. 214.
37. F. Barrett: *Evolution du capitalisme japonais*, Vol. III, p. 345.
38. G. Jacquemyns: *La Société belge sous l'occupation allemande 1940–1944*, Vol. I, pp. 123, 132-3, 138.
39. Bruno Gleitze: in *W.W.I. Mitteilungen*, March 1955, p. 55.
40. Leinberg, Ussing and Zeuthen: in *Income Redistribution and Social Policy*, ed. by Alan T. Peacock, p. 69.
41. Ibid., pp. 114, 156-7, 144–5, 81.
42. Rottier and J. F. Albert: in ibid., p. 114; *Rapport au congrès du P.S.B.*, 12-13 December 1959, p. 51.
43. Rottier and J. F. Albert: in *Income Redistribution and Social Policy*, pp. 135-6.
44. F. Weaver: "Taxation and Redistribution in the United Kingdom", in *Review of Economics and Statistics*, August 1950, p. 206.
45. Leinberg: etc., op. cit., p. 63.
46. Kuznets: *Shares of Upper Income Groups . . .*, passim and pp. 36-39.
47. *Studies in Income and Wealth*, published by N.B.E.R., Vol. CXXXII, p. 302, New York 1951.
48. *U.S. Statistical Abstract*, 1958.
49. *W.W.I. Mitteilungen*, October-November 1950.
50. Vance Packard: *The Status Seekers.*
51. Kuznets: *Shares of Upper Income Groups . . .*, p. 216, and *U.S. Statistical Abstract*, 1958.

CHAPTER ELEVEN

PERIODICAL CRISES

Pre-capitalist and capitalist crises

An economic crisis is an interruption in the normal reproduction process. The human and material basis of reproduction, the mass of productive labour power and of instruments of labour effectively employed is reduced. There follows a decline in both human consumption and productive consumption, that is, a reduction in the amount of labour both living and dead available for production during the next cycle. In this way a crisis reproduces itself spirally, the break in the normal production process causing a shrinkage in the starting-basis of this process.

In pre-capitalist societies crises took the form of *material destruction* of the elements of reproduction, whether simple or expanded, as a result of natural or social catastrophes: "Before and even during the eighteenth century, crops, wars, plagues, and so on were absolutely and relatively very much more important [than business fluctuations]."[1]

Wars, plagues and other epidemics, floods, draught, earthquakes, all destroy society's productive forces, the producers and the means of production. Depopulation and faminine condition one another and bring about an overall reduction in both current production and social reserves. As agriculture is the basis of all expanded reproduction, it is above all a reduction in agricultural production, in the output of agricultural labour, that lies at the root of pre-capitalist crisis. This reduction is usually caused by non-economic factors.[2] Causes inherent in the mode of production—increasing exhaustion of the soil, without any possibility of extending cultivation to fresh land, and flight of the producers from increasing exploitation—may, however in certain circumstances take the place of non-economic disasters as causes of crisis.

Crises occur in a different way in capitalist society. In this society the material destruction of the elements of production occurs not as the cause but as the result of crisis. It is not because there are fewer workers engaged in production that a crisis happens, it is because a crisis breaks out that there are fewer workers engaged in production. It is not because hunger reigns in people's homes that the output of labour declines and crisis breaks out, but the other way round.

Pre-capitalist crisis is a crisis of *under-production of use-values.* It is due to inadequate development of production, or to inadequacy of exchange and of transport facilities. A crisis like this, in a particular province or country, may coincide with normal conditions of reproduction in a neighbouring province or country. A capitalist crisis, however, is a crisis of *overproduction of exchange-values.* It is due to inadequacy not of production or physical capacity to consume, but of *monetarily effective demand.* A relative abundance of commodities finds no equivalent on the market, cannot realise its exchange value, remains unsaleable, and drags its owners down to ruin.

Unlike a pre-capitalist crisis, a crisis in the capitalist epoch thus presupposes the universalisation of commodity production. Whereas pre-capitalist crisis is by definition local and limited in space, capitalist crisis is by definition general, and involves most of the countries united in the capitalist system of production and exchange of commodities: *

"Whereas the crises of the Ancien Régime were phenomena of shortage suddenly experienced, and for thousands of years the very idea of crisis was linked with under-production and famine . . . crises since the Revolution are always, except during wars, phenomena of overabundance of an explosive nature, which also lead to deep-going social changes."[3]

General possibility of capitalist crisis

This new type of crisis, called a crisis of over-production, seems to result from the very characteristics of the commodity, and of the general development of commodity production. The intrinsic contradiction of the commodity, the contradiction between use-value and exchange-value, leads in fact to the *splitting of the commodity into the commodity itself and money.* This splitting is what creates the general possibility of capitalist crises.

So long as society essentially produces use-values, a situation of "poverty amid plenty", of masses of use-values being destroyed while masses of people are condemned to poverty, cannot occur. The direct appropriation of use-values by the consumers prevents any such paradoxical coincidence. As soon, however, as commodity production becomes general, this direct appropriation ceases to be possible. Henceforth, in order to consume a commodity, it is necessary to possess the equivalent of its exchange-value. To appropriate use-values one has to be able to *buy* them.

From this time forward crises of overproduction are theoretically possible. For them to occur, all that is needed is for the owners of

* This does not mean, of course, that all the crises of the capitalist epoch necessarily have to affect *all* countries. The universality of capitalist crisis is a matter of a predominant feature, not an absolute and mechanical rule.

commodities to find themselves unable, for whatever reason, to encounter customers who possess sufficient money-capital to realise the exchange-value of their commodities. The system of trade and credit tends to bridge over temporarily the separation between the commodity and its equivalent in money. The longer this bridge becomes, however, both in time and space, the more closely trade and credit bind all countries together in a single system, the more the contradiction inherent in the commodity and its divided condition is intensified.

If during the circulation of commodities *their price of production changes*, as a result, say, of the introduction of new methods of work, the intensifying of competition, or of a fall in the average rate of profit, a large number of commodities no longer find their equivalent on the market, and a large number of debts cannot be met. It is enough for an income not to be spent today but only tomorrow for it to be incapable of buying the same number of commodities, if their prices have risen in the meantime.[4] The contradiction between the commodity and the money equivalent which it has to find on the market thus develops into a contradiction between money as medium of circulation and money as medium of payment, a contradiction which in turn leads to the contradiction between the whole process of commodity circulation and the process of reproduction.

The law of markets

Vulgar political economy set up against this analysis of the theoretical possibilities of overproduction the idea that the value of commodities is by definition equal to the total incomes of the various classes of society which in one way or another take part in the production of these commodities. Deduced from this was the conclusion that all production of commodities is at the same time production of the incomes needed to absorb these commodities. Hence arose the well-known "law of markets" which is unjustly called "Say's law", since it was discovered not by the French economist J. B. Say but by the British economist James Mill, father of John Stuart Mill. This "law of markets" leaves no room for general overproduction; at most it allows of the existence of partial overproduction, overproduction in some sectors accompanied by underproduction in others, due to faulty distribution of the "factors of production" among the different sectors of the economy.

The mistake in the law of markets arises from the fact that it neglects the *time-factor*, that is, it assumes a static and immobile system instead of the dynamic capitalist system.* We know already that during the period between production and sale the prices of commodities can vary, in either direction, so creating either a surplus of

* This is admitted by Guitton.[5]

incomes or a surplus of commodities without counter-value in money on the market.*

On the other hand, the incomes distributed during a certain period of time will not necessarily be used to buy commodities during this same period; only the incomes of wage-earners, intended for the purchase of perishable consumer goods, will be so spent. This is not true of capitalist incomes, which *tend to be accumulated*, nor of that part of the value of commodities which represents not an income but the counter-value of used-up constant capital. The capitalists are under no obligation to invest these sums *immediately*, that is, to use them at once as purchasing power to acquire a certain category of goods. When the capitalists expect not a rise but rather a fall in their profits they may well put off such expenditure. The hoarding of incomes, non-productive saving, may thus give rise to a surplus of income which will correspond to an overproduction of certain commodities.[7] This brings about an initial reduction in employment which may entail overproduction spreading throughout all parts of the economy, which will cause a further decline in employment, and so forth.

In fact, the "law of markets" is valid only:

(*a*) if all problems of investment are eliminated,
(*b*) together with all problems of credit; and
(*c*) if the immediate sale, for cash, of all the commodities produced assumed, together with
(*d*) complete stability in the value of these goods and
(*e*) no difference of productivity between different enterprises.

These assumptions boil down to an assumption that production is not capitalist production, stimulated by thirst for profit and by competition, but petty commodity production.

Even in that case, monetary phenomena can upset the perfect equilibrium between incomes and commodity values. The law of markets is thus truly valid only for natural economy.[8] In this way we come again to the argument set forth at the beginning of this chapter, that a society which produces use-values cannot experience "overproduction"

The cyclical progress of capitalist economy

Increase in the organic composition of capital and a downward tendency of the average rate of profit, conditioned by this, are the general laws of development of the capitalist mode of production. By bringing about a periodical modification in the price of production of commodities they create the theoretical possibility of general crises of

* Marx notes that there is no automatic, immediate unity between production and realisation of value under capitalism. This unity results only from a process and is connected with a series of conditions.[6]

overproduction, if an interval between the production and sale of commodities is assumed. The capitalist mode of production thus acquires its characteristic rhythm of development—*uneven, unsteady,* proceeding by leaps which are followed by periods of stagnation and retreat.

The introduction of new machines and new production methods does not change the price of production in an imperceptible, gradual way. It changes it through sudden jerks, at more or less regular intervals, when society becomes aware *after the event* that too much social labour has been expended in producing certain commodities. This results, leaving all other factors out of account, from the rotation cycle of fixed capital, which embraces a whole succession of production cycles and rotation cycles of circulating capital. Keynes says:

"There are reasons, given firstly by the length of life of durable assets in relation to the normal growth in a given epoch, and secondly by the carrying-costs of surplus stocks, why the duration of the downward movement should have an order of magnitude which is not fortuitous, which does not fluctuate between, say, one year this time and ten years next time, but which shows some regularity of habit between, let us say, three and five years."[9]

A number of other writers express the same view, e.g., Aftalion, Pigou, Schumpeter, etc.[10] The "interval" factor operates in agricultural affairs too. There is a gap between the moment when, on the basis of favourable prices, a decision is taken to increase the cultivation of a certain product, or the raising of certain animal stock, and the moment when this decision actually results in an increase in production.[11]*

On the other hand, a certain period has to elapse before the market can react to the introduction of new production methods, that is, before it can be established whether these methods will continue to bring super-profits to their initiators or if they will lead, on the contrary, to an all-round lowering of prices of production. This period is precisely that during which the splitting of the commodity into the commodity itself and money is *stretched* to the utmost, which leads to the inevitable slump.

Capitalist production is production for profit. The variations in the average rate of profit are the decisive criteria of the actual condition of capitalist economy.†

* This leads to a phenomenon of inevitable cyclical fluctuations known as the "cobweb theorem".

† A large number of writers accept this view as self-evident, e.g. Aftalion, W. C. Mitchell, Keynes, Schumpeter, Hansen and Guitton.[12] Haberler, however, in his work on economic cycles, which is otherwise so clear, is guilty of the following enormity in order to remain faithful to the terminology of the marginalist school: "Variations in profits (or losses) are often regarded as the barometer of economic cycles. It does not, however, seem justified to put

The long-term tendency of the average rate of profit is a downward one. But this does not show itself in straight-line fashion. It becomes effective only through periodical adjustments and increases, in a *cyclical* movement the primary origin of which has just been shown. This cyclical movement can be briefly characterised in its main phases by the change in the average rate of profit:

(*a*) *Economic recovery*. Part of production capacity not having been used any more for a certain period, the stocks previously accumulated have been got rid of, and the demand for goods now exceeds the new supply. Prices and profits start to rise again. Some of the factories which have been closed now reopen, for the same reason, which encourages the capitalists to increase their investments—because when demand exceeds supply it means that *less* social labour is crystallised in the commodities present on the market than is socially necessary. This implies that the total value of these goods easily finds it equivalent on the market. The factories working at a level of productivity higher than the average will realise a substantial super-profit: the less productive enterprises still surviving after the crisis will realise the average profit. The circulation period of commodities is reduced, most enterprises undertaking production to order. The gap between the moment of purchase and the moment of payment for goods is very short.*

(*b*) *Boom and prosperity*. All available capital flows into production and trade, in order to take advantage of the increase in the average rate of profit.† Investments rapidly increase. During a whole period the establishment of new enterprises and the modernisation of existing

this factor on the same footing with the three fundamental criteria abovementioned. The term 'profit' is vague and ambiguous [!] . . . It is a combination of interest, rent, monopoly profits, etc. Profits in the doctrinal sense are part of the national income and are included under that head in 'real income'. The absence of profit (or loss) in the strict sense of the word is the very essence of the perfect equilibrium [!] of the economic system."[13] We are ready to lay odds that any business-man would explain to Mr. von Haberler that his "doctrine" is in conflict with reality . . . It is to be observed, furthermore, that Gayer, Rostow and Schwartz[14] have confirmed empirically that the cyclical movement of the textile industry coincides in the first part of the nineteenth century with cyclical fluctuations in the rate of profit.

* We leave aside for the moment many factors which enter into the cyclical movement and which we shall deal with later. It is above all necessary to grasp the *fundamental* mechanism of the rate of profit, which underlies the cyclical movement.

† It is thus not wrong to speak, as do Aftalion and Pigou, about "mistakes by too optimistic entrepreneurs". But it must be grasped that these are "mistakes" (of over-investment) from the *social* standpoint; because, from the point of view of the *private* entrepreneur, it is logical to try to increase production and sales to the maximum *at the moment when profit is highest*. Each one hopes he will survive the ensuing slump, that this will affect only the other man. And in fact, are not the most modern new plants those that stand up best to crises? "The trouble seems to be not so much that business men mistake their interests . . . as that their actual interests lie in doing the things

enterprises is the essential source of the general expansion of economic activity: "industry is industry's best customer". The newly-launched enterprises raise the average level of productivity well above the former average, but so long as supply is exceeded by demand prices continue to rise and the average rate of profit remains at a high level. The most modern enterprises realise substantial super-profits, which stimulates fresh investments and develops credit, speculation, etc.

(*c*) *Overproduction and slump.* As the newly-made investments increase more and more the total production of society, and thereby the quanity of commodities hurled on to the market, the relations between supply and demand change, at first imperceptibly, then more and more obviously. It is now seen that some of the commodities produced in the least favourabe conditions of productivity actually contain labour-time which is *wasted*, from the social standpoint. These goods have become unsaleable at their prices of production. For a certain period the factories where these unfavourable conditions exist nevertheless go on producing—*that is, wasting social labour-time*—thanks to the expansion of the credit system, and this is reflected in the accumulation of stocks, the lengthening of the circulation time of commodities, the widening of the gap between supply and demand, etc. At a certain moment it becomes impossible to bridge this gap with credit. Prices and profits collapse. Many capitalists are ruined; the enterprises which work at too low a level of productivity[17] have to close down.

(*d*) *Crisis and depression.* The fall in prices means that production is henceforth profitable only for the enterprises that work under the most favourable conditions of productivity. The firms that were realising super-profits now have to be satisfied with the average profit. In fact, a new level of average profit is thus established, corresponding to the new organic composition of capital. At the same time, however, the crisis, through the bankruptcy and closure of many factories, means the destruction of a mass of machinery, of fixed capital. By the fall in prices, capital, as exchange value, is also lowered in value, and the total value of society's capital is reduced. The smaller amount of capital which is left as a result of this destruction can more easily be utilised. It will be invested easily under conditions making possible, at the moment of economic recovery, a new rise in the average rate of profit.

which bring on the cycle, so long as they are acting as individual business men or representatives of individual business interests."[15]

Natalia Moszkowska does not understand the periodical coincidences of these "errors of judgment". Why does everybody make the same sort of mistake?[16] Perhaps because every entrepreneur is forced by competition to try for the highest profits? Is this not a vivid illustration of the contradiction between the *social* character of production and the *private* character of appropriation (the hunt for private profit) under capitalism?

The cyclical movement of capital is thus nothing but the mechanism through which the tendency of the average rate of profit to fall is realised. At the same time, it is the system's reaction to this fall, through the lowering of the value of capital during crises. Crises make possible the periodical adaptation of the amount of labour actually expended in the production of commodities to the amount of labour which is *socially necessary*, the individual value of commodities to their socially-determined value, the surplus-value contained in these commodities to the average rate of profit. Because capitalist production is not consciously planned and organised production, these adjustments take place not *a priori* but *a posteriori*. For this reason they necessitate violent shocks, the destruction of thousands of lives and enormous quantities of values and created wealth.

The internal logic of the capitalist cycle

The contradiction between use-value and exchange value, the contradiction between the commodity and its money equivalent, provide only the *general possibility* of capitalist crises of overproduction. They do not yet explain why, or in what specific conditions, these crises periodically follow one another. The variations in the rate of profit reveal the inner mechanism of the economic cycle. They explain the general significance of it as a periodical readjustment of the conditions of equilibrium of capitalist reproduction. But they do not reveal the "concrete causes" of crises. These factors can be distinguished from the causes of crises in the strict sense by contrasting, in the tradition of Aristotle's logic, and as the economist G. von Haberler does, the causes *sine qua non*—without which there would not be any crises—with the causes *per quam*—which explain the immediate reasons why crises break out. To analyse the latter requires a concrete analysis of all the elements of capitalist production.

For expanded reproduction to take place without interruption, the *conditions of equilibrium*, indicated in Chapter 10, must be constantly reproduced. The purchases of consumer-goods by all the workers and the capitalists engaged in producing capital goods must be equivalent to the purchases of capital goods by the capitalists engaged in producing consumer goods (including in both categories the purchases needed in order to expand production). The constant reproduction of these conditions of equilibrium thus requires a *proportional development* of the two sectors of production. The periodical occurrence of crises is to be explained only by a periodical break in this proportionality or, in other words, by an *uneven development* of these two sectors.

Up to now, however, we have not left the province of definition, that is, of tautology. To say that periodical crises occur because of disproportion between the two sectors of production is like saying that opium puts you to sleep because it has sleep-inducing properties. The crisis is the *expression* of the disproportion. But if we are to regard it as being *inherent* in the process of capitalist development, we have to show why this process gives rise *periodically and necessarily* to such a disproportion.

Capitalist production is production for profit. The periodical disproportion between the development of the capital goods sector and that of the consumer goods sector must be linked with periodical differences between the rates of profit in the two spheres. The causes of these periodical differences are to be observed in the different ways in which the basic contradictions of capitalism show themselves in the two sectors. We get the following picture, for the successive phases of the economic cycle:

(*a*) *The depression.* Stocks having accumulated during a whole period, their disposal takes time, since the incomes available for buying consumer goods have been severely reduced as a result of unemployment. All investment activity slows down considerably after the outbreak of crisis.[18] As, at the same time, many enterprises have had to use for other purposes the funds available to them for renewing fixed capital, the activity of the enterprises in the capital goods sector is much reduced.[19] The production of consumer goods likewise declines to a considerable extent, but not so much.[20] Even the unemployed do not stop eating, and the purchase of perishable goods cannot be put off till tomorrow; moreover, though the workers' wages have grown less, this reduction has often been less than the fall in prices since the onset of the crisis.[21] As for purchases of semi-durable consumer goods, they decrease less than purchases of durable consumer goods. The latter, the sale of which seriously declines, nevertheless sell more easily than capital goods.[22] During the period of depression we thus see the beginning, in the sphere of production, of the disproportion between the two sectors which, from the start of economic recovery, will spread to the sphere of prices and profits.

(*b*) *The turn to economic recovery.* While the economic depression lasts, industrial activity remains at an abnormally low level. When the rate of profit is very low, no reduction in the rate of interest can cause a revival of investment.[23] But the very logic of this stagnation creates the elements of a recovery. As stocks are disposed of, thanks to the lowering of production, the consumer-goods sectors whose sales have not been much reduced are able slightly to increase their activity; prices of these goods stop falling, though without at once rising. It is enough, however, for them to remain stable for a certain period, for the enterprises in these sectors to start thinking about re-equipment.[24]

Everything encourages this. The prices of raw materials and means of equipment are unusually low; re-equipment at this moment is therefore a profitable undertaking. Wages continue to remain low, under the pressure of unemployment, even after prices have been stabilised. These low wages likewise encourage expansion of production, since they give a promise of higher profits.[25]

The stoppage or reduction in investment activity during an entire period has made it possible to accumulate the funds needed for depreciating fixed capital. These funds, at first hoarded, start to make their way back to the banks, there to bring in interest which is still moderate but not, in a period of depression, negligible.[26]* The absence of any investment activity markedly reduces the demand for money capital, so that the average rate of interest falls in a period of depression: [29] another reason for the capitalists in the consumer goods sector to undertake investments on credit towards the end of this period. Finally, the still low rate of profit encourages them to seek out and to introduce new methods of production which have accumulated since the end of the boom without any possibility of being applied. (See Keynes and Hansen, as well as Aftalion, Pigou, Schumpeter, and a large number of others writers.)[30]

The resulting reduction in costs of production makes it possible to increase the rate of profit with the existing market prices. In this way, investment activity starts again in the consumer goods sector, which brings about economic recovery.†

(c) *Economic recovery.* The orders for equipment for the consumer goods sector which arise from the inner logic of the depression itself in their turn make possible the recovery of production in several sectors making capital goods. This recovery reduces unemployment, increases available purchasing power, and develops sales of consumer goods, which in its turn stimulates a new wave of investment. The *multiplier principle* comes into play.[32]

This explains that an initial investment increases the total final in-

* Woytinsky[27] notes that the total amount deposited in savings banks increased by 1932, as compared with the level at 31st December, 1929, to: 129 in the U.K., 137 in Germany, 140 in Holland, 140 in the U.S.A., 142 in Italy, 143 in Japan, 148 in Switzerland, 166 in Sweden, 193 in France, 192 in Belgium, etc. To these sums, and to those in bank deposits, must be added the considerable sums which were *hoarded.*[28]

† Supporters of the theory of pure underconsumption, like Natalia Moszkowska and Léon Sartre,[31] regard this way of describing the progress of economic recovery as question-begging. In assuming that the majority of enterprises renew their fixed capital at the same time, instead of supposing that this renewal is spread equally over each year, they say, we are already *presupposing* the existence of the cycle, that is, we are starting from what we have subsequently to prove. To this objection we answer: (*a*) it is enough to start from a *first cycle*—determined, e.g. by the initial introduction on a large scale of steam-driven machinery into the English textile industry—to see that this objection is historically invalid; and (*b*) we do not see in this renewal of fixed capital the "cause" of the cycle but only a convenient point of departure for our exposition.

come by a sum which exceeds the value of this investment; it explains likewise that one independent investment can give rise to one or more waves of investment stimulated in this way.[33] Statisticians have tried to work out the value of the multiplier in the industrially advanced countries for 1919–1939 and have evaluated it at between 2 and 3 (calculations by Kalecki and Kuznets).[34] These statistics are, however, to be handled cautiously. In any case, they do not apply to an entire historical epoch.[35]

Let us now see what happens with the rate of profit. The production of capital goods is much less elastic than that of consumer goods. To supply cotton mills with the spindles they require it is necessary to delve into the stock of steel and coal, increase the production of these raw materials when the stocks have been exhausted, put to full use the machines that build machines, or else build these first of all, when there are no more reserves of productive capacity. As soon as recovery is well under way an interval thus appears between the order for additional constant capital and its delivery. During this interval *competition* rages between the enterprises, all striving to acquire the equipment and raw materials already on the market. The prices of these goods will thus rise more than the prices of consumer goods, and this difference produces an equivalent difference between the rate of profit in the two sectors.[36] The disproportion between the two sectors is thus shifted from the sphere of production to that of prices and profit.

Moreover, the rate of profit recovers all round. Whereas prices start to rise as soon as excess stocks are dispersed, wages do not rise at all, or rise very little, at the beginning of recovery, owing to the pressure exercised by unemployment on the labour market. At the same time, the factories which were not working at full pressure during the depression start to re-engage workers without at first changing their plant. The organic composition of their capital thus declines momentarily, thereby raising the rate of profit. The reduction in the circulation time of commodities increases the number of production cycles in a year and works in the same direction.

The expansion of production being slow at first, the demand for capital remains at a level lower than the supply, which implies that the rate of interest remains very low. The coincidence of a low rate of interest with a rising rate of profit determines a growing rate of entrepreneur's profit, which likewise explains a general tendency on the part of entrepreneurs to renew their fixed capital and invest an increasing proportion of their profits at this moment of the cycle: *

* Keynes and other writers speak of the rise in the "value of capital in relation to its cost". This means that the income anticipated from the purchase of capital goods exceeds the cost of purchasing (or replacing) these capital goods. The more this difference exceeds the interest, the more favourable are conditions for investment.[37] The whole of this reasoning leads to the same conclusions that we have just been setting forth.

"Investment in new plant could not, of its nature, be undertaken in small increments. Assuming a constant rate of increase in output, an individual firm could not alter its fixed plant at a parallel constant rate, and if our data are at all reliable it would appear that [in the first half of the nineteenth century in Britain] increases in capacity capable of dealing with the secularly increasing volume of output tended to occur largely in a few years of each decade."[38]

(*d*) *Boom, prosperity.* The disequilibrium between prices and rates of profit in the two sectors, which appears from the start of economic recovery, is now transformed into disproportion between the rate of increase of their production, a disproportion opposite to that which occurred during the depression. At first, the available capital will flow for preference towards the capital goods sector, the rate of profit in this sector being the higher. Furthermore, the *accelerator principle* starts to operate.[39] We know that a very limited proportion of fixed capital is used up and renewed during each production cycle. This proportion is determined by the relative longevity of fixed capital.

Let us suppose that its average age is ten years. That means that the value of the total production of a one-year cycle contains only 10 per cent of the value of all the fixed capital available to society. If we assume that the value of the annual product is 1,500 (million), of which 500 represents the value of fixed capital used up, a stock of fixed capital to the value of 5,000 is implied. If all the fixed capital in existence is already fully employed in ensuring an annual production of 1,500, an increase of this production from 1,500 to 1,800 (or an increase in overall demand in the same proportion) requires the installation of fresh fixed capital to the value not of 100 but of 1,000, 10 per cent of which, or 100, will be embodied in the value of the extra production of 300. The increasing of production by 20 per cent thus requires that the current production of fixed capital be *tripled*. The manufacture of new industrial plant, the capital goods sector, then experiences a burst of frenzied activity. Production in this sector increases more markedly than in the consumer goods sector.[40]

This feverish development of the capital goods sector again sets going the multiplier principle and makes it possible to absorb the bulk of the unemployed labour. It again increases the purchasing power available for consumer goods, and even causes a temporary shortage of these goods, which once more stimulates investment and the purchase of fixed capital in this sector. Full employment comes about. Wages start to rise, though not so fast as prices, and for this reason the rate of surplus value continues to rise, and in fact real wages decline or stagnate at the beginning of the boom.[41]

Given that in both sectors supply is less than demand, the firms with the highest level of productivity realise lush superprofits. In general, the high level of the rate of profit favours vigorous activity in the fields of investment, speculation and credit. The capital hoarded during the depression is progressively absorbed into economic activity, and consequently the rate of interest starts to recover. But the banks give circulation credit all the more readily because many firms are working on orders, that is, with guaranteed outlets. The discount rate thus remains comparatively low.

The more enterprises producing capital goods finish re-equipping themselves and begin to fulfil the orders that have piled up, the more equipment (and consequently production) increases in the consumer goods sector. At a certain profit it becomes sufficient to meet the increased demand caused by full employment. At this moment, one might suppose that these enterprises would start progressively reducing their orders for capital goods. But the orders for these goods placed earlier have only just been fulfilled. The *delay* between the moment when an order is placed and the moment when it is fulfilled thus plays an important role in the preparation of the crisis (see Aftalion, Tinbergen, Frisch on the cycle of shipbuilding, Kalecki, Hansen, etc.).

The cycle thus reaches here its first critical point. The industries producing consumer goods ought now to halt all expansion of production, and even begin to reduce it. Such a "rational" attitude on their part is impossible, however, and not only because of the anarchy of production, which means that each enterprise waits for its competitor to give ground, and hopes that it will itself attain a maximum of profit with a maximum of sales and production. This rationality is also ruled out by the dictation of production for profit. These enterprises have just re-equipped themselves. A restriction of production would increase depreciation charges on current production. It would reduce the rate of profit. Wages have been rising since full employment has been attained. There is therefore a risk that the rate of surplus-value and the rate of profit will fall, a risk that the capitalists try to offset by rationalisation, more intensive use of the productive apparatus, and intensification of effort on the part of the producers, all of which implies an increase in production.[42] The gradual recovery of the rate of interest likewise reduces the rate of entrepreneur's profit. The increase in the amount of profit needed to offset the lowering of this rate again implies increased production.[43]

Finally, it must not be forgotten that it is very difficult for the capitalists of the consumer goods sector to know at what moment exactly the point of equilibrium between the supply of their products and the demand for them has been reached.

"When this point comes, few men are aware of the fact, because the volume of commodities offered for sale does not indicate either the large volume in the making or the invisible supply in the hands of speculators . . . On account of the time it takes to produce commodities and get them into the shops, the markets do not feel the full effects of maximum productivity until months after that stage has been reached. Production, therefore, continues at a high rate; and the volume of commodities coming upon the market, as a result of loans previously made, continues to increase . . . As there is a limit, however, to the expansion of bank credit, the time comes when there is a decrease in the amount of money advanced by banks to producers, that reaches consumers' hands."[44]

When the total amount of purchasing power available for consumer goods has already ceased to increase, a considerable part of current production still goes on being sold: the shopkeepers and the firms in the intermediate stages of production have to replenish their stocks, exhausted at the end of the depression and throughout the recovery and the boom.* The increase in their sales encourages industrialists to undertake a fresh increase in production, which may thus coincide with a stagnation or even a slight shrinkage of ultimate consumption, at any rate during an initial period.

(*e*) *The slump, the turn towards depression.* The disequilibrium between the capital goods sector and the consumer goods sector, which first shows itself in the sphere of prices and the rate of profit, thus spreads more and more into the sphere of production and then into that of demand, sales and markets. Full employment having been attained, the total amount of purchasing power for consumer goods does not increase any further, or at best, very little.† On the other hand, the production of these same goods continues to increase throughout an entire period, for the reasons indicated above. "There is a suggestion here that the accumulated financial difficulties are accompanied (perhaps in part produced) by a slower growth of distribution [or, more correctly, sales. E.M.] to consumers, at the same time that

* Often, at the start of a boom, and before the accelerator principle has begun to operate thoroughly, enterprises and shops begin to replenish their stocks, and when this movement remains unaccompanied by a corresponding increase in sales to the public, they may be led to dispose quickly of these stocks and in the meantime restrict their own purchases. This explains the occurrence of minor recessions in the middle of the economic cycle, first elucidated by the economist Kitchin,[45] and also known as *inventory* recessions (Metzler and Abramovitz).[46]

† This is to be understood in real and not monetary terms. Currency inflation may of course increase nominal wages at the end of a boom, but this rise is largely skimmed off by the rise in the cost of living. It is true that at this moment any fresh increase in production leads to an increase in real wages (overtime, etc.) which reduces the rate of profit. At the same time, at the top of the boom, the rate of surplus value tends to decline, average output per wage-earner tending to fall, particularly as a result of the employment of inexperienced workers and also of the following phenomena: "It cannot be denied that, in many establishments, the output of labour has declined since full employment has been exceeded, owing to the fluidity of the labour-force, absenteeism, and lack of conscientiousness."[47]

physical output is growing faster."[48] Stocks thus begin to grow, first at the final stage (retail trade), then at the intermediate stages, finally in the industrial enterprises themselves.

As this increase in stocks develops, the industrialists and traders to whom it is happening resist any immediate lowering of prices which would mean for them a reduction in the value of their stock, that is, a serious loss. They therefore increasingly apply to the banks, to get circulation credit. The banks themselves, which have already extended substantial credit to the enterprises in this sector, put off as long as possible any refusal of credit, which would risk bringing about the bankruptcy of these enterprises and so the loss of the capital already lent. A regular credit inflation thus occurs, a dangerous tension of the whole system, linked with many phenomena of speculation and pure and simple swindling, which flourish in the boom atmosphere. This tension on the money market and the finance market comes just before the reversal of the conjuncture, and is marked by a sharp rise in the rate of interest.[49]

The entrepreneurs are now obliged to put off, further and further, the carrying-out of their current investment projects. They have to use as circulating capital a part of the money capital intended for these investments. Their orders for capital goods thus fall off more and more, while production stagnates or starts to decline in the consumer goods sector. Thus, the production of consumer goods reaches its climax, stagnates, or even starts to fall off, before the same phenomenon occurs in the capital goods sector.[50]

We have now reached the second critical point in the cycle. The enterprises in the capital goods sector re-equipped themselves at the beginning of the cycle, so as to be able to meet orders for *increased* fixed capital coming from the consumer goods sector. It is enough for this increase to come to a halt for phenomena of over-production to start appearing in the capital goods sector, for the industries of this sector to begin working below their new maximum production capacity. Furthermore, a *slowing-down in the rate of increase* in investments leads to the same result:

"The rhythm of production in the industries producing equipment is governed by the *expansion* of production in the industries making consumer goods. If the latter stop expanding, the former lose part of their markets and are forced to cut down their activity, even supposing they can obtain the funds they need in order to keep their production up to the former level."[51]

The enterprises in this sector, too, have recently made substantial investments; they thus have substantial amounts of capital to depreciate. They work much more with borrowed capital than do the enterprises in the other sector, since it is into them that available money capital has mainly flowed, attracted by a higher rate of profit.

The rise in the rate of interest resulting from the increasing shortage which becomes apparent on the capital market* will thus hit them harder than the enterprises in the consumer goods sector. This will be felt all the more severely because about the same time the rate of profit will likewise tend to decline, owing to the rise in overheads, the rise in wages (overtime, etc.), the increase in wastage, etc.[52]

In view of the emptying of their order-books, these enterprises find themselves compelled, in turn, to restrict production, dismiss some of their employees, and adopt other economy measures. But all this means that the volume of purchasing power distributed by this sector tends to decline. There results from this, so far as consumer goods are concerned, a real decline in demand, a fresh increase in stocks, a further shrinkage in production, a new fall in profits.

At a certain point in this cumulative process of shrinkage, disequilibrium necessarily extends to the last phase, that of credit. Demand for circulation credit is accumulating on every side. The supply of money capital, however, declines, because the difference between the rate of profit and the rate of interest disappears. In the face of the increase in stocks and the stagnation in sales, the enterprises are, moreover, continually short of ready money, they draw out their bank deposits, and they sell off their property and securities, etc.[53]

Finally, all the reserves accumulated during the previous period of stagnation have been absorbed in the feverish activity of the boom. It is thus inevitable that during such a process the disequilibrium between supply of and demand for money capital should to a certain extent cause a stoppage in the expansion of the credit system. The banks start to refuse new requests for circulation credit, except at more and more exorbitant rates. Rates of interest and discount rates both increase rapidly.† Bankruptcies occur in increasing numbers, debtors dragging down creditors. Soon an avalanche sets in. Hundreds of enterprises shut their doors and dismiss their workers. In order to find the ready money which has suddenly become the only thing capable of keeping the worst disasters at bay, enterprises are forced to sell off their stocks at any price. Prices collapse, profits vanish, a new wave of bankruptcy spreads. Prices, profits, production, incomes, employment, fall to an abnormally low level.‡

* This shortage need not necessarily result from an actual shortage of capital. Often, the owners of this capital refuse to lend it at this moment, because the fall in the rate of profit implies a growing risk of instability on the part of the borrowers.

† It must not be forgotten that the rise in the rate of interest in relation to credits for production has only a minor effect nowadays in the advanced capitalist countries, where self-financing by enterprises plays a dominant role.[54] This is not true, however, of circulation credit.

‡ Kaldor[55] gives four reasons for the cessation of the boom: an increasing rate of interest, which halts investment; a fall in the rate of profit caused by

The extension of the basis of capitalist production

Our analysis of the cyclical progress of capitalist economy is based on the typical behaviour of capitalist enterprises, who at any moment of the cycle are seeking the maximum profit, under the whip of competition, without troubling themselves about the system or the market as a whole. But how does it happen that the periodical occurrence of crises does not induce enterprises to be more prudent, that is, to restrict their investments when recovery comes, so as to avoid overproduction at the end of the boom? How, in other words, does it come about that booms are every time as feverish and exaggerated as before, leading every time to an especially disagreeable collapse?

This question is all the more justified because the sectors especially subject to fluctuations in demand during the cycle do learn to adapt themselves to these fluctuations:

"Producers becoming familiar with the recurrent shift of demand in the course of the cyclical phases, learn to provide . . . for the peak demand of prosperity. Industries more subject than others to such fluctuations, . . . which we shall call cyclical industries, are particularly likely to do this. They will set up productive capacity which is intended to be fully used only in times of prosperity."[56]

It is not as though such foresight on the part of the capitalists could *prevent* the cyclical development of the economy. We have seen that the mere fact of the periodical renewal of fixed capital, determined by its expectation of life, is enough to account for this cyclical pattern. But the question that arises is this: why do we not simply see the renewal of fixed capital at the start of each recovery phase, accompanied by investment which broadly corresponds to the increase in population during the cycle? Why do we see, instead, a substantial expansion in production capacity proceeding by leaps, which, through the working of the accelerator principle, causes booms in the strict sense of the word?

Historically, there is only one reply to this question. The cyclical development of capitalist economy becomes particularly feverish through the *extension of the basis* of this economy at the beginning of each recovery, and this happens through the sudden appearance of *new markets* for important sectors of industry, which thus stimulates the activity of the capital goods industry.

These new markets may result either from the geographical extension of capitalist production[57] (penetration into a non-capitalist milieu),

this rise in the rate of interest; the inadequacy of the expansion of demand for consumer goods: the appearance of excess capacity, owing to the shortage of labour. We have commented on the operation of three of these four factors, even if not in the same order as Kaldor's. The fourth is quite exceptional. The influence of full employment is felt above all on the rate of profit.

from the appearance of new sectors of production (technological progress) or from sudden leaps in relations between competitors (disappearance of a powerful competitor as a result of war, of technological backwardness, etc.). To this must be added, in the twentieth century, the role of replacement markets played essentially by the armaments orders of the State*

Each successive boom in the history of capitalism can be explained in this way by such an extension of the basis of production:

(*a*) 1816–25 cycle. British industry conquers the markets of Latin America; building of gas-works and canals in Britain; beginning of Belgium's industrialisation.
(*b*) 1825–36 cycle. Rise in British exports to Latin America and U.S.A.; industrial expansion in Belgium, France, and the Rhineland; beginning of railway construction.
(*c*) 1836–47 cycle. Rise in British exports to Asia, especially to India and China (after the Opium War). Railway construction at a feverish pace throughout Western Europe.
(*d*) 1847–57 cycle. Expansion of the American market after the discovery of gold deposits in California. Railway building in the U.S.A. and throughout Europe. Establishment of new industries in the U.S.A., in Germany and in France. First expansion of joint stock companies.
(*e*) 1857–66 cycle. Expansion of the market in India and Egypt, especially through the development of cotton plantations, to replace the American cotton missing because of the American Civil War.
(*f*) 1866–73 cycle. Development of the iron and steel industry in Germany, Austria-Hungary, the U.S.A., especially stimulated by the wars of 1866 and 1870–71. Great railway building boom in the U.S.A.
(*g*) 1873–82 cycle. Feverish railway building in the U.S.A. and in Central Europe. Increase in naval construction. Expansion of markets in South America, Canada and Australia, due to their mechanised agricultural production.
(*h*) 1882–91 cycle. Last big expansion in railway building in the U.S.A., in Russia and in Latin America (especially in Argentina). Export of British and French capital. Development of the African market.
(*i*) 1891–1900 cycle. Building of tramways throughout the world; building of railways in Russia, Africa, Asia and Latin America; export of British, French and German capital. Development of the oil and electrical power industries.
(*j*) 1900–07 cycle. Expansion of the iron and steel industries (arms

* See Chapter 14.

race), of naval construction, of tramways, of electric power stations and telephone networks. Development of the Turkish, North African and Middle-Eastern markets. First development of heavy industry in Italy. Last wave of railway building in Africa and Asia.*

(*k*) 1907–13 cycle. Rise in iron and steel production, armaments and naval construction. End of the tramway-building boom. Development of the Middle-East market.

(*l*) 1913–21 cycle. In the U.S.A. and Japan, feverish industrial construction, boom in iron and steel, naval construction, armaments industries, boom in the chemical industry in these countries, as also in Germany and Britain; first expansion of the motor-car industry.

(*m*) 1921–29 cycle. World-wide expansion of the motor-car, rubber, oil, machine-tool, electrical-apparatus and chemical industries. Boom in American exports of capital, especially to Germany.

(*n*) 1929–37 cycle. Rise in the armaments industry, especially in Germany and Japan. Development of the Chinese and Latin-American markets. First expansion of the aircraft industry.

(*o*) 1937–49 cycle. Expansion of the armaments industry in the U.S.A., Canada, Australia, Germany (until 1944) and Britain. New division of world markets, especially in Western and Eastern Europe, Africa, Latin America and the Far East. Expansion of the aircraft, electronics and chemical industries. Beginnings of the atomic power industry. Industrialisation of the underdeveloped countries.

(*p*) 1949–53 cycle. Expansion of the armaments and aircraft industries. Development of the Atomic power industry. Renewed expansion of Germany heavy industry, focused on reconstruction needs. Development of the African market. Continued industrialisation of the underdeveloped countries.

(*q*) 1953–58 cycle. Expansion of the electronics, chemical (plastics) and engineering (industrial equipment of all kinds) industries. Capital construction for the armaments race and the industrialisation of the underdeveloped countries. Boom in building development, expansion of consumer-durable sectors in Europe; first large-scale development of automation.

* In Europe, apart from Russia, railway building reached its climax in the decade 1870–80, when there was an average annual increase in railway lines of 5,000 kilometres. In the U.S.A. this climax was reached in the decade 1880–90, with an average annual increase of 11,800 kilometres. From the decade 1890–1900 onward the annual construction in the rest of the world exceeded the total of railway construction in Europe and the U.S.A., reaching its climax between 1900 and 1908, with an annual average of 12,031 kilometres.[58]

Under-consumption theories

In the history of economic thought, two great schools of explanation of the capitalist economic cycle are to be distinguished: the underconsumption school and the disproportionality school. Each puts its finger on a fundamental contradiction of the capitalist mode of production, but goes astray in isolating this contradiction from the other features of the system.

In order to explain the periodical crises, the supporters of underconsumption theories start from the contradiction between the tendency to unlimited development of production and the tendency to limitation in consumption by the broad masses, a contradiction which is indeed characteristic of the capitalist mode of production. The periodical crises thus *appear as crises of the realisation of surplus-value*. The inadequacy of the purchasing power of the masses prevents them from buying all the goods manufactured during a particular period. The surplus value has been produced all right, but it remains crystallised in unsaleable commodities.

Among the representatives of this school may be listed pre-Marxist socialists such as Owen, Sismondi and Rodbertus, the Russian Populists, and a series of Marx's own disciples: Kautsky, Rosa Luxemburg, Lucien Laurat, Fritz Sternberg, Otto Bauer (in his last work), Natalia Moszkowska, Paul M. Sweezy, etc. Among non-Marxist representatives of this school may be mentioned Major Douglas, Professor Lederer, Foster and Catchings, Hobson, and Keynes, along with some of the latter's followers, such as Professor Hamberg.

The crudest defenders of this idea find the origin of crises in the fact that the workers receive as wages the equivalent of only *part* of the new value they produce. They forget that the other part of this value corresponds to the purchasing power of the bourgeois class (capitalist families and firms). Even a writer with such claims to scholarship as Fred Oelssner writes in his work *Die Wirtschaftskrisen*: [59]

"It follows from this contradiction between the worker's role as producer of surplus value and his role as consumer or buyer on the market that the development of the market can never [!] correspond to the extension of production. Demand always [!] develops more slowly than supply under capitalist conditions [of production]."

An idea like this does not explain why crises have to occur—it would rather serve to explain the *permanence* of overproduction, the impossibility of capitalism.

The workers are not at all expected to buy all the commodities produced. On the contrary, the capitalist mode of production implies that a part of these commodities, namely, capital goods, is *never* bought by the workers, but always by the capitalists. In order to uphold the theory of underconsumption one would have to show that under the capitalist mode of production the ratio between wages and the part of surplus value not transformed into constant capital, on the one hand, and the national income, on the other, is *necessarily and periodically less* than the ratio between the value of consumer goods and the value of production as a whole. This has never been shown in a convincing way.

Rosa Luxemburg,[60] though she starts from similar considerations, raises the discussion to a level more worthy of interest by inquiring into the origins of accumulation, of expanded reproduction. Expanded reproduction means, in fact, that the capitalists withdraw from commodity circulation, at the end of a rotation cycle of capital, more value than they have introduced into production. This surplus is nothing else but realised surplus value!

Now, Rosa Luxemburg goes on, both the workers' wages (variable capital) and the replacement value of the machinery and raw material used up in production (constant capital) were *advanced* by the capitalists. As for the capitalists' unproductive consumption (the unaccumulated part of surplus value) this is also paid for by the capitalists themselves. If, then, the whole of production were bought by the workers and the capitalists, that would simply mean that the capitalists recovered funds they had themselves put into circulation, and bought their own surpluses from each other.

This would make sense if one were to look on each capitalist enterprise as an isolated unit. But for the capitalist order taken as a whole the conclusion seems absurd. This capitalist order presents a picture of increase in wealth, in the value accumulated by the capitalist class, an increase which cannot be the result of exchange between capitalists. Rosa Luxemburg concludes, therefore, that the realisation of surplus value is possible only to the extent that non-capitalist markets are open to the capitalist mode of production. She sees these markets above all in the purchasing power of the non-capitalist classes (peasants) within the capitalist countries and in the external trade of the latter with non-capitalist countries.*

It is certain that, historically, the capitalist régime was born and developed within a non-capitalist setting. It is no less certain that the extension of its basis received a particularly dynamic stimulus from the

* Bukharin replied to this argument that in trade with non-capitalist classes or countries there is also exchange of commodities, and therefore no new outlets. He did not grasp that this trade can take the form not of an exchange of commodities but of an exchange of *non-capitalist incomes* (e.g. semi-feudal ground rent) arising from non-capitalist modes of production, against capitalist commodities. There are therefore, indeed, new outlets and transfers of value in favour of the bourgeoisie. Sternberg adds that if one starts from the hypothesis that only a residue of consumer goods is unsaleable in a "pure" capitalist society, these consumer goods could be exchanged against capital goods (raw materials) imported from non-capitalist countries, so favouring both the realisation of surplus value and the accumulation of capital.[61]

conquest of fresh space. But from that it does *not* follow that if a non-capitalist setting is absent then surplus value cannot be realised.

Rosa Luxemburg's mistake lies in treating the world capitalist class as a whole, i.e. in *leaving out competition.* It is true that Marx, in his calculations of the average rate of profit in Volume III of *Capital,* also starts from the capitalist class as a whole, and Rosa quotes this reference triumphantly, to confirm her view.[62] But she seems to be unaware that in his overall plan for *Capital* Marx stressed that *crises fall outside the sphere of "capital taken as a whole"; they result precisely from the phenomena which he calls those of "different capitals", i.e. competition.* It is competition that determines the whole dynamic, all the laws of development, of capitalism.

Now, competition implies exchange of commodities with other capitalists. This shift of value within the capitalist class may very well be at the basis of the "realisation of surplus value". Within the setting of these exchanges between capitalists, the "totality" of the capitalist class may see its total profits increase, realised *successively* by the circulation of one and the same sum of money.*

It is the unevenness of the rate of development[63] *as between different countries, different sectors and different enterprises that is the driving force of the expansion of capitalist markets,* without non-capitalist classes necessarily having to be brought in. This is what explains how expanded reproduction can go on even without any non-capitalist setting, how under these conditions the realisation of surplus value takes place through a market accentuation of the *concentration of capital.* In practice, exchanges with non-capitalist surroundings are only one aspect of the uneven development of capitalism.

Critique of models of "underconsumption"

Several writers have tried to give a more subtle form, supported by figures, to the theory of "underconsumption", that is, of the impossibility of realising surplus value as the ultimate cause of periodical crises. Otto Bauer (in his last work), Léon Sartre, Paul M. Sweezy and Fritz Sternberg provide the most interesting examples. Nevertheless, these various "models", arithmetical or algebraic, of underconsumption all suffer from a common weakness. They always *beg the question* by regarding as already shown, in their exposition of the problem, the solution which they wish to offer.†

* See Marx's very interesting observation in the *Grundrisse*: "Surplus value created at one point demands the creation of surplus value at another point, so that this may be exchanged for that."

† The same observation applies, incidentally, to most of the "models" of econometry used to demonstrate one theory or another of the cycle. See the more detailed comment given in Chapter 18, section on "The econometricians."

Thus, Paul M. Sweezy[64] sets up his model by starting from the assumption that a certain increase in the value of the production of capital goods is necessarily accompanied by a *proportionately increased* production capacity of consumer goods. In other words: the ratio $\frac{\text{value I}}{\text{value II}}$ remains stable, while the ratio

$$\frac{\text{surplus value accumulated in c}}{\text{wages + surplus value not accumulated in c}}$$

increases more and more, and along with it, the ratio

$$\frac{\text{purchasing power of I}}{\text{purchasing power of II}}$$

If one starts from this assumption, the "necessity" of the overproduction of consumer goods is, of course, proved, since it is already contained in the assumption.

Otto Bauer[65] follows a similar line of reasoning. He deduces the inevitability of the crisis from the fact that constant capital accumulates more rapidly than the need of constant capital for the production of the extra consumer goods bought by the extra workers taken on in the course of expanded reproduction. This follows logically from the employment of an increasing rate of surplus value. But Otto Bauer's model presumes that society absorbs new constant capital only *in the same proportion* as it increases its ultimate consumption. It thus presupposes a *stable proportion* between the value of production in the two sectors—which is just what has to be proved.

It should be observed that Otto Bauer is the first Marxist writer to introduce the idea of *stock of existing fixed capital* (total production capacity) and *rate of technical progress* into his model. These two ideas have been extensively used by the neo-Keynesian and econometric school, notably by Harrod, Domar, Pilvin and Hamberg.*

Léon Sartre[67] starts from the assumption that the ratio between the constant capital in the two main sectors of industrial production remains the same. He deduces this asumption from a basic hypothesis about the identity of the rate of surplus value and the rate of accumulation in the two sectors. But he supposes at the same time that the demand for capital goods increases more quickly than the demand for consumer goods. If $\frac{\text{value I}}{\text{value II}}$ remains stable while $\frac{\text{demand I}}{\text{demand II}}$ increases,

* Hamberg[66] shows that there is a stable proportion between the increase in the stock of existing fixed capital and the increase in production which results from the full employment of this stock. But he is careful not to claim that a stable proportion exists between the increase in the *total* stock of the fixed capital and the production capacity of *consumer goods* alone. He thus avoids the mistake common to all the supporters of the underconsumption theory.

crisis is obviously inevitable, and takes the form of a crisis of over-production of consumer goods.

Here we have not only question-begging but also an error of reasoning. Sartre, like Sternberg, deduces from capitalist competition the maintenance of a constant proportion between the productive forces engaged in the two sectors. This is a mechanistic, "idyllic" idea of competition. The latter does not at all lead to equalisation of the organic composition of capital in all sectors. On the contrary, it leads to an *overall increase in the organic composition of capital,* and thereby to a relative redistribution of the productive forces, in favour of the capital goods sector. This is one of the fundamental hypotheses of Marxism, which is moreover confirmed by statistical data.* But if one incorporates this assumption in a "model" of the cycle, all notion of a constant proportion between the value of production in the two sectors collapses, and therewith all "mathematical demonstration" of the inevitable overproduction of consumer goods through under-consumption.

Sternberg's theoretical model is the most interesting one. He proceeds from a twofold basis—on the one hand, the mathematical formulae illustrating expanded reproduction in Volume II of *Capital,* and on the other, the very nature of competition.

When she studied the formulae of expanded reproduction used by Marx in Volume II of *Capital,* Rosa Luxemburg had already insisted on the fact that equilibrium of exchange between the two sectors was made possible only by the fact that the rate of accumulation, which was 50 per cent of the surplus value in Sector I, fell during the same cycle to 20 per cent of the surplus value in Sector II. Sternberg[69] takes up this critique and carries it further. He declares that this inequality between the two rates of accumulation is indispensable for the achievement of equilibrium between the two sectors, with increasing organic composition of capital in both sectors.†

* In the U.S.A., according to Shaw,[68] the production of capital goods increased from 296 million dollars in 1869 to 6,033 million in 1919; the production of consumer goods increased in the same period from 2,428 million dollars to 28,445 dollars. Sector I thus increased its production more than 20-fold, Sector II only 12-fold (and the production of this sector is over-valued, since it contains in the category of "durable consumer goods", products which are actually capital goods). For the period between 1919 and our time we have no exact calculations of the same kind. But the figures of the *Statistical Abstract* relating to different categories of commodity are revealing. Between 1919 and 1952 the production of durable goods (mostly belonging to Sector I) increased 5-fold (growing from index 72 to index 340) whereas that of non-durables only trebled (growing from index 62 to index 190).

† An interesting variant: Kalecki[70] emphasises that it is the allocation of expenditure by the capitalists, that is, the rate of accumulation of surplus value, that underlies the cycle. According to him, this rate is a function of the gap between the *rate of profit expected* and the *present* rate of profit, a gap which shrinks as production capacity rises at the end of the cycle.

Sternberg goes on to say that there is no reason to suppose that the rate of accumulation of capital would be different in the two sectors; this rate would be equalised through capitalist competition. In his formula the disequilibrium results, however, not from an equal rate of accumulation in the two sectors but from the *opposition* between an equal rate of accumulation and a different organic composition of capital in I and II.

Now, both theory and empirically-established data confirm to us that this organic composition of capital must actually be different in these two sectors. It is enough, under these conditions, to follow the working of competition to understand that the rate of accumulation *must* also be lower in Sector II. The capitalists of sector I in fact annex part of the surplus value produced by the workers of sector II, because they exploit the fact that they are technologically ahead of light industry. This conclusion, which fits the facts, leaves Sternberg's argument without a leg to stand on.

Theories of disproportionality

The other school of economics sees the fundamental cause of crisis in the *anarchy of production*, which periodically upsets the conditions of equilibrium between the two main sectors, that of consumer goods and that of capital goods, conditions which we have explained in Chapter 10. In this category can be placed those disciples of Marx such as the Russian "Legal Marxists" Tugan-Baranovsky and Bulgakov, the Austrians Hilferding and Otto Bauer (in his youthful writings), the Pole Henryk Grossman, the Soviet theoretician Bukharin, etc. Among the non-Marxist economists of this school special mention must be made of Aftalion, Schumpeter and Spiethoff.

All these theoreticians see the origin of crises in the fact that each entrepreneur endeavours to increase his own profits to the utmost, without taking into account, in his investments, the tendencies of the market as a whole. It follows logically from this idea that if the capitalists were capable of investing "rationally", i.e. so as to maintain proportions of equilibrium between the two main sectors of production, crises could be avoided. Some theoreticians have even claimed that the production of capital goods could be separated completely from the ultimate consumption of consumer goods and that it would be quite possible to imagine a system in which the whole of economic activity consisted exclusively in the making of machines to make machines, without the consumption of consumer goods coming into the system, so to speak.

The American economist Myron W. Watkins writes: "It may be asked, 'Is there no economic limit to the deferment of consumption?' The answer is that there is none, save . . . the continuance of such consumption as is essential to the proper sustenance of life. In economic theory, the indefinite [!] extension of the roundabout process [of production] is a logical aim [!] A society is conceivable in which men may for several generations (which means indefinitely) be content [!] to get along with salt, bread, milk and a loin cloth the while they are industriously and profitably [!] engaged in the production of machines and equipment of every sort."[71]

What we have here is obviously an absurd idea. No maker of textile machinery is going to double his production capacity, if analysis of the market shows him that no expansion of sales of textile products is expected, since stocks are already fully adequate: "The ultimate aim of accumulation of capital is of course to increase the production of consumer goods."[72] The production of capital goods may separate itself for a whole period from this initial basis and undergo a big expansion without *for the moment* worrying about the increase in ultimate consumption. But it is precisely this *momentary* separation that has to be paid for in the form of a crisis.

It is, moreover, false to suppose that "rational organisation" of investment in a capitalist society, i.e. the "regulation" of competition, could fully do away with economic fluctuations. Experience, notably that of German and Japanese war economy, has given striking proof of this.* No reasoning will lead all the capitalists to restrict their production voluntarily when demand exceeds supply. No logic will induce them to maintain their investments at an average level, at the moment when their current production is no longer being absorbed by the market. To eliminate crises completely, the entire cyclical development of production must be abolished, i.e. every element of uneven development, i.e. all competition, all endeavour to increase the rate of profit and of surplus value, i.e. everything that is capitalist in production . . .

The anarchy of capitalist production therefore cannot be regarded as a cause in itself, independent of all the other characteristics of this mode of production, independent in particular of the contradiction between production and consumption which is a distinctive feature of capitalism.

The supporters of the disproportionality theory forget, moreover, that a *certain* proportion between production and consumption (not a *stable* proportion, as the supporters of the underconsumption theory suppose), between the production capacity of the entire productive apparatus, the production capacity of consumer goods and the purchasing power available for these same goods, is inherent in the conditions of proportionality necessary for avoiding a crisis, and that these conditions can never be realised for a long period under capitalism.

It is to be observed that some supporters of the underconsumption

* See Chapter 14.

theory, carried away by the symmetrical beauty of their "numerical" models, have arrived at conclusions very close to those of Tugan-Baranovsky and Co. This in particular is what has happened to Léon Sartre, who writes:

"One may wonder what would become of capitalism if a well-informed economic dictatorship were to insist that an increasing share of the accumulated surplus value at the disposal of the consumer-goods industries be invested in the capital-goods industries, to the same extent as purchasing power shifted in that direction. If this happened, Tugan-Baranovsky rightly says, basing himself on the diagram, equilibrium would be maintained. The result would be a perfectly viable [?] economy in which the production of means of production would increase faster and faster and that of consumer goods would grow only very slowly . . . But a capitalism like this, producing means of production only so as to produce more means of production, remains in the world of theory, being impracticable under a competitive system."[73]

N. Bukharin also upheld the view that a *state capitalism* would know no more periodical crises of overproduction.[74]

Such "solutions" would be impracticable not only because of the impossibility of establishing a "universal trust" embracing all enterprises but also because of the *technological ratio* that exists between a certain production capacity and a production capacity of consumer goods. They would be impracticable because it is impossible, as we have shown above, completely to separate production from consumption, which remains its ultimate purpose. They would be impracticable because no "logic" would induce the capitalists to buy more and more machinery at a time when the production capacity of their machinery already exceeds the market's capacity to absorb consumer goods.

Outline of a synthesis

An attempt at synthesising underconsumption theories and theories of disproportionality has been undertaken by a whole school, which bases itself on the accelerator principle: Aftalion and Bounatian in France, Harrod in Britain, J. M. Clark and S. Kuznets in the U.S.A., etc. This attempt has been continued by synthesising the multiplier principle with the accelerator principle, as is done by the neo-Keynesian econometry school, notably Samuelson, Goodwin, Hicks, Kalecki, Harrod and Joan Robinson. These syntheses, excessively simplified, succeed merely in showing the basic instability of the capitalist system.

They are only distant approaches to the real cycle, to the understanding of which they nevertheless make important contributions.

To show how this synthesis should be undertaken in Marxist terms, we must briefly reformulate the incorrect views about the ultimate causes of crises, which are, let us repeat, crises of *an economy which aims at profit realised by selling commodities*:

(1) The vulgar supporters of the under-consumption theory declare that crisis could be avoided by increasing the workers' purchasing power during the last phase of the boom. These theoreticians forget that the capitalists do not work simply in order to sell, but to *sell at a profit*. And when wages are raised at a moment when the rate of profit is already declining, the latter risks collapsing altogether—far from prolonging the boom, this additional increase in wages would strangle it.

(2) The vulgar supporters of disproportionality theories, and especially the supporters of what is called the "under-accumulation" school (von Hayek, von Mises, Pigou, Hawtrey, etc.),* declare that a crisis could be prevented if one were to resist any fall in the rate of profit during the last phase of the boom (for example, by freezing wages, reducing excessively high rates of interest, attempting to prevent any distortion of prices, etc.). But these theoreticians forget that if the rate of profit rises *at the same time as markets are shrinking*, this will not stop investment from slowing down. What interests the entrepreneur, indeed, is not the *theoretical* profit he can deduce from a certain rate of wages, a certain rate of interest and certain costs of production, but the *real* profit he expects to realise when he compares costs of production with the *selling possibilities* of his goods:

"High income and profit levels may be a necessary condition of investment, but they cannot be considered a sufficient one. It is questionable whether business firms have so little acumen as to expand capacity on the basis of currently high profits alone. Unless they have been operating at full capacity, with order backlogs piling up, and have been unable or unwilling to expand in the absence of more equity funds, or unless they anticipate further *growth* in sales, induced investment is likely to contract [at the peak of a boom] even in the face of high profits."[76]

And Moulton[77] opportunely recalls an example from history relevant to this subject:

"The increasing concentration of income in the higher brackets and also the rising level of urban incomes generally were serving more or less automatically [between 1919 and 1929] to increase the proportion of the aggregrate national income set aside as money savings. That is, although the current income into trade and service channels continued to expand, it expanded less rapidly than the flow of funds into investment channels. While an abundance of funds was thus available with which to construct new plant and equipment, it was evidently clear to business enterprisers that prospective consumptive demands were

* In 1927 Pigou confidently asserted that draconic [!] wage-cuts could avoid a crisis. Von Hayek proclaimed the same "truth" in 1932 [!] in the midst of huge masses of unsaleable consumer goods.[75]

not sufficiently large to warrant as much expansion as the available funds made possible."

There are, then, *two simultaneously-needed conditions* for economic recovery and the beginning of a boom: *an increasing rate of profit and expanding real markets*. At the start of the economic cycle, these two conditions may coincide for a certain number of reasons: reduction in the organic composition of capital (a larger number of workers with the same amount of equipment), comparatively low wages; increase in the rate of surplus-value, acceleration of the velocity of rotation of capital, on the one hand; and the other, increase in the overall purchasing power of the wage-earners as a whole (through the return of the unemployed to employment), investment of funds saved during the crisis and the depression (notably depreciation funds), and increasing profits quickly realised.

But the same forces that bring about the coincidence of these two factors at the start of the cycle undermine their existence more and more as the cycle progresses, and bring about their collapse towards the end of the cycle. We have already examined, above, the conditions which determine a fall in the rate of profit towards the end of the boom: increase in the organic composition of capital; fall in the rate of surplus value; slowing-down of the velocity of rotation of capital; credit becoming more expensive; increased overhead charges; rising wages, etc. We must now look at what happens as regards markets.

Demand for consumer goods rises very little after full employment has been more or less attained. As for capital goods, when the renewal of fixed capital has been completed, industry is re-equipped with a production capacity exceeding the possibilities of absorption by the market. New investment becomes increasingly improbable. Shrinkage of markets thus takes place in both sectors. The coincidence of the fall in the rate of profit with the shrinkage of markets brings about the crisis.

Is there general overproduction at the moment of the crisis? Undoubtedly there is. It follows necessarily from the two basic aspects of the boom.

Economic recovery, by causing a rise in the rate of surplus value and a rise in the rate of profit, changes the allocation of the national income among the classes, to the advantage of the bourgeoisie and at the expense of the wage-earners. Many writers confirm this opinion (Haberler, Schumpeter, Lederer, Foster and Catchings, Hobson, Moszkowska, Hicks, etc.)[78]* Sombart expresses the idea like this:

* Professor Guitton gives the following picture of the average cyclical variations in France during the nineteenth century: prices rise by 17 per cent in boom and fall by 16 per cent in depression; wages rise by 12 per cent in boom and fall by 3 per cent in depression; profits rise by 40 to 200 per cent [!] in boom and fall by 14 to 38 per cent in depression.[79]

"It is the conjuncture of expansion itself . . . which, in periods of recovery, has the effect that wages do not rise to the same extent as surplus value, owing to the rise in prices; this also, by regular movements of contraction, by expelling workers (from the production process), is what fills up the labour market to the desired degree, so creating the industrial reserve army which prevents an excessive rise in wages."[80]

But at the same time as the wage-earners' share of the national income relatively falls, the production capacity of the industries producing consumer goods is constantly growing. The moment has to come at which the increase in this production capacity exceeds the level of demand.

Furthermore, the increase in the production capacity of the sector producing capital goods corresponds to the need for renewing a substantial part of the fixed capital of all industry. When this renewal has been achieved, sector I will be able to avoid overproduction only on condition that investment *continues at the same pace*, which is obviously not possible.[81]

Society's greatly increased production capacity cannot be used to a more or less complete extent until after a preliminary destruction of value, adaptation of the value of the commodities to the new amount of labour socially-necessary to produce them, a smaller amount than that which determined the previous level of value of these commodities. *The collapse of the boom is thus the collapse of the attempt to maintain the former level of values, prices and rates of profit with an increased quantity of capital.* It is the conflict between the conditions for the accumulation of capital and for its realisation, which is merely the unfolding of all the contradictions inherent in capitalism, *all* of which enter into this explanation of crises: contradictions between the great development of production capacity and the not-so-great development of the consumption-capacity of the broad masses; contradictions arising from the anarchy of production resulting from competition, the increase in the organic composition of capital and the fall in the rate of profit; contradictions between the increasing socialisation of production and the private form of appropriation.*

The conditions of capitalist expansion

The historical conditions which ensure the expansion of the capitalist mode of production, have already been explained above. They arise essentially from the *uneven development* of different sectors, branches and countries drawn into the capitalist market. The creation of the world market, which precedes the great advance of the capitalist mode

* On crises in the epoch of declining capitalism, and the role of public expenditure in the economy, see Chapter 14, section on "A crisis-free capitalism?"

of production, establishes the general setting for this uneven development. The latter shows itself in:

(*a*) Unevenness of development as between industry and agriculture. As industry develops, its commodities drive out the products of the domestic and craft labour of the peasantry, ruining a section of the country people, who become proletarians and form a mass of labour available to expanding industry. The value of industrial production increases as compared with that of agricultural production; the industrial labour force increases as compared with the number of persons occupied in agriculture. The peasants buy more means of production (which previously they made for themselves) from large scale industry, which buys raw material from the peasants, though in smaller proportions.

(*b*) Unevenness of development as between the countries first to be industrialised and the colonial and semi-colonial countries. The industry of the first-industrialised countries destroys the craft and domestic production of the colonial and semi-colonial countries, which are transformed into markets of the advanced countries. The labour-power "released" as a result of this destruction of the age-old equilibrium between agriculture and industry cannot find occupation in an expanding national industry, because it is the expansion of industry in the *metropolitan* country that has made it possible to conquer this market. In consequence there appear the related phenomena of chronic under-employment and pressure of over-population on the land. "The results come quickly: in 1813 Calcutta exported £2 million worth of cotton goods; in 1830 it imported cotton goods to the same value. The import of cotton goods into India as a whole rose from £8 million in 1859 to £16 million in 1877 and £20 million in 1901, that of silks from £1·4 million to £7 million and £16 million, and that of cotton thread from £1·7 million to £2·8 million."

At the same time India became more and more agricultural, and in the same period 1850–1877 the export of raw cotton increased from £4 million to £13 million, that of jute from £0·9 million to £3 million, that of tea from £0·15 million to £2·6 million, and that of oil from £2·5 million to £5·4 million. [82]

A combination of four obstacles to the capitalist industrialisation of the colonial and semi-colonial countries resulted: competition from commodities produced in the metropolitan country; competition between the very cheap local labour-power and modern machinery; shortage of capital owing to investment of the accumulated income of the ruling class in landed property; and lack of adequate internal markets such as would make possible a rapid development of some industrial sectors.*

(*c*) Unevenness of development as between different branches of

* See Chapters 6, 9 and 13.

industry, especially between declining ones and those which are on the upgrade owing to successive technological revolutions. The declining branches see their markets, their turnover, the numbers employed in them, getting smaller and smaller, at first relatively, then absolutely. After trying to defend themselves by increasing the organic composition of capital and reducing prices (relatively or absolutely), they submit, and henceforth renew only part of their fixed capital. A share of the surplus value and the depreciation funds of these sectors spills on to the capital market, attracted by the sectors which are expanding rapidly. The latter carve themselves a place in the market by tearing resources (fixed capital, raw material, purchasing power) from the existing sectors, either by slowing down the growth of some of them or else by causing absolute setbacks to others.

(*d*) Unevenness of development as between different parts of a single country. This phenomenon, usually underestimated in Marxist economic writing, is in reality one of the essential keys to the understanding of expanded reproduction. *By creating depressed areas within the capitalist nations, the capitalist mode of production itself creates its own "complementary" markets, as well as its permanent reserves of labour-power.* This happened with Scotland and Wales in Britain, the Southern States in the U.S.A., the eastern and southern parts of Germany, Flanders in Belgium, Slovakia in Czechoslovakia, the South in Italy, the South and the North in the Netherlands, France south of the Loire, and so on. What is characteristic of the spasmodic, unequal, contradictory development of the capitalist mode of production is that it cannot industrialise systematically and harmoniously the whole of a large country. The gradual abolition of old depressed areas is itself accompanied by the appearance of new depressed areas: New England in the U.S.A., the Borinage and the la Louvière region in Belgium: Lancashire in Britain; Haute-Loire in France; Genoa in Italy, etc. The irony of history is such that often these new depressed areas were formerly the cradles of capitalist industry in these countries.

No growth without fluctuations?

Since the great crisis of 1929 the idea of a harmonious and balanced development of the capitalist order has finally fallen into discredit. The most fashionable bourgeois writers, such as Schumpeter, have, like Marx, put stress on the basic instability of the capitalist mode of production. For Schumpeter this instability results from the fact that "innovation", i.e. the application of technical discoveries to industry, cannot be spread evenly over the whole duration of the economic cycle, but tends to be concentrated in certain spaced-out periods.[88] For the econometricians the basic instability of the mode of production results from the fact that the conditions needed for unbroken growth are unrealisable in practice, owing to the special nature of investment under capitalism: * "The system will not remain in progressive equilibrium unless it is *completely adjusted* to it . . . A system is unlikely to be completely adjusted in a progressive equilibrium until it has been in approximate equilibrium for a long time. It is not sufficient that the capital stock should be adjusted to current output; it is also necessary that it should fall due for replacement at the right dates. The induced investment of the future which is already preconditioned (to a considerable extent) by past changes in output, the effects of which are embodied in existing equipment, must be such as to be consistent with steady development."[85]

Joan Robinson makes the same point: "An economy which existed in a state of tranquillity, lucidity and harmony would be devoted to the production and consumption of wealth in a rational manner. It is only necessary to describe these conditions to see how remote they are from the states in which actual economies dwell. Capitalism, in particular, could never have come into existence in such conditions, for the divorce between work and property, which makes large-scale enterprise possible, entails conflict; and the rules of the game have been developed precisely to make accumulation and technical progress possible in conditions of uncertainty and imperfect knowledge."[86]

And, further: "For each individual entrepreneur the future is uncertain even when the economy as a whole is developing smoothly, and the actions of each entrepreneur affect the situation for the rest. For this reason there is an inherent instability, under the capitalist rules of the game, which generates fluctuations, so to say, from within the economy, quite apart from any change in external circumstances. The typical entrepreneur, as soon as he finds his existing capacity operating at what seems to him a reasonable rate of profit, wants to operate more capacity. Unless investment just hits off the golden-age rate, at which demand grows with capacity (or unless it is effectively controlled), it will always be oscillating, for whenever it happens to rise it generates a seller's market, and so stimulates a further rise."[87]

Writers who conscientiously try to emphasise the advantages of the capitalist mode of production as the most progressive mode of production, like Arthur F. Burns and David McCorde Wright, have taken a step further and declared that it is *impossible* to conceive of an economy open to the benefits of technological progress or possessing a substantial stock of fixed capital which would not be subject to fluctuations. According to them, the choice is not between progress with or without fluctuations but rather between progress with fluctuations and complete stagnation.

Thus, David McCorde Wright writes: "The *fundamental* cause of the business cycle is the failure of changes in taste and technique to occur at rates which smoothly offset one another. It is *durability* of

* Including fluctuations in stocks: see Metzler, Abramovitz, Eckert.[84]

equipment plus asymmetrical *changeability* of wants plus inevitable frictions plus *consumer sovereignty* [!] which produces the business cycle . . . Any growing society which wants to meet the pattern of consumer spending will inevitably suffer certain [!] instabilities and insecurities."[88]

Let us first of all throw Noah's garment over the most absurd aspect of this apologia, namely, the allegation that the innovations which bring the big waves of investment result from "changes in taste on the part of the consumer". It was not, after all, the "need to have a car" that created the motor-car industry; it was this industry that created the need to have a car. It is the investment of enormous amounts of capital in new sectors of industry (and, to a subsidiary extent, publicity for their products) that changes the taste of consumers, and not the changing taste of consumers that brings about the flow of enormous amounts of capital into certain sectors, or, even less, technical inventions.

But would these innovations not occur in an irregular way in a planned economy, a socialist economy?*

Would not the durability of industrial equipment bring about equally in such an economy the phenomenon of "overproduction", through the need to meet *sudden demands* (e.g. the introduction of colour television; or the effect of a sudden increase in the population on the building industry, etc.)?

According to McCorde Wright,[90] *any* economic system has *a choice only between two evils*: either to keep up the planned pace of growth, of production, in these sectors, and so provoke prolonged irritation on the part of the consumers (reflected in a rise in prices, etc.), or else to increase rapidly the rate of progress of production by exceptional investments, and so expose oneself to over-equipment (the appearance of excess capacity) from the moment when the exceptional demand has been satisfied (e.g. when all the extra population has been provided with housing, and the demand for renewal declines owing to a changed age-structure of this same population).

Arthur F. Burns had already set forth the same view in his article *Long Cycles in Construction*, published in 1935 and reproduced in his collection *Frontiers of Economic Knowledge* (1954). He there explains the instability of the demand for housing in a "collectivist society", and strives to show that such a society would experience marked cyclical fluctuations in the building trade.[91] But his entire argument is based on a simplistic assumption, namely, that what is available to each family must remain *fixed* and that house building fluctuates exclusively in accordance with fluctuations in the population (and the more-or-less correct forecasting of this).

From the moment when we abandon this assumption and accept, on

* Schumpeter and Cassel[89] emphasise the same idea.

the contrary, that planned economy has a *twofold* aim—first and foremost, to provide each family with the indispensable "housing unit", constituting the minimum standard of comfort, but then, after that, to bring the minimum standard of housing up to the *optimum* standard (from the standpoint of comfort, town-planning, hygiene, upbringing of children, etc.)—the whole of Burns' theory collapses. As soon as a surplus of capacity, in relation to immediate needs, makes its appearance, this capacity can be used to bring about an improvement in the living conditions of part of the population. And as one may reasonably assume that this *optimum* itself has a tendency to rise, as a result of scientific and technical progress, no "excess capacity" is conceivable for a long period of time.

McCorde Wright's mistake is exactly the same. In order to demonstrate the "fluctuations" inevitable in a planned economy he imagines an economy which has abolished only one aspect of capitalism (private ownership of the means of production), while retaining all its other aspects. Thus, when a backlog of demand has been satisfied, he sees no other result than "overproduction" or "excess capacity"; it does not occur to him that it would be possible to make an additional and new range of consumer goods available to society.* When the productive apparatus is "hypertrophied", he does not realise that one can "adapt it to need" by reducing the producers' working time. When he brings in an "absolute excess capacity" without the possibility of making "new products", he does not realise that the putting into reserve of part of this machinery would be accompanied by no reduction of consumption or "income" for society, and so by no *economic* fluctuation, since this withdrawal of machinery would have been *caused* precisely by the fact that the *real needs* (and not merely effective monetary demand) of society had been *previously and completely satisfied*.

The fluctuations of production which entail fluctuations in income and consumption, through overproduction of commodities, and which thus imply periodical unemployment and poverty, are peculiar to capitalism. They did not exist before capitalism, and they will not survive it.†

* Hamberg[92] emphasises what a ceaselessly expanding range of products can be manufactured with the same modern equipment.

† See Chapter 17.

REFERENCES

1. J. Schumpeter: *Business Cycles*, Vol. I, p. 225.
2. W. Abel: *Agrarkrisen und Agrarkonjunktur in Mittelalter*, p. 158.
3. Jean Fourastié: *Le Grand espoir du XXe siècle*, p. 141.
4. J. M. Keynes: *General Theory*.

5. H. Guitton: *Les fluctuations économiques* (9th volume of Gaëtan Pirou's *Traité d'économie politique*), pp. 174-5.
6. Karl Marx: *Grundrisse*, Vol. I, p. 310.
7. L. R. Klein: *The Keynesian Revolution*, p. 8.
8. F. A. Von Hayek: *Geldtheorie and Konjunkturtheorie*, pp. 51, 103.
9. J. M. Keynes: op. cit., p. 317.
10. G. Von Haberler: *Prospérité et Dépression*, pp. 154-5.
11. Alvin H. Hansen: *Business Cycles and National Income*, p. 50; Hans Roth: *Die Uebererzeugung in der Welthandelsware Kaffee*, pp. 104-5; Richard B. Tennant: *The American Cigarette Industry*, pp. 192-4, etc.
12. A. Aftalion: *Crises périodiques*, Vol. I, pp. 359-64; W. C. Mitchell: *Business Cycles and Employment*, pp. 10-11; Keynes: op. cit–Schumpeter: op. cit., Vol. I, pp. 4, 123; Hansen: op. cit., p. 564; Guitton: op. cit., p. 321.
13. Von Haberler: op. cit., p. 298.
14. A. D. Gayer, W. W. Rostow and A. J. Schwartz: *Growth and Fluctuation of the British Economy*, p. 557.
15. J. M. Clark: quoted in Hansen, op. cit.
16. Natalya Moszkowska: *Zur Kritik Moderner Krisentheorien*, p. 62.
17. Schumpeter: op. cit., Vol. I, p. 148.
18. Von Haberler: op. cit., p. 414.
19. Keynes: op. cit.
20. Von Haberler: op. cit., pp. 32, 154-5; Abramovitz: *Inventories and Business Cycles*, pp. 360-9.
21. Schumpeter: op. cit., Vol. II, pp. 576-7.
22. W. C. Mitchell: *What Happens During Business Cycles?*, pp. 106, 116-17.
23. Von Haberler: op. cit., p. 429.
24. Ibid., p. 378.
25. Spiethoff: in von Haberler: op. cit., p. 90.
26. Keynes: op. cit.; von Haberler: op. cit., p. 442.
27. W. Woytinsky: *Conséquences sociales de la crise*, pp. 72-73.
28. Jan Tinbergen: *Les Cycles économiques aux Etats-Unis*, p. 105.
29. Schumpeter: op. cit., Vol. II, p. 637.
30. Hansen: op. cit., p. 60; Keynes: op. cit.
31. Moszkowska: op. cit., p. 62; L. Sartre: *Esquisse d'une théorie marxiste des crises périodiques*, p. 101.
32. Hansen: op. cit., p. 145.
33. Ibid., p. 173.
34. R. Eckert: *Les Théories modernes de l'expansion économique*, p. 35.
35. J. R. Hicks: *A Contribution to the Theory of the Trade Cycle*, p. 108.
36. Schumpeter: op. cit., Vol. II, p. 400.
37. Hansen: op. cit., pp. 123-4.
38. Hayer, Rostow and Schwartz: op. cit., p. 554.
39. Hansen: op. cit., pp. 182-3.
40. Hansen: op. cit., p. 60; G. von Haberler: op. cit., pp. 316-17.
41. Schumpeter: op. cit., Vol. II, pp. 576-7.

42. Hansen: op. cit., p. 125.
43. Von Haberler: op. cit., p. 404.
44. W. T. Foster and W. Catchings: *Money*, p. 274.
45. Eckert: op. cit., p. 12.
46. Abramovitz: op. cit., p. 498; Metzler: "Business Cycles and the Modern Theory of Employment", in *American Economic Review*, June 1946.
47. *Die Welt*, 22nd October, 1960.
48. W. C. Mitchell: *What Happens During Business Cycles?*, pp. 302-3 (see also pp. 32, 40, 73); Hansen: op. cit., pp. 82-83.
49. W. C. Mitchell: *What Happens During Business Cycles?*, pp. 161 *et al.*
50. Ibid., pp. 32, 34, 41.
51. Von Haberler: op. cit., p. 416.
52. Ibid., p. 120; W. C. Mitchell: *What Happens . . .*, pp. 132-3.
53. Von Haberler: op. cit., pp. 375-80.
54. Harold G. Moulton: *Controlling Factors in Economic Development*, p. 306.
55. N. Kaldor: *Stability and Full Employment*, reprinted in A. Hansen and R. V. Clemence, *Readings in Business Cycles and National Income*, pp. 499-500.
56. J. Schumpeter: *Business Cycles*, Vol. I, p. 158.
57. Gayer, Rostow and Schwartz: op. cit., p. 544; Schumpeter: op. cit., 499.
58. K. Kautsky: *"Finanzkapital und Krisen"*, in *Neue Zeit*, Vol. XXIX, No. 1, pp. 843-4 (1911).
59. Fred Oelssner: *Die Wirtschaftskrisen*, Vol. I, p. 38.
60. Rosa Luxemburg: *Die Akkumulation des Kapitals*, passim.
61. N. Bukharin: *Der Imperialismus und die Akkumulation des Kapitals*, pp. 95-108.
62. Luxemburg: op. cit., p. 407.
63. Karl Marx: *Theorien über den Mehrwert*, Vol. II, pt. 2, p. 315.
64. Paul M. Sweezy: *The Theory of Capitalist Development*, pp. 180-4.
65. Otto Bauer: *Zwischen zwei Weltkriegen?*, pp. 51-53, 351-5.
66. Hamberg: *Economic Growth and Instability*, pp. 55-56 *et al.*
67. Sartre: op. cit., pp. 62-66.
68. Shaw's estimates in *Historical Statistics of the U.S.A.*
69. Fritz Sternberg: *Der Imperialismus*, pp. 20 et seq.; *Der Imperialismus und seine Kritiker*, pp. 163 et seq.
70. Kalecki: "A Theory of the Business Cycle", in *Review of Economic Studies*, Vol. IV, 1936–7, pp. 77.
71. Myron W. Watkins: "Commercial Banking and Capital Formation", in *Journal of Political Economy*, Vol. XXVII, July 1919, pp. 584-5.
72. Von Haberler: op. cit., pp. 43-44.
73. Sartre: op. cit., p. 61.
74. Bukharin: op. cit., pp. 88-89.
75. In Hansen: op. cit., p. 518; Von Hayek: in *Weltwirtschaftliches Archiv*, July 1932, Vol. I, pp. 90, et seq.
76. Hamberg: op. cit., p. 323.
77. Moulton: op. cit., p. 70.

78. Von Haberler: op. cit., p. 324; Schumpeter: op. cit., pp. 155, 561; Moszkowska: op. cit., p. 26; Hicks: op. cit., pp. 126-7, etc.
79. Guitton: op. cit., p. 94.
80. Werner Sombart: *Der moderne Kapitalismus,* Vol. II, p. 586.
81. Hamberg: op. cit., p. 55; Hansen: op. cit., pp. 495-6.
82. André Philip: *L'Inde moderne,* p. 87.
83. Schumpeter: op. cit., Vol. II, p. 1033.
84. Eckert: op. cit., pp. 59-64.
85. Hicks: op. cit., pp. 63-64.
86. Joan Robinson: *The Accumulation of Capital,* p. 60.
87. Ibid., p. 209.
88. David McCord Wright: *Capitalism,* pp. 147, 153, 154.
89. Schumpeter: op. cit., Vol. II, p. 803; Cassel: in *Readings in Business Cycles and National Income,* p. 124.
90. Wright: op. cit., pp. 144-6.
91. Burns: op. cit., pp. 314-34.
92. Hamberg: op. cit., pp. 223-4.